P9-AEZ-947

The Seventy-sixth Congress and World War II

About the Author

David L. Porter is Associate Professor of History at William Penn College, Oskaloosa, Iowa. He has published numerous articles in scholarly journals.

The Seventy-sixth Congress and World War II
1939–1940

David L. Porter

University of Missouri Press
Columbia & London, 1979

Copyright © 1979 by the Curators of the University of Missouri
Library of Congress Catalog Card Number 79-4843
Printed and bound in the United States of America
University of Missouri Press, Columbia, Missouri 65211
All rights reserved

Library of Congress Cataloging in Publication Data

Porter, David L   1941–
    The Seventy-sixth Congress and World War II, 1939–
1940.

    Bibliography: p. 214
    Includes index.
    1. World War, 1939–1945—United States.   2.   United
States—Neutrality.   3.   United States—Politics and
government—1933–1945.   4.   United States—Foreign
relations—1933–1945.   5.   United States.   76th Congress,
1939–1940.   I.   Title.
D753.P64   940.53′73   79-4843
ISBN 0-8262-0281-0

To my parents,
Willis Hubert and
Frances Bowan Porter

Contents

Acknowledgments

Numerous individuals and groups helped immensely during the research phase of this study. The late Prentiss M. Brown graciously reminisced with me about his role in sponsoring legislation for a federal loan to Finland. Several members of the Seventy-sixth Congress, including the late Homer T. Bone, Emanuel Celler, John A. Danaher, the late Allen J. Ellender, the late Ernest W. Gibson, Jr., Albert Gore, Charles A. Halleck, the late Carl Hayden, the late Edwin C. Johnson, Warren G. Magnuson, the late Karl E. Mundt, John E. Miller, the late Gerald P. Nye, Claude D. Pepper, Jennings Randolph, Margaret Chase Smith, Carl Vinson, the late John M. Vorys, and the late Burton K. Wheeler, cordially answered my written queries. C. Jasper Bell, the late Clifford R. Hope, Eugene J. Keogh, Claude D. Pepper, the late John M. Vorys, and Lindsay C. Warren kindly gave me permission to examine their congressional correspondence. Relatives and friends of Clarence Cannon, Jr., Grenville Clark, Rush Dew Holt, and John Taber generously made their manuscript collections available. Arthur Kogan of the State Department and William S. Coker of the University of West Florida granted me access to the Cordell Hull and Pat Harrison papers.

Librarians and archivists facilitated the project enormously. Dr. Buford Rowland and staff of the National Archives, Elizabeth B. Drewry and personnel of the Franklin D. Roosevelt Library, and employees of the Library of Congress afforded invaluable assistance. I am also indebted to the considerable aid and hospitality provided by the manuscript divisions and staffs of Dartmouth College, University of Vermont, Syracuse University, Cornell University, New York Public Library, Rutgers University, West Virginia University, Washington National Records Center, Georgetown University, University of Virginia, Duke University, University of North Carolina, University of Florida, University of Southern Mississippi, Louisiana State University, University of Kentucky, Ohio State Historical Society, University of Michigan, University of Chicago, Herbert C. Hoover Library, University of Iowa, University of Missouri, Harry S. Truman Library, Nebraska State Historical Society, Kansas State Historical Society, University of Oklahoma, University of Texas, Arizona State University, University of California, Berkeley, and University of Wyoming. At various stages, Miriam Hess of the Pennsylvania State University Library, Marion Rains of the William Penn College Library, and the staff of the University of Iowa Libraries supplied pertinent secondary sources.

Several other sources deserve mention. Financial assistance from the National Science Foundation enabled me to learn more about the application of computers to the social sciences at the University of Michigan. I am also grateful to the National Endowment for the Humanities for a grant to participate in a summer seminar for college teachers at the Herbert C. Hoover Library. The Inter-University Consortium for Political Research at the University of Michigan graciously afforded me the use of relevant roll-call data, while the Oral History Collection at Columbia University contained the lucid memoirs by Rep. James W. Wadsworth, Jr.

This book benefited from the help of several professional colleagues. I am particularly indebted to Ari Hoogenboom of Brooklyn College, who helped foster my interest in both political history and the Seventy-sixth Congress. Robert James Maddox, Elton Atwater, and Harry Stein of Pennsylvania State University kindly read earlier drafts of the entire manuscript and made numerous constructive suggestions. During the latter stages, Robert Divine of the University of Texas at Austin, Walter LaFeber of Cornell University, and David Thelen of the University of Missouri carefully read the whole manuscript and made several perceptive comments. I also am grateful to John Garry Clifford of the University of Connecticut, George H. Lobdell, Jr. of Ohio University, Robert K. Murray of Pennsylvania State University, Martin L. Fausold of the State University of New York at Geneseo, and all the NEH summer seminar participants for enhancing considerably my understanding of the two decades leading to American entry into World War II.

My wife Marilyn has given me encouragement throughout the preparation of the manuscript and has helped me in numerous ways.

D.L.P.
Oskaloosa, Iowa
Summer 1979

1

Introduction

During the late 1930s, Congress acted very independently of the executive branch on domestic issues. President Franklin D. Roosevelt, after the election of 1936, experienced a rocky courtship with the legislative branch on political, economic, and social matters. Bipartisan conservatives thwarted the president's plans to increase the size of the United States Supreme Court and to reorganize the executive branch and reduced appropriations for several New Deal agencies. Roosevelt caused additional consternation among party conservatives by seeking unsuccessfully in the 1938 Democratic primaries to purge five senators opposing domestic measures.[1] What roles, however, did Congress and President Roosevelt play on major foreign policy and defense legislation during the same period?

Historians disagree about executive–legislative relations before American entry into World War II. Some argue that Roosevelt wielded extensive power and authority in national decisionmaking, indicating that Congress played a subordinate role. The chief executive, according to Charles A. Beard and Charles C. Tansill, maneuvered the United States into the European war by provoking Japan into attacking Pearl Harbor. The president, they charge, often conducted foreign policy in an inconsistent manner and made public statements incompatible with his private actions.[2]

Other historians stress that Congress played a moderate role in determining foreign policy. These historians, most notably William L. Langer, S. Everett Gleason, James MacGregor Burns, and Robert A. Divine, describe how isolationists on Capitol Hill limited Roosevelt's effectiveness as a diplomatic leader. Besides denying that the president deliberately led the United States into World War II, they maintain that Roosevelt gradually educated a reluctant nation about the dangers posed to American security by the Axis powers. The president, they believe, exaggerated the isolationist influence on Capitol Hill and should have acted more decisively. Burns pictures Roosevelt as a sly fox rather than a forthright lion, while Divine portrays the president as an inconsistent leader letting political expediency override ideological principles.[3]

A third group claims that Congress played a very dynamic role at this time. Denying that the legislative branch acted as a rubber stamp for the president, they

1. James T. Patterson, *Congressional Conservatism and the New Deal*.
2. Charles A. Beard, *American Foreign Policy in the Making, 1932–1940* and *President Roosevelt and the Coming of War, 1941: A Study in Appearances and Realities*; Charles C. Tansill, *Back Door to War: The Roosevelt Foreign Policy, 1933–1941*.
3. William L. Langer and S. Everett Gleason, *The Challenge to Isolation, 1937–1940* and *The Undeclared War, 1940–1941*; James MacGregor Burns, *Roosevelt: The Lion and the Fox*; Robert A. Divine, *The Illusion of Neutrality* and *The Reluctant Belligerent: American Entry into World War II*.

contend that the Senate and House were very independent of the White House. James T. Patterson describes how congressional conservatives blocked New Deal legislation, while Wayne S. Cole and Manfred Jonas emphasize the considerable influence of the Senate and House isolationists.[4] I hope to expand this view, indicating that the legislative branch played an even more significant and independent role in national decisionmaking than previously thought. Congress consistently limited the maneuverability of the president, continually placed the chief executive on the defensive, and often forced him to exhibit indecisive leadership.

Historians writing about American entry into World War II have concentrated on the White House and State Department. During the 1940s and 1950s, orthodox and revisionist scholars argued over whether the Axis nations threatened Western Hemisphere security and whether the president deliberately attempted to draw the United States into the conflict.[5] Until the 1960s, the legislative branch was given peripheral treatment. Although nearly two more decades have elapsed, there are still very few works tracing the legislature's role in framing American foreign policy during the critical prewar years.

There is no published overview of Congress covering the transitional 1939–1940 period. Historians instead describe specific aspects of the legislative branch. Langer, Gleason, and Burns concentrate on executive–legislative relations, while Divine, Robert Sobel, and Samuel R. Spencer, Jr., reiterate the congressional response on one specific international issue.[6] Several historians examine either prominent factions within or groups outside of Congress. Mark Lincoln Chadwin and Walter Johnson describe the internationalists, while Cole and Jonas concentrate on congressional isolationists.[7] In addition, there are several biographies of prominent senators and representatives who served in the Seventh-sixth Congress.[8] There is, however, no book analyzing the overall role of the legislative branch in determining American foreign policy in the prewar years.

4. Patterson, *Congressional Conservatism*; Wayne S. Cole, *Senator Gerald P. Nye and American Foreign Relations*; Manfred Jonas, *Isolationism in America, 1935–1941*.

5. Some orthodox works include Langer and Gleason, *Challenge to Isolation* and *Undeclared War*; Herbert Feis, *The Road to Pearl Harbor: The Coming of the War between the United States and Japan*; Basil Rauch, *Roosevelt from Munich to Pearl Harbor: A Study in the Creation of a Foreign Policy*; and Robert E. Sherwood, *Roosevelt and Hopkins: An Intimate History*. Revisionist works are Beard, *Foreign Policy* and *Roosevelt*; Tansill, *Back Door to War*; and Harry Elmer Barnes, ed., *Perpetual War for Perpetual Peace: A Critical Examination of the Foreign Policy of Franklin Delano Roosevelt and Its Aftermath*. The best descriptive accounts of historiography are Wayne S. Cole, ''American Entry into World War II: A Historiographical Appraisal''; Robert A. Divine, ed., *Causes and Consequences of World War II*; Justus D. Doenecke, *The Literature of Isolationism: A Guide to Non-Interventionist Scholarship, 1930–1972*; and John E. Wiltz, *From Isolation to War, 1931–1941*. An excellent overview on the role of the president is the recent Robert Dallek, *Franklin D. Roosevelt and American Foreign Policy, 1932–1945*.

6. Langer and Gleason, *Challenge to Isolation* and *Undeclared War*; Burns, *Lion and the Fox*; Divine, *Illusion of Neutrality*; Robert Sobel, *The Origins of Interventionism: The United States and the Russo-Finnish War*; Samuel R. Spencer, Jr., ''A History of the Selective Training and Service Act of 1940 from Inception to Enactment'' (Ph.D. diss.).

7. Mark Lincoln Chadwin, *The Hawks of World War II*; Walter Johnson, *The Battle Against Isolation*; Wayne S. Cole, *America First: The Battle Against Intervention, 1940–41*; and Jonas, *Isolationism*.

8. Two biographies featuring international affairs are Cole, *Nye and American Foreign Relations*,

This book attempts to fill that void. It describes the debate between the isolationists and the noninterventionists on one hand and the internationalists and the interventionists on the other hand and evaluates the shift of the Seventy-sixth Congress from basically an isolationist, noninterventionist body to a predominantly internationalist, interventionist group in the 1939–1940 period. The isolationists and noninterventionists opposed American involvement in the European war but disagreed over the best means of avoiding involvement. The two types of isolationists and noninterventionists were traditionalists and revisionists. The traditionalists, led by Republican Sen. William E. Borah of Idaho and Rep. Hamilton Fish, Jr., of New York, favored defending American neutral rights if endangered by the Axis powers. If a foreign nation attacked an American vessel on the high seas, traditionalists believed the United States should abandon strict neutrality and defend its rights under international law. Revisionists, on the other hand, contended the United States should avoid any entanglement in European affairs. Under the direction of Republican senators Gerald P. Nye of North Dakota and Arthur H. Vandenberg of Michigan, they counseled that the United States should not retaliate if its neutral rights were infringed upon by foreign powers. The neutrality legislation of the 1930s, described in Chapter 3, represented a compromise between these two isolationist groups. On the opposite side, internationalists insisted that the Axis powers threatened American security and maintained that the United States should provide at least indirect, limited aid to the Allies. Led by Democratic senators Key Pittman of Nevada and Elbert D. Thomas of Utah, they stressed that American cooperation with other nations afforded the best means of preserving both internal defense and world peace. On the other hand, they supported neutrality revision primarily as a means of keeping the United States out of European wars. Internationalists often were reluctant to commit the United States either to specific defense alliances or to direct intervention on behalf of particular nations in specific European conflicts.

---

and Robert James Maddox, *William E. Borah and American Foreign Policy*. Biographies of senators include J. Joseph Huthmacher, *Senator Robert F. Wagner and the Rise of Urban Liberalism*; Fred L. Israel, *Nevada's Key Pittman*; Ervin L. Levine, *Theodore Francis Green: The Washington Years, 1937–1960*; James K. Libbey, *Dear Alben: Mr. Barkley of Kentucky*; Richard Lowitt, *George W. Norris: The Triumph of a Progressive, 1933–1944*; Patrick J. Maney, *"Young Bob" La Follette: A Biography of Robert M. La Follette, Jr., 1895–1953*; Marian C. McKenna, *Borah*; John Robert Moore, *Senator Josiah William Bailey of North Carolina: A Political Biography*; James T. Patterson, *Mr. Republican: A Biography of Robert A. Taft*; Homer E. Socolofsky, *Arthur Capper: Publisher, Politician, and Philanthropist*; Martha H. Swain, *Pat Harrison: The New Deal Years*; and C. David Tompkins, *Senator Arthur H. Vandenberg: The Evolution of a Modern Republican, 1884–1945*. Studies of representatives are Edward C. Blackorby, *Prairie Rebel: The Public Life of William Lemke*; Joseph B. Gorman, *Kefauver: A Political Biography*; Martin L. Fausold, *James W. Wadsworth, Jr.: The Gentleman from New York*; and Alan Schaffer, *Vito Marcantonio: Radical in Congress*. Memoirs include Alben W. Barkley, *That Reminds Me*; Sol Bloom, *The Autobiography of Sol Bloom*; James F. Byrnes, *All in One Lifetime*; Thomas Connally and Alfred Steinberg, *My Name is Tom Connally*; Joseph W. Martin, Jr., *My First Fifty Years in Politics*; Merle Miller, *Plain Speaking: An Oral Biography of Harry S. Truman*; George W. Norris, *Fighting Liberal: The Autobiography of George W. Norris*; Jerry Voorhis, *Confessions of a Congressman*; and Burton K. Wheeler, *Yankee from the West: Turbulent Life Story of the Yankee-Born U.S. Senator from Montana*.

In this book, a case-study approach is utilized. This method involves the collecting and studying of data depicting either any portion or the entire life process of a given unit. Typical units examined may be an individual, family, institution, organization, social group, community, or nation. In this instance, the Seventy-sixth Congress is the subject, and legislative correspondence and published documents are the data examined. A case study of a particular Congress affords several benefits. One can gain a clearer understanding not only of how the legislative branch operates, but also of how it relates to the other branches of national government and to the American people. This method also provides a picture of the experiences, social forces, and influences to which Congress has been subjected. Third, it enables the exploration of legislative values and attitudes on specific problems. In this case study, roll-call votes are analyzed to determine the sources influencing congressional voting behavior.[9]

This work examines the role of the Seventy-sixth Congress in enacting three controversial measures—neutrality revision, aid to Finland, and selective service. The legislative branch spent more time in 1939 debating the neutrality issue than it did any other international question. The Senate and House argued over whether to maintain the ban on munitions sales or to permit the United States to send arms, ammunition, and other implements of war to victims of aggression. The second issue, which arose after Russia attacked Finland in 1939, involved whether the federal government should send military, economic, or other assistance to the Scandinavian nation. Selective service was the most controversial preparedness issue in the prewar period. Congress deliberated whether to continue voluntary recruitment or to implement the first peacetime draft in American history.

Several considerations influenced the selection of these particular issues. The legislation shows the four major phases through which the Seventy-sixth Congress passed—isolationism, internationalism, interventionism, and preparedness. Neutrality revision illustrates the isolationist and internationalist stages, while the Finnish question represents the interventionist phase and selective service portrays the preparedness theme. At the regular session in 1939, isolationists controlled congressional foreign policy decisionmaking and prevented repeal of the arms embargo. Following the outbreak of World War II in Europe, the internationalists prevailed over the isolationists by lifting the ban on munitions sales to belligerents. On the Finnish issue in early 1940, Congress entered a third major phase characterized by a debate between interventionists and noninterventionists. During that period, the interventionists secured the adoption of legislation providing economic assistance to the Finnish government. The interventionists, unlike the internationalists, argued that the federal government should intervene in specific conflicts to aid particular democratic countries against aggressor nations. On the other hand, the noninterventionists opposed federal aid to Finland and did not want to risk involving America in

9. Henry Pratt Fairchild, ed., *Dictionary of Sociology*, pp. 32–33; Julius Gould and William L. Kolb, eds., *A Dictionary of the Social Sciences*, pp. 74–75; and G. Duncan Mitchell, ed., *A Dictionary of Sociology*, p. 26.

the European war. In the summer of 1940, Congress shifted to a fourth stage typified by the battle between preparedness advocates and rearmament opponents. Following the Nazi invasion of Western Europe, preparedness advocates controlled legislative decisionmaking and enacted the first peaceime draft in American history. Rearmament opponents would have preferred to retain the traditional voluntary recruitment method for raising an armed force.

Other factors affected the selection of these measures. First, neutrality revision, Finnish assistance, and selective service influenced major aspects of American foreign and defense strategy. The extent to which the United States aided the Allies, intervened in the European conflict, and developed a preparedness program depended largely on how Congress responded to these three proposals. Second, these topics provoked very lively controversy in the Seventy-sixth Congress. These issues make excellent cases for studying the differences between the internationalists and isolationists, the interventionists and noninterventionists, and the preparedness advocates and rearmament opponents on Capitol Hill. Third, these subjects still remain vital. Congress continues to discourse over how much economic and military assistance the United States should send abroad. A national debate has revived over whether to retain voluntary recruitment, which was adopted in 1971, or return to the draft. Above all, few historians have examined extensively the reaction of the Seventy-sixth Congress to these topics.

Neutrality policies have received the most historical treatment, particularly the perceptive analysis by Divine entitled *The Illusion of Neutrality*. Divine traces the development of neutrality legislation in the 1930s, highlighting the debate between the internationalists and isolationists. The United States, he stresses, attempted in the 1930s to escape the realities of world affairs behind a wall of neutrality measures. According to Divine, the American people supported a policy of rendering aid to the Allies without directly committing themselves to intervening in the European war. Besides concluding that neutrality was an illusion, he criticizes President Roosevelt for failing to act decisively in rallying public and congressional opinion against isolationism. Congressional internationalists likewise exhibited lackluster leadership, enabling isolationists to control American foreign policy until the outbreak of World War II.[10]

Sobel, *The Origins of Interventionism: The United States and the Russo-Finnish War*, is considered the principal account of the congressional response to that conflict. The American people, Sobel states, overwhelmingly sympathized with Finland, while private organizations raised funds primarily for economic relief. In addition, he stresses that the Roosevelt administration proceeded cautiously and preferred providing only federal economic assistance to the Finnish government. Sobel pictures the congressional battle over Finnish aid as one between interventionists and noninterventionists, claiming that the debate between internationalists and isolationists ended with the outbreak of World War II. According to Sobel, the

10. Other works discussing neutrality revision are Dallek, *Roosevelt and American Foreign Policy*, and Donald F. Drummond, *The Passing of American Neutrality, 1939–1941*.

Finnish question also caused a considerable realignment among legislators on Capitol Hill. Numerous isolationists advocated federal intervention in the form of permitting Finland to purchase American military equipment, while several internationalists opposed any national intervention against the Soviet Union. The limited economic assistance approved by Congress, Sobel concludes, did not help the Finnish army very much but established a precedent for American intervention in the European war by aiding other victims of aggression.[11]

The principal account of the Selective Service Act of 1940 remains a doctoral dissertation by Spencer. Spencer ably describes how the Military Training Camps Association, comprising many veterans who had trained at Plattsburg, New York, during World War I, played the leading role in securing enactment of the first peacetime draft in American history. Besides framing the original legislation, the pressure group found congressional sponsors, testified before Senate and House committees, and lobbied strenuously on Capitol Hill and among the American people. Spencer also stresses how world events and increasing public acceptance facilitated the adoption of selective service and emphasizes the national debate between the preparedness advocates and rearmament opponents.[12]

This book uses a different approach than the above-mentioned works. Divine, Sobel, and Spencer devote more attention to the role of the executive branch, public opinion, and pressure groups. Divine features President Roosevelt and the State Department, while Sobel stresses the impact of public opinion, the media, private organizations, and the executive branch. Spencer highlights pressure groups in general and the Military Training Camps Association in particular. By contrast, I will concentrate almost exclusively on the part played by Congress in repealing the arms embargo, providing economic assistance to Finland, and enacting selective service.

These other works drew less extensively upon congressional manuscript sources. Divine, Sobel, and Spencer use numerous newspapers, magazines, and other published sources. Divine also relies heavily on unpublished correspondence of President Roosevelt and the State Department. Sobel cites relatively few manuscripts, while Spencer primarily uses the extremely valuable Grenville Clark Papers.[13] I have used mainly congressional correspondence, much of which was not open for scholarly research at the time the other works were written. Legislative collections disclosed the sources of the divisions between the isolationists and internationalists on the arms embargo, the interventionists and noninterventionists on Finnish aid, and the preparedness advocates and rearmament opponents on selective service measures. In addition, they furnished indispensable information

---

11. Andrew J. Schwartz, *America and the Russo-Finnish War*, is a general account.

12. Spencer, "Selective Training and Service Act." Other pertinent studies are John Joseph O'Sullivan, "From Voluntarism to Conscription: Congress and Selective Service, 1940–1945" (Ph.D. diss.), and Martin L. Fausold, *James W. Wadsworth, Jr.: The Gentleman from New York*, pp. 310–19.

13. The Grenville Clark Papers are housed at the Baker Memorial Library, Dartmouth College. Besides directing the Military Training Camps Association, Clark played a critical role in securing adoption of selective service.

concerning floor strategy and factions that influenced voting behavior. The Hiram W. Johnson and William Allen White papers, the latter containing several lucid letters from Republican Sen. Clyde M. Reed of Kansas, describe isolationist strategy at the regular 1939 session. In regard to the White House neutrality conferences, the infrequently cited Warren R. Austin Papers include penetrating insights made by a major Republican participant. On Finnish legislation, the Arthur H. Vandenberg Papers and particularly the recently opened Prentiss M. Brown Papers contain invaluable material. Vandenberg was a close friend of Finnish Ambassador Hjalmar Procopé, while Brown sponsored Finnish aid legislation in the Senate. Besides the Grenville Clark Papers, the Wadsworth Family Papers are an indispensable source on peacetime conscription. Wadsworth, who introduced the selective service bill in the House, illuminates both legislative strategy and the role of Republican presidential nominee Wendell L. Wilkie. Numerous other congressional papers clarify the isolationist and internationalist responses to these issues.[14]

Oral history, a research technique not common at the time the other works were written, is employed in this book. I conducted an extensive interview with Senator Brown of Michigan, who helped frame Finnish legislation. Brown disclosed considerable information not published previously about the background of his measure and about legislative strategy. The memoirs of Representative Wadsworth of New York clarified his role in securing enactment of a peacetime draft.[15]

This book also makes the first composite biographical sketches of the isolationists and internationalists serving in the Seventy-sixth Congress. Divine, Sobel, and Spencer did not trace the biographical backgrounds of the legislators deciding American foreign and military policy. The collective portraits, described in Chapter 2, sketch the educational, occupational, religious, military, and political backgrounds of the members determining neutrality, Finnish aid, and selective service programs.[16]

New historical techniques, not widely employed by historians at the time the other works were written, are used here. Divine, Sobel, and Spencer follow traditional approaches in studying the nature of congressional alignments. On significant roll calls, I use statistical data supplied by the Inter-University Consortium for Political Research to determine the alignments.[17] These figures not only provide a more definite means of measuring the impact of political party, sectionalism, and other voting determinants, but they also conflict with a few traditional assumptions concerning congressional alignments. With the aid of this "new history" approach, I also explore the effect of ethnic background on the three issues.

This book tests several interpretations concerning the nature of congressional

14. The Hiram W. Johnson Papers are located at the Bancroft Library, University of California, Berkeley; the William Allen White, Jr., Papers and Wadsworth Family Papers are at the Library of Congress; and the Arthur H. Vandenberg Papers and the Prentiss M. Brown Papers are at the Bentley Historical Library, University of Michigan.

15. Prentiss M. Brown, Interview with Author, and James W. Wadsworth, Jr., Memoirs.

16. Donald R. Matthews, *U.S. Senators and Their World*, provides an excellent model for conducting a career-line analysis of national legislators.

17. The Inter-University Consortium for Political Research is located at the University of Michigan.

alignments. For 1939 and 1940, Julius Turner, George L. Grassmuck, Robert A. Dahl, and Leroy N. Rieselbach picture the Democrats as avowed internationalists, interventionists, and preparedness advocates supporting Roosevelt's foreign policy. Republicans, on the other hand, are depicted as determined isolationists, noninterventionists, and rearmament opponents advocating greater congressional control over the White House. With the assistance of Consortium roll-call data, I assess the impact of political party affiliation on foreign policy and preparedness measures. Although considering partisanship an important variable, I stress that political parties often were more divided than previously thought. A sizeable number of Democrats opposed the president on neutrality and selective service, while several Republican senators supported the administration.[18]

Several reevaluations are made here concerning the sectional alignments of Congress on foreign policy. Grassmuck, Patterson, Wayne S. Cole, and Marian D. Irish describe the Southern members as the leading internationalists, interventionists, and preparedness advocates in the legislative branch in the 1939–1940 period. Internationalism appealed to Southerners because of their traditional military pride, highly Anglo-Saxon background, solid Democratic party allegiance, and the economic benefits they derived from defense spending.[19] On the other hand, Ray A. Billington, Selig Adler, Ralph H. Smuckler, and Jeannette P. Nichols portray the Great Lakes and Great Plains members as the primary spokesmen for nonentanglement. Isolationism prevailed in the Great Lakes and Great Plains because of their inland geographical location; their relatively high concentration of Republicans, Germans, and Scandinavians; and their belief in economic self-sufficiency.[20] As this book shows, the South did not always act as the most internationalist or interventionist, and the Great Lakes and Great Plains frequently were not the most isolationist or noninterventionist sections. Border and sometimes Middle Atlantic senators stood at the forefront of the internationalists and interventionists, while Pacific senators and New England representatives often led the isolationist, noninterventionist faction.

I attempt to employ a more precise means of measuring regional loyalties. Many social scientists use four standard sectional divisions—Northeast, Midwest, South, and West—for assessing geographical alignments. Since these divisions may be too broad, I have grouped legislators instead into the eight regional categories used in Consortium surveys. The eight sections are the New England, Middle Atlantic, Great Lakes, Great Plains, Southern, Border, Mountain, and Pacific states.

18. Julius Turner, *Party and Constituency: Pressures on Congress*; George L. Grassmuck, *Sectional Biases in Congress on Foreign Policy*; Robert A. Dahl, *Congress and Foreign Policy*; and Leroy N. Rieselbach, *The Roots of Isolationism*, have stressed the role of political parties in international affairs.

19. The internationalism of the South has been described in Grassmuck, *Sectional Biases*; James T. Patterson, "Eating Humble Pie: A Note on Roosevelt, Congress, and Neutrality Revision in 1939"; Wayne S. Cole, "America First and the South, 1940–1941"; and Marian D. Irish, "Foreign Policy and the South."

20. Ray A. Billington, "The Origins of Middle Western Isolationism"; Selig Adler, *The Uncertain Giant, 1921–1941: American Foreign Policy Between the Wars*; Ralph H. Smuckler, "The Region of Isolationism"; and Jeannette P. Nichols, "The Middle West and the Coming of World War II," have pictured the Middle West as the core of isolationist strength.

The Northeast is divided into New England and Middle Atlantic, the Midwest into Great Lakes and Great Plains, the South into Southern and Border, and the West into Mountain and Pacific.[21]

Several considerations influenced me to adopt these criteria. Although sharing some common traits, each subsection has distinct political party loyalties, economic interests, and ethnic configurations. Differences include predominant economic activity, extent of urbanization and industrialization, type of farming, and density of population. The New England states, for example, voted predominantly Republican, had moderate manufacturing and urban settlement, were not heavily populated, had numerous dairy and fruit farms, and comprised mainly English and Irish inhabitants. On the other hand, the Middle Atlantic states had a more competitive two-party system, were highly industrialized, urbanized, and populated, and had numerous Germans, Italians, and Eastern Europeans. The Great Lakes states generally supported Republicans, had extensive commerce, included numerous cities and vast populations, and contained a sizeable number of Poles, Italians, and Scandinavians. The Great Plains, meanwhile, aligned more heavily with Republicans, had smaller populations and fewer cities, depended mainly on grain and livestock farming, and comprised many Germans and Scandinavians.

Marked differences characterized the other subsections. The South solidly supported the Democrats, was primarily agricultural, had large cotton and tobacco farms, and did not have many ethnic groups. Although controlled by Democrats, the Border states were more industrialized, populated, and urbanized, and had at least four major ethnic groups. Germans resided in all Border states, while other common ethnic groups included the Italians, Irish, and Russians. The Mountain states overwhelmingly backed Democrats, engaged primarily in mining and agriculture, were sparsely populated, and included a sizeable number of Mexicans, Germans, and Russians.[22] Despite having similar ethnic groups, the Pacific states contained a larger Republican minority, were more populated and urbanized, had more industry, and were less agricultural.

Traditional views about ethnic alignments are reexamined in this work. Samuel Lubell and Louis L. Gerson, for example, describe the Germans as isolationist and noninterventionist in the pre-World War II period. Situated primarily in the Great Lakes and Great Plains, the 12 million Germans resented the chauvinistic discrimination by other Americans against their culture in World War I and feared that involvement in a conflict against Hitler might result in similar reprisals. Nazi organizations subjected them to enormous propaganda designed to divert their

21. The regional breakdown is as follows: *New England*: Connecticut, Maine, Massachusetts, New Hampshire, Rhode Island, Vermont; *Middle Atlantic*: Delaware, New Jersey, New York, Pennsylvania; *Great Lakes*: Illinois, Indiana, Michigan, Ohio, Wisconsin; *Great Plains*: Iowa, Kansas, Minnesota, Missouri, Nebraska, North Dakota, South Dakota; *South*: Alabama, Arkansas, Florida, Georgia, Louisiana, Mississippi, North Carolina, South Carolina, Texas, Virginia; *Border*: Kentucky, Maryland, Oklahoma, Tennessee, West Virginia; *Mountain*: Arizona, Colorado, Idaho, Montana, Nevada, New Mexico, Utah, Wyoming; *Pacific*: California, Oregon, Washington.

22. The Border states are located between the North and the South, while the Mountain states are those through which the Rockies run.

loyalties to the German fatherland.[23] Lubell, along with T. Ryle Dwyer, pictures Irishmen as a significant component in the isolationist, noninterventionist coalition. Anti-British sentiments inspired the noninterventionism of 15 million Irish residing mainly in the urban northeastern states. Irregardless of despising the totalitarian Nazi methods, the Irish protested that the British had denied them political independence and had disallowed religious freedom.[24] Mark Lincoln Chadwin portrays the Scandinavians as a third part of the isolationist, noninterventionist coalition. Residents of midwestern and upper northwestern regions, Scandinavians advocated strict neutrality because their native governments and clergy had espoused noninterventionism.[25]

These generalizations about ethnic groups, I believe, have been exaggerated. In order to assess the influence of ethnic background on voting behavior, I have used the family surnames of the legislators. The nationality of each member was determined by using the most common ethnic origin of the family surname as listed in Elsdon Coles Smith, *New Dictionary of American Family Names*. Although this process confirmed the Scandinavian isolationism and noninterventionism, I found that Irishmen and some Germans were quite internationalist and interventionist. Since this methodology has limitations, the conclusions must be regarded as tentative. The ethnic composition of the congressional district or state was not assessed because insufficient data were available. In some instances, a senator or representative was of a different nationality than the predominant ethnic group of the congressional district or state. Democrat Robert F. Wagner, a native of Germany, represented the heavily Irish and Italian New York State, while Progressive Robert M. La Follette, Jr., of French descent served German and Scandinavian Wisconsin.

In addition, traditional views about congressional party leadership are examined. Political scientists have contended that the majority party in Congress usually acts more cohesively than the minority party.[26] Democrats controlled both the Senate and the House in the 1939–1940 period, easily outnumbering the Republicans. Majority party leaders, I have found, often exhibited less effective control than the minority heads, especially in the upper chamber. In the Senate, Majority Leader Alben W. Barkley of Kentucky often encountered greater resistance from his party than did Minority Leader Charles L. McNary of Oregon. On the House side, Minority Leader Joseph W. Martin, Jr., of Massachusetts usually secured more party cooperation than did Majority Leader Sam Rayburn of Texas.[27]

Subsequent chapters treat several major questions. What role did the Seventy-sixth Congress play on neutrality revision, Finnish assistance, and selective service?

23. Samuel Lubell, *The Future of American Politics*; Louis L. Gerson, *The Hyphenate in Recent American Politics and Diplomacy*.

24. Lubell, *Future of American Politics*; T. Ryle Dwyer, *Irish Neutrality and the USA: 1939–47*. For further analysis, see Lawrence H. Fuchs, "Minority Groups and Foreign Policy."

25. Chadwin, *Hawks of World War II*.

26. Grassmuck, *Sectional Biases*, and Matthews, *U.S. Senators*, have found the majority party more united than the minority.

27. Studies of congressional leadership include Barkley, *That Reminds Me*; C. Dwight Dorough, *Mr. Sam*; Dwayne L. Little, "Man in the Middle: Sam Rayburn as Majority Leader, 1937–1940"; Walter J. Heacock, "William Brockman Bankhead: A Biography" (Ph.D. diss.); Walter K. Roberts, "The Political Career of Charles Linza McNary, 1924–1944" (Ph.D. diss.); and Martin, *Fifty Years*.

What individuals or groups originated each measure? What changes, if any, did congressional committees make? Who led the battles in Congress for and against the legislation? What were the basic issues at stake? What changes, if any, were made on the Senate and House floors? What factors influenced congressional voting behavior? What role did President Roosevelt, pressure groups, public opinion, and European events play? What was the impact of each measure?

Before examining these questions, however, it is essential to determine the nature of the isolationist and internationalist factions on Capitol Hill. In order to understand the congressional response on foreign policy and defense issues, it is helpful to know more about the legislators making those decisions. In the next chapter, therefore, I will describe who the isolationists and internationalists were and indicate how the two factions differed.

2

A Portrait of Congress

The Seventy-sixth Congress held the awesome responsibility of deciding the pace of American involvement in the European war. Before describing the legislative response to the coming of World War II, it may be helpful to provide composite biographical portraits of the internationalists, isolationists, and moderates. Basically, internationalists favored discarding the arms embargo and argued that national defense compelled American cooperation with other nations to prevent world chaos. At the other pole, isolationists preferred remaining aloof toward European affairs and continuing the ban on munitions sales to any belligerent nation. Moderates opposed the strict isolationist legislation because they believed the Axis powers threatened world peace. At the same time, they urged giving only limited assistance to Allied countries so that the United States would not become directly involved in war.

For the regular session in 1939, it is difficult to categorize the senators because no roll-call votes were conducted on the neutrality issue. Classification is based instead on a *Congressional Intelligence* survey taken on 7 April, less than one month after the German takeover of Czechoslovakia[1] (see appendix 1). In the poll, senators were asked if they favored increasing the authority of President Franklin D. Roosevelt to determine aggressors among belligerent nations. Members supporting the granting of such power are labeled internationalists, while opponents are categorized as isolationists, and undecided legislators are defined as moderates.

In early April, senators divided sharply on foreign policy questions. Thirty-four recommended giving the chief executive discretionary authority, but thirty-five urged retaining the arms embargo. Twenty-three were uncommitted, preferring to wait until the Foreign Relations Committee acted on neutrality revision. Four senators, including one internationalist, one isolationist, and two moderates, were not interviewed. Since neither internationalists nor isolationists held a numerical majority, the undecided members, composing over one-fourth of the Senate, held the balance of power on major foreign policy legislation.

A homogeneous group politically, internationalists came predominantly from east of the Mississippi River. Practically all the advocates of expanding commitments abroad were Democrats, including Foreign Relations Committee Chairman Key Pittman of Nevada, Tom Connally of Texas, and Claude D. Pepper of Florida. Middle Atlantic and Border members spearheaded the campaign for American military assistance to European nations, while Southern senators, ordinarily considered the bulwark of internationalism, were more cautious about revising American

---

1. "Congressional Poll on Neutrality," p. 4.

foreign policy[2] (see tables 1, 2). Southerners Pat Harrison of Mississippi, Carter Glass of Virginia, Josiah W. Bailey of North Carolina, James F. Byrnes of South Carolina, and Walter F. George and Richard B. Russell of Georgia still resented the earlier attempts by President Roosevelt to enlarge the Supreme Court and to defeat conservative Democratic party members in the 1938 primaries.

Averaging sixty-four years of age, internationalists came from rural, privileged backgrounds. A vast majority had been born in the same state they represented and had grown up on farms or in small towns, but often they had moved to larger communities. Democrats Sen. Robert F. Wagner of New York and Sen. James E. Murray of Montana had immigrated to the United States from Germany and Canada, respectively. Educationally, all had attended college and a vast number had matriculated at graduate or professional schools. Besides comprising mainly lawyers, the internationalists were affiliated with Methodist, Presbyterian, or other Protestant denominations[3] (see tables 3 through 8).

Considerable military and political experience characterized the internationalists. Nearly one-half had participated in the Spanish-American War, World War I, or peacetime military service. Although Democrats Carl Hayden of Arizona, James M. Mead of New York, and Charles O. Andrews of Florida had spent at least a quarter of a century in other political positions before they were elected to Congress, internationalists typically averaged around twelve years of apprenticeship in state legislatures and local judicial offices (see tables 9, 10, 11).

By contrast, isolationists were a more heterogeneous group politically and came predominantly from the western United States. The nucleus of the isolationist group was Republican, as were the more dynamic and vocal leaders, including Gerald P. Nye of North Dakota, Arthur H. Vandenberg of Michigan, and William E. Borah of Idaho. Led by Bennett Champ Clark of Missouri and Burton K. Wheeler of Montana, nearly one-fourth of the Democrats also favored continuing a neutral foreign policy. The Pacific delegation, which included a high proportion of Republicans serving an area insulated geographically from European affairs, directed the resistance to expanding American commitments abroad. The Great Lakes and Great Plains, normally pictured as the centers of isolationism, and the Mountain and New England blocs also supported the isolationist forces[4] (see tables 1, 2).

A considerably younger group than the internationalists, the isolationists came from rural, less prestigious socioeconomic backgrounds. They averaged fifty-eight

2. Wayne S. Cole, Marian D. Irish, George L. Grassmuck, and other scholars have described the South as most internationalist in the Roosevelt era.

3. U.S., Congress, *Biographical Directory of the American Congress, 1774–1961 (BDAC)*; Margaret Blackly, Library of Congress, Legislative Reference Service, "Religious Affiliation of Members of 75th Congress," Typewritten Manuscript, 9 October 1940. With the exception of religious affiliation, the *BDAC* provided the background information for the members of the Seventy-sixth Congress. The percentages in all tables have been rounded off and may not always equal 100 percent. Categories for education, main nonpolitical occupation, and religion are based on those used by the Inter-University Consortium for Political Research, University of Michigan.

4. Ray A. Billington, Selig Adler, Ralph H. Smuckler, Jeannette P. Nichols, and other scholars have pictured the Middle West as least internationalist in the Roosevelt period.

years of age, were all native Americans, had grown up in small towns, had remained in their native states, and had spent adult life in larger communities. In contrast with the internationalists, isolationists had received fewer years of formal education and had pursued less prestigious occupations. Although a majority had attended college, less than one-half had matriculated at professional or graduate institutions. Republicans John Townsend of Delaware and Clyde M. Reed of Kansas had only attended elementary school. Isolationists had usually engaged in law or journalism, but over one-quarter had performed more menial tasks. On the other hand, they belonged to slightly more status-oriented Protestant denominations, held much stronger religious ties, and were more often Roman Catholic (see tables 3 through 8).

Isolationists boasted fewer military and political credentials than did internationalists. A far smaller number had participated in military service or had served a decade of party apprenticeship. Of particular note, vocal isolationists Borah, Nye, and Vandenberg had each amassed only one year of previous political experience. Although some isolationists had used state legislative offices as a stepping-stone, they had most often held governorships and other state executive positions (see tables 9, 10, 11).

Moderates composed a bipartisan, highly mobile group transcending sectional lines. Democrats formed the nucleus of this faction and were joined by more than one of every five Republicans. Directed by New Englanders, the moderates also attracted support from among the Southern and Great Lakes delegations. Averaging sixty-two years of age, nearly one-half of them had moved from their native states, and many had migrated to different regions of the United States. After spending their childhoods on farms or in towns, they later settled in large cities (see tables 1 through 5).

In terms of socioeconomic class, they resembled the highly elite internationalists. Two-thirds had attended either professional or graduate schools and only one in six had not matriculated at college. Although most practiced law, the moderates as a group demonstrated greater diversification, since many of them had ventured into journalism, medicine, and other professions. Concerning religion, they identified more readily with the isolationists by belonging to Presbyterian and other elite Protestant denominations. On the other hand, there were more neo-Fundamentalists and fewer Roman Catholics in their camp (see tables 6, 7, 8).

The moderates had much more military and political experience than the isolationists. Moderates, at least one-third of whom had served in World War I or in other military service, had received the most political training. A substantial majority had spent over fifteen years in apprenticeship and Glass had even spent over forty years in sundry political positions. Before joining the Senate, nearly one-half had belonged to the House of Representatives (see tables 9, 10, 11).

In the lower chamber, meanwhile, three key roll-call votes were conducted in June 1939 on foreign policy legislation. Classification of representatives is based on these tallies, which included the Bloom bill to loosen the restrictions on American neutrality and two key isolationist amendments. The Vorys motion, approved 214 to

173 by the House, prevented repeal of the arms embargo, while the Tinkham amendment, barely rejected 196 to 194, sought to recommit the entire measure to the Foreign Affairs Committee. After acting on the two motions, the House adopted 201 to 187 the modified Bloom bill. The 179 representatives favoring the Bloom proposal and opposing any alterations are cited as internationalists, while the 188 congressmen rejecting the Bloom legislation and supporting the Vorys and Tinkham motions are defined as isolationists. Sixty-two members did not align consistently with either side and are placed in the moderate category (see appendix 2).

House internationalists, who resembled their Senate allies politically, fit traditional political and sectional stereotypes of the period. Nearly all the neutrality revision advocates were Democrats, including Majority Leader Sam Rayburn of Texas, Speaker William B. Bankhead of Alabama, Foreign Affairs Committee Chairman Sol Bloom of New York, and Military Affairs head Andrew J. May of Kentucky. Far more internationalist than their Senate compatriots, Southern representatives spearheaded the campaign in the lower chamber for military assistance to Great Britain and France. Border and Mountain delegations were slightly in favor of removing the arms embargo, but Middle Atlantic representatives were much more isolationist than their Senate counterparts (see tables 1, 2).

Age and geographical and socioeconomic considerations clearly distinguished the internationalist congressmen from their Senate allies. Averaging fifty-four years of age, internationalists had usually remained in the states where they were born, spent their childhood years on farms, and subsequently moved to much larger residential areas. In contrast to their Senate compatriots, they were much younger, fewer of them were foreign-born, they had changed residences more often, and more of them had settled in urban communities. Internationalists typically had studied at either professional or graduate institutions, practiced law, and belonged to prestigious Protestant churches, but many came from less elite backgrounds. One in every six had not completed high school, while nearly one-third had engaged in nonprofessional occupations. Neo-Fundamentalist faiths and, surprisingly, Roman Catholicism commanded the religious loyalties of around 40 percent of the internationalists. In historical works, Roman Catholic congressmen of Irish, German, and Italian descent usually are pictured as isolationists (see tables 3 through 8).

Compared to their Senate counterparts, internationalist representatives had much less previous military and political experience. Over two-thirds had neither participated in World War I nor trained for combat duty. A majority had served fewer than ten years in other political offices, with one-third spending less than the equivalent of one U.S. Senate term in prior party positions. State legislative and local judicial jobs provided the most common avenues to Congress for both internationalist groups (see tables 9, 10, 11).

As in the Senate, House isolationists formed a more politically heterogeneous group than did the internationalists and transcended sectional lines. Republicans still dominated the isolationist camp and furnished as its leaders party head Joseph W. Martin, Jr., of Massachusetts and Foreign Affairs Committee members Hamilton

Fish of New York and John M. Vorys of Ohio. Although attracting fewer Democrats than in the Senate, isolationists did receive support from war referendum spokesman Louis Ludlow of Indiana and around ten percent of the Democrats. Regionally, House isolationists formed different alignments than their Senate allies. New Englanders, surprisingly, led the isolationist forces proportionately in the lower chamber and coalesced with Great Plains representatives in defending neutrality policies.[5] Isolationists also received considerable backing from the Middle Atlantic and Great Lakes delegations, but attracted considerably less support among the Mountain and Pacific members (tables 1, 2).

In terms of age and geographical background, isolationist congressmen sharply contrasted with both their Senate compatriots and internationalist representatives. Averaging fifty-three years of age, they usually had remained in the states where they were born, had grown up in either towns or cities, and represented both large and small communities. In comparison with their Senate counterparts, they were five years younger and had spent both their childhood and adult years in more populous areas. They were more mobile and resided in smaller communities than the internationalists (tables 3, 4, 5).

Isolationists came from a relatively less elite socioeconomic background than their adversaries in the lower chamber. They usually had attended beyond college, practiced a profession, and were affiliated with prestigious Protestant Reformation denominations. Although they had received more years of formal education than their Senate allies, they exhibited less impressive academic credentials than the internationalist representatives and had not enrolled as often at professional schools. Comprising fewer lawyers, they had served in a wider variety of professions and in more menial tasks than their opposition. Isolationists identified much less with pietistic and fundamentalist Protestant sects and the Roman Catholic faith and often had little or no connection with organized religion (tables 6, 7, 8).

Isolationists had much more previous military service and less prior political experience than the internationalists. Three of seven isolationist congressmen either had fought in World War I or had received peacetime training in the armed forces. Politically, isolationists had averaged around six years in apprenticeship positions and most often had held state legislative or local executive offices. An astonishing 21 percent of the isolationists had occupied no other office or appointment before being elected to the lower chamber (see tables 9, 10, 11).

Moderate representatives, meanwhile, differed markedly from their Senate compatriots, both politically and sectionally. Even though wielding some power on foreign policy issues, the sixty-two moderate members asserted less influence than their allies in the upper chamber. Besides appealing mainly to Democrats, the moderate position had the most support proportionately among the Border and Pacific blocs, rather than among the New England and Southern delegations (see tables 1, 2). New York Republicans Bruce Barton and James W. Wadsworth, Jr.,

5. George L. Grassmuck, *Sectional Biases in Congress on Foreign Policy*; Julius Turner, *Party and Constituency: Pressures on Congress*; H. Bradford Westerfield, *Foreign Policy and Party Politics: Pearl Harbor to Korea*, pp. 45–47.

along with Democrat Robert G. Allen of Pennsylvania, stood at the forefront of the uncommitted faction.

Youth, geographical mobility, and a less elite image characterized the moderate congressmen. Averaging only forty-eight years of age, they typically had grown up on farms and spent their adult years in small towns. Considerably younger than other senators or representatives, they were all native Americans, had often moved to different sections of the United States, and resided in relatively small communities. Many had attended a professional school, practiced law, and belonged to Reformation Protestant denominations. In contrast with other congressmen, however, fewer uncommitted members had pursued education beyond college or had engaged in professional occupations. Several had held relatively less esteemed jobs in commerce, trade, services, and public-school teaching. Twenty percent practiced the Roman Catholic faith, a figure surmounting that of all other factions except internationalist Republicans (see tables 3 through 8).

Despite having considerable military experience, moderates demonstrated unimpressive political credentials. Nearly one-half either had fought in World War I or had participated in peacetime duty, exceeding both the internationalist or isolationist camps. Serving the least political apprenticeship, uncommitted representatives averaged only five years prior training and usually had used state legislative and local judicial spots as their route to the House. At least 25 percent never had held an elective or appointive party office before arriving on Capitol Hill (see tables 9, 10, 11).

The above capsule portraits are designed to provide a clearer picture of the internationalists, isolationists, and moderates in Congress at the regular session. Politically, the Democrats favored increasing involvement in European affairs and Republicans defended strict neutrality. Geographically, Southern members endorsed internationalism, especially in the House, and the Great Lakes and Great Plains legislators espoused isolationism. Representatives and particularly senators came from elite backgrounds, comprising highly educated lawyers identified with status-oriented Protestant denominations. Roman Catholics were vastly more prominent in the House, which was accorded wider representation from New York City, Chicago, and other metropolitan communities. Besides having more military experience than isolationist senators, internationalists in both chambers had received considerably more apprenticeship in political offices.

Several unusual sectional patterns emerged. During early 1939, Middle Atlantic senators proportionately led the battle for neutrality revision, and Pacific senators and New England representatives stood at the forefront of the isolationist faction. The Middle Atlantic senators, comprising mainly Democrats, remained loyal politically, backing Roosevelt's international policy. They also served states engaged in vast commerce with Great Britain and located closer geographically than most other sections to the European war. On the isolationist side, the Pacific Senate delegation included influential Republicans Charles L. McNary of Oregon and Hiram W. Johnson of California, who were against granting any additional authority to a

Democratic president. These members served states relying relatively little on European trade and containing numerous German and Russian constituents espousing strict neutrality policies. Geographically, the Pacific states were located the farthest from Europe and did not regard themselves as being endangered. In the House, the New England delegation proportionately led the isolationist camp in 1939 primarily because they were predominately Republicans rejecting any further foreign policy powers for the president. New England representatives also served a considerable number of Irish inhabitants counseling noninvolvement in the European war. Historians traditionally picture the Southern Democrats as the leading internationalist spokesmen and the Great Lakes and Great Plains Republicans as the most vocal isolationists in Congress. Regional delegations often differed significantly, as Southern, Mountain, and Pacific representatives and Middle Atlantic senators were more favorable than their sectional counterparts to repeal of the arms embargo.

Some trends concerning religious affiliation, formal education, and prior military and political experience conflict with traditional stereotypes. Roman Catholic representatives, who normally are pictured as strict neutrality advocates and who served predominantly isolationist Irish, German, and Italian constituents, aligned with the internationalists.[6] Irish congressmen, mostly Democrats, usually supported the president's foreign policy for political and ideological reasons. Despite the traditional Irish antipathy toward Great Britain, they insisted that the totalitarian nations were an immediate threat to world peace and warned that Hitler endangered the republican institutions and religious liberties of Roman Catholics. A substantial minority of the German Roman Catholic representatives also coalesced with the internationalists because they despised Hitler and feared the spread of totalitarian methods to non-German speaking countries. In order to stop the Nazis from further territorial expansion, they supported sending American military assistance to Great Britain and France. Isolationists in Congress also had amassed more military experience than their adversaries and had more formal education and political experience than isolationist senators.

The composite portraits likewise have significant ramifications concerning socioeconomic class and voting behavior. Internationalists usually came from more elite backgrounds and had more years or political training than neutrality advocates, especially in the Senate. Besides having had broader formal educational opportunities, they were employed in more prestigious occupations. Senators were more elite than representatives, giving them a more privileged background upon which to draw in making foreign policy decisions. As shown in subsequent chapters, political party loyalty, sectional alignments, ethnic background, and other factors influenced the diplomatic voting patterns of national legislators.

6. Mark Lincoln Chadwin, T. Ryle Dwyer, Lawrence H. Fuchs, Louis L. Gerson, Samuel Lubell, and other scholars have pictured Irishmen, Germans, and Italians as neutrality advocates in the pre-World War II era. For traditional views about the South and Middle West, see Footnotes 2 and 4.

3

The Maintaining of Isolationism

When the Seventy-sixth Congress convened in January 1939, Democrats numerically dominated both chambers. Roosevelt's party held 70 percent of the Senate seats and 60 percent of the House positions, while Republicans filled most remaining places. Third parties blossomed only in the Great Lakes and Great Plains and played the most crucial role in the Great Plains Senate delegation. The South exhibited the least competitive system, with the Democrats holding all the section's seats. To a lesser degree, Republicans controlled the New England bloc and Democrats dominated the Border and Mountain groups. Congressmen from these sections wielded a disproportionate amount of power in congressional committees because they had accumulated seniority more easily. Competitiveness between parties flourished most readily among the Middle Atlantic and Great Lakes delegations, which Republicans dominated in the House and Democrats controlled in the Senate[1] (see table 12).

Although Democrats maintained vast majorities in both chambers, President Franklin D. Roosevelt by early 1939 faced an increasingly rebellious Congress. In the Senate, Republicans had picked up eight seats in the 1938 elections, and twenty to thirty Democrats were disenchanted with New Deal programs. The situation looked even less promising for the administration in the House, where the Republicans had nearly doubled their strength by gaining eighty-one seats. Around one-third of the returning Democrats contemplated aligning with the minority party to oppose the extension of New Deal reforms.[2] Most senators and representatives expected a short session devoted almost entirely to domestic legislation, including financing work-relief programs, reorganizing the executive branch, extending the monetary policy, subsidizing agriculture, and reforming national campaigns and elections. Few realized the European situation would worsen, compelling them at once to reassess American neutrality policy.

At the regular session, Congress consequently devoted much more attention than anticipated to foreign policy. Isolationists and internationalists in early 1939 debated vigorously over the conduct of American relations abroad, with the former group still controlling legislative decisionmaking. Isolationists adamantly opposed American involvement in the European war, but disagreed over whether the nation should retaliate if its neutral rights were infringed on by any foreign belligerents. Besides championing the rigid neutrality laws, isolationists opposed both lifting the arms embargo and restoring the cash-and-carry system. Internationalists, on the

---

1. Statistics cited in this and subsequent chapters are based on data from the Inter-University Consortium for Political Research, University of Michigan.
2. Milton Plesur, "The Republican Comeback of 1938."

other hand, favored cooperating with other nations and providing at least limited, indirect aid to the Allies. Repeal of the arms embargo and revival of the cash-and-carry system, they stated, afforded the best means of keeping the United States out of European wars. Although internationalists, they were very reluctant to commit the United States either to defense alliances or to direct intervention on behalf of particular nations in specific conflicts. The debate between isolationists and internationalists intensified rapidly as the Nazis and other Axis powers continued to expand in Europe and Asia.

During the 1930s, dictatorships increasingly had endangered international peace and security. The Nazis, who had seized power in Germany in 1933, had proceeded within five years to rearm and remilitarize the Rhineland, annex Austria, and occupy the Sudetanland in northwestern Czechoslovakia. At the Munich Conference in September 1938, however, Chancellor Adolf Hitler pledged to the British and French governments that his country would seek no additional territory in Europe. Fascists, meanwhile, already had established firm control in Italy, marched into Ethiopia, and allied with Germany. On the Asian front, Japan had established a puppet state in Manchuria and since 1937 had made substantial territorial gains in China.[3]

The isolationist Congress, preoccupied with the severe economic depression, preferred to remain aloof from European affairs. In the New Deal era, the legislative branch had concentrated on establishing relief, recovery, and reform programs to combat massive unemployment, lagging production, declining agricultural prices, and enormous labor strife. Between 1934 and 1936, isolationist Republican Gerald P. Nye of North Dakota conducted a widely publicized Senate investigation of America's entrance into World War I. After holding extensive hearings, the Nye committee concluded that bankers and munitioners seeking financial profits had drawn the United States into that world conflict. The inquiry not only triggered numerous legislative proposals to prevent American involvement in future wars, but also intensified isolationist sentiments across the nation. Revisionist scholars and journalists further augmented the isolationist mood by publishing books denying that European nations had threatened Western Hemisphere peace and security in World War I.[4]

Throughout the New Deal period, isolationist Congress adopted policies avoiding involvement in European affairs. The Johnson Act of 1934 prohibited American loans to any foreign country, including World War I allies, that had defaulted on its debts. During the next two years, the Senate and House enacted a series of neutrality laws preventing the United States from exporting arms, ammunition, implements of

3. For European developments, see Robert A. Divine, *The Reluctant Belligerent: American Entry into World War II*, and Arnold A. Offner, *American Appeasement: United States Foreign Policy and Germany, 1933–1938*. For Asian developments, see Dorothy Borg, *The United States and the Far Eastern Crisis, 1933–1938*, and Herbert Feis, *The Road to Pearl Harbor: The Coming of the War between the United States and Japan*.

4. John E. Wiltz, *In Search of Peace: The Senate Munitions Inquiry, 1934–36*; Charles A. Beard, *The Devil Theory of War*; Charles C. Tansill, *America Goes to War*.

war, and noncombat goods to any belligerent nation. The embargo on nonmilitary commodities was lifted in 1937, but warring powers had to pay cash for such commodities and transport the goods from the United States in their own vessels. Numerous adamant isolationists, however, preferred even more complete American withdrawal from international affairs and supported the Ludlow war-referendum amendment. In 1938, though, representatives refused to consider the Ludlow proposal, which would have made any future involvement in war subject to popular approval unless an actual invasion of United States territory had occurred.[5]

After the Munich Conference the Roosevelt administration began contemplating revision of the neutrality laws. The State Department favored renewing the cash-and-carry provisions, which would expire in May 1939, and permitting the president to prevent American ships from visiting specified combat zones and to invoke the arms embargo. In mid-October, however, Senate Foreign Relations Committee Chairman Key Pittman of Nevada recommended a different approach. Congress, Pittman suggested, should remove the ban on munitions sales and put all trade, including armaments, on a cash-and-carry basis. Following intense discussions, State Department authorities in early November urged the administration to pursue the Pittman strategy and seek removal of the munitions embargo at the next legislative session.[6]

Shortly after the Seventy-sixth Congress convened, the president commented in a circuitous manner on the neutrality issue. In his annual message on 4 January, Roosevelt discussed the expansionist activities of Germany, Italy, and Japan and cautioned that aggression by these nations endangered American security. "There are many methods short of war," he stated, "but stronger and more effective than mere words, of bringing home to aggressor governments the aggregate sentiments of our own people." Concerning American foreign policy, the president remarked, "our neutrality laws may operate unevenly and unfairly—may actually give aid to an aggressor and deny it to the victim."[7] Roosevelt implied that the isolationist statutes had encouraged Italian aggression in Ethiopia and Japanese activity in China because the United States could not provide military assistance to the victims of foreign attacks. Although the president avoided specific recommendations, his speech was viewed by Congress as a request to revise the Neutrality Act.

Roosevelt did not want to risk another major confrontation on Capitol Hill. After the election of 1936, the president had suffered a series of setbacks causing his authority and influence to decline among both Republicans and conservative Democrats. Anti-New Dealers openly distrusted the president for seeking to increase his personal control over domestic policy and to usurp some congressional power. Besides raising federal expenditures, Roosevelt had attempted to increase the size of the U.S. Supreme Court, reorganize the executive branch, and purge conservative Democrats in Congress. The sizeable Republican comeback in the 1938 congres-

5. Robert A. Divine, *The Illusion of Neutrality*, pp. 57–161; Richard Dean Burns and W. Addams Dixon, "Foreign Policy and the Democratic Myth: The Debate on the Ludlow Amendment."

6. Divine, *Illusion*, pp. 231–33.

7. Samuel I. Rosenman, ed., *The Public Papers and Addresses of Franklin D. Roosevelt*, 8:1–4.

sional elections had further eroded the president's leadership on Capitol Hill. "We suffer under a severe handicap at this time," Republican Rep. James W. Wadsworth of New York remarked, "in that the leadership of the President in the Congress has been sadly impaired. His attack upon the Supreme Court, his insistence upon extravagence [sic] and the piling up of debt, his attempt to purge some of the very best men in his own party . . . are responsible."[8]

Roosevelt particularly proceeded cautiously because the distrust expressed by anti-New Deal Democrats extended into foreign policy. Several Southern senators still suspected the president's motives and believed his policies might entangle the United States in a European war. "I am afraid," Democrat Carter Glass of Virginia remarked, "that the 'war scare' is to be used as a red herring across the spendthrift record of the administration to divert attention from the reckless expenditures that have already bankrupted the nation." Democrat Josiah W. Bailey of North Carolina commented, "I am not going to take any step calculated to get this country into a war, as I know that even if we should win the war, we would lose the Republic." If a less ambitious president had occupied the White House, these anti-New Dealers probably would have supported neutrality revision. Besides disliking Hitler's overseas activities, they privately sympathized with Great Britain and France. Glass in early 1939 commented, "It makes me mad that we did not wipe out the entire crowd of huns when the allies had an opportunity to do it."[9] Roosevelt thus refused to direct any campaign to revise neutrality legislation, which still had considerable backing both on Capitol Hill and among the American people.

During the next week, Pittman persuaded the president to let him rather than the State Department command the battle. The son of a brilliant lawyer, the sixty-six-year-old native of Vicksburg, Mississippi, had attended Southwestern Presbyterian University and had then trekked westward to seek gold in the Yukon Territory and Alaska. Pittman in 1901 had moved to the silver boom town of Tonopah, Nevada, where he invested substantially in mines and became a prominent lawyer. Joining the United States Senate in 1913, he became the leading spokesman for Mountain silver interests and for monetary measures favorable to his state. The Nevada Democrat often united the eight silver-mining states into a formidable bloc, exaggerating the influence of the sparsely populated Mountain states. During World War I, he had sponsored legislation empowering the federal government to sell India 350 million ounces of bullion from silver dollars stored in the treasury. Pittman had served as a delegate to the London Economic Conference of 1933 and the next year had helped frame the Silver Purchase Act. This measure had authorized the Roosevelt administration to buy existing stocks of silver from domestic producers. Although adept at political maneuvers, the tall, lean Pittman often had exhibited the rough, crude

8. James W. Wadsworth, Jr., to Alexander Gordon, 9 March 1939, Box 27, Wadsworth Family Papers. For congressional disenchantment with President Roosevelt, see James T. Patterson, *Congressional Conservatism and the New Deal*, and Richard Polenberg, *Reorganizing Roosevelt's Government: The Controversy Over Executive Reorganization, 1936–1939*.

9. Carter Glass to Charles Stoll, 9 January 1939, Box 394, Carter Glass Papers; Josiah W. Bailey to George C. Warner, 25 March 1939, Personal File, Josiah W. Bailey Papers. James T. Patterson, "Eating Humble Pie: A Note on Roosevelt, Congress, and Neutrality Revision in 1939," pp. 409–10.

manner of a mining frontiersman, was plagued with alcoholism, and shunned the public spotlight.

Pittman also had played an instrumental role in international policy. He in 1916 had joined the Foreign Relations Committee and had supported President Woodrow Wilson's World War I and League of Nations programs. A loyal party member, Pittman in 1933 had become committee chairman and had helped steer prewar strategy. In cooperation with the Roosevelt administration, he had sought both limited internationalism and broader presidential discretion and had opposed the Senate isolationists. On the other hand, the Nevada Democrat had advocated Senatorial control over American neutrality policies and had kept his committee free of executive domination. The pessimistic senator feared the numerical strength of the isolationists on his committee and urged the State Department to exhibit more caution. Pittman adamantly resisted the economic internationalism embodied in Hull's reciprocal trade program and insisted that all agreements were treaties requiring Senate ratification. Besides supporting the World Court, he had partially drafted the Neutrality Act of 1935 banning the sale of munitions to all belligerents. Two years later, he had inserted a cash-and-carry principle permitting the United States to sell nonmilitary goods to warring nations. By early 1939, Pittman endorsed lifting the arms embargo and expanding cash-and-carry to cover all American exports. Roosevelt preferred repealing the entire Neutrality Act or applying the arms embargo against aggressor states only, but reluctantly cooperated with Pittman's strategy.[10]

For the next two months, however, Pittman exhibited weak leadership. Instead of introducing any arms embargo repeal legislation, he preferred serving as a mediator between the isolationists and internationalists. "My position as a compromiser," he insisted, "would be weakened if I presented bills and resolutions at this time setting forth my present opinions as to the character of legislation that should be adopted." Since he believed that isolationists controlled the Foreign Relations Committee, he was reluctant to press the neutrality question. "In fact," Pittman claimed, "any such bill or resolution that I introduced would be considered as an Administration proposal and would probably receive the united attack of all those holding diverging views."[11] Counseling against hasty action, Pittman wanted his group to explore the various alternatives and reach a consensus on a particular plan.

Pittman's committee on 19 January postponed indefinitely action on the neutrality question. Since the monetary bill was pending, the Nevada Democrat was engrossed in planning legislative strategy for raising prices on domestically mined silver. Committee deliberations, he also feared, would intensify the already spirited national debate over aiding the Loyalist government in the Spanish civil war. In

10. "Key Pittman," *Dictionary of American Biography* 8, supp. 2, pp. 530–31; Fred L. Israel, *Nevada's Key Pittman*; Wayne S. Cole, "Senator Pittman and American Neutrality Policies, 1933–1940."

11. Key Pittman to Franklin D. Roosevelt, 11 January 1939, President's Personal Files 745, Franklin D. Roosevelt Papers.

January 1939, numerous Americans were urging Congress to lift the arms embargo because the insurgent Nationalist forces of General Franco were defeating the Loyalists. Pittman's group, however, opposed American military intervention and instead favored continuing a neutral approach to the Spanish conflict.[12]

Four factions had developed within the committee. Despite controlling sixteen of the twenty-three seats, Democrats were divided so sharply over munitions sales that no group commanded a numerical majority. Internationalist Democrats Elbert D. Thomas of Utah, Claude D. Pepper of Florida, and James E. Murray of Montana definitely advocated military assistance to Great Britain and France and particularly urged repeal of the arms embargo. Pittman, Alben W. Barkley of Kentucky, Tom Connally of Texas, Robert F. Wagner of New York, and four other internationalist Democrats leaned toward revising the existing neutrality law but preferred to proceed more cautiously. A third faction, consisting of Democrats Walter F. George of Georgia, Pat Harrison of Mississippi, and Frederick Van Nuys of Indiana and Republican Wallace H. White of Maine, welcomed postponement because it gave them time to explore the various legislative alternatives. Seven isolationist members, including four Republicans, two third-party members, and one Democrat, definitely opposed American involvement in European affairs and urged retention of the arms embargo. Wielding a disproportionate influence, they typically represented either midwestern or western states and included vocal Republicans William E. Borah of Idaho, Arthur H. Vandenberg of Michigan, and Hiram W. Johnson of California and Progressive Robert M. La Follette, Jr., of Wisconsin.

Committee isolationists, however, disagreed over the best means to keep the United States out of war. Timid isolationists, such as La Follette and Vandenberg, favored retaining the Neutrality Act of 1937 and rejected American involvement in the European conflict under any circumstances. By contrast, Johnson, Borah, and other militant isolationists urged discarding the existing neutrality legislation and relying instead exclusively on international law. If any foreign power attacked the United States or infringed upon American neutral rights, Congress should consider declaring war. In an impassioned defense of international law guidelines, Johnson argued, "There would be no hardship in attempting it, and every nation would know what our position was, and how we were going to maintain it."[13]

Despite the committee stalemate, Roosevelt refused to comment publicly on the issue for several weeks. At a 7 March press conference, he stated that the existing neutrality legislation might have hindered international peace and security. "We might have been stronger," he remarked, "if we had not had it." But the president still did not support any specific plan and gave no hint when the White House would take the initiative. Prodded by Roosevelt's statement, Pittman on 8 March promised that his committee would begin hearings on the neutrality question within ten days. During the next few days, however, isolationist Republicans Borah, Vandenberg,

12. For background, see F. Jay Taylor, *The United States and the Spanish Civil War*, and Richard P. Traina, *American Diplomacy and the Spanish Civil War*.
13. Hiram W. Johnson to Hiram W. Johnson, Jr., 22 April 1939, Part VI, Box 7, Hiram W. Johnson Papers.

and Nye threatened to filibuster any administration endeavor to change the 1937 act. "Any effort to repeal or emasculate the Neutrality Act," Nye vowed, "will keep the Senate here all summer." Contrary to his earlier pledge, Pittman refrained from considering the neutrality issue at the 15 March committee meeting. Following the session, the chairman told reporters no senator had indicated interest in starting discussions on repealing the arms embargo. Pittman's refusal to commence hearings irked the administration, which wanted Congress to begin action. Privately, Roosevelt denounced "the extreme partisan mentality which is willing to subordinate patriotic considerations to the achievement of partisan objectives" and hoped "Nye, Vandenberg, and Borah will not force us into war."[14]

Hitler spurred both the president and Pittman to make a more decisive commitment. In violation of the Munich Pact, German armies on 15 March suddenly seized the remainder of Czechoslovakia. A day later, Roosevelt told committee member Connally of Texas, "We'll be on the side of Hitler by invoking the act. If we could get rid of the arms embargo, it wouldn't be so bad."[15] At a press conference on 17 March, the president insisted Congress should begin considering neutrality legislation. Pittman then held a series of conferences with State Department officials, who helped him considerably in drafting a measure.

On 20 March, Pittman introduced the bill, which he termed the "Peace Act of 1939." Declining to repeal the existing law outright or grant the president power to name aggressors, he instead suggested two major changes in the existing law. Since warring countries had been converting many American supplies to military use, the Nevada Democrat recommended eliminating the arms embargo. This change, he contended, would place all commerce with belligerent countries on a cash-and-carry basis and would eliminate the need to distinguish between munitions and noncontraband. In the other innovation, Pittman proposed authorizing the president to proclaim certain combat zones closed to American vessels and citizens so as to avoid provocative incidents on the high seas. Seeking to attract isolationist support, he recommended retaining the other sections of the 1937 act. The existing measure had denied loans to foreign nations, prohibited travel on the ships of belligerent nations, and disallowed the arming of American merchantmen. In a radio address the night before he introduced the bill, Pittman stressed that the cash-and-carry provision would keep the United States out of the European war and prevent a repetition of the World War I experience. He also claimed the proposal would insure American assistance to England and France because those two nations held supremacy on the high seas.[16]

Ardent internationalists, led by Thomas of Utah, criticized Pittman's compromise bill. Advocates of collective security and of an alliance with Great Britain,

14. *New York Times*, 8, 17, March 1939; Elliott Roosevelt, ed., *FDR: His Personal Letters, 1928–1945*, 2:862; Franklin D. Roosevelt to William G. McAdoo, 9 March 1939, Box 468, William G. McAdoo Papers.

15. Thomas Connally and Alfred Steinberg, *My Name is Tom Connally*, p. 226.

16. *Congressional Record (CR)*, 76th Cong., 1st sess., vol. 84, 20 March 1939, pp. 2923–25. For background, see R. Walton Moore to Franklin D. Roosevelt, 18 March 1939, President's Secretary's File (PSF), Box 57, Roosevelt Papers.

France, and China, they protested that Pittman's measure did not empower Roosevelt to determine aggressors and would not prevent armaments from reaching the Axis countries. Five weeks earlier, Thomas had introduced a resolution authorizing the president to name aggressors and to prevent the sale of war supplies and raw materials to belligerents. If Congress consented, the chief executive would be able to authorize American economic and military aid for victims of foreign attacks. His proposal, Thomas insisted, would place "the economic and moral force of our country in a position to be able to be used in such a way that the war maker among nations may be curbed." Although internationalists welcomed the proposal, a majority of senators feared the Thomas motion would overcommit the United States abroad. "The Thomas amendment," Nye charged, "is one which would have us taking steps which would certainly be war-like and ultimately inviting us to war. There isn't a chance in the world of the Thomas proposal winning the approval of Congress."[17]

Nye led the isolationist forces in attacking the Pittman bill. The son of a newspaper editor, he was born in Hortonville, Wisconsin, in 1892 and had pursued a career in journalism. After writing for the *Des Moines Register*, he in 1916 became editor of the *Fryburg* (North Dakota) *Pioneer* and had ardently defended agricultural interests. Besides supporting agrarian radicalism, Nye also began to endorse the Nonpartisan League activities in local politics. Farm problems, he remarked in editorials, were caused by northeastern big business and Wall Street financial interests. Nye was appointed in 1925 to the U.S. Senate to fill a vacancy caused by the death of Edwin F. Ladd and was a political maverick in the Coolidge-Hoover years. An emotional liberal, he eagerly had supported consumer causes and some early New Deal measures. On the other hand, he had opposed the National Industrial Recovery Act of 1933 because the legislation favored big business and encouraged monopolies. Nye's agrarian radicalism also influenced his foreign policy views. Since economic conditions at home were still depressed, he had urged the federal government to concentrate on helping the farmers and other impoverished groups rather than become embroiled in European commitments. Between 1934 and 1936, he had headed a special committee conducting an extensive investigation of the American munitions industry. Greedy northeastern bankers and munitioners, the Nye committee had concluded, deliberately had drawn the United States into World War I. The North Dakota Republican, who contended the United States had no legitimate rationale for entering that conflict, strongly had supported in the mid-1930s strict neutrality legislation. Nye wholeheartedly backed both the arms embargo and the cash-and-carry system and had disapproved of granting the president discretionary authority. He believed the United States could best stay out of future European conflicts by retaining the Neutrality Act of 1937.[18]

17. *CR*, 13 February 1939, p. 1347; Elbert D. Thomas CBS Radio Address, 16 March 1939, Box 8, Elbert D. Thomas Papers; Gerald P. Nye to Rev. Clarence Parr, 8 May 1939, Box 26, Gerald P. Nye Papers.
18. Manfred Jonas, *Isolationism in America, 1935–1941*, pp. 58–62; Wayne S. Cole, *Senator Gerald P. Nye and American Foreign Relations*.

Nye, along with Democrats Bennett Champ Clark of Missouri and Homer T. Bone of Washington, countered the Pittman bill on 28 March with a proposal continuing the arms embargo and all other provisions of the existing legislation. Nye affirmed, "I believe the existing law, while not all that it should be or could be, good law nevertheless. It is far better than having no law in its field whatever." Besides favoring the ban on loans, credits, and munitions sales to belligerents, he opposed empowering the president to determine aggressors and favored invoking the entire act upon outbreak of war. His isolationist measure, Nye argued, would make neutrality "a far better anchor than it now is against one hundred thirty million people being drifted [sic] into war by an unrestricted conduct of foreign policy by a few administrators."[19]

By early April, senators were debating more vigorously over American foreign policy. As the April *Congressional Intelligence* poll disclosed, thirty-five isolationist members favored the arms embargo, thirty-four internationalists advocated removal of the ban, and twenty-three were undecided. "About half," Democrat Elmer Thomas of Oklahoma remarked, "contend the United States should keep its nose out of the affairs of foreign nations, and the other half are favorable to the United States taking a a necessary and proper part in world affairs." Isolationists, who held a slim numerical advantage, comprised most of the Republicans and 25 percent of the Democrats and were from the Pacific, Mountain, Great Plains, Great Lakes, and New England states. On the opposite side, internationalists consisted almost exclusively of Democrats serving Middle Atlantic, Southern, and Border constituents. The moderate camp included mainly Democrats, along with over 20 percent of the Republicans, from New England, the South, and the Great Lakes states.[20]

The issues dividing the three camps, meanwhile, were becoming more sharply defined. In attacking the Pittman bill, isolationists placed high priority on economic considerations. Isolationists stressed that the United States had spent $33 billion in World War I and noted that 116,000 American men had died on European battlefields. Citing the Nye committee findings, isolationists feared profit-seeking munitioners and Wall Street interests might draw the nation into another global conflict. Senate Minority Leader Charles L. McNary of Oregon argued that removal of the arms embargo "would bring bigger profits to the munitions makers." "Let them fight their own battles," Republican Rep. Fred L. Crawford of Michigan remarked, "and clean up their own back yard. What visible, tangible evidence can the world produce today to show that any country gained anything by or through the World War?"[21] Since nearly all European countries had defaulted on repaying World War I debts, isolationists opposed making any future loans to belligerents.

19. *New York Times*, 29 March, 1 April 1939; Gerald P. Nye to Walter Lippman, 26 April 1939, Box 26, Nye Papers; Cole, *Nye and American Foreign Relations*, p. 160.
20. "Congressional Poll on Neutrality," p. 4; Elmer Thomas to Louis McKnight, 28 February 1939, Legislative Correspondence, Box F-G, Elmer Thomas Papers.
21. Charles L. McNary to Mrs. Harriet Gilbert, 21 July 1939, Box 7, Charles L. McNary Papers; Fred L. Crawford to Constituents, 17 January 1939, Box 5, Fred L. Crawford Papers.

The United States, Borah of Idaho complained, "loaned millions of the taxpayers [*sic*] money to them and they repudiated their debts." "Our Americans," Republican Rep. John Shafer of Wisconsin vowed, "will not go to slaughter on foreign battlefields in a tie-up with the ungodly, unchristian, bloody red butchers from Moscow, and the debt defaulting French."[22]

Cautioning against massive American financial and manpower commitments abroad, isolationists implored American legislators to solve lingering problems concerning unemployment, housing dislocation, and agricultural overproduction. Sen. Henrik Shipstead of Minnesota, a Farmer-Laborite, insisted, "The best way to discourage the dictators is to make our democracy secure by solving our own problems" and "by putting our own house in order." "America," Republican Ernest W. Gibson of Vermont counseled, "should mind her own business and take care of her own problems."[23] Inasmuch as 3 million Americans were on federal relief rolls and another 12 million were jobless, Republican Rep. Karl Stefan of Nebraska warned, "It is ill time for the United States to meddle in foreign affairs" and advised, "We should give most of our attention to the rehabilitation of our people."[24]

Ideological ramifications of the Pittman bill also were stressed by the isolationists. Since American entry into World War I had not prevented the eventual rise of European dictatorships, isolationists opposed making future crusades to preserve democracy abroad. "We made the world safe for democracy," Republican Sen. Arthur Capper of Kansas recalled, "and got the worst of it." Nye cautioned "against any course that would in any way drag our American cause into the deep mud that holds Europe like a vice," while Democrat Sen. Rush Dew Holt of West Virginia suggested, "The way to preserve our democracy is to stay out of this insane game of European diplomacy."[25]

Isolationists distrusted giving Roosevelt control of foreign affairs primarily for political reasons. A predominantly Republican group, isolationists usually had rejected the president's New Deal programs and charged that Roosevelt deliberately had sought to aggrandize his personal power. His attempts to add several U.S. Supreme Court justices and to reorganize the executive branch, they feared, would upset the balance of power between the various branches of the federal government. Isolationists predicted the president would exploit the European situation to seek additional personal authority. "Roosevelt," Sen. Hiram Johnson of California charged, "is afflicted with 'delusions of grandeur' " and endeavoring "to knock down two dictators in Europe, so that one may firmly be implanted in the United

22. William E. Borah to Mrs. C. H. Mesling, 16 January 1939, Box 426, William E. Borah Papers; John Schafer to Amos Pinchot, 18 April 1939, Box 66, Amos Pinchot Papers.

23. May Rene Lorentz, "Henrik Shipstead: Minnesota Independent, 1923–1946" (Ph.D. diss.), pp. 190–91; Ernest W. Gibson Press Statement, 14 April 1939, Newspaper Statements, Ernest W. Gibson Papers.

24. Karl Stefan to Ludwig Stanek, 4 February 1939, Box 24, Karl Stefan Papers.

25. Arthur Capper to Managing Editor of *Philadelphia Inquirer*, 21 March 1939, Box War, National Defense, Arthur Capper Papers; Gerald P. Nye to Rabbi Joseph Hager, 13 July 1939, Box 17, Nye Papers; Rush Dew Holt to Herbert O'Brien, 20 April 1939, A&M 1701, Box 36, Rush Dew Holt Papers.

States.'' Isolationists not only disapproved of giving the president more freedom to apply arms embargoes and define combat zones, but also insisted that Congress should regulate strictly the president's foreign policy maneuverability. To a lesser extent, ethnic and ideological considerations influenced isolationists to reject the enlargement of Roosevelt's international prerogatives. Several Great Plains and Great Lakes senators who held progressive attitudes and backed New Deal programs represented districts containing Germans, Scandinavians, or other nationalities opposed to American intervention in the European conflict. Denying that European developments threatened American security, isolationists claimed Roosevelt really was hoping to increase American military commitments to Great Britain and France. Republican Rep. Clifford R. Hope of Kansas warned, ''It is rather dangerous to have a man at the head of our government in times like these who is as impulsive as the President and who apparently believes in taking a lot of chances when it comes to international affairs.''[26]

Besides disbelieving war would occur in Europe, isolationists claimed Germany did not endanger American defense. When gathering information, the isolationists often relied on optimistic assessments of American visitors to Europe and on isolationist newspapers and magazines in the United States and Western Europe. Nye predicted in early March, ''There will be no war in Europe this spring, this year, or next year unless the United States encourages, urges and eggs Europe into it.'' ''I have never felt that war would break out in Europe,'' Democrat Sen. Burton K. Wheeler of Montana told reporters, ''or that Hitler would go through with his threats.''[27] If war occurred, isolationists claimed that the Atlantic and Pacific oceans would prevent the Axis nations from launching effective air and land assaults upon the Western Hemisphere.

Moderates, meanwhile, were undecided about whether to repeal the arms embargo or to maintain the existing neutrality law. On the one hand, they feared that the administration's foreign policy was too internationalist, and they hoped to keep the United States out of global wars. Charging that ''Roosevelt's course is calculated to get us into war,'' Democrat Josiah W. Bailey of North Carolina stated, ''I am profoundly opposed to our country becoming involved either diplomatically or actually in the European situation.'' At the same time, moderates were more apprehensive about worsening developments abroad and contemplated lifting the arms embargo against victims of foreign aggression. Independent George W. Norris of Nebraska remarked, ''I can not comprehend how it can be possible for human beings [Hitler, Mussolini] so to disregard the rights of innocent people'' and urged the United States ''to do everything we can honorably do to refuse to supply the dictator countries with the sinews of war to kill innocent people.'' Democrat Clyde L. Herring of Iowa succinctly summarized the moderate position: ''The hands of the President should not be tied by fanatical legislation passed in a desperate effort to

26. Hiram W. Johnson to Hiram W. Johnson, Jr., 19 March, 29 April 1939, Part VI, Box 7, Johnson Papers; Clifford R. Hope to Don Shaffer, 25 April 1939, Legislative Correspondence, Box 150, Clifford R. Hope Papers.
27. *CR*, 3 March 1939, p. 2197; *Great Falls Tribune*, 30 August 1939.

insure peace, any more than they should be raised against other nations by inspired legislation inciting belligerency.''[28]

Internationalists, meanwhile, countered primarily with ideological arguments stressing that the United States should support the democracies fighting against totalitarian aggression. American foreign policy, internationalists insisted, had encouraged aggressor nations because the existing neutrality laws prevented the United States from sending arms to the victims. Thomas of Utah asserted that the 1937 act had spurred "a revival of a rearmament race" abroad, while Democrat Lewis P. Schwellenbach of Washington cautioned, "We must not lull ourselves into a sense of security through any legislative panacea.''[29] In order to stem the expansion of the Germans, Italians, and Japanese, internationalists favored lifting the munitions embargo and cooperating with those governments seeking to preserve more democratic institutions. If Congress repealed the ban, the United States could give more assistance to both Great Britain and France.

Invoking a domino theory, internationalists warned that the Germans and Japanese threatened American defense and security. In early 1939, Senate Military Affairs Committee hearings had disclosed that the Nazis were intending to penetrate the Western Hemisphere with commercial airplanes easily convertible to military uses within striking range of the Panama Canal and the southern United States. Democrat Pepper of Florida feared that America would become "hemmed in between a dominant Japan on the West and a dominant Germany on the East."

Internationalists urged an American foreign policy based on international law. Since the arms embargo violated global statutes, the internationalists argued that Congress should permit the sale of munitions to belligerents. The Hague Convention of 1907 had authorized nonaligned states either to adopt new measures or to revise old statutes to safeguard their rights and to engage in foreign commerce. Republican Sen. Warren R. Austin of Vermont claimed the legislative branch should change guidelines in midcourse because "we cannot be bound by rules imposed upon us by belligerents elsewhere on earth.''[30]

Internationalists, almost exclusively Democrats, favored granting Roosevelt principal power over foreign affairs. Since the president belonged to the Democratic party, internationalists insisted Congress should not hinder his flexibility on foreign policy questions. Many Democrats, particularly the New Dealers, denied Roosevelt was seeking to increase his own power and supported permitting him to determine aggressors and designate combat zones. Democrat Rep. Lindsay C. Warren of North Carolina, for example, claimed, "The President and Secretary Hull have admirably

28. Josiah W. Bailey to J. H. McAden, 13 April 1939, Political, Bailey Papers; George W. Norris to Miss Louise Newhall, 14 January 1939, Tray 104, Box 4, George W. Norris Papers; Clyde L. Herring Address on Neutrality, Des Moines, Iowa, 11 May 1939, Box 4, Clyde L. Herring Papers.

29. Elbert Thomas Radio Address, 16 March 1939; Lewis P. Schwellenbach Address on Neutrality, Charlottesville, Virginia, 6 July 1939, Box 1, Lewis P. Schwellenbach Papers.

30. Alexander R. Stoesen, "The Senatorial Career of Claude D. Pepper" (Ph.D. diss.), p. 136; Warren R. Austin to W. S. Kies, 11 October 1939, Senatorial Correspondence, Box 21, Warren R. Austin Papers.

handled the very delicate foreign situation." To a lesser degree, ethnic and ideological factors influenced party members to back Roosevelt's foreign policy programs. Several anti-New Dealers from Southern or Border states served English constituents advocating aid short of war to Great Britain. Ideologically, internationalists believed Roosevelt earnestly was trying to prevent the United States from becoming more embroiled in the European conflict. Enlarging executive power, internationalists contended, would enhance the president's ability to respond quickly to emergency situations. "This barking at the heels of the President," Democrat Theodore F. Green of Rhode Island protested, "and trying in the first place to hamper, and in the second place to misrepresent his every effort, is passing the bounds of mere partisanship and becoming unpatriotic."[31]

Pittman, meanwhile, convened his committee on 29 March to commence action on neutrality. The internationalists and isolationists were deadlocked on whether to even hold hearings, but eventually voted 11 to 8 to permit them. Since the cash-and-carry section was scheduled to expire 1 May, Pittman preferred to summon few witnesses and to limit testimony to two weeks. Isolationists and uncommitted members, however, blocked the chairman's strategy, insisting the committee proceed more slowly and permit unlimited discussion. Pittman, isolationists warned, would invite only internationalists defending either his or the Thomas bill to speak. "I think," Johnson of California warned, "that Pittman has the idea that he will call ten or fifteen 'disinterested' parties, like [Henry L.] Stimson, to give their views upon neutrality."[32]

Submitting to the isolationist pressure, the committee between 5 April and 8 May held exhaustive hearings. Numerous witnesses representing four schools of thought appeared before Pittman's group. Ardent internationalists, who furnished the largest number of witnesses, favored the Thomas bill. They advocated empowering the president to use economic sanctions and urged munitions sales to victims of aggression. Led by New York City financier Bernard M. Baruch, a few lobbyists espoused more cautious internationalism and defended the Pittman measure repealing the arms embargo. Militant isolationists argued that no neutrality legislation would be impartial completely and preferred relying exclusively on international law. Under the direction of Socialist Norman Thomas, timid isolationists considered the Neutrality Act of 1937 too permissive and preferred an embargo on all merchandise.[33]

Throughout April, the committee remained deadlocked. Hearings not only revealed the complexity of the issue, but also left the members sharply divided. Johnson of California observed, "We're as confused, as uncertain now as we were when we commenced," while Green of Rhode Island remarked, "The question is

31. Lindsay C. Warren to Elder B. S. Cowin, 22 February 1939, Box 20B, Lindsay C. Warren Papers; Theodore F. Green to Paul Christie, 17 April 1939, Box 92, Theodore F. Green Papers.
32. *New York Times*, 30 March 1939; Hiram W. Johnson to John Bassett Moore, 25 March 1939, Part III, Box 18, Johnson Papers.
33. Divine, *Illusion*, pp. 246–51. For testimony, see U.S., Congress, Senate, Committee on Foreign Relations, "Neutrality, Peace Legislation, and Our Foreign Policy," *Hearings*, 5 April–8 May 1939.

far more complicated than it seems at first sight." "It is a difficult question," Green indicated, "as to which of these acts, or combination of them or some act not yet drafted, or no act at all, will best serve that purpose [avoiding war]."[34] In a survey conducted on 19 April, nine internationalist members favored repeal of the arms embargo, nine isolationists preferred retaining the existing law, and four were uncommitted. A week later, Chairman Pittman claimed ten of the twenty-three members already supported his measure and was "sure that two more will come to me after the Thomas amendment is defeated." The Nevada Democrat, though, did not succeed in rallying internationalist backers of the Thomas proposal behind his plan. Minority Leader McNary simultaneously intensified efforts to persuade committee colleagues to postpone action on neutrality for one year. At the end of the month, Pittman conceded privately that divisions within the committee "will tend to prevent any legislation at all."[35]

Since the cash-and-carry provisions expired on 1 May, two committeemen proposed compromise solutions. In late April, Pittman already had warned that the termination of cash-and-carry would compel the United States to rely exclusively on international law. Democrat Guy M. Gillette of Iowa urged Congress to reenact cash-and-carry for nonmilitary goods and to permit the president to fix combat zones as off limits for American ships. On the Republican side, Vandenberg of Michigan suggested restoring cash-and-carry and retaining all other sections of the existing law. Furthermore, Vandenberg recommended delaying committee consideration of neutrality revision until the 1940 session. These plans appealed to some moderates favoring early adjournment but did not secure majority support. Internationalists insisted upon repeal of the arms embargo, while isolationists opposed reviving the cash-and-carry system.

Due to the stalemate, Pittman preferred to postpone the neutrality issue. On 8 May he journeyed to the State Department and persuaded Secretary of State Cordell Hull to cancel his scheduled appearance before the committee. Hull already had drafted a statement supporting repeal of the arms embargo, but Pittman tartly replied that "that sort of presentation would do no good." According to Pittman, isolationists Borah of Idaho and Johnson of California were prepared to interrogate the secretary intensively about American foreign policy toward Great Britain, France, and China. After hearings ended on 8 May, Pittman postponed indefinitely committee consideration of neutrality revision. On 16 May he wrote Hull, "The situation in Europe does not seem to induce any urgent action on neutrality legislation" and suggested, "For a time Hitler should be left in doubt as to what our Government will do."[36]

34. Hiram W. Johnson to John Bassett Moore, 6 April 1939, Part III, Box 18, Johnson Papers; Theodore F. Green to Joseph Rainville, 25 April 1939, Box 107, Green Papers.

35. *New York Times*, 20 April 1939; Key Pittman to Bernard M. Baruch, 26 April 1939, Key Pittman to Henry L. Stimson, 30 April 1939, File 76A–F9, Legislative Division, National Archives. There was one vacancy on the committee due to the death of Democrat James Hamilton Lewis of Illinois. Democrat Bennett Champ Clark of Missouri subsequently filled that vacancy.

36. Divine, *Illusion*, pp. 257–62; Israel, *Pittman*, pp. 162–66; R. Walton Moore to Franklin D. Roosevelt, 12 May 1939, PSF, Box 57, Roosevelt Papers; Key Pittman to Cordell Hull, 16 May 1939, File

The prevalent influence of the isolationists, coupled with the ineffective leadership of the Roosevelt administration and of Senate leaders, had contributed to the delay. Vocal isolationists, although divided on specific plans, had wielded considerable influence in the committee in preventing legislative action on neutrality revision. Despite Nazi activity in Europe, isolationists still controlled legislative decisionmaking on American foreign policy and adamantly upheld strict neutrality laws. The Roosevelt administration, although favoring repeal of the arms embargo, had exhibited little direct leadership and had relied too much on Pittman. Besides publicly discussing neutrality revision in terms of keeping the United States out of the European conflict, the executive branch also was reluctant to commit the United States to either defense alliances or direct intervention on behalf of specific European nations. In an effort to avoid alienating southern conservatives, Majority Leader Barkley decided to let Pittman handle the neutrality question. Pittman, cognizant of the isolationist influence over foreign policy decisionmaking, had procrastinated in the winter and had exhibited ineffective leadership over his committee. "There was, unfortunately, a tendency even on the part of the leadership of our party," Pepper of Florida commented, "to compromise this matter without letting the country know that the issue was up."[37]

Public opinion, although sharply divided, was slightly more internationalist than the committee. On 16 February, a Gallup poll showed that 52 percent of those interviewed approved repeal of the arms embargo in event of war. After Germany seized Czechoslovakia a month later, 66 percent surveyed supported selling military supplies to England and France. The percentage subsequently dropped a few points, but nearly three of five still endorsed the Pittman measure or other internationalist solutions. Newspapers likewise indicated growing public acceptance of neutrality revision. During March, 38 percent of editorials preferred either outright repeal or more flexible legislation, 30 percent favored maintaining rigid isolationism, only 10 percent espoused the Pittman plan, and 22 percent had no definite opinion. Within the next two months, however, editorials supporting the Pittman amendment rose to 33 percent and exceeded by nine percentage points those defending strict isolationism.

Pressure groups likewise were divided. Most business organizations favored repeal of the arms embargo but disagreed over the Thomas and Pittman bills. On the labor front, the American Federation of Labor supported retaining the ban on munitions sales, and the Congress of Industrial Organizations urged removing the restriction. Roman Catholic churches advocated keeping the existing laws, while Protestant denominations and peace organizations split openly. Internationalist peace societies, such as the League of Nations Association, the National Conference on the Cause and Cure of War, and the Carnegie Endowment for World Peace, urged permitting the sale of military supplies. On the other hand, the National Council for

76A–F9, Legislative Division, National Archives.

37. Claude D. Pepper to Cornelius Vanderbilt, Jr., 7 April 1939, 66A–82, Box 112, Claude D. Pepper Papers.

the Prevention of War, the Women's International League, and the Fellowship of Reconciliation opposed lifting the embargo.[38]

Americans thus still disagreed considerably over the best means to keep the United States out of war. Hitler's expansion in Europe, coupled with the developments in China and Spain, had convinced a majority that strict isolationist policies could no longer guarantee internal peace and security. They were not ready, however, for the United States to align directly with Great Britain and France in the European conflict. This deadlock threatened to continue, unless President Roosevelt intervened with more decisive leadership.

The executive branch, irate over the Senate procrastination, shifted attention to the House. For several weeks, Sol Bloom of New York, the acting chairman of the Foreign Affairs Committee, had been asking the State Department for permission to direct the administration campaign for neutrality revision in Congress. Roosevelt and the State Department, though, had declined the chairman's overtures and had preferred to work through the far more experienced Pittman. Although Bloom was a long-time Democratic member of the Foreign Affairs Committee, the Roosevelt administration did not believe he had astute knowledge of the complexity of the neutrality issue or skill at framing such legislation. After Pittman postponed committee action indefinitely, however, Hull permitted Bloom to take charge.

Bloom's career had resembled the Horatio Alger rags-to-riches stories. The son of poor Jewish immigrants, the sixty-nine-year-old Bloom had been born in Pekin, Illinois, and had had little formal education. Before reaching adulthood, he had sold newspapers, worked in a brush factory, served as a bookkeeper, and headed a theater ticket office. Bloom had developed a profitable music publishing chain in Chicago and had then prospered in real estate and construction projects in New York City. A generous supporter of Tammany Hall, Bloom in 1923 was elected by sixty-seven votes to the United States House of Representatives from a solidly Republican district. During the 1930s, he had attracted considerable national attention as publicity director for the George Washington Bicentennial celebration and the Constitution Sesquicentennial. A domestic liberal, he had endorsed federal relief agencies, labor legislation, and other Roosevelt New Deal measures. Bloom, whose amusing antics and off-color jokes often were criticized, was short statured, radiant, popular, and friendly.

Bloom had also played a prominent role in foreign policy matters. The New York Democrat loyally supported the president's international and defense programs and argued that the strict neutrality legislation of the mid-1930s benefited aggressor nations. In 1937, he favored a flexible neutrality measure permitting Roosevelt to exercise his judgment in applying cash-and-carry. When Democrat Sam McReynolds of Tennessee suffered a crippling heart attack in the fall of 1938, Bloom became acting chairman of the Foreign Affairs Committee. He directed the battle in 1939 for revising neutrality legislation in the House and particularly advocated repeal of the arms embargo and giving the president authority to determine aggres-

38. Divine, *Illusion*, pp. 252–56.

sors. Since the Nazis already had begun conquering non-German-speaking territories, Bloom warned that both the democratic institutions and the security of the Western European nations were threatened. One of the few Jewish congressmen, the New York Democrat was alarmed at Hitler's anti-Semitic policies and at the persecution of Jews within Germany. Bloom also represented an industrial area likely to derive benefits from arms sales abroad.[39]

On 19 May, Roosevelt summoned Secretary Hull, Bloom, Speaker William B. Bankhead of Alabama, and Majority Leader Sam Rayburn of Texas to the White House to discuss administration strategy. In an emphatic plea for lifting the arms embargo, the president argued, "This would actually prevent the outbreak of war in Europe" or "would make less likely a victory for the powers unfriendly to the United States." Bankhead and Rayburn both warned that isolationist representatives might reject munitions sales to belligerents, but Roosevelt was determined to proceed. Although favoring the combat-zone discretionary power and not objecting to cash-and-carry, he expressed no preference regarding the other aspects of the legislation. Roosevelt hoped the House would complete action before mid-June, when the king and queen of England were scheduled to visit the United States.[40]

The White House conference symbolized a major administration shift. Following four months of indecision, the executive branch had made a more definite stand to remove the arms embargo. Roosevelt, though, refused to make a personal appeal, opting instead to work through Secretary Hull. Between 24 and 26 May, Secretary Hull invited all Foreign Affairs Committee members except isolationist Republicans Hamilton Fish of New York and George Holden Tinkham of Massachusetts to his Hotel Carlton apartment to stress the president's commitment to revising the neutrality legislation. Hull had feared Fish would quiz him persistently, while Tinkham had vowed to discuss with reporters any comments made by the secretary at the secret sessions.

In a letter to Pittman and Bloom made public on 27 May, Hull clarified the adminstration's foreign policy stand. Since modern combat had obliterated the distinction between munitions and raw materials, he urged the United States to revert to traditional international law by repealing the arms embargo. Hull insisted that the transit of American ships and citizens into belligerent territory endangered internal peace far more than did sending exports abroad. The secretary proposed a six-point program, which included lifting the munitions ban and permitting domestic vessels to transport cargoes abroad. In addition, Hull suggested authorizing the president to designate combat zones as off limits to all American ships and personnel. All other features of the Pittman bill, including the restrictions on loans and credits and the registering of arms shipments with the National Munitions Control Board, would be

39. Sol Bloom, *The Autobiography of Sol Bloom*; U.S., Congress, *Biographical Directory of the American Congress, 1774–1961 (BDAC)*, p. 566; "Sol Bloom," *Current Biography* 4 (1943):55–58; "Bloom's Rise," *Newsweek* 14 (17 July 1939): 15–16.
40. R. Walton Moore to Franklin D. Roosevelt, 19 May 1939, PSF, Box 57, Roosevelt Papers; Cordell Hull, *The Memoirs of Cordell Hull*, 1:643; William L. Langer and S. Everett Gleason, *The Challenge to Isolation, 1937–1940*, pp. 138–39.

retained. According to the secretary, his plan "would make easier our two-fold task of keeping this nation at peace and avoiding imposition of unnecessary and abnormal burdens upon our citizens."[41]

Bloom on 29 May introduced a neutrality bill and immediately scheduled hearings. The measure, which contained the Hull program, proposed lifting the arms embargo and revising the cash-and-carry system. American vessels could carry merchandise to any area outside combat zones, but the title to all shipments would have to be transferred to belligerents before cargoes departed from domestic ports.[42] Since internationalists controlled the Foreign Affairs Committee numerically, Bloom anticipated encountering fewer obstacles than Pittman. Hearings were scheduled to begin on 5 June.

Freshman Republican John M. Vorys of Ohio, however, threatened to block committee action. The second of four sons, the forty-two-year-old Vorys had been born in Lancaster, Ohio, and had begun his public education there. His father, Arthur, had practiced law in Lancaster and Columbus and was a Republican national committeeman. After earning a degree from Yale University, John Vorys had taught in Changsha, China, and had performed secretarial duties for the American delegation to the Washington Naval Disarmament Conference. In 1923 Vorys had received a law degree from Ohio State University and had joined his father's firm. Dabbling in politics, he had served successive two-year terms in the Ohio General Assembly and Senate and subsequently had become the state's first director of aeronautics. The dark-haired, square-jawed Republican in 1938 had joined the U.S. House of Representatives, where he opposed New Deal measures and became a member of the prestigious Foreign Affairs Committee. An isolationist, Vorys strongly favored continuing American neutrality policies toward Europe and hoped to avoid a recurrence of the World War I experience. He cited not only the massive spending and heavy casualties stemming from the American involvement, but suspected that eastern bankers and munitioners had drawn the United States into the conflict for their financial profits against the national interest. Besides claiming that European developments did not endanger American security, he insisted that the three-thousand-mile-wide Atlantic Ocean would prevent Germany from launching an effective air and land assault upon the United States. Since New Deal programs already had enhanced Roosevelt's power considerably, the Ohio Republican hoped to maintain congressional control over the president's movement into European affairs. Vorys particularly opposed granting Roosevelt broad authority either to determine aggressors or to sanction the sale of arms to belligerent nations, because such leeway would permit the president to declare war. The isolationist Ohio Republican criticized the portions of the Pittman bill intended to repeal the arms embargo but liked the other sections preserving the existing neutrality law and prohibiting the president from defining an aggressor. Following in the Republican tradition, he preferred more active American responses on the Asian front and

41. *New York Times*, 25, 27 May 1939; U.S., Department of State, *Peace and War: United States Foreign Policy, 1931–1941*, pp. 461–64.
42. *New York Times*, 29–30 May 1939.

specifically urged an embargo on the shipment of scrap iron, oil, and arms to Japan. Japanese expansion in China, he claimed, posed a greater threat to American security than did German or Italian activity at that moment.[43]

Displaying unusual activity for a first termer, Vorys urged the committee to give top priority to legislation placing embargoes against Japan. Bloom, who advocated quick approval of his own measure, feared that hearings on the Asian bill might take several days or weeks and used his authority as chairman to prevent the Ohio Republican from speaking. On 3 June Vorys wrote committee colleagues urging them to insist upon consideration of the Japanese question. Besides arguing that Congress was making "a great mistake" by determining American policy toward European conflicts first, he warned, "we have let our excitement about what *may* happen to our remote interests in Europe blind us as to what is *now* happening to our immediate interests in the Pacific." "I can't see, from a diplomatic standpoint," Vorys remarked, "why it is a bad thing for the United States simply to name Japan, recite her violation of treaties, and slap on an embargo, but that is considered, down here, as too provocative."[44] Despite his determined resistance, however, Vorys could not prevent committee hearings from beginning on 5 June as scheduled.

Isolationist Republicans Vorys, Fish of New York, and Tinkham of Massachusetts were determined, however, to weaken the Bloom bill with restrictive amendments. Fish, who still was miffed at not being invited to Hull's secret sessions at the Hotel Carlton, had denounced the secretary's tactics as "undemocratic and un-American." On 6 June the House barely rejected 11 to 9 a Vorys proposal to prohibit the export of arms and ammunition to all belligerents. Although Vorys rallied enthusiastic support from New England, Middle Atlantic, Great Lakes, and Great Plains party colleagues, Southern Democrats effectively directed internationalist opposition. Uncommitted Republicans Bruce Barton of New York and Foster Stearns of New Hampshire did not vote, diminishing the isolationist hopes of restoring the embargo. The closeness of the margin alarmed Secretary Hull and other State Department officials, who had expected internationalists to wield firmer control in the committee. To the further dismay of the administration, the committee voted the next day to postpone further action until the British royalty had completed their 12 June visit to the United States.[45]

Despite the formidable isolationist resistance, the internationalists ultimately prevailed. After recessing for nearly one week, the committee approved the Bloom measure by a 12 to 8 margin. The twelve internationalist Democrats favored adopting the flexible neutrality legislation, while the eight isolationist Republicans preferred retaining the 1937 statute. Since the committee overwhelmingly followed political lines, party affiliation was the only important variable. Granting the president more maneuverability, the Democrats claimed, would assist in "dis-

43. "John M. Vorys," *Current Biography* 11 (1950):588; David L. Porter, "Ohio Representative John M. Vorys and the Arms Embargo in 1939," pp. 103–5.

44. John M. Vorys to Members of Foreign Affairs Committee, 3 June 1939, Box 3, John M. Vorys to Mrs. Harold Kaufman, 22 April 1939, Box 4, John M. Vorys Papers.

45. *New York Times,* 27 May, 6–8 June 1939.

couraging war and preventing this country from being involved in any foreign war that may possibly occur.'' These internationalists were reluctant to commit the United States to defense alliances or to direct intervention on behalf of particular nations attacked by aggressor states. In the opposition camp, the isolationist Republicans feared that the chief executive might commit the United States to aiding victims of aggression militarily and especially protested against empowering the president to declare combat zones. The measure, they complained, had given Roosevelt permission to invoke the act for security purposes, to choose when to enforce the exchange of title provisions, and to determine the selected exports to be included. They warned, ''We should not evade our responsibility by granting the President additional power.''[46]

The outcome uplifted administration spirits. In a note to Bloom, Secretary Hull commended ''the very helpful assistance'' given by the chairman and remarked, ''All of my associates tell me how uniformly courteous and considerate you and the Committee were in the attention you gave to these problems.'' State Department counselor R. Walton Moore, who had helped draft the Bloom bill, considered the vote ''very, very satisfactory'' and was ''extremely hopeful'' the measure would ''soon go through the House.'' According to Moore, Republicans would not ''make solid opposition to the Bill'' because Barton of New York and Stearns of New Hampshire already had abstained from voting in committee.[47]

Since isolationist Republicans had furnished formidable resistance in committee, administration leaders made their first major attempt to discipline Democrats. Roosevelt on 31 May personally urged Democratic congressional leaders to secure enactment of the Bloom bill before adjournment and to resist isolationist attempts to filibuster the legislation in the Senate. A week later, the president wrote Moore, ''I am pushing the Neutrality matter and hope you will see as many people in the House and Senate as you can.'' At a 20 June press conference, Roosevelt urged prompt congressional approval of the Bloom measure to ''help our influence for peace.'' Otherwise, he cautioned, war might occur and ''we would find it very difficult to change legislation to create neutrality without having it said that we were favoring one side or the other.''[48] Secretary Hull, meanwhile, conferred in early June with several Democratic representatives at his Hotel Carlton suite and urged them to support munitions sales. ''I gave the legislation top priority on my schedule, he stated, ''since I considered it crucial in our foreign relations.''[49] Several prominent State Department officials were requested by Hull to draft speeches supporting repeal for use in upcoming floor debates. In addition, the secretary mailed every congressman a copy of his 27 May letter and sent several assistants to a 19 June meeting of the House Democratic Steering Committee. These combined administra-

46. U.S., Congress, House of Representatives, Committee on Foreign Affairs, ''Neutrality Act of 1939,'' *Reports*, no. 856.

47. Cordell Hull to Sol Bloom, 24 August 1939, Box 45, Sol Bloom Papers; Edwin Watson Memorandum for Franklin D. Roosevelt, 13 June 1939, Official File 1561, Roosevelt Papers.

48. *New York Times*, 1, 21 June 1939; Franklin D. Roosevelt to R. Walton Moore, 7 June 1939, PSF, Box 57, Roosevelt Papers.

49. Hull, *Memoirs*, 1:645.

tion efforts still failed to sway around sixty isolationist Democrats opposing either removal of the arms embargo or the discretionary power to declare combat zones. In an attempt to make the Bloom measure more attractive to anti-Roosevelt Democrats, Speaker Bankhead and Majority Leader Rayburn agreed on 26 June to support removal of the controversial belligerent zone clause.

Before crowded galleries, representatives on 27 June began four days of heated debate on the Bloom bill. Representatives used colorful, lively language, frequently spoke in dramatic terms, and often used histrionics to stress their arguments. The debate, however, shed little new insight on the issue and probably influenced very few members to change their previous sentiments. House members divided along internationalist, moderate, and isolationist lines in floor discussions.

Administration leaders relied on Democrat Luther A. Johnson of Texas rather than on Bloom to direct the debate for the internationalists. Six years younger than Bloom, Johnson was regarded on Capitol Hill as more knowledgeable on foreign affairs, a more effective speaker, and an abler tactician and organizer. Unrelated to party colleague Lyndon Baines Johnson, the sixty-three-year-old native of Corsicana, Texas, had studied law at Cumberland University in Tennessee. He had developed a large, varied practice, impressing others with his astute understanding of the statutory system and forceful presentation of cases. After serving as attorney for Navarro County, Texas, and the Thirteenth Judicial District, he had been elected in 1923 to the U.S. House of Representatives. A loyal Democrat, Johnson had aligned wholeheartedly with the internationalists and ardently had defended Roosevelt's diplomatic programs. The ranking member of the Foreign Affairs Committee, he had opposed the strict neutrality legislation of the mid-1930s and instead had favored granting the president authority to use the arms embargo only against aggressor nations and to control application of the cash-and-carry system. The neutrality measures, Johnson argued, discriminated unfairly in favor of aggressor nations and should be replaced by reliance on the principles of international law. Besides representing mainly pro-British constituents, the Texas Democrat warned that territorial expansion by Axis countries threatened the security and safety of Western Europe. Johnson also realized that Southern states relied heavily on Latin American trade, which might be endangered by Nazi aggression. At the 1939 session, he urged repeal of the arms embargo and more American military assistance to Great Britain and France. The United States, he complained, prohibited the sale of munitions and yet allowed the trading of oil, steel, and other war supplies.[50]

Almost exclusively Democrats, the 179 internationalists came primarily from the South and included at least one-half of the Border and Mountain representatives. Johnson carefully arranged speakers who believed Germany, Italy, and Japan endangered both American security and interests. Denying that neutrality revision was designed to provide assistance for Great Britain and France, Johnson, Bloom, and others instead argued that the Bloom bill was the best means to avoid involvement in foreign war.

50. *BDAC*, p. 1128; *New York Times*, 7 June 1965.

Isolationists, under the direction of Fish and Vorys, held a slight numerical advantage. Cutting across party lines, the 188 isolationists comprised practically all the Republicans and around 20 percent of the Democrats and came mainly from New England, Middle Atlantic, Great Plains, and Great Lakes regions. Dominating floor debate, they opposed giving broad authority to the president and feared Roosevelt would align the United States with Great Britain and France. Selling munitions to belligerents, isolationists contended, was an immoral action likely to plunge the nation into armed combat. Great Lakes and Great Plains isolationists particularly argued that retention of the present law would avoid a repetition of the massive cost and bloodshed of World War I.

Moderates, meanwhile, hoped to discard neutrality legislation altogether. Under the direction of Democrat Robert G. Allen, a thirty-five-year-old Harvard graduate and one-time department store sales manager, the sixty-two moderates included primarily Border and Pacific Democrats. They complained the arms embargo had encouraged overseas conflict by discriminating in favor of aggressor nations, but argued that repeal would ally the United States with Great Britain and France. Since any congressional measure would discriminate unevenly against nations abroad, moderates urged using international law as the guideline for conducting foreign affairs.[51]

In an effort to avert a showdown on the arms embargo issue, Allen on 29 June introduced a compromise amendment. The Pennsylvania Democrat proposed eliminating all neutrality legislation and using international law in diplomatic relations. Besides noting that the United States had relied before 1935 principally on global statutes, Allen claimed his amendment would afford protection against entangling alliances or commitments abroad. His plan, Allen argued, would "declare our unwillingness to shackle our foreign policy so as to render it impotent or dependent upon the acts of other nations."[52]

Democratic internationalists and Republican isolationists, however, combined to reject decisively 195 to 68 the compromise amendment. Many Americans, internationalists argued, might interpret the elimination of the entire existing measure as a step toward war because constituents frequently identified neutrality with peace. On the other hand, isolationists charged that international law would not avert the sending of youth to European battlefields and stressed that the existing laws had kept the United States out of foreign conflicts. "The Bloom bill is bad enough," Fish of New York protested, "but this proposal is a thousand times worse than the Bloom bill."[53] In addition, several Democratic moderates may have been subjected to administration pressure to oppose the compromise plan. Republican Wadsworth of New York claimed "a great many of them told me personally they were for it" and believed that Roosevelt "at the last minute" passed word that "complete repeal was going too far and might be politically dangerous." Since former President Herbert

51. *CR*, 27–30 June 1939; Divine, *Illusion*, pp. 269–71.
52. *CR*, 29 June 1939, pp. 8288–91.
53. *CR*, 29 June 1939, pp. 8304, 8311.

C. Hoover had endorsed a similar approach, over forty Republicans supported the Allen proposal. They argued that the existing law discriminated in favor of aggressors, but they opposed aligning with Great Britain and France. As Republican W. Sterling Cole of New York remarked, "The best way we can obtain the neutrality which we all seek is by strict observance of the international laws on the subject which have been built up over generations and are recognized by most of the nations of the world."[54]

Isolationists, in hopes of outmaneuvering the administration forces, seized the offensive. Following intense pressure by isolationists, Bloom agreed to eliminate the provision authorizing the president to declare combat zones. Vorys on 29 June introduced his committee amendment prohibiting the sale of arms and ammunition to all belligerents. In an attempt to attract support from moderate Democrats, though, he specifically excluded aircraft, trucks, automobiles, food, raw materials, and other items that could be converted to military use. The House initially rejected the isolationist plan the same night in a straw vote, but Fish shrewdly requested a more precise count. Several Democrats either switched sides or abstained, thus enabling the House to narrowly approve 159 to 157 the arms embargo amendment.[55]

House administration leaders, chagrined that prospects for repeal were jeopardized, resorted to a rarely used parliamentary device. A day later, Johnson of Texas sought another test vote on the munitions sales and made certain more internationalists were present. Johnson introduced a substitute resolution containing the terms of the original Bloom bill minus the Vorys amendment. This strategy backfired, as internationalists fell four votes short, 180 to 176 this time. It unfortunately is impossible to determine specific voting patterns because the ballot was taken without any published roll call.

Internationalists, however, still refused to concede defeat. In an attempt to persuade uncommitted Democrats to support munitions sales, Speaker Bankhead and Majority Leader Rayburn both joined the floor debate and vigorously defended the Bloom bill. Congress, Bankhead claimed, had made "a supreme and colossal mistake" by departing from "the time-honored and time-tested Constitutional principle of leaving the management of our foreign and diplomatic affairs in the hands of the President." "Is it immoral," Rayburn queried, "when ambitious men have the desire to control the earth, to ship arms to some little, weak country that it may let the dictator know it can get arms somewhere to protect its liberty?"[56]

These twin pleas represented the most concrete attempt by House leaders of either party to solidify ranks on neutrality. Although a majority of Democrats favored repeal of the arms embargo, Louis Ludlow of Indiana led a vocal minority opposing munitions sales and granting discretionary authority to President Roosevelt. In view of these divided sentiments, Bankhead and Rayburn had not

54. James W. Wadsworth, Jr., to William Chadbourne, 5 July 1939, Box 27, Wadsworth Papers; W. Sterling Cole to Mr. & Mrs. Fred Koecker, 29 June 1939, Box 21, W. Sterling Cole Papers.
55. CR, 29 June 1939, pp. 8320–25; Porter, "Vorys," p. 110.
56. CR, 30 June 1939, pp. 8502–11; New York Times, 1 July 1939.

attempted previously to develop a party consensus on this issue. Minority Leader Joseph W. Martin of Massachusetts, meanwhile, had disclosed in early April that his party would not make neutrality legislation a political issue. Martin noted, "There are too many varieties of opinions on our side of the House. Every man will have to speak for himself."[57]

On 30 June the House held one of its most dramatic sessions in several years. Before overflowing galleries, undaunted internationalists insisted a roll call should be taken on the Vorys amendment. In anticipation of a close margin, several representatives kept scorecards counting each tally. Democrat J. Hardin Peterson of Florida described the situation as "a tug of war," while Republican Hope of Kansas remarked, "It is going to be a close fight" because the "Administration is straining every nerve to get this bill through." To the astonishment of many representatives and spectators, isolationists easily restored 214 to 173 the arms embargo.[58]

Partisan considerations largely determined the outcome. Despite Martin's decision against making neutrality a political issue, nearly all Republicans rallied behind the isolationist Vorys amendment. Distrusting Roosevelt, they claimed the president already had assumed enormous power on domestic issues. Minority party representatives had protested numerous attempts by Roosevelt since 1937 to increase his personal authority on New Deal questions and were determined to restrict his maneuverability in foreign policy. Since the president had not revealed his personal intentions for 1940, Republicans feared he might seek an unprecedented third term in office. A large majority of Democrats favored repeal of the arms embargo, remaining loyal politically to the administration. Totalitarian nations, they also believed, upset the European balance of power and threatened American security. Over 25 percent of the Democrats ignored the pleas by Bankhead and Rayburn and aligned with the Republicans (see table 13). In a buoyant mood, Vorys boasted, "It would have been impossible for the Republicans to have put through the Vorys amendment . . . without Democratic support."[59] Mountain representatives led the rebellion against the administration, but approximately one of every five Border and Middle Atlantic Democrats also favored restoring the arms embargo. Several defecting party members believed Roosevelt had seized too much personal power and objected to his seeking another term in office. Other Democrats represented either inland regions more insulated geographically from the European conflict or more pronounced German or Irish districts.

Sectionally, the isolationist Vorys proposal fared well among representatives from the north and west. Great Plains representatives led proportionately the battle for retaining the arms embargo and allied with the New England and Great Lakes delegations. Primarily Republican isolationists, the Great Lakes and Great Plains members charged that Roosevelt already wielded too much authority over American

57. *New York Times*, 8 April, 1 July 1939.
58. *CR*, 30 June 1939, pp. 8511–13; *New York Times*, 1 July 1939; J. Hardin Peterson Newsletter, 6 July 1939, Box 20, J. Hardin Peterson Papers; Clifford R. Hope to Herman Rome, 30 June 1939, Legislative Correspondence, Box 150, Hope Papers.
59. John M. Vorys to Dr. Edward Hume, 18 July 1939, Box 4, Vorys Papers.

policy. They contended that their regions were protected from foreign invasion by the Atlantic Ocean. Economically, they served many constituents believing that greedy eastern bankers, munitioners, and industrialists deliberately were conspiring to ally the United States with Great Britain. Their grain markets relied relatively little on European trade. Numerous progressives believed the United States should concentrate on solving domestic problems and argued that repeal of the arms embargo would embroil the nation too much in international affairs. In addition, some Great Lakes and Great Plains representatives served districts including numerous Germans opposing American entry into war against their fatherland. The predominantly isolationist New England delegation also comprised primarily anti-Roosevelt Republicans and represented a considerable number of Irish constituents favoring neutrality. On the other hand, Southern and Border Democrats directed resistance to the isolationist Vorys amendment because they believed their political differences with Roosevelt should stop at the water's edge. Besides serving sections having close commercial relations with Great Britain, these internationalists had been elected largely by Anglo-Saxon voters. In addition, they recognized that the Southern and Border states were not well insulated geographically from the European war and had depended extensively on the British navy for military security. Although Southern and Great Plains delegations displayed impressive unity, regionalism played a less dominant role than political party in influencing voting behavior (see table 13).

A sampling of surnames indicates that ethnic considerations helped provide the decisive margin in favor of isolationist forces. Nearly all of the thirty-five to forty German representatives declined to place American influence against their homeland, influencing the outcome more than any other nationality. They identified with their ethnic heritage and had resented American discrimination against their nationality in World War I. Besides believing that Roosevelt had pursued a policy hostile to their native land, they were exposed to the propaganda of German-American organizations. If German members had opposed unanimously the Vorys amendment, isolationists probably could not have restored the ban on munitions sales. Around twenty Irish congressmen also supported the restoration of the arms embargo. Although disliking Hitler, isolationist Irishmen disapproved of any American military assistance to Great Britain. The British, they argued, for centuries had persecuted their Catholic religion and denied them political independence. Casting aside traditional allegiances to Roosevelt's party in this instance, they instead sympathized with the isolationist appeals of Father Charles E. Coughlin. Of striking importance, however, over thirty of the Irish Democrats remained loyal to the administration and rejected the Vorys motion. Historians usually picture the Irish members as isolationists, but a clear majority in this instance aligned with the internationalists. Along with being influenced by party loyalties, this Irish faction disdained the restrictions on Catholic worship and the other totalitarian policies of Hitler. The immediate dangers to European security posed by Nazi Germany, they insisted, outweighed any long-range animosities toward the British. Of the dozen

Scandinavians, two-thirds coalesced with the isolationists. The pacifist sentiments of their clergy, coupled with traditional nonalignment policies pursued by their native governments, convinced the Scandinavians to oppose American intervention abroad[60] (see table 31). It should be noted, however, that the above findings equate ethnicity only to surname and do not consider the nationalities within particular districts. German, Scandinavian, and especially Irish constituents may have held differing views than their congressmen on the neutrality issue.

The outcome likewise was affected by ideology. Led by Ludlow of Indiana, several Great Lakes and Great Plains Democrats did not follow the majority party position because they feared further American commitments abroad would embroil the nation in war. Wadsworth, Barton, and four other Middle Atlantic and New England Republicans bolted from their party on this question because they perceived the European struggle as a battle for the survival of democracy against dictatorships. "I know of no measure," Vorys summed up, "that has come up here since I have been here where there has been more searching of hearts and attempting to vote our real convictions as to the ultimate best way to keep America out of war."[61]

Isolationists attempted to continue their assault on the Bloom measure. Republican Tinkham of Massachusetts, a sixty-eight-year-old Boston lawyer, proposed returning the complete bill to the Foreign Affairs Committee and thus killing all efforts to repeal the arms embargo. In an extremely close tally, the lower chamber barely rejected 196 to 194 the isolationist Tinkham proposal. Although supporting the Vorys amendment earlier, twenty-six Democrats primarily from Southern and Border delegations opposed recommittal. Since the House had restored the arms embargo, they no longer found the Bloom bill objectionable and did not want to block further consideration of the measure. This time, the more united, better organized Republicans could not overcome the vast numerical superiority of Roosevelt's party. The Republicans unanimously endorsed the Tinkham plan, preferring that no action be taken at all on neutrality revision.

In an anticlimactic fashion, the House approved the modified Bloom measure by a 201 to 187 tally. Political considerations figured much more prominently than on the Vorys amendment. Democrats, including nearly one-half of those defecting from the administration side earlier, overwhelmingly backed the legislation. Supporters of the original Bloom bill considered the modified legislation better than no action at all. Inasmuch as the House had reversed the munitions sales provision, several members who had bolted the party earlier aligned with the administration this time. By contrast, Republicans almost unanimously opposed even the revised version of the Bloom measure. Although the arms embargo had been restored, they feared the legislation would increase the power of the president over American foreign policy (see table 13). With the exception of Vorys, Fish, and three others, the minority party still preferred that the House reject any neutrality revision.

60. The ethnic origins of members are derived from Elsdon Coles Smith, *New Dictionary of American Family Names*.

61. Vorys to Hume, 18 July 1939.

Sectionalism and ethnicity made considerable impact this time. Regionalism particularly played an important role in the predominantly one-party Southern, New England, and Border delegations, where five of every six congressmen endorsed a common position (see table 13). On the other hand, geographical elements still were overshadowed by political loyalties. Irish members aligned even more solidly in the internationalist camp this time, providing crucial votes enabling adoption of the modified proposal. A majority of the German and Scandinavian congressmen still resisted changing the present law in any way[62] (see table 31).

In the House, isolationists had continued to dominate legislative decisionmaking. Under the able direction of Vorys and Fish, they were well organized and waged a very effective battle. Isolationists had made limited concessions permitting the sale of aircraft and other implements of war but had kept the existing legislation largely intact. Besides reviving the arms embargo, isolationists had forced removal of the combat-zone clause. As isolationist Hope of Kansas remarked, "the bill, as passed, was much less harmful than the one which was originally introduced" because "the House adopted a number of good amendments." Roosevelt privately denounced the isolationist-inspired House action as "a stimulus to war" and contended that defeat of the proposal "would have been a definite encouragement to peace," while Secretary Hull argued that the arms embargo jeopardized both American peace and security.[63]

Internationalist and administration forces, by contrast, had been indecisive. Luther Johnson of Texas performed ably in floor debates and in arranging speakers, but other congressional Democrats were less effective. Although energetic, Bloom overestimated the willingness of members to increase presidential authority on foreign policy and lacked a profound understanding of the neutrality question. Bankhead and Rayburn, extremely cognizant of the isolationist influence, did not attempt to command party loyalty on this critical issue and intervened too late to be persuasive. The White House also had proceeded too cautiously and only belatedly had exhibited more dynamic leadership. Instead of taking direct charge, Roosevelt had designated Secretary Hull and State Department aides to lobby privately for the Bloom bill. Even though Democrats often had criticized the president since 1937, Roosevelt probably could have commanded more party loyalty by either addressing the House on arms embargo repeal or discussing the issue with more isolationist Democrats. Since a slight majority of Americans favored lifting the munitions ban, this strategy perhaps could have prevented adoption of the Vorys amendment.

At any rate, several congressmen criticized the executive branch for an ineffective performance. "This whole thing," Wadsworth of New York remarked, "has been wretchedly managed by the Administration and by the Democratic leaders in the House. I have done my best for three months to stir the State Department into action, especially with respect to the embargo against the exportation of arms, etc.

62. *CR*, 30 June 1939, pp. 8512–14; *New York Times*, 1 July 1939.
63. Clifford R. Hope to Rev. Stanley Esser, 3 July 1939, Legislative Correspondence, Box 150, Hope Papers; Roosevelt, ed., *Personal Letters*, 2:900–901; Hull, *Memoirs*, 1:646–49.

They let the whole thing drift all winter long and only at the last moment, comparatively did Mr. Hull make his views known. It was then too late."[64]

Since Congress was planning to adjourn shortly, the administration intensified activity on Capitol Hill and privately began to bridge the chasm between it and conservative party members. At an impromptu press conference on 4 July, Roosevelt urged Pittman's Foreign Relations Committee to reconsider the neutrality question as soon as possible. The president also threatened to prevent adjournment until the legislative branch had sanctioned sales of munitions to belligerents. In an attempt to prevent domestic disagreements from hindering the conduct of foreign policy, the president tried to reestablish cordial relations with several disenchanted senators. Roosevelt implicitly endorsed a move to put Democrat James F. Byrnes of South Carolina on the Foreign Relations Committee and renewed friendship with Democrat Connally of Texas, who had been shunned by the White House since he had opposed the 1937 Court reform measure. The president also was more affable toward Harrison of Mississippi, whom he had helped defeat in 1937 when Harrison had tried for the majority leadership. Assuming more personal control, Roosevelt urged Harrison in July to delay a trip home so as to be present for any committee votes on neutrality legislation. "I need you here on lots of things," Roosevelt wrote Harrison, "including the next big thing on the Neutrality Bill." Other conservative Democrats, however, continued to suspect Roosevelt's foreign policy moves and thus declined to support neutrality revision. "I can't help a feeling," Bailey of North Carolina stated, "that the President's gestures have indicated that he is very much disposed to ally us with England or France."[65] At the same time, Secretary Hull and other cabinet officials exhorted several wavering Democrats to support neutrality revision.

Pittman initially shunned the president's request and continued to procrastinate. Although believing that a majority of his committee favored the original Bloom bill, he sidestepped the neutrality question during the 5 July meeting. At that time, Pittman was embroiled in a complex legislative battle over securing higher rates for domestic silver producers. The Nevada Democrat postponed a special session scheduled for Saturday, 8 July, because too many members were out of town, and he did not bring the issue up for consideration until three days later.[66]

Senate isolationists, meanwhile, already had begun plotting counterstrategy. On 16 June, thirteen isolationists met at Hiram Johnson's office to discuss combating neutrality revision. Borah, McNary, Vandenberg, La Follette, and Clark were among the participants. Although unanimously opposed to repealing the arms embargo and granting the president discretionary authority, the isolationists deadlocked over endorsing an alternative program. "We were agreed upon our opposi-

64. Wadsworth to Chadbourne, 5 July 1939.
65. New York Times, 5 July 1939; James F. Byrnes, All in One Lifetime, pp. 108–16; Patterson, "Eating Humble Pie," p. 409; Franklin D. Roosevelt to Pat Harrison, 6 July 1939, PSF, Box 57, Roosevelt Papers; Martha H. Swain, Pat Harrison: The New Deal Years, p. 221; Josiah W. Bailey to Peter G. Gerry, 8 July 1939, Foreign Policy File, Bailey Papers.
66. New York Times, 5–9, 12 July 1939.

tion,'' Johnson noted, ''but we could not agree upon the tactics or strategy.'' Despite the stalemate Johnson predicted, ''We probably will arrive at some unity of action in a very short time.'' He also vowed, ''We'll kick the views of the 'interventionists' into Wilson's cocked hat on the question of neutrality.''[67]

During the next three weeks, however, the isolationist impasse continued. On 7 July, Johnson summoned the same group of thirteen isolationists to his office to develop a consensus on legislative strategy. ''I took hold of our forces on the so-called Neutrality Bill,'' Johnson remarked, ''in order to prevent a thorough disintegration.'' At the session, isolationist participants again rejected unanimously the original Bloom bill. According to Republican Clyde M. Reed of Kansas, ''everybody turned thumbs down'' because ''it was full of jokers that entitled it to be called a 'Presidential discretion plan!' '' Reed suggested that the isolationists accept the modified Bloom bill containing the Vorys amendment, but most other participants opposed endorsing any specific measure. ''There was no chance to get any affirmative action on legislation,'' Reed stated, because ''the conference couldn't possibly have agreed on what form that legislation should take.''

In an attempt to break the deadlock, Democrat Clark of Missouri and Progressive La Follette of Wisconsin proposed a general method for attacking the internationalists. Isolationists, they proposed, should persuade the Foreign Relations Committee to postpone consideration of all neutrality bills until the next session of Congress. If that tactic failed, they recommended that the isolationists should filibuster the measure in the Senate and then seek adjournment before 1 August. Johnson, however, initially objected to this strategy because isolationists controlled only nine of twenty-three committee seats and no longer wielded a numerical majority in the Senate. He warned, ''If we were to fool with a bill in committee, it would very soon get out and be upon the floor of the Senate, and then our only recourse would be to filibuster.'' In addition, Johnson pointed out that delaying tactics usually go awry. ''I cannot and will not filibuster,'' he declared. Several colleagues promised to sustain a filibuster, but the California Republican still objected. ''Many times,'' he noted, ''very blithely, a number of men will talk about filibustering, and tell you how many hours they will talk, but when it comes down to the hard grind, very few will stick. Bodies, as well as minds, give out, irritability succeeds the determination with which the filibuster began, and finally, a loophole is sought to escape proceeding further.''[68]

Johnson eventually dropped his opposition to the Clark–La Follette plan. Conferees assured Johnson that a majority of the Senate Foreign Relations Committee might favor postponing until 1940 any concrete action on neutrality. Clark even volunteered to introduce such a motion at the next meeting. In addition, Clark offered to try to convince several Democratic colleagues, including George of Georgia and Gillette of Iowa, to support the delay. All conferees consented to seek

67. Hiram W. Johnson to Hiram W. Johnson, Jr., 17 June 1939, Part VI, Box 7, Hiram W. Johnson to Boake Carter, 1 July 1939, Part III, Box 18, Johnson Papers.
68. Hiram W. Johnson to Hiram W. Johnson, Jr., 16 July 1939, Part VI, Box 7, Johnson Papers; Clyde M. Reed to William Allen White, 13 July 1939, Box 222, William Allen White Papers.

postponement in committee first and then, if necessary, to resort to filibuster tactics. "When I counted noses in the Foreign Relations Committee, and found we had nine which might be stretched into twelve," Johnson stated, "I concluded to play the game that way." The California Republican added, "Even if we were not successful, we could still go on with a filibuster."

Within three days, however, the fragile isolationist agreement nearly shattered. In remarks to newspaper reporters, Borah indicated he opposed any committee efforts to postpone action on neutrality and wanted the Senate to consider the thorny issue before adjournment. Isolationists, he claimed, definitely had support from at least thirty-four members opposing munitions sales to belligerents. At the 11 July meeting of Pittman's committee, Johnson tried to make certain Borah did not renege on his earlier pledge to support the Clark motion for postponement. "I took my seat immediately next to Borah, my usual place at the table," Johnson admitted, "and tried to look my severest, never taking my eyes off him."[69]

The Clark–La Follette strategy ultimately succeeded. On the evening of 10 July, Clark met secretly with fellow Democrats George of Georgia, who was uncommitted, and Gillette of Iowa, who leaned in favor of repealing the arms embargo. The two senators, Clark realized, still resented President Roosevelt's attempt to purge them in the 1938 Democratic primaries. Capitalizing on their hostile attitudes toward the president, Clark convinced both men to vote in committee for postponement of the neutrality issue until the 1940 session. At the last minute, Republican White of Maine also improved prospects for the Clark motion by joining the members favoring delay. "I am not willing," White asserted, "to grant discretionary powers in this field to the President in addition to those Constitutionally his."[70]

On 11 July, the Foreign Relations Committee held one of its shortest sessions on record. After Pittman called the meeting to order, Clark caught the internationalists off guard by proposing to postpone until 1940 consideration of all neutrality legislation. Clark's motion passed by a slender 12 to 11 margin, as five Democrats, five Republicans, and two third-party members favored delay. On the other hand, eleven internationalist Democrats, principally from Southern and Mountain regions opposed procrastination on the neutrality question. Pittman, who had been confident beforehand that the internationalists controlled the committee, had suffered another major setback and adjourned the session in fifteen minutes.

The committee action showed that several conservative Democrats continued to suspect Roosevelt's foreign policy motives. Four anti-New Dealers, including George of Georgia, Gillette of Iowa, Clark of Missouri, and Van Nuys of Indiana, voted with the committee majority against reporting neutrality revision to the Senate floor. Even though Clark was the only real isolationist, the four conservatives

69. Johnson to Johnson, 16 July 1939; "34 in a Lair," *Time* 34 (17 July 1939):13.
70. *New York Times*, 12 July 1939; *Portland Press Herald*, 12 July 1939.

refused to help the president partly because Roosevelt had either opposed or declined to endorse them in their 1938 election campaigns.[71]

The tally merely determined the time of consideration. The 12 to 11 margin did not reflect the attitude of the committee on repeal of the arms embargo, presidential discretionary power, or other substantive aspects of the neutrality issue. By 11 July, it is quite possible a majority of members favored the original Bloom bill. Secretary Hull had met often with both Gillette and George and had made progress in converting them toward flexible legislation. Since eleven members had already aligned with internationalists, a shift by either Gillette or George would have kept the Bloom measure alive.

Isolationists, nevertheless, still controlled congressional decisionmaking. Although disagreeing among themselves over particular approaches, the isolationists again had prevented legislative action on neutrality revision. Despite changing conditions abroad, isolationists adamantly rejected altering the strict neutrality laws. Isolationists welcomed the committee's vote as a rejection of Roosevelt's foreign policy and as vindication for their crusade against American involvement in the European conflict. A few isolationists, however, feared the president might attempt to revive the legislation before adjournment. Roosevelt, Johnson warned, "often transmutes defeat into victory, and very often he will remain quiescent after a knock long enough to get himself in shape for a successful flank charge." If the president attempted to renew the battle, the isolationists expected to triumph. Johnson vowed, "If it has to be begun again, we'll go to the limit. I am sure that they are enough determined men to stand with me to prevent any legislation." On the other hand, several internationalists attributed their setback to distrust of President Roosevelt rather than to the substance of neutrality revision. The vote, Republican Austin of Vermont claimed, "shows what a bad actor he is, for many who voted against action would have preferred to repeal the neutrality act if the President had been less ambitious personally."[72]

Many isolationists openly distrusted Roosevelt. The president, numerous anti-New Deal Republicans and Democrats believed, already had usurped too much domestic authority from Congress and was threatening the balance of power between the three branches of federal government. Besides resisting Roosevelt's attempt to increase the membership of the U.S. Supreme Court by adding liberal justices, they also protested the president's plans to enhance his personal power through executive reorganization. Conservative Democrats, moreover, resented Roosevelt's attempts to oust anti-New Deal party members from Congress. On the other hand, some liberal Republicans supporting New Deal programs distrusted the president on the foreign policy front. Roosevelt, they feared, was seeking to align the United States

71. *New York Times*, 12 July 1939; T.R.B., "Politics at the Water's Edge," *New Republic* 99 (2 August 1939):360; Divine, *Illusion*, p. 278; Patterson, "Eating Humble Pie," p. 410.

72. Johnson to Johnson, 16 July 1939; Warren R. Austin to Mrs. Chauncey Austin, 12 July 1939, Correspondence with Mother, Box 1939–1940, Austin Papers.

on the side of Great Britain and France against the national interest. These Republicans with progressive attitudes wanted Congress to control decisionmaking over foreign policy and opposed granting the president power to determine either aggressors or combat zones. Besides charging that businessmen from Roosevelt's Middle Atlantic region were encouraging American entry into the European conflict, these liberals preferred spending federal monies on solving unemployment and other domestic problems.

Roosevelt, meanwhile, was infuriated with the committee decision. He initially planned to send Congress a message accusing the isolationists of making "unspeakable and unsupported charges" because of "personal and partisan" considerations but was convinced by Secretary Hull that such a response would further alienate the legislative branch. In a more conciliatory note, the president on 14 July wrote, "For the cause of peace and in the interest of American neutrality and security, it is highly advisable that Congress at this session should take certain much needed action." Secretary Hull attached a message urging Congress to enact the original Bloom bill because any further delays would diminish American prestige abroad and encourage Hitler to launch further aggression.[73]

The administration wanted the Senate to override Pittman's committee and initiate floor consideration of the original Bloom bill. To accomplish this, Roosevelt summoned Vice-president John Nance Garner, Secretary Hull, and Democrats Barkley and Pittman to participate in an informal strategy session on the evening of 18 July at the White House. Although he had shunned Republicans in previous neutrality discussions, the president attempted to rally bipartisan support by inviting Borah, McNary, and Austin to attend. Borah was the ranking Republican on the Foreign Relations Committee and already had indicated to reporters a preference to have Senate consideration. McNary headed the opposition party, while Austin was assistant minority leader and the most vocal Republican internationalist. This administration strategy irked the other Republicans, who accused the president of attempting to split the opposition party on neutrality. "Roosevelt was too damn smart," Johnson of California charged, "in selecting a committee and calling them to the White House." Before the conference, Johnson urged all three Republicans to recommend indefinite postponement of the question. "It is not a pleasant thing to give your colleagues hell," he remarked, "but this was the time when it was needed in order to hold them together."[74]

Before the 18 July conference began, the scene at the White House resembled a Hollywood extravaganza. "A great throng of photographers and news men crowded the front porticos of the White House," Austin remarked, "and we had to pass through a barrage of flashing cameras and questions." After conversing with the press, the guests were ushered to the Blue Room and sat in a crescent around the president's sofa.

73. Divine, *Illusion*, pp. 278–79; Rosenman, ed., *Public Papers*, 8:380–81; *CR*, 14 July 1939, pp. 9127–28.
74. Hiram W. Johnson to Hiram W. Johnson, Jr., 22 July 1939, Part VI, Box 7, Johnson Papers.

Roosevelt and Hull, in unusually somber moods, opened the conference with impassioned pleas for neutrality revision. Besides insisting that a European war was imminent, Roosevelt complained that the arms embargo prevented victims of totalitarian aggression from securing American weapons. Legislative inaction, the president protested, severely restricted his attempt to mediate the European conflict. "I have been deprived," he asserted, "of my last cartridge by the failure of Congress to act." If the Senate and House repealed the arms embargo, Roosevelt claimed, the Axis nations might not continue expansionist activity. Hull, citing daily reports from American ambassadors abroad, predicted war would result within two months and claimed lifting the arms embargo would "reduce the chance of war by at least half." In an unrestrained tone, the secretary even threatened to close his State Department office if Congress adjourned without revising the neutrality law.[75]

Hull's comments provoked an intense debate with isolationist Borah. The tenth child of a prosperous and industrious Illinois farmer, Borah had attended Southern Illinois Academy at Enfield and had acted briefly in a Shakespearean Company. After studying law at the University of Kansas, he had become a successful attorney in Boise, Idaho, for several lumber and mining companies. He was elected in 1907 to the U.S. Senate as an insurgent Republican and became one of the leading critics of the Old Guard within his party. Although crusty and unpredictable, the highly principled Borah had become one of the most influential senators. A brilliant orator, he had been an active member of the Foreign Relations Committee and from 1925 to 1933 had served as its chairman. On the one hand, Borah had advocated American involvement with other countries. Since Germany had violated America's maritime rights as a neutral country, he had supported American entry in 1917 into World War I. Borah also had helped convene the Washington Naval Disarmament Conference of 1921–1922 and steer through the Senate the Kellogg-Briand Pact of 1928 to outlaw war as an instrument of national policy. In 1933 he had backed the renewal of diplomatic relations with the Soviet Union so as to promote commerce. On other issues, however, Borah had held strict isolationist views. He had rejected the Treaty of Versailles and American entrance into the League of Nations and had opposed the Nine Power Treaty of 1922. During the 1930s, he had supported the militant isolationists fully prepared to defend American neutral rights on the high seas. Since he denied that world events threatened domestic interests and security, Borah had opposed vigorously intervention abroad. With depressed conditions still prevalent in the United States, he had urged the federal government to concentrate on the needs of farmers and miners rather than become embroiled in European conflicts. Borah had favored the Neutrality Act of 1935, although preferring to forbid Americans from traveling on any belligerent vessels even at their own risk. One of six senators opposing the Neutrality Act of 1937, he had argued that the cash-and-carry section would sacrifice American maritime rights and foreign trade. Cash-and-carry, Borah

75. Warren R. Austin Memorandum on White House Conference, 19 July 1939, Senatorial Correspondence, Box 20, Austin Papers; David L. Porter, "Senator Warren R. Austin and the Neutrality Act of 1939," pp. 232–33; Joseph W. Alsop and Robert Kintner, *American White Paper*, pp. 43–44.

also warned, meant discriminating in favor of sea powers like England and Japan. In 1939 he vigorously had denounced efforts to repeal the arms embargo as a provocative step involving the United States further in the European war.[76]

During Secretary Hull's presentation, Borah interrupted by accusing the State Department of exaggerating world problems. The isolationist Idaho Republican insisted, "We are not going to have a war" because "Germany isn't ready for it." Borah, Hull replied, would change his mind upon seeing cables portraying "the extremely dangerous outlook in the international situation." Borah countered that his source, a Socialist British newspaper, had denied a European conflict was imminent. The senator's brashness in questioning the competence of the State Department upset the secretary. "Never in my experience," Hull subsequently remarked, "had I found it nearly so difficult to restrain myself and refrain from a spontaneous explosion." Although Borah gave assurance that "there was no intention to charge the Secretary with inefficiency," Hull abruptly terminated his presentation and declined to respond to further queries.[77]

Tensions characterized the entire three-hour conference. Roosevelt vowed that if Congress adjourned without taking any action on the Bloom bill, he would take his case to the American people and blame the legislative branch for inaction. Vice-president Garner, who preferred abandoning all neutrality measures and relying exclusively on international law, warned that Roosevelt could not afford to further alienate Capitol Hill. The presidential strategy, Austin interjected, might jeopardize the administration defense program in Congress. Austin disapproved of granting Roosevelt broad discretionary authority and preferred international law over the Bloom bill. If "war should occur while Congress is not here," Austin stated, "we could answer the call for munitions as efficiently" by depending on global statutes. Of the senators present, only Pittman and Barkley favored the original Bloom version permitting the sale of armaments to warring nations.

As midnight approached, Garner asked each member whether neutrality legislation could be passed at the 1939 session. To Roosevelt's dismay, Barkley and McNary contended that a majority of their colleagues opposed immediate action on the Bloom bill and favored postponing the issue until 1940. Barkley remarked that nearly all Republicans and around 33 percent of the Democrats opted for delay, while Pittman warned that isolationists would filibuster the Bloom measure. "Well, Captain," Garner told Roosevelt, "we may as well face the facts."[78]

The conference thus produced no major changes. Within the next twelve hours, the White House issued press statements placing responsibility for the delay upon Congress. Postponement, the administration stressed, "would weaken the leadership of the United States" in the effort to preserve international peace "in the event

76. Jonas, *Isolationism*, pp. 45–50; "William E. Borah," *Current Biography* 1 (1940):99–102; Robert James Maddox, *William E. Borah and American Foreign Policy*.

77. Alsop and Kintner, *White Paper*, pp. 58–59; Hull, *Memoirs*, 1:649–50; Austin Memorandum, 19 July 1939; Langer and Gleason, *Challenge to Isolationism*, pp. 143–44. For Borah's position, see Maddox, *William E. Borah*, pp. 239–41, and Marian C. McKenna, *Borah*, p. 362.

78. Alsop and Kintner, *White Paper*, pp. 58–59; Hull, *Memoirs*, 1:649–50; Austin Memorandum, 19 July 1939; Langer and Gleason, *Challenge to Isolationism*, pp. 143–44.

of a new crisis in Europe between now and next January."[79] Besides confirming the president's earlier belief that Congress opposed taking immediate action on arms embargo repeal, the conference indicated that a wide gap still separated the internationalists and isolationists on Capitol Hill. Above all, the Roosevelt administration had failed dismally in a last-minute attempt to secure legislative action before adjournment.

Isolationists thus continued to prevail on Capitol Hill. In addition to thwarting the president's maneuver to revive the issue, they ostensibly had procrastinated further consideration until the 1940 session. Although divided on specific neutrality legislation, McNary, Borah, and Austin all had agreed to support postponement. "They held, thank the Lord," Johnson of California commented, "and the bitterness of the President is unspeakable." After the confrontation with Hull, Borah was more determined to retain the arms embargo. "I am so certain I am doing the right thing," Borah wrote, "according to the information which I have that I shall continue to pursue the course I have been pursuing."[80]

At the regular session, therefore, internationalist neutrality revision failed. Anti-Roosevelt sentiment influenced the outcome especially in the House, signifying that the legislative branch was not prepared yet to subordinate political differences. Conservative representatives and senators, who had attacked several presidential actions on the domestic front, rejected increasing Roosevelt's control over foreign policy. Ethnic factors affected voting patterns of congressmen, while ideological considerations prevailed in the more independent Senate. In order for Congress to lift the arms embargo, German representatives would have had to deemphasize loyalties to their nationality, and antiwar senators would have had to subordinate ideological considerations. Ineffective presidential and majority party leadership also diminished the prospects for removing the arms embargo. Besides not intervening directly until the summer months, Roosevelt had designated too much responsibility to an overworked State Department and an indecisive Pittman. Although confronting formidable isolationist opposition, the president probably could have achieved more satisfactory results by taking a greater personal role. Barkley, Bankhead, and Rayburn likewise did not attempt much to command party loyalty, principally because their political colleagues were divided so sharply on munitions sales. If House administration leaders had intervened more decisively at an earlier date, they might have registered triumphs on some crucial teller votes. Above all, legislative efforts to repeal the arms embargo did not succeed because actual war had not occurred yet in Europe. Despite Hitler's expansionist activities, Congress was reluctant to change neutrality policies unless it perceived a more direct threat to American security and institutions.

Isolationists, even though holding only a slight numerical majority in each chamber, had controlled foreign policy decisionmaking at the regular session. Although prevailing much less in the House than the margin on the Vorys amend-

79. Rosenman, ed., *Public Papers*, 8:387–88.

80. Johnson to Johnson, 22 July 1939; William E. Borah to Rev. John Haynes Holmes, 19 July 1939, Box 426, Borah Papers.

ment indicates, they nevertheless restored the controversial arms embargo. Senators were more internationalist minded than representatives and might have approved a roll-call vote on arms embargo repeal, but the vocal, well-organized isolationists in Pittman's committee prevented floor action on neutrality revision and thus kept the existing measure intact. The isolationist blocs in both the Senate and the House provided much more effective leadership than did the internationalist Democratic party heads on Capitol Hill. Isolationist Republicans particularly were more cohesive than Democrats in the lower chamber, reflecting the rebellious mood of conservatives against Roosevelt.

At the regular session, Congress rather than the executive branch controlled foreign policy decisionmaking. Roosevelt had wielded considerable power over Congress in his first term, but since 1937 increasingly had lost much influence there. The Supreme Court "packing" incident, the attempted purge of Democratic party conservatives in primaries, and other presidential actions had made Roosevelt a much less effective force than previously on domestic issues in Congress. The decline in presidential prestige also had extended to foreign policy legislation, as illustrated by the neutrality issue. Although favoring complete repeal of the strict neutrality laws, Roosevelt had treaded very cautiously and let Congress handle the specific details. But the House, along with the Senate Foreign Relations Committee, rejected the chief executive's wishes.

In the final analysis, postponement may have been the only course Congress could have agreed upon. Although European events soon confirmed the dire predictions made by Secretary Hull, a majority of legislators preferred to adjourn early rather than consider a controversial neutrality measure. At the 1939 session, Congress would have experienced difficulty in reaching a consensus on any particular legislation and would have confronted a formidable filibuster in the Senate. The legislative branch adjourned in early August, little realizing Eastern Europe would be engulfed in flames within four weeks, compelling reassessment of American neutrality policy.

4

The Shift to Internationalism

Within one month, the rapidly changing situation in Europe profoundly affected Congress. Germany, after signing a nonaggression pact with Russia, on 1 September suddenly attacked Poland. Two days later, Great Britain and France came to the defense of Poland and declared war against Hitler's Germany.[1] Up until the outbreak of World War II, the isolationists had controlled foreign policy decision-making on Capitol Hill. After the German attack on Poland, however, the internationalists secured a numerical majority in Congress and determined the legislative course of American foreign policy. The eruption of the war provoked another intense debate between the internationalists and isolationists over whether the United States should lift the embargo on selling ammunition and implements of war to belligerents.

Several internationalists, particularly in the House, immediately requested a special session. Since Congress already had adjourned, the neutrality question could not be reconsidered unless President Roosevelt reconvened Congress. In letters or telegrams, ten Democratic representatives urged Roosevelt to summon Congress as soon as possible to revise neutrality legislation. Internationalists recommended repeal of the arms embargo as a means of cooperating with other nations and favored providing at least limited aid to the Allies through the cash-and-carry system. William I. Sirovich of New York, for example, advocated legislation enabling Western European nations "to buy arms implements and ammunition in our country to protect their nations from being destroyed by Nazi atrocities and barbarisms." Besides hoping to increase presidential authority in foreign affairs, internationalists believed removing the ban on munitions sales afforded the best means of keeping the United States out of the European conflict. Military Affairs Committee Chairman Andrew J. May of Kentucky suggested a measure giving Roosevelt "greater latitude in dealing with foreign relations," while John W. McCormack of Massachusetts argued that neutrality revision would "keep us out of war."[2] Although internationalists, they usually were very reluctant to commit the United States either to defense alliances or to direct intervention on behalf of particular nations in specific conflicts. Despite the eruption of the European war, they usually did not state arms embargo repeal in terms of assistance to Great Britain and France.

Other members, though, advised either procrastinating or not holding a special session. Postponement of action for several weeks, Speaker William B. Bankhead of

1. Robert A. Divine, *The Reluctant Belligerent: American Entry into World War II*, pp. 65–66.
2. William Sirovich to Franklin D. Roosevelt, 1 September 1939, Andrew J. May to Franklin D. Roosevelt, 24 August 1939, Official Files (OF) 419, Box 9, John W. McCormack to Franklin D. Roosevelt, 2 September 1939, President's Personal File (PPF) 4057, Franklin D. Roosevelt Papers.

Alabama argued, would provide additional time to develop broader legislative support for repealing the arms embargo. Besides advising Roosevelt to "await further and fuller developments in the war situation," he predicted that continued German aggression would cause "a most substantial change in the views of many members of Congress on neutrality revision." Isolationists, meanwhile, still opposed removing the ban on munitions sales and adamantly disapproved of reconvening Congress. Republican William E. Borah of Idaho cautioned that changing the neutrality laws might culminate in the sending of "our young men into the hell-holes of Europe," while Arthur H. Vandenberg of Michigan predicted that lifting the restriction on armaments would promote "still more effective aid" to Great Britain and France.[3]

The administration played a more dynamic role this time. When Germany attacked Poland, Roosevelt decided the same day to urge Congress to repeal the arms embargo. In a fireside chat on 3 September, he indicated a desire to keep the United States out of the conflict and yet no longer insisted that Americans should remain impartial in thought. The president deliberately delayed for two days issuing the mandatory proclamation invoking the existing legislation. During the same period, Roosevelt held frequent strategy sessions with Democratic congressional leaders in an effort to ascertain the public mood. Since telephone surveys indicated that around sixty senators favored repeal of the arms embargo, he discarded his earlier timid approach and launched instead an extensive campaign to revise the neutrality legislation.[4] At a press conference on 8 September, the president revealed plans to convene Congress in a special session and asked for legislation permitting the sale of military supplies. Three days later, Roosevelt wrote British Prime Minister Neville Chamberlain, "I hope and believe that we shall repeal the embargo next month and this is definitely a part of the Administration's policy." He soon requested the legislative branch to meet in special session on 21 September to approve a bill sanctioning the trade of munitions to belligerents. An advocate of limited debate, the president advised, "The less said on either floor, the better." Isolationist senators, he feared, might filibuster the neutrality revision and make the issue "a political football to be booted about the halls of Congress." Roosevelt also enlisted administration aides and prestigious businessmen to persuade conservative Democrats who had favored retaining the arms embargo to support neutrality revision. "I am limiting the hands of the Executive Branch," he wrote, "to more action and less words."[5]

3. William B. Bankhead to Franklin D. Roosevelt, 5 September 1939, PPF 4142, Roosevelt Papers; William E. Borah to Student Body of Twin Falls Business University, 22 September 1939, Box 426, William E. Borah Papers; Arthur H. Vandenberg, Jr., ed., *The Private Papers of Senator Vandenberg*, p. 2.

4. Samuel I. Rosenman, ed., *The Public Papers and Addresses of Franklin D. Roosevelt*, 8:460–63; *New York Times*, 6 September 1939; Harold L. Ickes, *The Secret Diary of Harold L. Ickes*, 2:709; Stephen Early to Myron Taylor, 8 September 1939, OF 1561, Box 2, Roosevelt Papers; Stephen Early to Pat Harrison, 11 September 1939, File 1, Pat Harrison Papers.

5. *New York Times*, 9, 14 September 1939; Elliott Roosevelt, ed., *FDR: His Personal Letters, 1928–1945*, 2:919; Franklin D. Roosevelt to Guy M. Gillette, 7 September 1939, PPF 6176, Roosevelt Papers.

On 20 September, the president summoned eleven congressional leaders to the White House for a strategy session. Although deliberately shunning Borah this time, he invited four Senate participants of the ill-fated 18 July conference: Democrats Alben W. Barkley of Kentucky and Key Pittman of Nevada and Republicans Charles L. McNary of Oregon and Warren R. Austin of Vermont. Two prominent Democratic senators—Majority Whip Sherman Minton of Indiana and floor strategist James F. Byrnes of South Carolina—were among the new faces at this conclave. In hopes of improving prospects for neutrality revision in the House, the president asked five prominent representatives to attend. These congressmen were Speaker Bankhead, Majority Leader Sam Rayburn of Texas, and Foreign Affairs Committee Chairman Sol Bloom of New York from the Democratic side and Minority Leader Joseph W. Martin of Massachusetts and Carl Mapes of Michigan from the opposition party. Seeking bipartisan support for arms embargo repeal, the president requested Alfred M. Landon and Frank Knox, the Republican presidential and vice-presidential candidates in the 1936 election, to join the conclave.[6]

At the conference, Roosevelt continued displaying more leadership. Stressing that Europe was engulfed in war, the president urged the Senate to adopt within thirty days the original Bloom bill and requested the House to follow suit. Roosevelt endorsed repeal of the arms embargo, but preferred to leave other details up to Congress. Lifting the ban on munitions supplies, the president argued, would hurt Hitler, since "he can't get over here to get our arms and munitions and England and France can." When Austin of Vermont interjected that the legislative branch should "support the democracies," Roosevelt was "tickled to death." In marked contrast to his approach during the regular session, the president was determined to be less cautious from the outset. "Roosevelt," Democrat Tom Connally of Texas observed, "appeared to be a different man. He now spoke with sureness about foreign affairs and kept a firm grip on the rein as he detailed what he wanted from Congress. This was his first direct international leadership."

Although less volatile than the July conclave, the conference produced tension. Austin suggested that Congress should repeal the entire act and restore presidential prerogatives over foreign policy, provoking a sharp rebuttal from Pittman. "If you try that," Pittman interjected, "you'll be damn lucky to get five votes in my committee." According to Pittman, a majority of committee members probably would reject making any major changes in the existing law except to repeal the arms embargo.

Despite occasional clashes, most conferees insisted Congress should alter the existing measure. They recommended either removing the ban on the sale of munitions or relying exclusively on international law for keeping the United States out of foreign wars. In order to avert the torpedoing of American vessels and the destruction of American property in combat zones, participants favored restoration of cash-and-carry limitations. Pittman's committee, they suggested, should begin

6. Joseph W. Alsop and Robert Kintner, *American White Paper*, pp. 75–76; William L. Langer and S. Everett Gleason, *The Challenge to Isolation, 1937–1940*, p. 222.

considering legislation "as soon after Congress convenes as possible."[7]

Roosevelt failed to achieve complete bipartisan cooperation, but diffused the measure politically. Besides resenting Democratic domination of strategymaking, most Republicans still opposed repeal of the arms embargo. On the other hand, McNary and Martin did not make munitions sales a partisan issue because the minority party was divided on neutrality policies. Senators George W. Norris of Nebraska, Robert A. Taft of Ohio, and Wallace H. White of Maine, alarmed over European developments, joined internationalists this time. The National Republican Club in late September overwhelmingly endorsed 46 to 6 lifting the arms embargo. Landon and Knox, two Republican participants in the conference, also adamantly supported sending American military supplies to belligerents.[8]

Roosevelt also defended neutrality revision publicly. The president on 21 September addressed a joint session of Congress and requested quick approval of arms sales and other basic features of the original Bloom bill. After summarizing how Europe was plunged into war, he charged that the existing neutrality legislation violated international law. "I regret," Roosevelt admitted, "that Congress passed that act. I regret equally that I signed that act." In order to restore "the ancient precepts of the law of nations," he urged Congress to repeal the arms embargo. The president, though, recommended that American citizens, vessels, and property be barred from combat zones. Refusing to concede that neutrality revision was intended to sell arms and munitions to England and France, he argued instead that removal of the ban on arms would keep the United States out of the European conflict. During the speech, he did not indicate publicly his concern for the dangers facing England and France. A shrewd tactician, Roosevelt did not want to jeopardize legislative prospects by making assistance to the democracies a major issue. He hoped to diffuse isolationist resistance by stressing that his approach would afford the nation better protection against involvement in World War II.[9] Although Roosevelt sought bipartisan consensus, congressional reaction to the presidential address divided along party lines. Democrat Samuel Dickstein of New York labeled the speech "the greatest exposition possible of the historical record of the country," while Republican John M. Vorys of Ohio claimed the chief executive "misstated facts, law and history."[10]

Pittman, meanwhile, provided much more effective leadership this time in the Foreign Relations Committee. No longer preoccupied with silver legislation, he concentrated on repealing the munitions embargo. With the assistance of Democrats Connally of Texas and Elbert D. Thomas of Utah, he on 21 September began

7. Transcript, White House Conference, 20 September 1939, PPF 1-P, Box 263, Roosevelt Papers; Thomas Connally and Alfred Steinberg, *My Name is Tom Connally*, p. 228; David L. Porter, "Senator Warren R. Austin and the Neutrality Act of 1939," p. 235.
8. *Newsweek* 14 (18 September 1939): 28; *New York Times*, 27 September 1939; George W. Norris, "American Neutrality."
9. Rosenman, ed., *Public Papers*, 8:512–22; Cordell Hull, *The Memoirs of Cordell Hull*, 1:684; Robert A. Divine, *Roosevelt and World War II*, p. 28.
10. Samuel Dickstein to Franklin D. Roosevelt, 26 September 1939, PPF 314, Roosevelt Papers; John M. Vorys to Wesley Stout, 13 October 1939, Box 3, John M. Vorys Papers.

drafting a bill permitting the sale of arms to belligerents and invoking cash-and-carry for all commerce in wartime. In order to prevent possible dilatory tactics by Republicans, Pittman met with Democratic committee members the next three days to finalize the draft. Pittman, though, sought to placate isolationists by retaining the other sections of the 1937 measure. Upon completing the draft, he phoned the White House remarking, "We got as much as we could."[11]

The Pittman bill, although repealing the arms embargo, espoused mandatory neutrality. Based on rigid cash-and-carry, the measure compelled, for all American exports to belligerents, that the titles be transferred before the merchandise departed from the United States and that the items be transported in foreign vessels. Besides applying to England and France, the restrictions encompassed commerce with European, African, and Asian nations. The president could determine combat zones where American citizens, vessels, and airplanes could not enter. Retaining certain features of the 1937 act, the legislation prohibited citizens from traveling on the ships of belligerent nations or making loans to warring governments. In concessions, the bill limited Roosevelt's authority and refused American businessmen the right to barter with British and French colonial possessions.

The cash-and-carry plan afforded a means of aiding belligerents without repeating the World War I experience. Between 1914 and 1917, the United States had loaned a vast amount of money and shipped numerous goods to warring countries. Nearly every European nation had defaulted on repaying extensive loans made by the Wilson administration. Trade practices not only had contributed to the destruction of American property on the high seas, but also had led to the loss of American lives. To avoid a repetition of these problems, belligerents would be required to pay cash for goods and to transport them from American shores in their own vessels. On the other hand, cash-and-carry enabled the United States to furnish economic and military assistance to European nations attacked by aggressors. The authors of the Pittman bill realized that neither applying embargoes nor restricting commerce would keep the nation out of the overseas conflict.

Internationalist Democrats solidified ranks this time, enabling Pittman to steer the measure through the Foreign Relations Committee by a 16 to 7 margin. With the exception of isolationist Bennett Champ Clark of Missouri, all members of Roosevelt's party joined Pittman in supporting the neutrality revision. Democrats Guy M. Gillette of Iowa, Walter F. George of Georgia, Robert R. Reynolds of North Carolina, and Frederick Van Nuys of Indiana, along with Republican White of Maine, favored immediate floor consideration of the Pittman measure this time because of the German attack on Poland. "It is certain," White remarked, "I am in no sense neutral in spirit. I find myself anxious to do whatever we can for the allied cause short of getting involved in the war."[12]

11. Connally and Steinberg, *Tom Connally*, p. 228; John C. Donovan, "Congress and the Making of Neutrality Legislation, 1935–1939" (Ph.D.diss.), p. 319; Edwin Watson Memorandum for Franklin D. Roosevelt, 25 September 1939, President's Secretary's File (PSF), Box 57, Roosevelt Papers.
12. *New York Times*, 29 September 1939; U.S., Congress, Senate, Committee on Foreign Relations, "Neutrality Act of 1939," *Reports*, no. 1155; Wallace H. White, Jr., to Warren R. Austin,

Seven isolationists, including Borah, Clark, Vandenberg, and Hiram W. Johnson of California, opposed the Pittman bill. A heterogeneous group politically, they consisted of four Republicans, one Democrat, and two third-party members and were principally from the Great Lakes and Great Plains. These isolationists denied that the outbreak of World War II threatened American security and protested designating so much authority to the chief executive. According to Vandenberg, Roosevelt would interpret repeal of the arms embargo "as the go sign for him to help the Allies in any way he can."[13]

For the first time, internationalists controlled congressional decisionmaking on the neutrality issue. At the regular session, isolationists had influenced a majority of Foreign Relations Committee members to retain the existing neutrality legislation and to prevent any floor action on neutrality revision. Internationalists had now overcome the vocal isolationist resistance and averted any further delay in considering legislative changes. Internationalists not only had secured committee approval of the Pittman bill, but also had given the Senate its first opportunity in 1939 to debate repeal of the arms embargo.

In the Senate, meanwhile, the internationalists were broadening their political and sectional bases of support. Around twenty-five members converted to the internationalists side at the special session, mainly from uncommitted ranks, giving the internationalists more bipartisan and cross-sectional backing (see table 14). Democrats still provided the core of the internationalist wing, but were joined this time by nearly one-third of the Republicans. Subordinating previous political differences with Roosevelt, Southern Democrats almost unanimously aligned with the internationalists this time and proportionately replaced the Middle Atlantic members at the helm of the repeal movement. "President Roosevelt," Democrat Theodore G. Bilbo of Mississippi summed up, "has been and is doing his best to keep this country out of war and I will be glad to cooperate with him in this respect."[14] Border senators also stood proportionately at the forefront of the internationalist bloc and coalesced with a majority of New England, Middle Atlantic, Great Lakes, and Mountain members. Historians usually picture the Great Lakes and Mountain states as isolationist in 1939, but these sections cooperated with the internationalists at the special session. On the other hand, the isolationists formed a more homogeneous group consisting largely of Republicans. Pacific senators proportionately still led the dwindling isolationist ranks but secured majority backing only from the Great Plains delegation.

Presidential intervention, along with ideological considerations, figured prominently in the Senate shift toward involvement abroad. Following the outbreak of World War II, Roosevelt had intensified his effort to lure conservative votes.

---

8 September 1939, General Correspondence, Warren R. Austin Papers.

13. *New York Times*, 29 September 1939; Arthur H. Vandenberg Diary, 15 September 1939, Scrapbook, vol. 12, Arthur H. Vandenberg Papers.

14. Theodore G. Bilbo to A. A. Phillips, 10 September 1939, File W, Theodore G. Bilbo Papers. The tables referred to in this chapter are based on data from the Inter-University Consortium for Political Research, University of Michigan.

Besides asking Byrnes to woo anti-New Dealers behind-the-scenes, the president had enlisted Connally to play a major role in floor debates for the repeal camp. Roosevelt also acted more conciliatory toward Carter Glass and Harry F. Byrd of Virginia, who earlier had been deprived of patronage appointments. Glass was invited to the White House for the first time in several years to discuss with the president the possible selection of judges from Virginia to serve on the federal courts, while administration aide Edwin Watson promised Byrd that the Treasury Department would appoint a conservative Virginian to a vacant post. Democrat Josiah W. Bailey of North Carolina, who also was invited to the White House, found Roosevelt quite cooperative and began delivering speeches supporting neutrality revision. "The President," Bailey admitted, "is in a conciliatory humor and I have reason to believe he is disposed to make friends of men like myself."[15] These senators, along with other anti-New Deal Democrats, supported lifting the arms embargo at the special session. German global strategy also convinced these legislators that Hitler endangered American security and Western democracy. Byrd warned Congress to "avoid opposition to the President and his foreign policies," while Democrat Gillette of Iowa insisted, "Partisan views must be subordinated" because of the threat to American safety. On the House side, Democrats Ross A. Collins of Mississippi and Jerry Voorhis of California switched in the middle of September to the internationalist camp.[16]

Considerable impetus also came from the fact that the public was more receptive to repeal. Within two weeks of the German attack on Poland, Gallup polls indicated the proportion of persons favoring repeal of the arms embargo jumping from 50 percent to 57 percent. During the next six weeks, those supporting military assistance to Great Britain and France ranged between 56 percent and 62 percent. Southerners proportionately led the grass-roots campaign for lifting the ban, but a majority from every section urged removing the restriction. At the same time, Americans insisted on restoring the cash-and-carry system. In mid-September, at least 90 percent urged requiring belligerents to pay cash for all merchandise purchased in the United States and opposed American vessels transporting goods into combat zones.

The mass media and pressure groups fostered the more conducive climate for neutrality revision. In a *Newsweek* survey conducted in early September, thirty-two of fifty leading newspaper editors advocated immediate removal of the arms embargo and only five adamantly opposed this step. With the exception of the *Saturday Evening Post*, the major mass circulation news magazines supported the sale of

15. James T. Patterson, "Eating Humble Pie: A Note on Roosevelt, Congress, and Neutrality Revision in 1939," pp. 411–12; Carter Glass to Judge Armistead Dobie, 19 October 1939, Box 398, Harry F. Byrd to Carter Glass, 12 September 1939, Box 345, Carter Glass Papers; Josiah W. Bailey to Dr. J. M. Ruffin, 18 September 1939, Personal File, Josiah W. Bailey Papers.

16. Harry F. Byrd to Josiah W. Bailey, 9 September 1939, Political File, Bailey Papers; Guy M. Gillette to Franklin D. Roosevelt, 6 September 1939, PPF 6176, Edwin Watson Memorandum to Franklin D. Roosevelt, 15 September 1939, Adolf A. Berle to Franklin D. Roosevelt, 20 September 1939, OF 1561, Box 2, Roosevelt Papers.

armaments to warring nations. Ten of thirteen prominent international lawyers surveyed in mid-October by the *New York Herald-Tribune* agreed with Secretary Hull that the United States and other neutrals could alter foreign policy to meet changing circumstances. The Non-Partisan Committee for Peace, a pressure group consisting of several hundred prominent Americans headed by nationally known editor William Allen White, lobbied very effectively at the grass-roots level in October for neutrality revision. Besides operating local units in thirty states, this group issued numerous press releases, conducted polls of professional groups, and arranged radio broadcasts to counter isolationist arguments. Businessmen, labor leaders William Green and John L. Lewis, the American Farm Bureau Federation, college educators, and internationalist peace organizations also helped in rallying both public opinion and Congress behind the Pittman bill.[17]

Administration officials and senators, therefore, were very optimistic about the prospects for the Pittman bill. During early September, two surveys by the executive branch disclosed that around sixty internationalist senators approved of lifting the embargo on armaments, while approximately twenty-four still resisted changes in the existing law and the remainder were undecided. Roosevelt remarked near the end of the month that "he hadn't had to buy a Senator yet" and was pleased that several conservative Democrats planned to support neutrality revision. Vice-president John Nance Garner did not "see how things on the Hill could look better," while isolationist Johnson of California remarked, "the President took his time, and has chiseled away from us quite a number of those who were with us."[18] "There is no question," Democrat Bailey of North Carolina predicted, "of the passage of the pending measure in the Senate." Roosevelt even contended, "we can get the votes in the House and the Senate but . . . the principal difficulty will be to prevent a filibuster in the latter."[19]

Senate isolationists already had begun discussing opposition strategy. On 11 September, Republicans Borah of Idaho, Vandenberg of Michigan, and Gerald P. Nye of North Dakota met at Hiram Johnson's office to commence plans for blocking neutrality revision. Isolationists attempted to organize resistance during the next few days but found few participants. "Since I have been here," Johnson admitted, "I have been every hour engaged in trying to draw together again our shattered forces. I have not been very successful except with the 'die-hards.' "[20] At the same time, Borah and aviator Charles A. Lindbergh made radio speeches urging Americans to influence Congress to retain the arms embargo. Delighted with the public response, the small, spirited group gathered nearly every morning in Johnson's office to devise plans for prolonging floor consideration. "I have no intention of debate in order to

17. Robert A. Divine, *The Illusion of Neutrality*, pp. 307–9.

18. Stephen Early Memorandum for Franklin D. Roosevelt, 7 September 1939, OF 1561, Early to Taylor, 8 September 1939, Stephen Early to Bernard M. Baruch, 14 September 1939, PPF 88, Roosevelt Papers; Ickes, *Diary*, 3:27; Hiram W. Johnson to Hiram W. Johnson, Jr., 24 September 1939, Part VI, Box 7, Hiram W. Johnson Papers.

19. Josiah W. Bailey to Franklin D. Roosevelt, 4 October 1939, PSF, Box 61, Roosevelt Papers; Roosevelt, ed., *Personal Letters*, 2:919.

20. *Washington Times-Herald*, 12 September 1939; Johnson to Johnson, 24 September 1939.

kill time," Borah remarked, but "a matter of such great importance is entitled to be considered, to be discussed and debated, in a sincere and honorable way."[21] Rejecting compromise solutions, these isolationists vowed to fight neutrality revision from "Hell to breakfast" and expected to wage a successful battle. Nye declared, "This stand is going to be a winning one." In addition, the isolationists conducted public rallies in Washington, D.C., and New York City to build support from the American people. As Johnson remarked, "we hope to convince the public, and in that way, have our influence on the Senate."[22]

Several pressure groups and a vocal segment of the public sustained the determination of the isolationist senators. Most farm organizations, Protestant and Roman Catholic groups, along with several pacifist organizations, adamantly rejected repeal of the arms embargo and overwhelmed members of Congress with countless printed forms. In an especially effective nationwide protest, Father Charles E. Coughlin of Royal Oak, Michigan, urged Americans to deluge Capitol Hill with telegrams and letters opposing the sale of munitions to belligerents. During the next two weeks, Americans sent senators and representatives 1 million pieces of mail ranging from 5 to 1 to 100 to 1 against neutrality revision. The Senate post office estimated receiving on 20 September over 175,000 letters, mostly hostile to the Pittman bill.[23] Congressmen, Republican Clyde M. Reed of Kansas commented, could not remember "a flood of written expression such as had come to all members, especially the Senators, in the last week or ten days." Although he usually received only twenty-five communications daily, Rep. James W. Wadsworth of New York remarked, "On September twenty-first the number suddenly jumped to one thousand and continued at the rate of about a thousand a day for four days. All of these letters were on the same subject—neutrality. In the proportion of nine to one they expressed opposition to repeal of the arms embargo." Besides relying heavily on the mail, constituents also made approximately 48,000 telephone calls daily to members of Congress. Republican Rep. Usher L. Burdick of North Dakota even reversed plans to support the Pittman measure because of the intense lobbying activities by peace organizations and because letters were "decidedly the other way."[24]

These communications did not provide an accurate indicator of public sentiment on the issue, however. Approximately 15 percent of the correspondence

21. Hiram W. Johnson to William E. Borah et al., 5 October 1939, Part III, Box 18, Johnson Papers; *New York Times*, 22–24, 27 September 1939; William E. Borah Press Release, 11 September 1939, Box 433, Borah Papers.

22. Gerald P. Nye to Constituents, 28 September 1939, Box 26, Gerald P. Nye Papers; Wayne S. Cole, *Senator Gerald P. Nye and American Foreign Relations*, p. 166; Johnson to Johnson, 24 September 1939.

23. Divine, *Illusion*, pp. 298–99; William E. Leuchtenburg, *Franklin D. Roosevelt and the New Deal, 1932–1940*, p. 294; L. E. Gleeck, "96 Congressmen Make Up Their Minds."

24. Clyde M. Reed to William Allen White, 26 September 1939, Box 224, William Allen White Papers; James W. Wadsworth, Jr., to F. M. O'Connell, 11 October 1939, Box 27, Wadsworth Family Papers; Clarence Cannon, Jr., Washington Newsletter, 4 November 1939, Scrapbook, vol. 40, Clarence Cannon, Jr., Papers; Usher L. Burdick to Edwin Watson, 23 September 1939, OF 1561, Roosevelt Papers.

received by two congressmen consisted of form letters inspired primarily by pacifist organizations. The largest proportion of mail came from the Great Lakes and Great Plains, where radio listeners of Father Coughlin petitioned congressmen with communications hostile to neutrality revision. Democrat Clyde L. Herring of Iowa on 29 September commented, ''In the past ten days we have received thousands of letters and telegrams, the plea in each being 'KEEP US OUT OF WAR.' '' German-American groups likewise persuaded thousands of people to deluge senators and representatives with antirepeal correspondence. In addition, numerous German and Irish constituents sent letters and telegrams urging their legislators to oppose lifting the arms embargo. At the same time, public opinion polls indicated that a majority of Americans actually favored removal of the ban on munitions sales to belligerents, but internationalist citizens, particularly those from the Southern states, mailed comparatively little correspondence to their national legislators on this issue.[25]

At the special session, the basic areas of disagreement between the internationalists and isolationists remained the same. Relying principally on ideological themes, internationalists pictured the European conflict as a battle between dictatorship and democracy and insisted that the Neutrality Act of 1937 had benefited aggressor nations. Democrat Elmer Thomas of Oklahoma charged, ''The United States is not a neutral nation'' because ''we are helping Germany and injuring Great Britain and France,'' while Prentiss M. Brown of Michigan contended that the ban on munitions sales had ''acted to strengthen Hitler's determination.''[26] Internationalists touted repeal of the arms embargo as the most effective method of preventing further German assaults in Europe. Claiming that Hitler's ''doctrine, his aim, is repulsive to every sense of justice and humanity,'' Independent Norris of Nebraska urged lifting the restriction so that ''such a horrible nightmare shall not be brought and thrust upon a civilized world.'' Neutrality revision at an earlier date, internationalists claimed, perhaps could have circumvented World War II. ''I feel certain,'' Democrat Joseph C. O'Mahoney of Wyoming stated, ''that if this bill had been repealed during the regular session when the President and the State Department asked it and Great Britain and France had been able to secure all the aircraft they needed, Hitler would have hesitated to invade Poland.''[27] In order to enhance American security and to help prevent further expansion by Hitler, internationalists advocated munitions sales to Western European democracies on a cash-and-carry basis. Glass of Virginia recommended ''selling to England and France anything and everything that would help them win the war'' and ''shoot Hitler off the map.'' Unless the United States dropped the arms embargo, Claude D. Pepper of Florida warned, ''we shall have to make this fight alone and probably without adequate

25. Divine, *Illusion*, p. 299; Gleeck, ''96 Congressmen,'' pp. 14–16; Clyde L. Herring, CBS Radio Address, 29 September 1939, Box 3, Clyde L. Herring Papers.

26. Elmer Thomas to Francis Kramer, 3 November 1939, Legislative Correspondence, Box M-N, Elmer Thomas Papers; Prentiss M. Brown Press Statement, 29 August 1939, Box 24, Scrapbook 9, Prentiss M. Brown Papers.

27. George W. Norris to William Allen White, 30 October 1939, Tray 25, Box 9, George W. Norris Papers; Joseph C. O'Mahoney to Paul Greever, 14 October 1939, Box 46, Joseph C. O'Mahoney Papers.

protection." On the other hand, the internationalists still were reluctant to intervene directly on behalf of particular European nations and argued that the measure would avert direct American involvement in World War II. "If Gerald Nye and his crowd could have their way," Bilbo of Mississippi warned, "we would be in war in twelve months." "Our purpose," Herring of Iowa added, "is to strengthen our position as a neutral, not to weaken it. We do not propose to abandon neutrality, but to make it more easily enforceable."[28]

Several Republicans, principally from New England, opposed combining arms shipments with an increase in presidential discretionary authority. Although espousing munitions sales, Austin of Vermont, Styles Bridges of New Hampshire, White of Maine, and Reed of Kansas were "dead set against giving the President specific powers." Congress, Austin and Reed suggested, should "pass a straight out neutrality bill without giving the President undue discretion." Reed promised, "The two of us will help Roosevelt and Hull out if they will let us," but feared that "the President and Hull would insist upon something like the degree of 'Presidential discretion' contained in the Bloom bill." If the administration refused to delete the prerogatives of the executive branch, Reed warned, "they may force enough fellows to vote to continue the present law."[29]

Isolationists likewise employed earlier themes, highlighting ideological, economic, and political considerations. In denouncing the Pittman bill, they believed the ban on arms shipments still afforded the best means of avoiding involvement in foreign conflicts. Borah of Idaho charged that the "most sordid and cowardly" measure would "utterly destroy any reasonable contention that we are any longer neutral," whereas youthful Democrat Rush Dew Holt of West Virginia argued, "A vote for the revision of the Neutrality Act is a vote for war."[30] Ever mindful of the World War I experience, isolationists still stressed that selling armaments to belligerents might lead eventually to larger military and financial commitments abroad. The "repeal of the arms embargo," Nye of North Dakota asserted, "is only a step which will be immediately followed by other steps by this Administration which will have us wrapped up in Europe's war overnight." In a similar vein, Progressive Robert M. La Follette, Jr., of Wisconsin cautioned that the "manpower, resources, and wealth of the nation must not be wasted in other nation's wars," while Minority Leader McNary recalled, "We got mixed up twenty years ago and the tragic results are known to all."[31] Politically, Republican isolationists still resisted empowering a Democratic president to determine aggressors without

---

28. Theodore G. Bilbo to Axel Rapp, 21 October 1939, File N, Bilbo Papers; Herring Radio Address, 29 September 1939; Carter Glass to George Allen, 14 September 1939, Box 383, Carter Glass to R. B. Stephenson, 16 September 1939, Box 383, Glass Papers; Claude D. Pepper to John Cabot, 8 October 1939, 66–A–82, Box 106, Claude D. Pepper Papers.

29. Clyde M. Reed to William Allen White, 4 September 1939, Box 224, White Papers.

30. William E. Borah to Jess Hawley, 31 October 1939, Box 426, Borah Papers; Rush Dew Holt to J. Shirley Ross, 27 September 1939, A&M 873, Series 1, Box 5, Rush Dew Holt Papers.

31. Gerald P. Nye to Mrs. C. J. McCarthy, 22 September 1939, Box 26, Nye Papers; Robert M. La Follette, Jr., Newsletter, October 1939, OF 1561, Roosevelt Papers; Charles L. McNary to Scott Beeler, 29 September 1939, Box 7, Charles L. McNary Papers.

congressional approval. Besides claiming that "the hierarchy of the New Deal are anxious to have us get into the war," Charles W. Tobey of New Hampshire argued that the Pittman measure granted "tremendous powers to the President in the event of war, under the emergency, greater powers than any man ever had before." "I think the gentleman in the White House, not withstanding his late asservations [sic]," Johnson of California remarked, "is determined to carry us into war, and that he sees himself a world military leader."[32]

Administration leaders, meanwhile, finalized strategy for the impending floor debate. Following his 21 September address, Roosevelt played a subordinate role because of fears that direct intervention might make neutrality revision a personal issue. "I am almost literally walking on eggs," Roosevelt stated; "having good prospects of the bill going through, I am at the moment saying nothing, seeing nothing, and hearing nothing." Vice-president Garner advised Majority Leader Barkley to conduct six-hour sessions for a week and implored him to "keep their [the administration spokesmen's] mouths shut and to shut off debate." If isolationists filibustered, Garner counseled holding night sessions so as to insure favorable action by 1 November on the measure. Since isolationists would "take up a good deal of time in talking," Democrat Pat Harrison of Mississippi advised Barkley to "hold their feet to the fire—by early meetings and late adjournments."[33]

To aid Pittman, the Roosevelt administration enlisted two dynamic Southern Democrats to help direct the Senate battle. Connally of Texas, who had assisted in framing the neutrality bill, managed floor operations and arranged the list of speakers for the internationalists. A native of McLennan County, Texas, the sixty-one-year-old Connally had graduated in 1896 from Baylor University and had studied law at the University of Texas. After briefly practicing law, Connally had served in the Texas House of Representatives and had been prosecuting attorney for Falls County. The tall, energetic Democratic party member, who was an effective "rough and tumble" debater, had belonged to the U.S. House of Representatives from 1917 to 1929 and then had joined the U.S. Senate. Although supporting most New Deal legislation, he had helped direct resistance to Roosevelt's Supreme Court plan and had played an instrumental role in killing the judicial reform plan. Connally not only had wielded considerable influence on the Finance and Judiciary committees, but also was a ranking member of the Foreign Relations group.

For a long time, Connally had exhibited interest in international affairs. The Texas Democrat, an ardent defender of neutral maritime rights, had supported American entrance into World War I against Germany. During the postwar period, he had attended meetings in Geneva and Paris of the Interparliamentary Union. He had endorsed Roosevelt's internationalist foreign policy programs, including resumption of relations with the Soviet Union, reciprocal trade, and American entrance into the World Court. Besides rejecting the Nye committee findings about the

32. Charles W. Tobey to Elwin Page, 21 September 1939, Box 79, Charles W. Tobey Papers; Hiram W. Johnson to Earl Warren, 29 October 1939, Part III, Box 18, Johnson Papers.

33. Roosevelt, ed., *Personal Letters*, 2:934; John Nance Garner to Pat Harrison, 22 September 1939, Pat Harrison to Sephen Early, 16, 23 September 1939, File 1, Pat Harrison Papers.

role of munitioners in World War I, Connally in 1935 had opposed placing an arms embargo on belligerent nations. This step, he argued, would be an unneutral act aligning the United States with aggressors against attacked countries. The Texas Democrat, however, reluctantly agreed to vote for the Neutrality Act of 1935 after receiving promises that the measure would not be permanent. Since he was embroiled in the Supreme Court controversy, Connally did not figure prominently in the 1937 debate over cash-and-carry. Hitler's moves into Austria and Czechoslovakia, coupled with Japanese expansion in China, persuaded the Texas Democrat to seek repeal of the arms embargo. An exponent of the domino theory, he believed Nazi and Japanese aggression endangered democratic institutions and the security of Western Europe and the United States. In July 1939, the Texas Democrat had supported lifting the arms embargo both at Foreign Relations Committee sessions and at the turbulent White House conference.[34] Byrnes of South Carolina ably assisted Connally by conversing with senators in cloakrooms and by encouraging several conservative colleagues over the telephone to cooperate with the president. "I devoted my time to this cause," Byrnes later recalled, "to the exclusion of everything else."[35]

Isolationists countered with even more effective leadership. Several experienced, articulate, influential members, including Borah of Idaho, Nye of North Dakota, and Vandenberg of Michigan, directed the campaign against the Pittman bill. Vandenberg, the fifty-five-year-old son of a penniless harnessmaker, had grown up in Grand Rapids, Michigan, and had worked as a newsboy and billing clerk. After studying law at the University of Michigan, he had edited the *Grand Rapids Herald*. Before joining the U.S. Senate in 1928, he had served only one year in politics as a member of the Grand Rapids Charter Commission. Vandenberg quickly had befriended Borah of Idaho and, within a decade, had become the real leader of the Senate Republican minority. Although stern and not particularly popular, he was industrious, intelligent, a persuasive and influential speaker, and flexible. The Michigan Republican initially concentrated on commercial and financial measures and usually opposed New Deal measures, including the National Recovery Act, the Agricultural Adjustment Act, and the Wagner Act. Vandenberg belonged from the outset to the Foreign Relations Committee but did not exhibit keen interest in international affairs until participating on the Nye committee. From the Great Lakes region, he had agreed with the committee findings that eastern financial interests and munitioners had drawn the United States into World War I against the national interest. The Atlantic Ocean, he believed, adequately safeguarded the United States against any invasion by Hitler. In order to avoid involvement in war, the Michigan Republican had disapproved of federal loans to foreign governments and in the mid-1930s had supported the strict neutrality laws. Vandenberg also had backed a comprehensive arms embargo and a rigid cash-and-carry policy. Along with other Republicans, he claimed that the president already had gained too much power and thus rejected granting Roosevelt discretionary authority. At the regular

34. "Tom Connally," *Current Biography* 2 (1941):167–68; Connally and Steinberg, *Tom Connally*; Frank H. Smyrl, "Tom Connally and the New Deal" (Ph.D. diss.).
35. *New York Times*, 29 October 1939; James F. Byrnes, *All in One Lifetime*, p. 111.

1939 session, he had preferred retaining the existing neutrality legislation because international conditions were too volatile to allow any experiments. In accordance with Republican tradition, Vandenberg warned that Japanese aggression in the Pacific endangered American security more than did German expansion in Europe and, therefore, urged the State Department to terminate the 1911 trade treaty.[36]

Before overflowing galleries, the senators on 2 October began the long-awaited debate. In a 170-hour period covering three weeks, over 1 million words were uttered by seventy of the ninety-six members concerning what Pepper of Florida described as "one of the great decisions of American History." Most legislators, including Austin of Vermont and Tobey of New Hampshire, found the sessions tedious mentally and exhausting physically. "Crowds are here," Austin remarked, "to listen to the debate on neutrality. My desk is filled with letters. Visitors of importance and helpful service are calling. I have been on the job since eight A.M. with only time out for an oyster stew. Even at table debate goes on." "Life," Tobey commented, "has been as intense as I have ever known it. We are working day and night. In fact I slept in the office last night as we worked so late. Telephones, telegrams, pressmen, photographers, all the paraphernalia of such an experience has been present."[37]

During lengthy floor debates, few internationalists admitted their real concerns about the European situation. Despite the outbreak of World War II, Pittman, Connally, Byrnes, and other internationalists described the measure as legislation intended solely to keep the United States from becoming involved in the European war. In the opening presentation on 2 October, Pittman urged the United States to rely on international law and "prevent our citizens from subjecting themselves to destruction in the mad war raging in Europe." The arms embargo, internationalists charged, was an unneutral action aiding the Axis nations. Pittman claimed that the ban on munitions sales not only violated global statutes, but also "helps Germany while injuring Great Britain and France." On the other hand, the vast majority of internationalists deliberately avoided stating that the real objective of the Pittman bill was to furnish American military assistance to Western European nations and preserve American security. From the outset, Pittman emphatically denied that "we are fighting for either Great Britain or France."[38] Lifting the restriction on military supplies provided the best solution for preventing involvement in foreign affairs. Connally of Texas maintained, "We are going just as far as any people can go in this legislation to stay out of war." Ever mindful of the extensive loss of American life and property in World War I, internationalists urged a strict cash-and-carry system

36. "Arthur Hedrick Vandenberg," *Current Biography* 1 (1940):821–23; Manfred Jonas, *Isolationism in America, 1935–1941*, p. 65; C. David Tompkins, *Senator Arthur H. Vandenberg: The Evolution of a Modern Republican, 1884–1945*.

37. Pepper to Cabot, 8 October 1939; Warren R. Austin to Mrs. Chauncey Austin, 3 October 1939, Correspondence with Mother, Box 1939–1940, Austin Papers; Charles W. Tobey to Elwin Page, 11 October 1939, Box 79, Tobey Papers.

38. *Congressional Record (CR)*, 76th Cong., 2d sess., vol. 85, 2 October 1939, pp. 50–56; Key Pittman to Paul Thurston, 6 November 1939, Box 38, Key Pittman Papers. For a concise summary of the floor debate, see Divine, *Illusion*, pp. 315–18.

for all trade with belligerents. During 1917, Connally charged, "we were dragged in by repeated insults and repeated outrages, and repeated murder of American citizens." The avalanche of hostile telegrams and letters sent to Capitol Hill by isolationist citizens and organizations convinced most internationalist senators to avoid stating the real purpose of the legislation. Although the isolationists did not represent a majority of public opinion, the internationalists realized that they were very vocal and wielded a national influence considerably beyond their actual numbers. Some internationalists privately indicated their desire to discuss more candidly in debates how German aggression endangered Western European democracies and threatened internal defense. "I wish the present state of opinion," Austin stressed, "would permit legislators to discuss the real situation frankly and recognize the great interest which animates us."[39]

Isolationists, who dominated floor debate, used more colorful terminology than the internationalists and yet added few insights. For over three weeks, twelve isolationists filibustered effectively against neutrality revision. Rejecting Pittman's view, they argued that the ban on the trading of armaments was consistent with global law. Borah, who on 2 October delivered the initial address for the isolationists, asserted, "I know of no rule of international law" that "denies the right of a nation to prohibit the sale of arms and munitions." Removal of the embargo, isolationists charged, was designed to assist England and France. According to Borah, the Pittman bill meant the United States would become an actual belligerent in "another bloody volume of European power politics."[40] Besides denying that German activity threatened domestic security, isolationists warned that permitting the sale of ammunition would encourage direct American financial and military intervention in the European conflict. Vandenberg cautioned, "To repeal the arms embargo is to strike down a great, indispensable, insulating defense against our involvement in this war." Defending strict cash-and-carry provisions, the isolationists opposed any American loans to Great Britain or France. Nye of North Dakota stated, "I hope to see both the arms embargo and the cash-and-carry plan made the law of the land."[41]

Since the isolationists objected primarily to lifting the ban on munitions sales, Tobey of New Hampshire urged action first on the remaining sections of the Pittman bill. A fifty-nine-year-old native of Roxbury, Massachusetts, Tobey had attended Latin School and had engaged in insurance, banking, and farming. After moving to Temple, New Hampshire, he had headed a shoe company and lived on a one-hundred-acre farm. The Republican had been elected to a wide variety of state offices, including representative, senator, lieutenant governor, and governor. After being elected in 1932 to the U.S. House of Representatives, he had served three terms there and in early 1939 had entered the U.S. Senate. A frank, candid

39. *CR*, 4 October 1939, pp. 83–94; Warren R. Austin to Arthur Krock, 28 September 1939, General Correspondence, Austin Papers.
40. *CR*, 2 October 1939, pp. 65–75; Robert James Maddox, *William E. Borah and American Foreign Policy*, pp. 244–45.
41. *CR*, 4 October 1939, pp. 95–104, 11 October 1939, pp. 269–70.

individual, Tobey had specialized on commercial and monetary legislation and vigorously had opposed New Deal programs. He frequently had participated in floor debates, speaking both succinctly and rapidly. During the 1930s, Tobey adamantly had supported strict neutrality policies primarily for political and geographical reasons. The New Hampshire Republican claimed Roosevelt already held too much power over domestic policy and rejected granting him discretionary power to determine aggressors. Roosevelt's foreign policy, Tobey charged, was a "gigantic conspiracy" to "drive the American people to war." He believed that the three-thousand-mile-wide Atlantic Ocean afforded the United States adequate protection against foreign invasion. Tobey, therefore, had backed neutrality legislation implementing the arms embargo and cash-and-carry. After cash-and-carry expired in May 1939, the New Hampshire Republican sought to revive the trade system and continue the other provisions of the 1937 statute. Tobey protested the Pittman bill, which included both the restoration of cash-and-carry and arms embargo repeal, and preferred delaying any action on the sanctioning of munitions sales to belligerents.[42]

On 4 October, Tobey introduced an amendment to dispose of cash-and-carry sections prior to discussion of the arms embargo repeal. Tobey, along with other isolationists, wanted to restore the cash-and-carry system and to retain the ban on munitions sales. Isolationists strongly disapproved of linking resumption of cash-and-carry and repeal of the arms embargo in the same bill. Floor debates on munitions sales, Tobey predicted, would take "many weeks and perhaps months" and jeopardize American neutral rights. If the United States failed to restore cash-and-carry, he warned, belligerents might sink vessels transporting materials abroad. Such incidents, Tobey insisted, would place the nation at "the brink of entrance into a war" requiring "billions of dollars" and "thousands of men." If they could secure enactment of the cash-and-carry restrictions first, isolationists then would be able to concentrate efforts on prohibiting shipment of military supplies.[43]

In a highly partisan vote, however, the Senate on 10 October soundly rejected 65 to 25 the Tobey amendment. Democrats solidly opposed the motion, refusing to separate the arms sales issue from the rest of the bill. Exploiting their vast numerical advantage, Barkley and Minton secured cooperation from 85 percent of Roosevelt's party in resisting the Tobey proposal. Besides remaining loyal politically to the administration, Democrats opposed the Tobey motion on ideological grounds. The German attack on Poland, they warned, endangered the European power balance and American security. Following the vote, Tobey remarked, "you can't lick a steam roller. The Administration ganged up on me, brought two sick men in to vote, and had a new Senator sworn in just 15 minutes before so he could vote too." Although more divided than the Democrats, Republicans favored the Tobey amendment. They contended that Roosevelt already exercised too much power and protested that neutrality revision would increase his authority. Since the president

42. "Charles W. Tobey," *Current Biography* 2 (1941):862–63; U.S., Congress, *Biographical Directory of the American Congress, 1774–1961*, p. 1719.

43. *CR*, 4 October 1939, pp. 104–8; Charles W. Tobey to Alben W. Barkley, 28 September 1939, Box X–43, John H. Overton Papers.

still had not disclosed his plans for the future, Republicans suspected he might entertain third-term aspirations. Despite the outbreak of World War II, they denied that Nazi Germany threatened the security of the United States or of other Western Hemisphere nations[44] (see table 15).

Regional considerations profoundly influenced Senate voting behavior. The Democratic-dominated Southern and Border delegations proportionately directed the onslaught against the Tobey plan. Although often defecting from Roosevelt's party on New Deal issues, they cooperated with the White House on this foreign policy question. Southern and Border members came from sections trading extensively with Great Britain and containing overwhelmingly Anglo-Saxon constituents. Besides having a military tradition, the Southern and Border sections enjoyed less geographical protection from the European war than did most other sections. In addition, at least 75 percent of the Middle Atlantic, Great Lakes, and Mountain senators opposed the Tobey motion. Controlled by Democrats, the Middle Atlantic delegation maintained party loyalty by supporting the president's foreign policy. Similarly, the Middle Atlantic states had traded extensively with Great Britain and were situated closer to the European scene. The outbreak of World War II persuaded this bloc that Hitler threatened the safety of Europe and the Western Hemisphere. Although the Great Lakes and Mountain blocs usually have been identified as isolationist in this period, they aligned with the internationalists this time. Democrats controlled these delegations—especially the Mountain bloc—and enthusiastically backed the president's neutrality program. Despite serving interior regions, they despised Hitler's totalitarian methods and believed Nazi Germany constituted a menace to democracy in the Western world (see table 15).

The Pacific states, surprisingly, proportionately led the campaign for the Tobey proposal, allying with the Great Plains members. Historians often have pictured the Pacific states as internationalist, but they sided with the isolationists this time. Republicans, most notably Minority Leader McNary of Oregon and Johnson of California, wielded considerable influence in this delegation and repudiated designating any further power to a Democratic president. In addition, the Pacific states engaged relatively little in commerce with Great Britain and included numerous nationalities supporting neutrality. German and Russian constituents opposed American entry into the war against their homelands, which were allied at this point. Geographically, Pacific states were far removed from the European conflict and did not consider themselves threatened by Nazi expansion in Europe. Great Plains senators composed the only other regional bloc with a majority defending the Tobey amendment. The largely Republican group opposed granting Roosevelt any additional control over American international policy. As with the Pacific delegation, they believed the eastern United States and the Atlantic Ocean provided an adequate buffer zone against any German attack. Besides engaging in limited business with European nations, they still suspected that eastern bankers, munitioners, and indus-

44. *CR*, 10 October 1939, p. 237; *New York Times*, 11 October 1939; Charles W. Tobey to Mrs. Daphne Prescott, 11 October 1939, Box 79, Tobey Papers.

trialists intended to draw the United States into the conflict on the British side. Great Plains senators also represented numerous German constituents opposing American entry into war against their native land and also insisted that the United States should give priority to solving domestic problems (see table 15).

Ideological considerations and international developments contributed significantly to the rejection of the Tobey amendment. Internationalists feared that German expansion endangered Western democratic institutions. On the other hand, isolationists argued that Hitler did not threaten American security and were determined to keep the United States out of foreign wars. Senators stressed ideology more often than did representatives because they faced reelection fewer times and could act more independently of constituent pressures. The outbreak of World War II likewise influenced the Senate to defeat the Tobey motion. Before Germany attacked Poland, the isolationist amendment probably would have attracted much larger numerical support.

Ethnic background, meanwhile, did not figure prominently in the outcome. In sharp contrast to the lower house at the regular session, no single nationality decisively influenced the Senate tally. Irish and German members, contrary to traditional historical stereotypes, aligned with internationalists in opposing the Tobey proposal. A majority of Irishmen, despising both Hitler's authoritarian tactics and his suppression of individual liberties, remained loyal to President Roosevelt and the Democratic party. At this juncture, they were more concerned about the immediate dangers posed by Nazi Germany to the Western world than by any longstanding hostility toward Great Britain. German senators, who shared similar attitudes, likewise aligned with the internationalists against the Tobey motion. Although proud of their German heritage, they believed Hitler's dictatorial policies jeopardized democratic nations and individual civil liberties across the European continent. The Nazi attack on Poland convinced these legislators that Hitler intended to conquer other non-German-speaking peoples and that the United States should respond by providing more assistance to Great Britain. Several Irishmen, however, joined Scandinavian members in urging postponement of the arms embargo issue. Sympathetic to the isolationist preachings of Father Charles E. Coughlin, they discarded political loyalties to President Roosevelt on this occasion. The British refusal to grant home rule to Ireland, coupled with its discrimination against Roman Catholics, largely provided the impetus for the isolationist behavior of this faction. Scandinavian senators likewise supported the Tobey amendment, being influenced by the isolationist sentiments of their native governments and pacifist clergy[45] (see table 31).

The rejection of the Tobey amendment marked the first time Senate internationalists had defeated isolationists on a major neutrality roll call. At the regular session, vocal Foreign Relations Committee isolationists had prevented floor action on the neutrality revision question. Internationalists this time controlled Senate

45. The ethnic origins of members are derived from Elsdon Coles Smith, *New Dictionary of American Family Names*.

decisionmaking, blocking the isolationist attempt to delay floor action on repeal of the arms embargo. The outcome, which virtually assured eventual adoption of the Pittman bill, enhanced the optimism and courage of the internationalists. Since the margin was decisive, Majority Whip Minton predicted "an overwhelming vote" in favor of the neutrality measure. Administration leaders hoped the tally would demonstrate to the isolationists the futility of stalling techniques. Pittman insisted, "Further debate will accomplish nothing," while Byrnes believed rejection of the Tobey amendment would take "all the punch out of the debate."[46] For the first time, internationalists admitted that the Pittman legislation was intended to provide American military assistance to Great Britain and France. Democrat Edward R. Burke of Nebraska remarked, "If by selling arms to nations that are risking everything in the cause we can aid in the struggle to restrain and hold within bounds the spread of nazi-ism and communism, then I am willing to share whatever guilt anyone may choose to say is involved in such a course." On the Republican side, Taft of Ohio asserted that the ban on munitions sales "discriminates against England and France and against peaceful nations."[47]

Isolationists, however, still monopolized floor debate. During the next two weeks, Borah, Vandenberg, La Follette, Clark, Nye, and a few other isolationists delivered lengthy speeches preventing the Senate from voting on amendments. Since the internationalists held numerical control, the isolationists considered the filibuster the only effective means of resistance. "The fact is," Johnson of California remarked, "the big boys and the Administration have taken every man of doubtful courage there is, and save for some lucky break, we're in a bad way."[48]

Several internationalists, including O'Mahoney of Wyoming and Austin of Vermont, complained that the isolationists were wasting time by making redundant arguments. After the Senate had debated neutrality revision for one week, O'Mahoney charged, "Almost every argument that can be made has been made." Isolationists continued their dilatory tactics, provoking internationalists to intensify their protests. Austin particularly was irritated on 19 October when Nye handed Republican Rufus C. Holman of Oregon a typewritten speech to deliver. "This is clearly unnecessary," Austin interjected, "for the purpose of educating anyone. The subject has been exhausted."[49] "We have been here now a month," Republican Ernest W. Gibson of Vermont protested, "doing work that could have been

46. Sherman Minton to William Allen White, 21 October 1939, Box 225, White Papers; *New York Times*, 11 October 1939.
47. *CR*, 11 October 1939, pp. 285–92, 13 October 1939, pp. 358–59.
48. Hiram W. Johnson to Bennett Champ Clark and Robert M. La Follette, Jr., 14 October 1939, Hiram W. Johnson to Frank Doherty, 15 October 1939, Part III, Box 18, Johnson Papers.
49. Joseph C. O'Mahoney to Dr. Thomas Cassidy, 9 October 1939, Box 46, O'Mahoney Papers; Warren R. Austin to Mrs. Chauncey Austin, 19, 24 October 1939, Correspondence with Mother, Box 1939–1940, Austin Papers. Throughout this period, the "peace bloc" insisted they were performing the United States a valuable service and refused to consider their tactics a filibuster. "There has not been the slightest attempt to waste time, except by Senator Pittman," Johnson of California claimed, "and there has not been the slightest evidence of a filibuster." Johnson to Doherty, 15 October 1939.

accomplished in a week. I often get disgusted at the length of time it takes to debate a question to finality in the Senate."[50]

Despite condemning the filibuster, internationalists made no organized effort to seize the initiative. Majority Leader Barkley, criticized by *Time* as "dazed" and "fumbling," did not arrange speakers to counter the filibuster. Satisfied that administration forces would triumph ultimately, Barkley instructed internationalists to let the isolationists dominate floor debate. "Supporters of the bill," O'Mahoney of Wyoming observed, "have generally agreed it is not necessary to talk" or "draw up more speeches." Barkley attempted several times to secure a unanimous consent agreement to begin considering amendments, but did not succeed until 24 October in breaking the filibuster.[51]

At the same time, numerous pressure groups sought to loosen shipping restrictions. Pittman's legislation prohibited American vessels and aircraft from transporting passengers or merchandise to any belligerent nation. Several trade associations and foreign chambers of commerce protested that the comprehensive language would prevent American companies from shipping military products to ports far removed from the European conflict. In addition, these organizations contended that the restrictions would deprive the United States fleet of nearly 130 million tons of cargo and might cause the unemployment of nine thousand seamen. Commerce Committee Chairman Bailey of North Carolina sympathized with these concerns, calling the limitations "an unnecessary abandonment of our rights." In response, the State Department gladly drafted an amendment confining cash-and-carry restrictions to the North Atlantic. From the outset, the administration had favored sanctioning trade with British and French ports in Africa, Asia, and the Pacific. Pittman objected to this approach, preferring to keep all trade on a cash-and-carry basis. With the assistance of Connally, he submitted a compromise proposal permitting American vessels to sell nonmilitary goods to British and French colonial possessions. Since the Connally-Pittman amendment did not satisfy business groups, Pittman reluctantly consented to let Connally introduce the State Department version. The Senate on 24 October approved the plan, thus restricting cash-and-carry to the North Atlantic.[52]

Following the lengthy filibuster, isolationists concentrated on inserting an amendment by Clark of Missouri to restore the arms embargo. A native of Bowling Green, Missouri, Clark was the son of a prominent U.S. congressman and noted speaker of the house. By age fourteen he had campaigned for his father and had served as a Democratic party precinct captain. After studying law at George

50. Ernest W. Gibson to Miss Beryl Atherton, 23 October 1939, Ernest W. Gibson to Willsie Brisbin, 23 October 1939, Personal, 1939, Ernest W. Gibson Papers.

51. "The Great Fugue," *Time* 34 (25 September 1939):12; O'Mahoney to Cassidy, 9 October 1939. Unanimous consent is consent, indicated by the absence of objection on the part of any senator, for proceeding contrary to a rule or rules. Unanimous consent is a time-saving device usually used in a variety of minor matters for expediting the passage of unopposed bills.

52. Divine, *Illusion*, pp. 319–24; Josiah W. Bailey to Key Pittman, 13 October 1939, Sen. 76A–E6, National Archives; Josiah W. Bailey to Franklin D. Roosevelt, 14 October 1939, PSF, Box 57, Roosevelt Papers; Hull, *Memoirs*, 1:694–95; *CR*, 24 October 1939, p. 776.

Washington University, the tall, broad-shouldered, barrel-chested Clark briefly had practiced in St. Louis and had become parliamentarian for the U.S. House of Representatives. On the side, he had written a congressional procedural manual, a biography of former President John Quincy Adams, and a social science textbook. Clark had been appointed in 1933 as senator to fill a vacancy caused by the resignation of Harry B. Hawes. Although having a magnificent voice, he frequently had ridiculed opponents in floor debates. Unlike most isolationists, Clark had rejected nearly all New Deal programs. Besides distrusting greedy bankers, he had advocated strict neutrality because of an intense hatred of Communism and a desire to prevent the president from encroaching on Senate foreign policy powers. Geographically, Clark believed the Atlantic Ocean afforded the United States adequate protection against any foreign invasion. A member of the Nye committee, he had drafted a plan for eliminating war profits and had opposed munitions sales to belligerent nations. Clark not only had strongly favored the mandatory neutrality legislation of the mid-1930s, but also had in particular championed the ban on the sale of arms to all belligerents. An advocate of cash-and-carry, he had opposed granting the president discretionary authority and had endorsed the war referendum movement. These policies, he had insisted, would best keep the United States out of any European conflict. At the regular session in 1939, he had continued to espouse strict neutrality and had opposed repeal of the arms embargo. Clark had joined the Foreign Relations Committee in late April and had played an instrumental role in securing a delay until 1940 of the entire issue. Without Chairman Pittman's knowledge, he had conferred with anti-New Deal Democrats George of Georgia and Gillette of Iowa and had persuaded them to vote with the isolationists in committee for postponement.[53]

Since the internationalists held numerical control, the Senate on 27 October soundly rejected 60 to 33 the Clark motion. Political and sectional alignments resembled those on the earlier Tobey proposal. Democrats overwhelmingly rejected the retention of the ban on munitions sales and vastly outnumbered the isolationist Republicans favoring the Clark amendment. Southern and Border senators again proportionately led the prorepeal forces and received support from all delegations except those of the Pacific and Great Plains states. Although often depicted as isolationists, Mountain and Great Lakes senators again supported American military assistance to belligerents. In another unusual pattern, the Pacific bloc rather than the Great Plains members proportionately led the isolationist resistance to the arms embargo (see table 15).

In anticlimactic fashion, the Senate quickly approved 63 to 30 the Pittman neutrality measure. Democrats Gillette of Iowa and Edwin C. Johnson of Colorado and Republican Reed of Kansas, all supporters of the Clark amendment, shifted to the internationalist camp this time. Great Plains senators, who previously had allied with the isolationist Pacific delegation, were divided sharply this time. Otherwise, political and sectional coalitions changed little[54] (see table 15).

53. "Bennett Champ Clark," *Current Biography* 2 (1941):153–55; Jonas, *Isolationism*, p. 64.
54. *CR*, 27 October 1939, pp. 1023–24; *New York Times*, 28 October 1939.

Partisanship played a moderate role on the Clark amendment and the Pittman bill. Democrats continued acting cohesively, with nearly four of five supporting the internationalists. Conservatives, who had opposed New Deal measures, set aside personal differences with Roosevelt to help insure the wide margin of victory for the neutrality revision. Every senator on Roosevelt's purge list in the 1938 primaries consented to the Pittman legislation, prompting Republican Vandenberg of Michigan to label them "the most faithful of rubber stamps." "There's a certain class of Democrats," Johnson of California explained, "the kid-glove group of the Southern States, who have always felt uneasy since the purge last year, and have been looking for a more comfortable seat in the Democratic Party. They have found it on the war issue."[55] Republicans sided with the isolationists, but Minority Leader McNary could not attain even 70 percent solidarity among his ranks. In marked contrast to their votes on domestic measures, many Republicans were influenced by nonpolitical considerations on foreign policy.

These roll calls signified a remarkable political transformation in the attitudes of anti-New Deal Democrats. Before, conservatives not only had distrusted the president, but also had opposed both his domestic and foreign policies. At the regular session, Glass and Byrd of Virginia, Bailey of North Carolina, and other anti-New Dealers opposed repeal of the arms embargo because they believed the president might embroil the nation in the European conflict. Democrats George of Georgia, Gillette of Iowa, and Van Nuys of Indiana had voted in July with the majority of the Foreign Relations Committee members against the administration to postpone consideration of neutrality revision. Following the German attack on Poland, however, Roosevelt had acted more cordially toward Glass, Byrd, Bailey, and other conservatives and had won their support for lifting the arms ban against belligerents.[56]

Regional and ideological forces continued to figure prominently and overshadowed the effect of ethnic background. Most Border, Southern, and Middle Atlantic senators supported the internationalists, while the opposite pattern occurred among the Pacific delegation. Sectional and philosophical considerations particularly influenced fifteen western senators who held progressive attitudes and eagerly supported both New Deal and isolationist measures. Serving areas more remote from Europe, they insisted the Pittman bill would draw the United States into foreign conflicts and urged instead concentrating on agricultural and labor problems. Nearly every ethnic group, including the traditionally isolationist Irish and Germans, backed neutrality revision (see table 31).

Senate internationalists once again had defeated the isolationists on major roll calls. Internationalists had enhanced their control of Senate decisionmaking, blocking isolationist attempts to restore the ban on munitions sales to belligerents. Despite providing vocal resistance, the isolationists could not overcome the numerical

55. Vandenberg Diary, 27 October 1939; Hiram W. Johnson to Hiram W. Johnson, Jr., 28 October 1939, Part VI, Box 7, Johnson Papers.

56. Patterson, "Eating Humble Pie," pp. 407–12.

advantage enjoyed by the internationalists following the outbreak of World War II. Borah claimed, "From the beginning, of course, we could not win" because the repeal "influences were too powerful," while Johnson of California remarked that the result was "long ago a foregone conclusion."[57] Most isolationists, nevertheless, reacted bitterly to the Senate approval of the internationalist Pittman measure. Democrat Holt of West Virginia, who denounced munitions sales to belligerents as a "great mistake," stressed, "Let us hope that the future does not bring us the tragedy that seems imminent." Besides being "exceedingly tired and mentally fatigued," Johnson of California admitted, "I still feel as if I had been run over by a truck in the neutrality fight."[58] Republican Arthur Capper of Kansas blamed the Roosevelt administration for the isolationist setback and argued that, otherwise, "the legislation would not have stood any chance." On the other hand, a few isolationists did not consider the filibuster fruitless. "I am convinced," Republican John A. Danaher of Connecticut stated, "that the debates served a most useful purpose and that every moment given to the proposition was well worth while."[59] The House of Representatives, isolationists believed, would either overturn or at least provide more effective resistance to the Pittman legislation. "Looks like we may have a very close vote," Republican Fred L. Crawford of Michigan observed, "but the repeal may carry by 10 to 20 votes or lose by about 10 to 15." Republican Karl Stefan of Nebraska anticipated "a very very close vote" and stated, "We of the opposition believe we have a 50–50 chance to win."[60] Republican Clifford R. Hope of Kansas likewise predicted, "The vote is going to be much closer than in the Senate" and promised, "Those of us who favor retaining the arms embargo are going to make every fight possible."[61]

The Roosevelt administration, in fact, grew increasingly restive. In the middle of October, Vice-president Garner warned cabinet colleagues that the result would be "much closer in the House than in the Senate." Since Majority Leader Rayburn was at home in Bonham, Texas, Roosevelt requested Postmaster General James A. Farley to check the mood among representatives. A few days later, Farley reported that several Irish Catholics from New York City intended to oppose the Pittman bill. Roosevelt, therefore, assigned the postmaster general to work exclusively on preventing widespread defections by Irish Democrats.[62]

57. William E. Borah to Ray McKaig, 31 October 1939, Box 426, Borah Papers; Hiram W. Johnson to John Neylan, 1 November 1939, Part III, Box 18, Johnson Papers.

58. Rush Dew Holt to Hudson DePriest, 3 November 1939, A&M 873, Series 1, Box 8, Holt Papers; Hiram W. Johnson to Frank Doherty, 30 October, 3 November 1939, Part III, Box 18, Johnson Papers.

59. Arthur Capper to Alfred M. Landon, 7 November 1939, Political, 1939, Alfred M. Landon Papers; John A. Danaher to Gerald P. Nye, 2 November 1939, Box 26, Nye Papers.

60. Fred L. Crawford to D. Kinahan, 20 October 1939, Box 1, Fred L. Crawford Papers; Karl Stefan to A. C. Gardner, 1 November 1939, Box 26, Karl Stefan Papers.

61. Clifford R. Hope to Mr. & Mrs. W. S. Fritmeier, 26 October 1939, Legislative Correspondence, Box 179, Clifford R. Hope Papers.

62. Ickes, *Diary*, 3:27, 43; Edwin Watson Memo for Franklin D. Roosevelt, 19 October 1939, PSF, Box 57, Roosevelt Papers.

Nationally prominent Republicans William Allen White and Frank Knox were enlisted to secure minority support for the Pittman measure. On 30 October, White, the editor of the *Emporia* (Kansas) *Gazette*, cautioned several Republican spokesmen against making neutrality revision a partisan issue. White asserted, "I would hate to have my party put itself in a position where it can be charged that we played Mr. Hitler's game in the matter of the embargo." Once again, Minority Leader Martin agreed not to discipline party members, freeing them to follow personal convictions. Knox, publisher of the *Chicago Daily News*, sent every Republican congressman a copy of his editorials defending munitions sales to belligerents.[63]

Majority Leader Rayburn of Texas, who returned to Washington in the latter part of October, began rounding up votes for the Pittman legislation. From a poor family, the fifty-seven-year-old Rayburn had been born in Roane County, Tennessee, and at age five had moved with his parents to a farm near Windom, Texas. After attending rural schools, he had studied at East Texas Normal College and at the University of Texas Law School and had opened an office in Bonham. Following a six-year stint in the state legislature, Rayburn in 1912 had been elected to the U.S. House of Representatives. Friendly with both President Roosevelt and Vice-president Garner, he had consistently supported New Deal programs. Rayburn had chaired the Interstate Commerce Committee, where he had helped frame the Wheeler-Rayburn public utilities bill and the Securities and Exchange Act. As majority leader, the Texas Democrat seldom delivered speeches on pending legislation and yet maneuvered shrewdly and diligently behind-the-scenes. Usually standing at the back of the chamber, Rayburn carefully observed floor developments and often gave advice, encouragement, or orders to party members on major legislation. Roosevelt frequently invited the majority leader to the White House to exchange information and map strategy. In addition, the president phoned and corresponded numerous times with the Texas Democrat to review major legislative problems and to provide encouragement. Washington correspondents considered Rayburn the most influential representative on the basis of his leadership role and his expertise on interstate commerce, the stock exchange, and public utilities. Besides being humorous, the bachelor, a heavy smoker, was considered shrewd, diligent, wise, dynamic, vigorous, and flexible.

Rayburn wholeheartedly endorsed internationalist foreign policy and defense programs. Besides advocating reciprocal trade and naval preparedness measures, the Texas Democrat also considered the neutrality legislation of the mid-1930s to be too strict. The majority leader believed Nazi expansion threatened the security of both Western Europe and the Western Hemisphere and thus insisted the United States should provide aid short of war to the Allies. A dedicated Democrat, he did not object to designating Roosevelt additional authority to determine aggressors.

63. Walter Johnson, *William Allen White's America*, pp. 517–20; William Allen White to Joseph W. Martin, Jr., 23 October 1939, Box 225, White Papers; Frank Knox to Franklin D. Roosevelt, 30 October 1939, PPF 4083, Roosevelt Papers.

Rayburn had participated in the May 1939 White House conference plotting strategy for neutrality revision and had urged adoption of the Bloom bill. In June 1939, he had made a determined yet abortive effort to defeat the Vorys amendment restoring the arms embargo. At the special session, the majority leader continued to battle for neutrality revision and encountered greater success this time.[64]

Rayburn, along with Majority Whip Patrick J. Boland of Pennsylvania, secured a majority in favor of neutrality revision. Internationalists, who attracted between forty-five and seventy-one new members, particularly gained converts from Roosevelt's party (see tables 13, 16). In late August, Democrat John W. Boehne of Indiana wrote the president, "You were right and I was wrong." "I will support administration program," Boehne pledged, "because I am convinced of the correctness of your position as regards our foreign policy."[65] Fourteen Republicans also joined the prorepeal forces at the special session, but relatively fewer shifted allegiances than in the Senate.

Geographically, internationalist representatives strengthened their position in every section. Southern Democrats proportionately still directed the internationalists and cooperated closely with the Border congressmen in supporting the Pittman bill. For the first time, a majority of the Pacific, Mountain, and Middle Atlantic delegations aligned with the internationalists (see table 16). Since the outbreak of World War II, over 20 percent of the Pacific members and 15 percent of the Mountain and Middle Atlantic blocs had shifted to the administration side.

Worsening European developments, changing public opinion, and more dynamic Democratic leadership had helped produce the shifts among the Pacific, Mountain, and Middle Atlantic delegations. The eruption of World War II convinced several moderates to advocate both repeal of the arms embargo and increased assistance to Great Britain and France. According to Gallup polls, inhabitants of those sections were more internationalist than they had been in the spring. After the outbreak of World War II, a clear majority of Middle Atlantic, Mountain, and Pacific citizens favored lifting the arms embargo against belligerent nations. Effective administration organization, along with Martin's decision not to make neutrality revision a partisan issue, brightened the prospects for the internationalists. Exhibiting more forthright direction, Rayburn and Boland persuaded several Democrats from these sections to vote for the Pittman bill. Roosevelt's party held a majority of seats in these three delegations, facilitating somewhat the task facing Rayburn and Boland. Due to the shifting momentum toward the internationalists, Democrat Lyle H. Boren of Oklahoma contended that the representatives would "not take as long to pass it."[66]

Isolationist representatives formed a more homogeneous group politically and

64. "Sam Rayburn," *Current Biography* 1 (1940):673–74; C. Dwight Dorough, *Mr. Sam*; "Washington Correspondents Name Ablest Members of Congress in *Life* Poll," *Life* 6 (20 March 1939):13–17; Alfred Steinberg, *Sam Rayburn: A Biography*.

65. John W. Boehne, Jr., to Franklin D. Roosevelt, 30 August 1939, PPF 6203, Roosevelt Papers.

66. Divine, *Illusion*, pp. 307–8; *Public Opinion Quarterly* 4 (March 1940):105–8; Lyle H. Boren to Lloyd Umberger, 21 October 1939, Box 66, Lyle H. Boren Papers.

sectionally than at the regular session. Although still commanding the loyalty of 88 percent of the Republicans, isolationists included only 12 to 14 percent of the Democrats and had experienced substantial numerical losses in all sections except the Great Plains and the Great Lakes. Great Plains congressmen proportionately directed the opposition to the Pittman measure but received majority backing only from the New England and Great Lakes members.

Internationalists and isolationists both stressed ideological themes. According to internationalists, munitions sales afforded the best means to keep the United States out of foreign conflicts. Republican Wadsworth of New York claimed, "No one has ever been able to explain just how and why repeal of the arms embargo would get us into war," while Democrat Lindsay C. Warren of North Carolina believed, "The changes proposed in our present Neutrality Act would do more to keep us from being involved in the conflict than our present law."[67] Internationalists, though, still preferred providing limited aid through cash-and-carry and were reluctant to commit the United States either to defense alliances or to direct intervention on behalf of particular nations in specific conflicts. On the other hand, isolationists warned that selling armaments would exacerbate tensions abroad. Republican John Taber of New York criticized the Pittman measure as "a menace to the peace of America." If Congress repealed the arms embargo, Democrat Frank Fries of Illinois feared, "The tides of hate will run stronger and the war may soon include all countries of the globe."[68]

The two sides disagreed sharply over the legality of the existing Neutrality Act. Besides insisting that the arms embargo violated American neutral rights, internationalists favored a return to traditional foreign policy based on international law. "Initially established rights," Democrat Thomas V. Smith of Illinois argued, "are a very good touchstone against the very temptation which all of us feel toward treating persistent problems with ad hoc remedies." On the other hand, isolationists asserted that the Pittman bill contradicted global statutes. Noting that "under international law belligerents have no 'right' to buy arms," Republican Vorys of Ohio cautioned about "the dangers of changing the rules after the game started." "To change the balance of power while the war is in progress," Republican Karl M. LeCompte of Iowa warned, "seems to me to be committing an act that is neither neutral nor non-combatant" and would signify "the first step toward involving our country in trouble with Germany."[69]

In contrast to the senators, internationalist and isolationist representatives highlighted the political ramifications at stake. Several internationalist Democrats supported neutrality revision as a means of enhancing the president's maneuverability in foreign affairs. Warren of North Carolina wrote President Roosevelt, "Your

67. Wadsworth to O'Connell, 11 October 1939; Lindsay C. Warren to Mrs. Vernon Ward, 2 November 1939, Box 22–A, Lindsay C. Warren Papers.
68. John Taber to Rev. Guy Morrill, 25 November 1939, Box 63, John Taber Papers; Frank Fries to Franklin D. Roosevelt, 28 October 1939, Box 7, Thomas V. Smith Papers.
69. Thomas V. Smith to Mrs. M. Whitcomb Hess, 18 September 1939, Box 5, Smith Papers; Vorys to Stout, 13 October 1939; Karl M. LeCompte to Mrs. Louis V. Phelps, 7 November 1939, Box 13, Folder 53, Karl M. LeCompte Papers.

Presidential leadership would be much more effective if the present unneutral act was repealed.'' Democrat Joe Hendricks of Florida remarked, ''I am not one of those who, just because the President is ending his second term, feel that whatever he may suggest is crazy and that he is trying to get us into war.''[70] Alarmed at the rapid expansion of presidential power, isolationists alleged that the Pittman legislation gave excessive authority to the executive branch. ''I am sure,'' Republican Hope of Kansas asserted, ''there is a mighty strong sentiment in Congress, among both parties, against giving the President any more power of any kind.''[71]

Geographical and economic issues also were highlighted by the isolationists. Denying that German expansion threatened American security, isolationists urged the United States to concentrate on solving domestic problems. ''Even if Hitler should win,'' Hope of Kansas admitted, ''I wouldn't consider his victory a menace to this hemisphere any time in our lifetime, because it will take any nation that wins this war a long time to get over it.'' If Congress focused on settling economic and social questions, Fries of Illinois advised, ''we would be doing far more good for civilization and humanity than we could accomplish by any battle ever won on any battlefield.''[72] Democrat Voorhis of California likewise feared a ''dislocation which may take place in our American economy as a result of the repeal,'' while Republican Stefan of Nebraska stressed, ''The United States of America should seek to preserve its democracy, and cannot afford another war.'' Eastern financial interests, isolationists charged, hoped to reap substantial profits from repeal of the arms embargo. Republican Ben F. Jensen of Iowa contended, ''There are so many high government officials, as well as Eastern capitalists, who have all their interests tied up in steel factories, munitions plants and foreign securities that they are greedy enough to want our American money and men to protect them against possible financial ruin.''[73]

Internationalists outmaneuvered the isolationists this time on the House floor. Most isolationists advocated sending the Pittman bill to the House Foreign Affairs Committee, where they hoped to restore the arms embargo amendment. On 31 October, however, the internationalist-minded House approved a Rules Committee recommendation to consider the Pittman bill as an amendment to the original Bloom resolution. Thus, the legislation would bypass the House Foreign Affairs Committee and be sent instead to a conference committee. Since numerous Republicans wished to speak, isolationists sought to have unlimited floor debate on neutrality. In order to avoid prolonged debate and restrictive amendments, however, the internationalist representatives accepted a Rules Committee suggestion limiting floor discussion to

70. Lindsay C. Warren to Franklin D. Roosevelt, 4 September 1939, PPF 2412, Roosevelt Papers; Joseph Hendricks to Lewis Tribble, 12 October 1939, Box 10, Joseph Hendricks Papers.
71. Clifford R. Hope to Arthur Martin, 7 October 1939, Legislative Correspondence, Box 179, Hope Papers.
72. Clifford R. Hope to Jay Scovel, 3 October 1939, Legislative Correspondence, Box 180, Hope Papers; Frank Fries to Constituents, 28 October 1939, Box 7, Smith Papers.
73. Jerry Voorhis to Franklin D. Roosevelt, 3 November 1939, PPF 5595, Roosevelt Papers; Karl Stefan to Andrew Soulek, 23 September 1939, Box 24, Stefan Papers; Ben F. Jensen to Willard Archie, 7 October 1939, Personal Correspondence, Box 18, Folder 97, Ben F. Jensen Papers.

ten hours. Republican isolationists denounced this action, which they claimed "prevented any intelligent analysis of the Senate bill."[74] These two actions indicated that the internationalists controlled decisionmaking in the House for the first time and probably could secure favorable action on arms embargo repeal.

During the next three days, representatives engaged in a more emotional and candid debate than had the senators. Under the direction of Democrats Luther A. Johnson of Texas and James P. Richards of South Carolina, most internationalists argued that neutrality revision afforded the best means of keeping the United States out of the European war. Internationalists insisted the Pittman bill would preserve domestic security because cash-and-carry would eliminate the possibility of attacks on American ships and citizens. Some bolder internationalists, however, admitted the legislation was intended to provide direct military assistance to the European democracies against the atheistic dictators. Isolationists, led by Democrat James A. Shanley of Connecticut and Republican Hamilton Fish of New York, charged that removal of the ban on munitions sales would violate international law and would embroil the United States in World War II. Besides disapproving of sending destructive military weapons to belligerent nations, they denied that the Axis dictatorships threatened American security. The Atlantic Ocean, isolationists asserted, adequately protected the Western Hemisphere from any German attack.[75]

Wadsworth of New York, an internationalist, delivered the most effective speech of the brief debate. On the final day, Wadsworth urged his Republican colleagues to place the national interest above political party allegiance by supporting the Pittman bill. Invoking the spirit of former President Theodore Roosevelt, he insisted the United States should repeal the arms embargo and "carry a big stick" in world affairs. Following the speech, "large numbers of Democrats rose and cheered him and finally the Republicans rose and joined in the applause." Republican Donald H. McLean of New Jersey wrote Wadsworth, "You emerged as the big man of the Neutrality fight! I am sure you must have felt the reaction and it should give you a great deal of satisfaction."[76]

Isolationists hoped to weaken the measure with restrictive amendments. As in June, Vorys proposed prohibiting the sale of arms and munitions to belligerents and sanctioning the shipment of aircraft and other implements of war. On 2 November the internationalist-minded House easily rejected 245 to 179 the Vorys motion (see table 17). The outbreak of World War II, coupled with more effective Democratic party leadership, had caused forty-five members to reject essentially the same amendment they had supported in June.

Both parties displayed more solidarity on the Vorys amendment than on any

74. Albert C. F. Westphal, *The House Committee on Foreign Affairs*, pp. 228–29; *CR*, 31 October 1939, p. 1103; John Vorys to Henry Luce, 3 November 1939, Box 3, Vorys Papers.

⁻ 75. *CR*, 31 October–2 November 1939. For a concise summary of the debate, see Divine, *Illusion*, pp. 327–29.

76. *New York Times*, 3 November 1939; J. Hardin Peterson Washington Newsletter, 9 November 1939, Box 20, J. Hardin Peterson Papers; Donald H. McLean to James W. Wadsworth, Jr., 6 November 1939, Box 27, Wadsworth Papers.

other neutrality roll call. Securing more party harmony than at the regular session, 87 percent of the Democrats opposed restoration of the arms embargo and thus insured rejection of the isolationist Vorys proposal. Party heads, most notably Rayburn of Texas, played a more active role in promoting political unity this time. The Rayburn forces, Vorys later conceded, had "settled the wet and dry issue in the House before the Senate bill had reached us" and had the votes "in the bag." Vorys had favored an earlier tally because the isolationists were "losing votes each hour through individual high pressure" by Democratic leaders. Republican Jensen of Iowa charged, "This whole question centers around partisan politics" and contended, "The administration, of course, is doing their work behind closed doors."[77] In addition, conservative Democrats believed political differences with Roosevelt over New Deal policies and the growth of presidential power should terminate at the water's edge. Since World War II already had begun, they increasingly realized the extent to which Nazi Germany jeopardized international peace and American security.

The vastly outnumbered Republicans, still hostile to the president, overwhelmingly supported the isolationist Vorys amendment (see table 17). They insisted that Roosevelt already had usurped too much authority on the home front and feared the president might use neutrality revision to enhance his personal control over American foreign policy. Like the Republican senators, the Republican representatives suspected the chief executive might attempt to shatter the two-term tradition and seek another term in office. Several Republicans, who leaned toward selling munitions to belligerents, consented to the isolationist Vorys motion because of anti-Roosevelt sentiments. "I argued and argued," Wadsworth of New York remarked, "with a lot of them personally. When backed into a corner many would agree that the embargo was unwise but unvariably they burst out into expressions of utter distrust of the man in the White House." He added, "A large number of the votes against repeal came from men activated by that utter distrust." Besides denouncing the outcome as "a great pity," Wadsworth warned, "It may embarrass the party later on."[78]

In some instances, however, other considerations prevailed. Thirty-four members of Roosevelt's party aligned with the isolationists supporting the Vorys amendment. Several Democrats represented interior regions more remote geographically from the European conflict and did not believe German expansion overseas harmed American security. In a letter to Roosevelt, Democrat Fries of Illinois wrote, "I consider you the greatest President and the greatest leader the United States has ever been privileged to have. However, the neutrality issue is a matter of deepest principle with me." "I have spent sleepless nights and anxious days," he added, "and I cannot come to any other conclusion." Other Democrats continued to endorse isolationism because they came from German or Irish districts or thought the president already held too much power over national

77. *CR*, 2 November 1939, pp. 1343–44; Vorys to Luce, 3 November 1939; Jensen to Archie, 7 October 1939.

78. James W. Wadsworth, Jr., to Harper Sibley, 9 November 1939, James W. Wadsworth, Jr., to Richard Scandrett, Jr., 7 November 1939, Box 27, Wadsworth Papers.

government. On the other hand, twenty-one Republicans bolted their party on the Vorys amendment because they favored American military assistance to Great Britain and France. These internationalists came principally from New England and Middle Atlantic states, situated closer than most other sections to the European conflict, and believed that German expansion overseas jeopardized the safety of the Western Hemisphere. "It was not easy for me to desert the majority of my party," Republican W. Sterling Cole of New York remarked, "but I felt that I could not conscientiously agree with their attitude."[79]

Most sections divided sharply on the Vorys amendment. Southern Democrats proportionately led internationalist resistance to restoring the embargo and coalesced with the Border and Mountain representatives to reject the Vorys motion. Although solidly Democratic, the Southern and Border state delegations often had disagreed with Roosevelt on New Deal issues. On this foreign policy issue, however, they remained loyal to the president. These sections had thrived on commerce with Great Britain and included predominantly Anglo-Saxon residents favoring neutrality revision. Besides having an internationalist tradition, the Southern and Border states were considered more vulnerable geographically to foreign invasion. Since Hitler already had begun attacking non-German-speaking nations, these representatives urged immediate American assistance to Great Britain. The Mountain representatives, contrary to traditional interpretations, also aligned with the internationalists in rejecting the Vorys proposal. Mainly Democrats, they rallied behind the president's neutrality policy. Although serving an inland region, they protested Hitler's authoritarian tactics and contended that the United States should help Western European nations halt Nazi expansion (see table 17).

Great Plains and Great Lakes representatives proportionately directed the isolationist campaign to continue the ban on munitions sales and were joined by New England and Middle Atlantic colleagues. A largely Republican group, the Great Plains and Great Lakes congressmen insisted Roosevelt already had too much personal power and might use neutrality revision to aggrandize his authority. In regard to geography, they stressed that the Atlantic Ocean safeguarded the United States from any European invasion. Economically, these isolationists realized that Great Lakes and Great Plains grain markets bartered comparatively little with Great Britain and also suspected that eastern financial interests hoped to profit from American intervention abroad. Some Great Plains and Great Lakes representatives held progressive viewpoints and feared that neutrality revision would hinder Roosevelt's efforts to resolve domestic economic and social problems, while numerous German constituents residing in the Great Lakes and Great Plains regions opposed any intervention against their homeland. Historians usually describe the Northeast as internationalist, but the New England and rural Middle Atlantic representatives supported the isolationist Vorys proposal. These delegations comprised mainly Republicans opposed to designating the president with any additional

79. Fries to Roosevelt, 28 October 1939; W. Sterling Cole to Dr. Royden Vose, 13 November 1939, Box 21, W. Sterling Cole Papers.

domestic or foreign policy powers. In addition, the New England and Middle Atlantic members served a sizeable number of Irish constituents favoring nonentanglement in the European war. With the exception of the largely one-party Southern and Border sections, no delegation demonstrated even 75 percent cooperation for either position (see table 17).

Ethnic forces played a less dynamic role than in June. At the special session, nearly 10 percent of the Irish members and around 20 percent of the German congressmen joined the internationalists for the first time. Continuing to defy traditional stereotypes, over seven of every ten Irish Representatives subordinated anti-British sentiments and opposed restoring the arms embargo. Irish legislators typically remained loyal to the Democratic party, submitting to appeals by Rayburn and other leaders to support the president's foreign policy. In addition, they warned that Hitler endangered both republican institutions and the religious freedom of Roman Catholics. Subordinating the traditional Irish hostility toward Great Britain, they contended that Nazi Germany posed a more immediate danger to international safety. Around 40 percent of the German congressmen also joined the internationalists in disapproving of the Vorys motion. The Nazi invasion of Poland, coupled with the outbreak of World War II, persuaded them that Germany might seek to conquer additional territory. In order to prevent Hitler and his totalitarian methods from overtaking other non-German-speaking countries, they favored sending American military assistance to Great Britain. On the isolationist side, approximately 60 percent of the German members and 70 percent of the Scandinavian congressmen favored continuing the ban on selling armaments. Besides having pride in their national heritage, they had disliked American treatment of the Germans during World War I. In addition, several German-American organizations encouraged them to oppose American entry into the European war against their homeland. German representatives were less internationalist than their Senate counterparts, while the opposite situation prevailed among the Irish. Once again the Scandinavian legislators supported neutrality in adherence to the nonalignment practices of their native governments and pacifist clergy (see table 31).

Isolationists furnished further resistance. Democrat Shanley of Connecticut, who had aligned with the internationalists earlier, preferred a more rigid proposal insuring strict neutrality. Broadening the scope of the Vorys amendment, he suggested forbidding the export of airplanes and all other possible implements of war. In a highly partisan vote, the House on 2 November rejected the Shanley motion by a 243 to 181 margin. Politically, 86 percent of the Democrats refused to revive the arms embargo and used their enormous numerical advantage to defeat the isolationist Shanley plan. Although 87 percent of the Republicans supported the amendment, only 14 percent of the Democrats coalesced with the minority party this time. Sectionally, Southern and Border Democrats effectively resisted an attempt by the Great Plains, Great Lakes, and New England delegations to insert the motion (see table 17). Irishmen continued sympathizing with the internationalists, while isolationist German representatives still disapproved of neutrality revision.[80]

The Vorys and Shanley amendments both indicate that House alignments on neutrality differed substantially from the Senate coalitions. At the special session, congressmen acted less internationalist on roll calls. Despite vocal resistance by isolationists, senators favored repeal of the arms embargo by a wider margin. Internationalist representatives attracted less following among Republicans and among all regions except the Southern and Pacific ones. Southern and Border members proportionately led the campaign to permit trade of military supplies but received strongest support from Pacific and Mountain representatives rather than New England and Middle Atlantic congressmen. As in the Senate, several unusual patterns occurred on this issue. Border and Mountain congressmen from inland regions coalesced with the internationalists, while New England and some Middle Atlantic representatives from coastal areas located nearer to the European conflict sided with the isolationists.

Motivations of representatives and senators also sharply contrasted. Political partisanship influenced voting behavior to a much greater extent in the House, where 87 percent of party members cooperated on neutrality. Democrats overwhelmingly followed internationalism, while Republicans solidly opposed the sale of armaments abroad. In the Senate, only 73 percent of all members clung to their party position. Partisanship was more effective in the House mainly because party leaders exhibited more dynamic control there. Representative Martin of Massachusetts, although he did not make neutrality a political issue, was more vocal than Senator McNary and consistently commanded more loyalty among Republican ranks. On the Democratic side, Congressman Rayburn kept tighter rein over party conservatives than did Senator Barkley. Anti-New Deal Democrats still resented Roosevelt's support in 1937 of Barkley over the popular, more experienced, and more influential Harrison for majority leader. Representatives also faced reelection every two years as compared to every six years for senators, so they probably were subjected more to party and other district political pressures. Ethnic considerations also had more impact in the lower chamber because numerous Irish congressmen supported trading military supplies to Great Britain and France.

On the other hand, regional and ideological factors affected the outcome less in the politically minded House. Over one-half of the Senate delegations consistently achieved at least 75 percent solidarity because Republicans were more inclined to cooperate with Democrats there. The one-party Southern and Border blocs were the only blocs in which representatives registered comparable unity. Ideological factors also loomed larger in the Senate, where antiwar elements delayed legislative action for weeks. Several Republicans who feared that Nazi expansion endangered democracy in Western Europe aligned with the internationalists.

Following the outbreak of World War II, internationalists had controlled decisionmaking in the House. At the regular session, isolationist representatives had restored the arms embargo and had nearly recommitted the entire Bloom bill.

80. *CR*, 2 November 1939, pp. 1344–45; *New York Times*, 3 November 1939.

Internationalists this time not only had blocked isolationist attempts to have the House Foreign Affairs Committee consider the legislation, but also had thwarted the Vorys and Shanley amendments to attach to the Bloom bill the arms embargo. Most internationalists, however, still were reluctant to commit the United States to direct military intervention in the European conflict and preferred instead to provide limited assistance through cash-and-carry.

A conference committee, consisting of six senators and five representatives, met on 3 November to decide the final form of the legislation. Since representatives had not attached any amendments, House conferees quickly accepted the Senate version. Four isolationist Republicans, including Senators Borah and Hiram Johnson and representatives Fish and Charles A. Eaton of New Jersey, refused to sign the final report.[81] Following the meeting, Johnson noted, "The conference had everything their own way, and I amused myself making an occasional sarcastic remark." Later the same day, the Senate approved the internationalist conference report 55 to 24 and the House followed suit by a 243 to 172 margin.[82]

Roosevelt welcomed the news from Capitol Hill. To reporters, he commented, "I am very glad that the bill has restored the historic position of the neutrality of the United States." Twelve congressional leaders, including four Republicans, were invited at noon the next day to the White House to see the president sign the measure. "This is the most important action," Roosevelt boasted, "that has taken place in our foreign policy during my administration." Before numerous photographers, he attached his signature to the legislation and promptly handed ceremonial pens to Pittman and Bloom. The president, Senator Connally observed, had seldom looked happier and gave no indication on this occasion of his strained relationship with Capitol Hill.[83]

The moods in the internationalist and isolationist camps contrasted sharply with those during the regular session. The internationalists greeted the congressional action revising the neutrality legislation, while the isolationists were disheartened over the outcome. Speaker Bankhead, an internationalist, described the measure as "a historic landmark in the annals of the modern history of our Republic." "One of the happiest moments of my life," internationalist Democrat Emanuel Celler of New York wrote Roosevelt, "was voting to sustain you on the Embargo Act. It is a great and well deserved victory for you."[84] On the isolationist side, Representative Vorys admitted, "I am sore from the game and sick of losing." "It was a big victory for the President," isolationist Sen. Hiram Johnson conceded, "and there is no question about that."[85]

81. Gilbert Y. Steiner, *The Congressional Conference Committee: Seventieth to Eightieth Congresses*, p. 75; U.S., Congress, House of Representatives, Committee on Conference, "Neutrality Act of 1939," *Reports*, no. 1475.

82. Hiram W. Johnson to Hiram W. Johnson, Jr., 5 November 1939, Part VI, Box 7, Johnson Papers; *CR*, 3 November 1939, pp. 1356, 1387–88.

83. Rosenman, ed., *Public Papers*, 8:559; *New York Times*, 5 November 1939.

84. William B. Bankhead to Sol Bloom, 22 November 1939, Box 45, Sol Bloom Papers; Emanuel Celler to Franklin D. Roosevelt, 2 November 1939, PPF 2748, Roosevelt Papers.

85. Vorys to Luce, 3 November 1939; Johnson to Johnson, 5 November 1939.

By passing the Neutrality Act of 1939, the legislative branch indicated that it no longer wanted the United States to remain impartial in World War II. Great Britain and France legally could buy arms, ammunition, implements of war, and other materials, provided they paid cash on delivery and transported their goods. Boosting the Allied morale, the legislation symbolized increased willingness to support the European democracies against Hitler. France immediately ordered numerous military supplies, while Great Britain by mid-1940 followed suit. In addition, the act empowered Roosevelt to designate combat zones where ships or citizens could not enter. On 4 November, he proclaimed that American vessels could not travel in the North Atlantic areas comprising the Bay of Biscay, waters surrounding England and Ireland, the English Channel, and the North and Baltic seas. No American ship could travel to any port in the area from the Baltic to Spain. All coastal cities in the Pacific, Indian, and South Atlantic oceans were open to American vessels and cargo.[86]

Although taking internationalist steps, Congress did not commit the United States to direct intervention in World War II. The legislative branch permitted the United States to provide limited, indirect aid to the Allies and did not involve the nation in specific defense alliances. Under cash-and-carry, belligerents would have to pay money for all merchandise and transport supplies in their own ships. In addition, vessels from the United States could not enter combat zones in the North Atlantic. As in the 1937 act, Americans could not travel on belligerent vessels or extend credit to warring governments. Isolationists, including Vandenberg of Michigan, praised these precautionary steps to prevent direct involvement abroad. These restrictions, Vandenberg claimed, made it "much more difficult for F.D.R. to lead the country into war." On the other hand, internationalists argued that Congress had put too many limits on American commerce and presidential authority. "In some ways it is a bad bill," Senator Thomas of Utah conceded, "but it is the best we could do."[87]

At the special session, several congressmen had played major roles in securing neutrality revision. Senators Pittman, Connally, and Byrnes, along with representatives Rayburn, Johnson, and Bloom, had helped guide the legislation through Congress. Pittman and Bloom, who had sponsored measures and chaired pertinent committees, especially received recognition for their performances. Secretary Hull wrote Pittman, "No one could have striven more constantly or more effectively than you have. I thank and congratulate you for the magnificent results in which your leadership played so large a part." Speaker Bankhead commended Bloom for "the very able and effective methods" he used to bring the "highly controversial issue to such a complete victory in the House of Representatives" and remarked, "In large measure this notable legislation bears the sign and seal of your patriotic handiwork."[88]

86. For a summary of the provisions of the Neutrality Act, see Divine, *Illusion*, p. 331.
87. Vandenberg Diary, 27 October 1939; Elbert D. Thomas to Dr. William Snow, 6 November 1939, Box 28, Elbert D. Thomas Papers.
88. Cordell Hull to Key Pittman, 3 November 1939, Box 44, Pittman Papers; Bankhead to Bloom, 22 November 1939.

Political, sectional, and ethnic forces also aided the internationalists. Democrats, especially in the House, responded to appeals by party leaders to support the president on neutrality revision. At this special session, conservative Southern and Border members subordinated their anti-Roosevelt sentiments. Roosevelt had acted more affably toward Byrnes, Connally, and Harrison after the outbreak of World War II and had given the first two senators leadership roles at the special session. During September and October, the administration also had acted more conciliatory toward Glass, Byrd, and Bailey and consequently had received much more cooperation than usual from these staunch anti-New Dealers. "It may be," Bailey quipped, "that he will realize that he cannot keep up with the left but can rely on the right."[89]

Arms embargo repeal was facilitated by several external groups. The executive branch, notably Roosevelt and Hull, solidified Democratic support for changing neutrality policy. Before the outbreak of World War II, the president had proceeded cautiously to avoid alienating either public opinion or an already rebellious Congress. The impact of the German attack on Poland upon the national mood, however, influenced Roosevelt to intercede in the legislative struggle. Although the measure contained strict cash-and-carry features, Roosevelt desired lifting the ban on trading military supplies. In addition, the White committee urged Congress to permit the sale of military supplies to the Allies. This pressure group, Senator Pepper of Florida remarked, intervened "when the opposition was literally pushing us around" and quickly put the isolationists "weakly on the defense."[90] The American people increasingly became alarmed over ominous developments abroad and could no longer be impartial toward the European conflict. Adjusting to changing realities overseas, a majority of citizens wanted Congress to alter the neutrality laws. The mass media, particularly the press, helped rally public opinion behind internationalism. "There were practically no newspapers in all the land with us," commented Johnson of California, "save the Chicago Tribune and the Hearst papers."[91] Of course, the beginning of the European war had prompted removal of the arms embargo. If Germany had not invaded Poland in September, the Neutrality Act of 1937 would have remained on the statute books.

Congress still wielded considerable control over foreign policy decisionmaking. Roosevelt, who still preferred complete repeal of neutrality legislation and a return to traditional principles of international law, once again had let congressional leaders handle the specific details. The legislative branch still acted quite independently of the president, retaining several restrictions from the isolationist Neutrality Act of 1937. Besides prohibiting American vessels from entering combat zones, Congress still denied Americans from traveling on belligerent vessels or extending credit to warring nations. By inserting the cash-and-carry system, the Senate and House permitted only limited, indirect American assistance to the Allies. On the

89. Patterson, "Eating Humble Pie," pp. 411–12; Josiah W. Bailey to David Lawrence, 31 October 1939, Political File, Bailey Papers.
90. Claude D. Pepper to William Allen White, 3 November 1939, Box 226, White Papers.
91. Johnson to Johnson, 5 November 1939.

other hand, Roosevelt had begun to recover some prestige lost in legislative skirmishes on domestic issues with Capitol Hill. Two specific provisions desired by the president—repeal of the arms embargo and wider discretionary authority for the chief executive—were included in the congressional measure.

At the special session, senators and representatives alike had taken major steps toward abandoning strict neutrality and had sanctioned limited American assistance to the Allies. Despite the vocal isolationist resistance, internationalists had attracted a much wider numerical backing than at the regular session. The pace of European developments and the response of the legislative branch would determine if these patterns would continue.

5

The Origins of Interventionism

During early 1940, Congress entered a third phase characterized by relative calm on the Western European scene. Germany did not launch further attacks for several months and concentrated instead on preparing for another military offensive. In this period, the British, French, and Americans were lulled into believing Hitler would not continue the war. The legislative branch, meanwhile, proceeded cautiously in international affairs and shifted attention from Germany to the Russo-Finnish conflict.[1]

On the Finnish issue, congressional focus changed from a debate between internationalism and isolationism to one involving interventionism against noninterventionism. At the special session in 1939, the internationalists and isolationists had clashed over neutrality legislation and the general American foreign policy toward the European war. Internationalists had supported removing the arms embargo and restoring cash-and-carry to assist the Western European democracies, while isolationists had favored maintaining mandatory neutrality laws. The nature of the debate changed in late November 1939, when the Soviet Union invaded Finland and attacked the capital city of Helsinki. Congress considered whether the federal government should intervene in a specific conflict to aid a particular democratic country against an aggressor nation. Interventionists argued that the United States should help halt the Russian expansion by providing direct military or economic assistance to the Scandinavian country. On the other hand, noninterventionists opposed federal aid to Finland and did not want to risk either involving the United States in the European war or driving the Soviet Union further into the German camp.

The United States for over two decades had sympathized with Finland. Americans had welcomed Finnish independence from the Russians in 1917 and had sent a small relief mission there two years later following the formation of a republic. In addition, the achievements of Olympic trackster Paavo Nurmi and musical composer Jean Sibelius enhanced American awareness of the Scandinavian nation. Americans generally had accepted the small number of Finns who had migrated to the United States to escape economic hardships and had settled in Michigan. The Scandinavian nation also had repaid its World War I debts regularly, while Great Britain, France, and other larger Western European democracies had defaulted. Americans largely

---

1. For background on the war, see Max Jakobsen, *The Diplomacy of the Winter War: An Account of the Russo-Finnish War*; Robert Sobel, *The Origins of Interventionism: The United States and the Russo-Finnish War*; Andrew J. Schwartz, *America and the Russo-Finnish War*; and Peggy M. Mulvihill, "The United States and the Russo-Finnish War" (Ph.D. diss.).

overlooked that Finland had owed only $9 million—a much smaller amount than most other countries.

On the other hand, Americans held hostile attitudes toward the Soviet Union. Americans viewed the Communist regime, which had seized power in the second Russian Revolution of 1917, as a dictatorship threatening capitalism, religion, democracy, and other highly cherished systems and values. Although the United States had recognized the Soviet Union in 1933, the American press still pictured the Bolsheviks in unfavorable terms. The Soviet Union had violated pledges not to interfere in American domestic affairs or to provide most-favored-nation treatment in commercial relations. Tensions had increased in August 1939 when the Soviets signed a nonagression pact with the Nazis and secretly negotiated protocols granting the Russians spheres of influence in eastern Poland, Latvia, Estonia, and Finland. During subsequent months, the Soviet occupation of eastern Poland and of bases in Latvia, Estonia, and Lithuania had further aroused American indignation.[2]

Soviet activity in Finland had caused an additional erosion in relations. After Germany attacked Poland, the Russians sought to use Finland as a buffer zone against possible Nazi expansion eastward. In order to gain strategic control of the Baltic Sea, Stalin in October demanded that the Finnish government cede territory in southern Finland. Stalin agreed to let the Scandinavian nation have in exchange a vast timberland in the northern part of the Soviet Union. The Russians and Finns negotiated for several weeks beginning 5 October, during which time the former made several concessions. Diplomatic discussions terminated, however, when the Finnish government refused to grant the Soviet Union territory for a western approach to Leningrad. On 26 November seven shots were fired in a Soviet village near the Finnish border. The Russians blamed the Finns for the incident and claimed four of their soldiers had been killed and nine others wounded. The Stalin regime quickly retaliated, recalling its political and economic representatives from Helsinki. In a radio address in November, Russian Foreign Minister Vyacheslav Molotov denounced the Scandinavian nation as a menace and declared the Finnish government "entirely responsible" for the worsening situation. Without an official declaration of war, the Soviet Union the following day invaded Finland by land, sea, and air.[3]

The American public responded angrily to the invasion. In a Gallup poll taken on 31 December, 88 percent of those interviewed sympathized with the Finns, only 1 percent sided with the Russians, and 11 percent were undecided. At the same time, Americans now viewed Russia as the second worst influence in Europe, next to Nazi Germany. Nearly all segments of the population across the United States backed the Finnish people. Americans overwhelmingly favored providing economic assistance for the Scandinavian country, but disagreed over whether the United States should

2. Sobel, *Interventionism*, pp. 67–72, 135–36; Robert Paul Browder, *The Origins of Soviet-American Diplomacy*, pp. 197–214; Robert A. Divine, *The Reluctant Belligerent: American Entry into World War II*, pp. 64, 76, 78.

3. Schwartz, *Russo-Finnish War*, pp. 5–16; John Henry Wuorinen, ed., *Finland and World War II, 1939–1944*, pp. 53–54, 59.

send arms, ammunition, and other implements of war. In order to avoid becoming further embroiled in the European war, they opposed sending military forces there.[4]

Numerous American citizens, along with the media, more actively supported the Scandinavians. Over three hundred Finnish-Americans fought in the conflict against the Russian army, while several hundred Americans sent to President Franklin D. Roosevelt letters and telegrams urging the administration to intervene more directly on behalf of the Finns. Newspapers likewise helped rally public opinion behind the Scandinavians by publishing stories exaggerating the accomplishments of the Mannerheim army and denouncing Soviet military tactics. By publishing distorted accounts, the press misled the American people into believing that the Finnish army was inflicting extremely heavy casualties and suffering minimal losses. Over twelve hundred newspapers assisted organized relief efforts by serving as collecting agents for private donations.

Many private organizations substantially aided relief efforts. Under the direction of former President Herbert C. Hoover, the Finnish Relief Fund held numerous rallies and parades and collected over $3.5 million to enable the Scandinavian country to purchase food, medicine, and other supplies. Hoover's organization, which consisted of volunteers, did not provide military assistance urgently required by the Finnish army. Gen. John F. O'Ryan, a World War I veteran, organized Fighting Funds for Finland and raised nearly $1 million to be used for purchasing war materials. In addition, the American Red Cross donated around $300,000 and sent two surgeons from the Public Health Service to advise on how to prevent the spread of epidemics. Specialized interest groups, including the National Ski Association and the National Lutheran Council, likewise conducted drives for donations.[5]

Both major political parties also sympathized with Finland. Roosevelt's Democratic party overwhelmingly favored American assistance to the Scandinavian nation, but disagreed over whether the aid should be military or merely economic. With the exception of two groups, Roosevelt held together the Democratic party coalition on this issue. Some rural Democrats, particularly from the South, believed the federal government should increase subsidies for farmers rather than help distant Finland, while very liberal party members disliked taking firm action against the Soviet Union. The Republican National Committee condemned the Russian invasion and supported private and limited federal assistance to the Finnish government. Besides stressing that prominent Republicans had opposed American recognition of the Soviet Union in 1933, they charged that the Roosevelt administration had contributed to the development of the Finnish problem by cooperating too much with the Stalin regime. National Republican leaders represented a wide variety of opinions on this issue, with Wendell L. Willkie favoring American intervention and Gov. Thomas E. Dewey taking a noncommittal position. Sen. Arthur H. Vandenberg of Michigan represented the midwestern isolationists favoring American intervention in the Finnish conflict, while colleague Robert A. Taft of Ohio endorsed noninter-

4. Hadley Cantril and Mildred Strunk, eds., *Public Opinion, 1935–1946*, p. 1159; *Fortune* 21 (March 1940):102.

5. Schwartz, *Russo-Finnish War*, pp. 25–26; Sobel, *Interventionism*, pp. 109–15.

ventionism.[6]

Finnish Ambassador Hjalmar Procopé, meanwhile, appealed for federal support. A youthful, friendly diplomat, he easily identified with the United States and its democratic institutions and values. Following the Soviet attack, Procopé reacted very courageously and vowed that his Scandinavian homeland would provide formidable resistance to the Russians. In early December, he requested the Roosevelt administration to provide $60 million in either a direct government loan or credits through the Reconstruction Finance Corporation. Procopé predicted an optimistic outcome to the war if Finland could purchase military supplies, transportation equipment, and other assistance from the United States. The Roosevelt administration, he also urged, should terminate diplomatic relations with the Soviet Union. On 8 December, Procopé pleaded with Secretary of State Cordell Hull for the United States government to furnish some type of help.[7]

The Roosevelt administration, however, moved very cautiously. The president on 1 December denounced the Soviet military and naval bombings as "a profound shock" and deemed it "tragic to see the policy of force spreading." Roosevelt at once asked both Russia and Finland to refrain from bombing civilian populations, but the Stalin regime refused to make such a pledge. At the same time, however, the president opposed furnishing direct American military assistance to Finland or breaking diplomatic relations with the Soviet Union. Such actions, he feared, might provoke the Russians to launch additional attacks and solidify further the nonaggression pact between Stalin and Hitler. In a telephone conversation with Republican Sen. Warren R. Austin of Vermont, Roosevelt on 30 November urged taking "no haste" in reassessing American ties with the Moscow regime. He also contended his administration "would be in a better position to help if we did not sever relations."[8] Congressional isolationists, he anticipated, might consider such assistance as the first step toward helping England and France and might attempt to block his recommendations on other important legislation. In a reply to journalist Herbert Bayard Swope, Roosevelt on 4 December wrote, "How I wish I could help you and Finland—brave souls both—but whether we like it or not Congress and God still live."[9] A pragmatic politician, he also believed that supporting direct American military assistance might affect adversely his and the Democratic party's prospects in the upcoming 1940 elections.

Roosevelt instead recommended very limited steps. The president rejected taking decisive actions against the Soviet Union, preferring merely to utter protests on Finland's behalf. Although consenting to terminate past practices aiding Russia,

6. Sobel, *Interventionism*, pp. 149–54, 159.

7. Arthur H. Vandenberg Diary, 30 November 1939, vol. 12, 1939–1940, Arthur H. Vandenberg Papers; Schwartz, *Russo-Finnish War*, p. 19; Hjalmar Procopé to Cordell Hull, 28 December 1939, Official Files (OF) 434, Franklin D. Roosevelt Papers.

8. Samuel I. Rosenman, ed., *The Public Papers and Addresses of Franklin D. Roosevelt*, 8:588–89; Warren R. Austin Memorandum, 1 December 1939, General Correspondence, Box 1939–1940, Warren R. Austin Papers.

9. Franklin D. Roosevelt to Herbert Bayard Swope, 4 December 1939, President's Personal Files, Swope, Roosevelt Papers.

he adamantly refused to impose new limitations on the Soviet Union. On 2 December, Roosevelt urged American manufacturers to stop selling airplanes and airplane parts to any nation that had bombed civilian populations. He targeted the action against the Stalin regime, even though the message also could have been applied to Japan. The president placed the moral embargo against the Soviet Union so that the latter could not purchase aluminum, nickel, tungsten, or machinery from the United States. Since the executive branch lacked effective enforcement mechanisms, however, American businesses virtually ignored the embargo. Roosevelt also did not invoke the recently revised Neutrality Act because neither the Soviet Union nor Finland officially had declared war. If the president had determined a belligerent state to exist, he would have been compelled to apply cash-and-carry to both nations. Since Finland did not have a large fleet, such action would have benefited the Russians. Declaring the Stalin regime a belligerent, Roosevelt and Hull feared, might solidify further the alliance between the Soviet Union and Germany. Hull believed the Western European nations eventually would need the Soviet Union to assist them in the fighting against the Germans. "I could not but feel," Hull subsequently wrote, "that the basic antagonisms between Communist Russia and Nazi Germany were so deep and Hitler's ambition so boundless, that eventually Russia would come over to the side of the Allies."[10]

The Roosevelt administration, after exploring alternative means of administering aid to Finland, devised a loan program. Since the Scandinavian nation had paid its financial obligations on schedule, the executive branch could bypass the usual Johnson Act restrictions. Secretary of Interior Harold L. Ickes recommended that the United States suspend Finland's debt payments, but the president insisted that a moratorium required prior congressional approval. On 11 December, Federal Loan Agency Administrator Jesse H. Jones announced that the Export-Import Bank would grant the Risto Ryti government $10 million for the purchase of agricultural products. Finland guaranteed this loan through its agency, the Finnish-American Trading Corporation. Roosevelt, however, declined to permit a loan for guns, planes, or ammunition without advance congressional approval.[11]

The restrictions placed on the Export-Import Bank loan, coupled with the small amount, disappointed the Finns. Procopé complained, "Ten million dollars does not help us very much" and insisted that his country needed "much more money" for airplanes, guns, and shells. On 14 December, Procopé requested permission to use the $10 million loan toward purchasing military supplies in the United States, but Secretary Hull vetoed this idea.[12] By mid-December, the Russian army was penetrating Finnish forces at all points along the 1,000-mile front. Prime Minister Ryti delivered a radio appeal urging all nations to send Finland military equipment and

10. Sobel, *Interventionism*, pp. 91–96; *New York Times*, 3 December 1939; Cordell Hull, *The Memoirs of Cordell Hull*, 1:706–7.

11. Harold L. Ickes, *The Secret Diary of Harold L. Ickes*, 3:80–81; Jesse H. Jones to Franklin D. Roosevelt, 9 December 1939, OF 643, Roosevelt Papers; *New York Herald-Tribune*, 11 December 1939; Hull, *Memoirs*, 1:707.

12. John Morton Blum, *From the Morgenthau Diaries*, 2:130.

transportation supplies to help it defend its democratic republic against the vast Soviet armed forces. In late December, Procopé requested the Roosevelt administration to furnish an unrestricted loan "to be used in accordance with the Country's requirements." Hull suggested that the president should recommend that Congress grant a loan for an amount equivalent to what Finland had paid on its debt after the time other nations had defaulted. The Finnish government simultaneously had ordered over $3 million in armaments, including 44 fighter planes and 60,000 gas masks, from American defense firms.[13]

Several congressional Democrats, meanwhile, launched a campaign to provide Finland with more substantial assistance. Sen. William H. King of Utah, along with Rep. Martin Dies of Texas, urged the United States to terminate its diplomatic relations with the Soviet Union. Rep. Frank E. Hook, who represented the Finnish district both numerically and geographically the largest in the United States, on 5 January introduced an interventionist bill for the Reconstruction Finance Corporation to loan $60 million to the Ryti government. Since no restrictions were imposed, the money could be used to purchase either American military or economic supplies. Inasmuch as Russia had not declared war on Finland officially, Hook stressed that the aid would not violate the existing neutrality legislation. At the same time, Democrat John D. Dingell of Michigan proposed selling the Scandinavian country 200 rounds of ammunition and 10,000 new semiautomatic rifles at one dollar each. "Aid to Finland," Dingell insisted, "is an obligation of civilization. You can't have a bunch of half-breed mongrels ravishing civilization."[14]

Three days later, Democrat Prentiss M. Brown of Michigan introduced the interventionist Hook measure in the Senate. A forty-eight-year-old native of St. Ignace, Michigan, he was the son of a prominent lawyer and prosecuting attorney of Cheboygan and Mackinac counties. He had graduated in 1911 from Albion College, where he had excelled in baseball. After studying at the University of Illinois, the short, stocky Brown had practiced law in St. Ignace. Brown had served twelve years as prosecuting attorney for Mackinac County and had belonged to the St. Ignace School Board. In 1932 he had become the first Democrat ever elected to the U.S. House of Representatives from his district. A member of the Banking and Currency Committee, he had helped draft legislation creating the Home Owners Loan Corporation, the Federal Deposit Insurance Corporation, and the Federal Housing Administration. Brown was appointed in 1936 to the U.S. Senate to fill the unexpired term of James Couzens. Noted for opposing Roosevelt's Supreme Court reorganization proposal, he sponsored legislation controlling inflation and subjecting government employees to the income tax. An industrious, courageous, and intelligent senator, he delivered clear, concise speeches and was popular with the press. The *Washington Post* had considered Brown, the father of seven children and an ardent baseball enthusiast, to be the most typical American in the Senate. An inter-

13. Schwartz, *Russo-Finnish War*, pp. 19–20, 25; *Business Week* 546 (17 February 1940):55; Hjalmar Procopé to Franklin D. Roosevelt, 29 December 1939, OF 434, Box 2, Roosevelt Papers.
14. Rosenman, ed., *Public Papers*, 8:594–95; *Detroit Free Press*, 6 January 1940; *Detroit News*, 6 January 1940.

nationalist, the Michigan Democrat had favored the resumption in 1933 of American diplomatic relations with the Soviet Union and had endorsed the reciprocal trade program. Following the German expansion into Eastern Europe, Brown argued that the strict neutrality legislation of the mid-1930s discriminated in favor of aggressor nations. At the special session in 1939, he backed the Pittman bill repealing the arms embargo and restoring the cash-and-carry system. The Michigan Democrat espoused the domino theory, maintaining that Nazi activity jeopardized both the security and the democratic institutions of the Western world.[15]

Ethnic considerations especially had influenced Brown to offer the interventionist legislation. He not only represented the state with the largest Finnish population in the nation, but also came from the heavily Scandinavian Upper Peninsula. Besides including numerous Scandinavian iron and copper workers, the Upper Peninsula resembled Finland geographically. Around fifty Scandinavians had sent Brown correspondence urging the Roosevelt administration to make unrestricted loans to the Ryti government. Professor Jennie Salmi of Suomi College, the only Finnish institution of higher learning in the United States, visited Brown's residence at St. Ignace in December. Since Finland desperately needed American military assistance, she asked the Michigan Democrat to draft a comprehensive measure for an unrestricted loan. Similar appeals later were made by Florence Harriman, ambassador to Norway, and Martha Bacon, the wife of a former diplomatic official.[16]

Brown also emphasized economic and ideological forces. He particularly admired the Scandinavian country for not defaulting on debt payments arising from $9 million in World War I grants. "Finland," he stressed, "happens to be the one nation in Europe to which we loaned money before 1930, that has fulfilled its promise to pay in every respect." On the other hand, the Russians had borrowed nearly $200 million from the United States and owed $395 million including interest. "She has not," Brown protested, "paid back one cent of that tremendous sum."[17] He commended the bravery and determination of Marshal Carl Mannerheim, who directed the Finnish resistance against the Russian aggression. Brown described Finland as a "little inoffensive nation that has been brutally attacked by a foe 50 times its size."[18] The Scandinavians, he noted, sought to preserve the same ideals of integrity, honesty, industry, and justice cherished by Americans. Brown warned that if the United States did not act quickly, the Stalin government might attempt to expand the Communist ideology. American assistance, he believed, could "remove a possible danger of the spread of the nefarious doctrines of Stalin and his cohorts to the splendid peoples of all Scandinavia."[19]

Brown argued that the interventionist loan program had recent historical precedents. In 1938, the Export-Import Bank of Washington had loaned the Chinese

15. "Prentiss M. Brown," *Current Biography* 4 (1943):78–81; Prentiss M. Brown to Author, 1 March 1968.
16. Prentiss M. Brown, Interview with Author.
17. Prentiss M. Brown Press Release, 26 January 1940, Prentiss M. Brown Radio Address, 28 January 1940, Speech File, Box 10, Prentiss M. Brown Papers.
18. Brown Press Release, 26 January 1940.
19. Brown Radio Address, 28 January 1940.

government $25 million to purchase nonmilitary items. There were several similarities between the Chinese and Finnish situations. Japan in 1937 suddenly had attacked China, which subsequently had asked for and received economic assistance from the United States. On the other hand, significant differences marked the two situations. Chiang Kai-shek's regime was more autocratic than that of the Ryti administration. The earlier loan had involved only nonmilitary aid and had not required congressional approval.[20]

Brown, however, opposed unlimited help. Despite disliking the Communist ideology, he disapproved of breaking diplomatic relations with the Soviet Union. The Stalin regime, Brown pointed out, controlled "the nation it represents with apparent approval of its people." Although conceding that the Russian attack upon Finland could be legitimate grounds for breaking diplomatic relations, he concluded, "I am not sure that it is altogether desireable [sic] to do so." [21] Brown rejected sending American combat units overseas to fight for the Ryti government because "we are unwilling to take any steps that will sacrifice our sons on the field of battle."[22]

From the outset, Senate leaders supported aid to Finland. Democrats Alben W. Barkley of Kentucky, James F. Byrnes of South Carolina, and Key Pittman of Nevada immediately favored the Brown measure, while minority head Charles L. McNary of Oregon recommended loaning nonmilitary materials. At a Republican caucus in early January, John A. Danaher of Connecticut cast the lone vote against federal assistance to the Scandinavian country.[23]

The Roosevelt administration, still opposing direct combat aid, sought limited federal intervention. On 10 January Secretary of the Treasury Henry Morgenthau discussed legislative strategy with Ways and Means Committee Chairman Robert L. Doughton of North Carolina and Appropriations Committee head Edward T. Taylor of Colorado. Doughton and Taylor were requested to designate some Democrat to introduce a bill authorizing an undetermined amount of money for nonmilitary purposes. As on the neutrality question, the White House preferred to leave the specific details up to Congress. Despite prodding by Doughton and Taylor, Morgenthau did not cite an explicit sum for the loan. Following the luncheon, Doughton and Taylor asked Speaker William B. Bankhead of Alabama to draft such legislation. Bankhead, however, declined to cooperate because he opposed disciplining party members this time and believed a credit arrangement might intensify the European war. He also was reluctant to seize the initiative on foreign policy, a topic normally considered first by the Senate.[24]

Roosevelt summoned congressional leaders to the White House on 15 January for a strategy session. Senators Barkley, Byrnes, and Brown, along with representatives Bankhead and Rayburn, attended the conference. At the outset, the president

20. Brown Interview with Author; *Washington Star*, 11 January 1940.
21. Prentiss M. Brown to F. J. Hall, 26 January 1940, Speech File, Box 10, Brown Papers.
22. Brown Radio Address, 28 January 1940.
23. *Washington Star*, 11 January 1940.
24. Blum, *Morgenthau Diaries*, p. 131.

criticized the interventionist Brown measure because an unrestricted loan enabling purchases of military supplies would violate the existing Neutrality Act. Roosevelt instead suggested that the Export-Import Bank intervene on a limited basis by lending around $25 million to the Scandinavian country for acquiring noncombat materials. Although willing to compromise, Brown replied that Finnish diplomats had requested a much larger amount. Brown added, "What Finland needs most now is war equipment." Other congressional leaders urged the federal government to provide a credit, but disagreed over whether the aid should include war supplies. Before the conferees adjourned, Roosevelt promised to draft a statement outlining his views.[25]

The next day, Roosevelt sent his recommendation for limited federal intervention to Capitol Hill. In identical messages to Vice-president John Nance Garner and Speaker Bankhead, he urged that the Export-Import Bank be authorized to loan Finland an undesignated amount for the purchase of farm surpluses and industrial goods. "There is without doubt," Roosevelt stated, "in the United States a great desire for some action to assist Finland to finance the purchase of agricultural surpluses and manufactured products." Such action, he contended, would not violate existing statutes or risk embroilment abroad. Besides vowing, "This matter will be kept within the realm of our neutrality laws and our neutral policies," he claimed that extending credits "does not in any way constitute or threaten any so-called involvement in European wars." Although rejecting the idea of funds for the acquisition of armaments, the president did not indicate whether he supported the Brown bill and preferred to let Congress decide the specific details. Besides figuring that congressional noninterventionists would block a military loan, he did not want to provide Hitler with an opportunity to strike again soon on the European front. He also feared that alignment with Finland would hinder Soviet-American relations and solidify Russian-German cooperation. Roosevelt's proposal disappointed Finnish Prime Minister Ryti, who disliked the exclusion of implements of war and warned that the Scandinavian nation required an adequate amount of military supplies quickly to counter the Russian army.[26]

Two different Senate committees debated the Brown bill. Since the measure involved increasing the revolving fund of the Export-Import Bank, the Banking and Currency Committee initially was assigned to consider the legislation. Democrat Tom Connally of Texas, however, insisted the measure primarily involved American international policy, therefore he requested that the Foreign Relations Committee instead handle the Brown bill. Majority Leader Barkley, nonetheless, preferred that the Banking and Currency Committee receive the legislation because that group always had examined Export-Import Bank financing. Democrat Robert F. Wagner of New York, who chaired the Banking and Currency Committee, arranged a compromise whereby his committee would explore the economic ramifications and Foreign Relations would investigate the general implications of the federal loan.[27]

25. *Washington Post*, 16, 19 January 1940.
26. Rosenman, ed., *Public Papers*, 9:50; *New York Times*, 17 January 1940.
27. *Congressional Record (CR)*, 76th Cong., 3d sess., vol. 86, 16 January 1940, pp. 360–62.

This maneuver diminished prospects for quick Senate action because noninterventionists on the Foreign Relations Committee would more closely scrutinize the Brown measure.

On 17 January, the Banking and Currency Committee began conducting hearings. Chairman Wagner invited Federal Loan Agency Administrator Jones to present the executive branch's viewpoints because Secretary Hull did not want to testify. At the outset, Jones contended that an unrestricted loan for military purposes transgressed the neutrality laws. Jones instead suggested increasing the lending authority of the Export-Import Bank from $100 million to $200 million to permit the continuation of credits to Latin America and Finland. Besides considering the loan "a good risk," he stressed that the Ryti government already had received $10 million from the United States. Jones testified that the bank could provide an additional $25 million for nonmilitary supplies but suggested that Congress determine the precise amount. Wagner recessed the committee for one week so that Jones and Brown could adjust their differences.[28]

Two days later, a compromise measure for limited federal intervention was drafted. Brown, who still believed Finland needed military supplies quickly, denied that an unrestricted, direct loan would conflict with neutrality statutes. Nevertheless, the Michigan Democrat reluctantly accepted a substitute bill for limited federal intervention. Jones proposed doubling the Export-Import Bank capital to $200 million, with no money available for military supplies. A $30 million ceiling would be established on credits available to any one country. Although not mentioning any specific countries, the bill would permit Finland to get loans up to $30 million. The Ryti government, which already had used $10 million, could receive an additional $20 million from the United States.[29]

The Banking and Currency Committee supported limited federal intervention. Wagner's group opposed massive intervention, wanting to restrict credits for any one nation to $30 million and forbid any transactions for the acquisition of armaments or in contravention of international law. On the other hand, they rejected an amendment by Republican noninterventionist Taft of Ohio reducing the increase in bank capital to $50 million. With noninterventionists Taft and Danaher of Connecticut dissenting, the committee on 24 January overwhelmingly approved 18 to 2 the limited intervention measure. According to noninterventionists Taft and Danaher, the bill was intended to help Latin America rather than Finland.[30]

For the first time, a Senate committee in the Seventy-sixth Congress had authorized federal intervention in the European conflict. At the special session, internationalists had permitted private business firms to sell arms, ammunition, and implements of war to belligerents on an indirect cash-and-carry basis. Wagner's committee now had resoundingly approved restricted intervention to aid Finland

28. U.S., Congress, Senate, Committee on Banking and Currency, "Extension of Lending Authority of Export-Import Bank of Washington," *Hearings*, 17 January 1940.

29. *Washington Post*, 19, 20 January 1940.

30. U.S., Congress, Senate, Committee on Banking and Currency, "Extension of Lending Authority of Export-Import Bank of Washington," *Reports*, no. 1166; *New York Times*, 25 January 1940.

against the Soviet Union. Although preferring more direct federal assistance, Brown issued a press statement praising the committee's vote. "The committee action," he remarked, "virtually assures passage of the Brown measure in the Senate without serious opposition since it is confidently expected the Foreign Relations Committee will add its approval." Finland could receive $20 million in additional credits for acquiring trucks, raw materials, agricultural goods, and other nonmilitary commodities. "I want to do all that can be done," Brown concluded, "within the limits of neutrality." Exuding confidence, he believed "Congress can reach a result which will greatly aid the heroic Finns."[31]

At the same time, Brown conferred with Army Department personnel. During late January, he met with Major General O'Ryan to compile lists of merchandise the United States could furnish without endangering American security. These included transportation, communication, food, shelter, hygiene, and personal items. Under the Brown bill, the Ryti government could be supplied with horses, mules, harnesses, automobiles, saddles, wagons, railroad engines, rolling stock, motor trucks, oil, and gasoline. Since Finland had 2,500 miles of navigable interior waterways, the United States could provide steel for bridge construction, motorboats, rowboats, and pontoons. Loans could be used to purchase telephone and radio equipment, hay, forage, oats, first-aid kits, splints, surgical instruments, and medicines. Additional nonmilitary goods included tents, blankets, sleeping bags, mittens, socks, shoes, boots, earmuffs, clothing, civilian gas masks, binoculars, and parachutes. On the other hand, the Ryti administration could not purchase armaments or airplanes.[32]

Brown also sought to rally public opinion behind the measure. By late January, he had received only 150 letters relating to Finland. In cooperation with Procopé, Brown planned an extensive publicity campaign before the measure reached the floor of Congress. On 26 January, the Michigan Democrat told reporters about conditions in the Scandinavian country and explained that if Congress approved the interventionist Brown bill, Finland could receive $20 million in additional loans for purchasing transportation, equipment, raw materials, and agricultural products. He urged wholehearted public support for the Ryti government. "I want to give all the aid I can," Brown remarked, "to this suffering nation attacked by a brutal bullying foe."[33]

Two days later, Brown made a nationwide radio broadcast. At the outset, he stressed that most Americans favored helping Finland. "They want to do it quickly," he contended, "and they want it to be effective." In addition, he lauded the Ryti government for providing determined resistance. "Our people," Brown stated, "see a brave little nation fighting against the most extensive nation in the world. We see a people outnumbered fifty to one, unjustly attacked without a semblance of provocation." The Finns, moreover, were struggling for "defense of their homeland and their homes, of themselves and their loved ones." Finland had

31. Brown Press Release, 26 January 1940.
32. Brown Interview with Author; Prentiss M. Brown NBC Radio Address, 26 February 1940, Speech File, Box 10, Brown Papers.
33. Brown Press Release, 26 January 1940.

repaid its entire World War I debt, while the Russians had defaulted on their entire $200 million credit. Brown considered the loan a small sacrifice for Americans to make because the Scandinavians were battling for survival against communist aggression. Besides figuring that the limited interventionist bill would cost each citizen only twenty-five cents, he predicted, "The average man would be willing to risk the pay of a part of an hour's labor." If the United States did not act, Brown claimed Russia might seize control of the whole Baltic area. "That refusal," he warned, "might result in the spread of an unholy doctrine that will plague us, may possibly destroy us in the years to come." "We can do this thing," Brown claimed, "without serious risk. Not to do it may be much more dangerous to our democracy."[34] Brown hoped that following the broadcast listeners would deluge senators with mail urging approval of his measure.

In late January, Brown also was invited to join the Foreign Relations Committee. Chairman Pittman, who was preparing to conduct hearings, feared isolationists might delay action on the measure. Since Brown had written the legislation and was a financial expert, Pittman believed the Michigan Democrat could steer the measure quickly through the committee. Pittman offered Brown a committee seat, but the latter declined. Besides enjoying economic and monetary matters, the highly respected, well-mannered Brown shared little in common with the coarse, hard-drinking Pittman.[35]

The twenty-two-member committee was divided into four factions. Eight internationalist Democrats, including Pittman, Wagner, and Claude D. Pepper of Florida, favored limited interventionist loans for purchasing nonmilitary supplies. Led by Vandenberg of Michigan and Progressive Robert M. La Follette, Jr., of Wisconsin, four traditional isolationists supported the mildly interventionist Brown bill because they served Scandinavian constituents. Under the direction of Walter F. George of Goergia and Pat Harrison of Mississippi, a third faction of erstwhile internationalists opposed extending federal credits. They vowed that the interventionist loan not only would raise taxes, but also would increase the national debt limit. Since the economic depression had caused hardship especially for the American farmer, they contended that the federal government should augment agricultural subsidies rather than assist distant Finland. Three isolationists, including Democrat Bennett Champ Clark of Missouri and Republican Hiram W. Johnson of California, claimed the interventionist measure would contravene neutrality legislation and might establish a dangerous precedent for assisting other European governments. Although "anxious to see Finland 'whip the tar' out of Russia," noninterventionist Johnson declared, "We do not want to do anything which may under any circumstances involve this country in war."

At the hearings, Federal Loan Agency Administrator Jones faced rigorous interrogation. George, Harrison, and other noninterventionists warned that financial assistance to Finland would embroil the United States in the European war. In an

34. Brown Radio Address, 28 January 1940.
35. Brown Interview with Author; in the interview, Brown did not indicate having any political reasons for declining the appointment.

effort to alleviate these fears, Jones vowed that the loans would not finance the Finnish war effort and thus would not violate neutrality legislation. The bank, he categorically stated, would reject granting any loans for arms, ammunition, or implements of warfare. Future credit applications, he promised, would be considered primarily on ability to repay the United States. Jones proceeded so cautiously during the hearings that Republican Wallace H. White of Maine wondered whether the bill really was intended to help Finland.[36]

Despite this resistance, interventionists ultimately triumphed. On 7 February, Pittman's committee approved 12 to 6 the Brown measure. To the dismay of noninterventionists, the committee defeated 13 to 5 an amendment reducing in half the proposed $100 million increase in lending authority. On the other hand, they rejected 15 to 3 an attempt by militant interventionists to authorize credits for purchasing military materials. The action marked the first time the Foreign Relations Committee had approved a measure sanctioning limited federal intervention to aid a specific country in the European conflict. Although it had shifted from isolationism to internationalism at the special session, Pittman's group had approved only indirect aid by private American businesses and had not allowed direct federal intervention against aggressors.

Committee Democrats did not exploit their vast numerical advantage. Historians usually picture the majority party as more united than the opposition, but several conservative Democrats this time split with Chairman Pittman. Supporters of the bill included eight Democrats, two Republicans, and two third-party members and represented all sections of the United States. They included Republican Vandenberg of Michigan, Progressive La Follette of Wisconsin, and Farmer-Laborite Henrik Shipstead of Minnesota, who served the Scandinavian upper Midwest, and Republican Johnson of California, who reluctantly approved reporting the measure. With the exception of Republican Arthur Capper of Kansas, all opposition votes were cast by Southern, Great Lakes, and Great Plains Democrats.[37] The Democratic opponents, including Harrison, George, Clark, Robert R. Reynolds of North Carolina, and Frederick Van Nuys of Indiana, were either noninterventionists or anti-Roosevelt. The president in 1937 had influenced the Senate to accept Barkley over Harrison for majority leader and the next year had attempted to purge George and Van Nuys in the Democratic primaries. On this issue, the committee interventionists had gained converts among Great Lakes and Great Plains Republicans and third-party congressmen and had witnessed defections by Southern Democrats. Defying historical stereotypes, Republicans and third-party members acted more interventionist than did the Democrats.[38] These members typically came from

36. U.S., Congress, Senate, Committee on Foreign Relations, "Increasing the Lending Authority of the Export-Import Bank," *Hearings*, 31 January–7 February 1940, pp. 3–29; Sobel, *Interventionism*, pp. 125–27. For Harrison's view, see Pat Harrison Press Release, 30 January 1940, File 1, Pat Harrison Papers, and Martha H. Swain, *Pat Harrison: The New Deal Years*, pp. 222–23.

37. U.S., Congress, Senate, Committee on Foreign Relations, "Increasing the Lending Authority of the Export-Import Bank," *Reports*, no. 1185; *New York Times*, 8 February 1940.

38. Julius Turner, George L. Grassmuck, Robert A. Dahl, Leroy N. Rieselbach, and other scholars have pictured the Democrats as more internationalist than the Republicans in the Roosevelt era.

the geographical section comprising the highest proportion of Scandinavian constituents.

Around the same time, the Finnish military situation steadily worsened. The well-equipped Russian troops launched an offensive in February, forcing the Finnish army to retreat at several places and battering the nation's second largest city. Finnish Field Marshal Carl Mannerheim on 5 February cabled Roosevelt about the bleak situation and hoped "the mighty people of America and its noble President will not leave us without effective support." The Ryti government contended the American Congress did not comprehend the problems confronting the Mannerheim army and urged the legislative body to divorce the issue from domestic politics. As the Senate prepared to begin floor debate, the Soviet forces rapidly were placing the Finnish troops in an untenable position.[39]

A poll conducted by *Congressional Intelligence*, meanwhile, encouraged interventionists and showed the nature of shifting Senate alignments. In the 3 February survey, forty-eight of eighty-three senators sampled favored federal loans to the Ryti government. Thirty-five members, mostly noninterventionists, opposed credits, while thirteen were either undecided or absent. Since the special session, the political and geographical composition of the Senate had changed slightly. Interventionists, still led by Democrats, were distributed more evenly geographically and controlled every section except the Great Plains. Middle Atlantic members proportionately replaced Southern Democrats at the forefront and received considerable support from Border and Mountain senators. Interventionists recorded their most significant gains among the Pacific bloc, which had led the isolationist resistance to neutrality revision. On the noninterventionist side, the Great Plains delegation proportionately replaced the Pacific members at the helm. Noninterventionists gained several converts from the heavily Democratic Southern bloc and the Great Lakes delegation[40] (see table 18). Southern Democrats served hardly any Scandinavian constituents, urged decreasing federal spending, and insisted charity should begin at home rather than with far-away Finland. Although representing the most heavily Scandinavian section in the nation, several Great Lakes members distrusted the president and disliked increasing funding for his New Deal agencies. Since a substantial portion of the aid probably would go to Latin American countries, Taft of Ohio and other Republicans preferred reducing the allocation considerably and designating the total amount for Finland. The Great Lakes region also was quite removed geographically from the European war, included numerous noninterventionist ethnic groups, and depended relatively little on foreign trade.

Interventionist senators stressed anti-Communism. Although they had concentrated on Nazi expansionist activity when considering the neutrality issue, they shifted attention eastward this time to note the danger inherent in the spread of the Soviet Union and Communism. Besides deploring "the Red Menace," Democrat Peter G. Gerry of Rhode Island remarked, "American indignation is growing in

39. Schwartz, *Russo-Finnish War*, pp. 23, 33.

40. "Congressional Poll on Loans to Foreign Governments," p. 4. The tables cited in this chapter are based on data from the Inter-University Consortium for Political Research, University of Michigan.

leaps and bounds against anything from Moscow."[41] Republican Austin of Vermont criticized the "brutal aggression" by Russia as "unwarranted, unprovoked, and ruthless," while Wagner of New York pictured the Stalin government as "international brigands, whose only excuse is power."[42]

Wanting to protect democracy in the Western world, interventionists hoped Finland would withstand totalitarian pressure. Since the Soviet Union had a much larger army, they lauded the ability, courage, and determination of the Finnish government. "I don't know," Democrat Joseph C. O'Mahoney of Wyoming remarked, "when any people have aroused more admiration than have the Finns in their splendid resistance to Russian aggression." "If ever a race or a nation deserved to survive," Democrat J. Wilburn Cartwright of Oklahoma declared, "it is these sturdy Finns whose integrity, intelligence, and fortitude demands [sic] the admiration of all the world." "We have not seen the like," he concluded, "since 1776!"[43]

Interventionists also concentrated more on economic considerations than they had during the neutrality debate. Although Finland had repaid its $9 million debt from World War I, every other European nation had defaulted on payments. Democrat Theodore F. Green of Rhode Island admired "what it had done in the past" to keep up the regular monthly installments. Foreign loans, interventionists claimed, ultimately would improve the American economy. Wagner of New York maintained that since Finland would purchase American goods, the money "really goes to our own industries, thus increasing employment opportunities in the United States."[44]

Advocates of Finnish assistance otherwise raised issues similar to those that had been stressed by proponents of arms embargo repeal. They favored overseas commitments to deter future aggression but disagreed over the assistance Finland should receive. In order to prevent excessive involvement in the European war, mild interventionists recommended restricting credits to nonmilitary supplies. Republican Ernest W. Gibson of Vermont cautioned, "The only way aid can be safely given is by way of loans, regular in form, and limited in use so that no excuse would exist for joining in the conflict." Similarly, Democrat Carl Hayden of Arizona hoped the Senate could find "a suitable method by which assistance can be rendered to that embattled Republic without in any way endangering our own neutrality structure."[45]

By contrast, more militant interventionists argued that permitting the acquisition of armaments afforded the only effective means of averting a complete Com-

41. Peter G. Gerry to Josiah W. Bailey, 13 December 1939, Political File, Josiah W. Bailey Papers.

42. Warren R. Austin Radio Address, 3 January 1940, Speech File, Box 1939–1940, Austin Papers; Robert F. Wagner Speech, New York City, 20 December 1939, Shelf, Robert F. Wagner Papers.

43. Joseph C. O'Mahoney to James Burgess, 19 January 1940, Box 49, Joseph C. O'Mahoney Papers; J. Wilburn Cartwright Washington Newsletter, 20 January 1940, Box 168, J. Wilburn Cartwright Papers.

44. Theodore F. Green to Miss Sonja Matson, 16 January 1940, Box 145, Theodore F. Green Papers; Robert F. Wagner to Arthur Diamondstein, 14 February 1940, S. 3069, Legislative Division, National Archives.

45. Ernest W. Gibson Press Release, 15 January 1940, Newspaper Statements, Ernest W. Gibson Papers; Carl Hayden to Mr. & Mrs. Walter Bopp, 20 January 1940, 590/5, Carl Hayden Papers.

munist takeover. "The proceeds of this loan," Austin of Vermont urged, "should be without restriction so that ammunition, arms, and whatever may be necessary to strengthen the defensive morale and gallant resistance of the Finns may be made promptly available." O'Mahoney of Wyoming added, "what the Finns need is not so much medical and agricultural supplies which are being offered, but military supplies."[46] On the other hand, more militant interventionists recognized that a majority of members probably would reject sending arms, ammunition, or implements of war. Democrat Carter Glass of Virginia, who advocated "a much larger loan to Finland," conceded that nommilitary assistance "would appear to be about all we can get out of Congress at the present time."[47]

Although sympathizing with Finland, noninterventionists opposed the Brown measure for ideological reasons. Noninterventionists admired the bravery and courage demonstrated by the Ryti government in defending its homeland against Russian aggression. Labeling the Soviet attack "shocking," Republican William E. Borah of Idaho affirmed, "I have great sympathy for Finland and her heroic and almost unparalleled defense of her country."[48] Recalling the heavy American commitment in World War I, noninterventionists feared the loan might lead to more direct American involvement in the European war. "I am not doing anything," Democrat Elmer Thomas of Oklahoma remarked, "calculated to involve our country in any sort of an entanglement with any foreign nation." Youthful Democrat Rush Dew Holt of West Virginia added, "I cannot cast my vote for a step, even though it may be a small step that might mean the death or destruction of Anerican boys."[49]

Antiwar sentiments also influenced noninterventionist attitudes toward the Soviet Union. Besides considering the loan a provocative action against Russia, noninterventionists urged continuing diplomatic recognition. If "we press Russia too far we may force Russia and Japan together," Republican Clyde M. Reed of Kansas warned. "I cannot see," Borah of Idaho added, "that breaking off diplomatic relations will serve in any way the cause of peace nor stay the wings of a single Red Plane."[50] Noninterventionists, moreover, were afraid a federal loan would establish an unfortunate precedent for American foreign policy. "If we are going to help Finland," Republican Clifford R. Hope of Kansas queried, "then how in all fairness can we refuse to help Belgium and Holland should they be invaded, or other countries such as Switzerland, Denmark, Norway and Sweden?"[51]

Noninterventionists again insisted that the Roosevelt administration should

46. Austin Radio Address, 3 January 1940; Joseph C. O'Mahoney to Paul Greever, 5 February 1940, Box 49, O'Mahoney Papers.
47. Carter Glass to Miss Ann Cabell, 9 February 1940, Box 388, Carter Glass Papers.
48. William E. Borah Press Statement, 1 December 1939, Box 433, William E. Borah to Dean Driscoll, 9 January 1940, Box 434, William E. Borah Papers.
49. Elmer Thomas to N. O. Conner, 23 February 1940, Legislative Correspondence, Foreign Legislation, Box F–G, Elmer Thomas Papers; Rush Dew Holt to Associated Press, 13 February 1940, A&M 1701, Box 102, Rush Dew Holt Papers.
50. Clyde M. Reed to William Allen White, 12 February 1940, Box 230, William Allen White Papers; Borah Press Statement, 1 December 1939.
51. Clifford R. Hope to E. F. White, 26 January 1940, Legislative Correspondence, Box 177, Clifford R. Hope Papers.

concentrate on solving domestic economic problems and lowering fiscal expenditures. Since the economic depression still persisted, noninterventionists urged that federal priority be given to expanding employment opportunities and providing adequate housing and food for needy citizens. Holt of West Virginia counseled, "If we have $100,000,000 there are thousands of hungry, naked and homeless Americans who could use part of that money." Farmer-Laborite Ernest Lundeen of Minnesota, who represented Scandinavian constituents, mentioned how a woman was compelled to give away her two sons because she could not support them with a $15 a week paycheck. With the national debt approaching $2 billion, noninterventionists claimed the Roosevelt administration should restore the nation to financial prosperity rather than lend money abroad. Harrison of Mississippi declared, "We are in no financial condition to make loans through government agencies, no matter how sympathetic we are to certain foreign governments whose plight appeals to us." Although sympathetic with Finland, Republican Karl M. LeCompte of Iowa warned, "This government is running behind daily" and cautioned, "We have no money to loan."[52]

Although politics played a more subordinate role this time, several noninterventionists preferred using private resources. They denounced the measure as a devious attempt to increase the power of the executive branch and administrative agencies. "The whole thing," Republican Johnson of California charged, "was a fraud, a delusion, and a snare. A very astute and cunning man, Mr. Jesse Jones, the head of the Export-Import Bank, had succeeded in changing the bill to an additional appropriation for his Bank with no mention whatever of Finland." Instead, noninterventionists encouraged Americans to send private donations, food, and clothing to the Finnish government. Finland, Harrison of Mississippi suggested, should utilize the Securities and Exchange Commission to sell bonds in the United States. "I have no doubt," Harrison predicted, "that the American people who are able to purchase these bonds will do so in large amounts."[53] The federal government, noninterventionists claimed, could not afford to furnish the type of assistance the Scandinavians needed. Republican John M. Vorys of Ohio disapproved of making a federal loan "until we are ready to follow it up with support that will guarantee the success of Finland in the magnificent struggle she is making." "There is no bill pending and none in sight," Republican John Taber of New York added, "that would provide a loan to Finland for what they do need."[54]

Brown directed the floor debate for the interventionists. Although chairman of the Banking and Currency Committee, Wagner of New York selected the younger, financially astute, eloquent Michigan Democrat to manage floor operations. Committee heads often designate more dynamic committee members to conduct floor

52. Holt to Associated Press, 13 February 1940; CR, 13 February 1940, p. 1399; Harrison Press Release, 30 January 1940; Karl M. LeCompte to Verne Marshall, 12 December 1939, Box 15, Folder 61, Karl M. LeCompte Papers.
53. Hiram W. Johnson to Hiram W. Johnson, Jr., 24 February 1940, Part VI, Box 8, Hiram W. Johnson Papers; Harrison Press Release, 30 January 1940.
54. John M. Vorys to Carl Norman, 22 January 1940, Box 4, John M. Vorys Papers; John Taber to Mrs. Florence De La Mater, 26 February 1940, Box 67, John Taber Papers.

maneuvering. Unlike neutrality strategists, Brown made no organized effort to buttonhole colleagues in cloakrooms or to telephone members. Besides believing that a clear majority of the senators already favored his measure, he realized that American public opinion and newspapers had deplored the Russian actions.[55] For the interventionists, Democrats King of Utah and Kenneth D. McKellar of Tennessee assisted the sponsor of the measure.

Harrison of Mississippi, the fifty-seven-year-old chairman of the Finance Committee, led the noninterventionist campaign. His father, an impoverished Crystal Springs, Mississippi, storekeeper, had died of a crippling disease in the late 1880s and had left four children. In order to help support his family, young Pat had sold newspapers and had driven a two-mule hack. After attending Louisiana State University, the tall, lanky Harrison had returned to Mississippi to teach public school and to play semiprofessional baseball. He had practiced law for several years and had served from 1911 to 1919 in the U.S. House of Representatives. A shrewd and witty campaigner, Harrison in the 1918 Democratic primary had ousted veteran James K. Vardaman from the U.S. Senate. The Mississippi Democrat, who was an exceptional leader and persuasive debater, had guided the National Recovery Act and other New Deal legislation through the Senate. When Roosevelt selected the more liberal Barkley of Kentucky over Harrison for majority leader in 1937, Harrison began aligning with the anti-New Dealers. Although not dynamic or outstanding intellectually, he was very popular, amiable, courtly, and a skillful parliamentarian. Brown did not enjoy opposing Harrison, who shared his interest in economic legislation and in the Washington Senators baseball club. According to Brown, Harrison was the most influential and ablest senator of the pre-World War II era and was one Southern Democrat who usually placed national interests above sectional considerations.

Harrison usually had aligned with the internationalists on foreign policy questions. During World War I, he had supported President Woodrow Wilson's programs and particularly had championed American military preparedness. The Mississippi Democrat subsequently had approved the Treaty of Versailles and had urged American entrance into both the League of Nations and the World Court. During the 1930s, Harrison normally had cooperated with the Roosevelt administration on international and defense legislation. In 1934 he had piloted through the Senate the administration's Reciprocal Trade Act, which had lowered tariff rates considerably. The Mississippi Democrat had played an instrumental role in 1937 in securing an extension of reciprocal trade and was preparing to wage another intense battle to preserve the program. Harrison likewise had supported the White House on neutrality legislation and believed the arms embargo discriminated in favor of aggressor nations. At the president's request, he had remained in Washington, D.C., during July 1939 and voted in the Foreign Relations Committee against postponing neutrality revision. At the special session, Harrison had endorsed the Pittman bill permitting munitions sales to belligerents. On the other hand, he opposed the interventionist

Brown bill extending Export-Import Bank loans to the Finnish government. Besides favoring a more balanced budget, the Mississippi Democrat preferred that federal aid be given to farmers and other depressed groups in the United States rather than to distant Finland. Harrison, who had favored resumption of American diplomatic relations with the Soviet Union in 1933, also did not want the Roosevelt administration to take any action jeopardizing those relations.[56] During the debate, Democrat George of Georgia and Republican Taft of Ohio assisted Harrison in the battle against the Finnish measure.

Opening floor debate on 9 February, Brown defended limited federal intervention primarily on ideological grounds. He assured noninterventionists that the bill prohibited loans for combat purposes but claimed the credits still could help the Scandinavian country resist the Russian army. Finland could purchase food, medicine, clothing, shelter, and transportation materials, thus enabling the Ryti government to designate a higher proportion of its own budget for securing weapons and mobilizing troops. He warned that in view of the Russian activity, the Finns soon might lose their individual freedoms. "If they are going to have any aid in their battle against Russia," the Michigan Democrat insisted, "they need it quickly."[57]

During the two-day debate, some members remarked that the bill was too ambiguous. Although Brown insisted the measure would aid Finland, his bill did not name the Scandinavian country specifically and hence was interpreted in a variety of ways. Democrat Henry F. Ashurst of Arizona, who did not comprehend the intent of the legislation, commented, "I intend to be a candidate for re-election to the Senate and beyond any doubt I shall be asked whether or not I voted for the loan to Finland!" In reply to Ashurst, Democrat Josiah W. Bailey of North Carolina observed that the legislation could be viewed as an attempt either to aid Finland or merely "to give the Export-Import Bank some money."[58] On the other hand, several noninterventionists warned that the measure was too pro-Finnish and would involve the United States in the European war.

Interventionists concentrated on ideological and anti-Communist considerations. Besides denouncing the Stalin government as the enemy of "international law, basic justice, and Christianity," King of Utah stressed that the "Bolshevik regime is now revealing its hatred of democracy" by "attacking in a savage and brutal way a free and independent people."[59] McKellar of Tennessee condemned "the cowardly, dastardly, and miserable fight which Russia is making in Finland" and asserted, "The present Government of Russia ought to be wiped off the face of the earth." Since the Finns had exhibited tenacious resistance, interventionists regarded a loan as the minimum the United States could do to help the Scandinavian country. "Finland's struggle against barbarous, cruel, and despotic power," Repub-

56. "Byron Patton Harrison," *Dictionary of American Biography* 8, supp. 3 (1973):384–85; William Sidney Coker, "Pat Harrison: The Formative Years," *Journal of Mississippi History* 25 (October 1963): 251–78; David Porter, "Senator Pat Harrison of Mississippi and the Reciprocal Trade Act of 1940," p. 364; Brown Interview with Author; Swain, *Harrison*, pp. 220–23.
57. *CR*, 9 February 1940, pp. 1281–82.
58. Sobel, *Interventionism*, pp. 124–25.
59. *CR*, 13 February 1940, pp. 1390–91.

lican White of Maine contended, "will be the subject of heroic stories told to generations yet unborn."[60]

During the debate, economic and ideological themes were highlighted by noninterventionists. Convinced charity should begin at home, they complained that the United States already had spent too much money abroad making loans to over fifty nations. Farmer-Laborite Lundeen of Minnesota advised colleagues that the "time has come to think about America and forget Europe" because "one-third of our people are ill-housed, ill-clothed, and ill-fed." "To all the world," Republican Johnson of California remarked, "we have become a wet nurse and all regard us as a sort of Santa Claus."[61] Ideologically, noninterventionists reiterated that the Brown measure violated international law and would drive the United States closer to involvement in the European conflict. George, who contended that global statutes forbade a neutral state from granting loans to belligerent nations, pictured the Finnish credit as "a step in the direction of war," while Republican Alexander Wiley of Wisconsin denounced the Brown bill as "an overt act in violation of international law and the Constitution."[62]

For nearly a month, noninterventionists had been developing legislative strategy. On 16 January, Republican Danaher of Connecticut offered a concurrent resolution to invoke the Neutrality Act in the undeclared war between Russia and Finland and aid neither country. Danaher's proposal dismayed interventionists in Congress and at the White House. "The same cleavage in the Republican ranks that existed regarding the Repeal of the Embargo of 1935 during the Extraordinary session appears this morning," Austin of Vermont noted.[63] At a cabinet meeting in late January, Roosevelt claimed, "There was a bunch of 'Uriah Heeps' in Congress, especially in the Senate, who disclaimed responsibility in this vital matter." These legislators, Roosevelt charged, "did not realize that what was going on in Europe would inevitably affect this country sooner or later."[64]

Most noninterventionists also considered the Danaher proposal too drastic and instead favored reducing the lending authority of the Export-Import Bank. Taft of Ohio and other noninterventionists favored federal credits to Finland but opposed financial assistance for other European or Latin American countries. "The Finnish loan," Taft remarked, "is justified. I do not see that it is an infringement on neutrality. Our sympathies have always been with struggling small nations." Taft proposed lowering the contemplated increase from $100 million to $50 million and designating the entire amount for the Ryti government. "If this bill could be reduced to the one question of a loan to Finland," Taft remarked, "I would be glad to vote for it."[65]

The Senate, however, rejected 50 to 27 the noninterventionist Taft amendment.

60. *CR*, 9 February 1940, p. 1299, 13 February 1940, p. 1393.
61. *CR*, 9 February 1940, p. 1298, 13 February 1940, p. 1402.
62. *CR*, 8 January 1940, p. 101, 13 February 1940, p. 1378.
63. *New York Times*, 17 January 1940; Warren R. Austin Memorandum to Mrs. Chauncey Austin, 16 January 1940, General Correspondence, Box 1939–1940, Austin Papers.
64. Ickes, *Diary*, 3:112.
65. *Washington Star*, 13 February 1940.

Although neither Majority Leader Barkley nor Minority Leader McNary disciplined party colleagues, members followed political loyalties more closely than they had at the regular session. Democrats, who largely opposed any reduction in the original amount, utilized their vast numerical superiority to block the Republican-sponsored amendment. Numerous Democrats, particularly New Dealers, liked the work the Export-Import Bank had accomplished and viewed the agency as an integral part of Roosevelt's foreign policy. On the other hand, Republicans nearly unanimously supported the noninterventionist proposal made by their influential Ohio colleague. Besides being distrustful of Roosevelt, they usually had opposed Export-Import Bank loans. Several Republicans sympathetic to Finland claimed Roosevelt's agency held too much legislative power and might use much of the increased lending authority to aid Latin American nations. Along with opposing deficit spending, most minority party members preferred that federal expenditures be made on the domestic front. Both parties, particularly the Republicans, stressed political considerations more than they had in October. McNary's party was more united than the Democrats, a striking contrast with the usual pattern in this period[66] (see table 19).

By contrast, sectionalism had less influence. Regionalism affected the voting behavior of Southern, Border, and Middle Atlantic senators, who displayed at least 75 percent cohesion. Of the five remaining delegations, only the Mountain bloc approached a comparable degree of solidarity. Southern Democrats proportionately led the resistance to the noninterventionist Taft amendment and were joined by Border, Middle Atlantic, and Mountain members. Southern and Border senators opposed the noninterventionist motion by the Ohio Republican because they traditionally had liked the work of Roosevelt's economic agency. The Export-Import Bank had made numerous loans to Latin American nations, which in turn had traded extensively with the Southern and Border states. Besides serving interventionist-minded Anglo-Saxon constituents, they disliked the Communist ideology and feared the Russians might attempt to spread their influence elsewhere. The Middle Atlantic delegation, controlled by Democrats, likewise disapproved of the noninterventionist Taft amendment. Since only the Atlantic Ocean separated their section from Europe, they were alarmed over international developments. Several Middle Atlantic senators were staunchly anti-Communist and worried that the Russian attack on Finland would threaten democracy in other European countries. Economically, they considered Finland a good risk because the Scandinavian nation had repaid its World War I debts. Mountain senators, contrary to traditional stereotypes, also opposed the noninterventionist Taft proposal. Primarily Democrats, they supported allocating the full amount for this major New Deal agency (see table 19). Although serving an inland region, they disliked the Communist ideology and believed Soviet expansion endangered the security of the Western world.

On the noninterventionist side, the New England and Pacific senators proportionately directed the campaign for the Taft amendment. Historians usually picture

66. *CR*, 13 February 1940, pp. 1403–4; *New York Times*, 14 February 1940.

both sections as interventionist, but they aligned with the noninterventionists this time.[67] The New England delegation included several conservative Republicans leery of increasing funding for New Deal agencies. The Export-Import Bank primarily had aided Latin American nations, which had not traded primarily with New England states. In addition, noninterventionist Irish constituents viewed the loan as further involving the United States in the European war. Pacific Republicans—most notably Minority Leader McNary of Oregon and Johnson of California—likewise disapproved of granting a New Deal agency any additional financial authority. In that region, German and particularly Russian constituents opposed American economic assistance to a nation engaged in war against their homelands. The Pacific states moreover had traded considerably with Asian nations and did not want to see the United States take any action that might lead to the breaking of diplomatic relations with Russia.

Great Lakes and Great Plains senators, often considered the leading proponents of noninterventionism, divided very sharply. As on neutrality revision, a slight majority of these senators continued to support noninterventionism. A considerable number of Great Lakes and Great Plains members who had advocated retaining the arms embargo, however, aligned with the interventionists on the Taft amendment. Michigan, Wisconsin, and North Dakota legislators represented Scandinavian constituents favoring American intervention this time on the Finnish side. Republicans Vandenberg of Michigan and Lynn J. Frazier of North Dakota, along with Progressive La Follette of Wisconsin, sought reelection in 1940 and hoped to placate the voters at home. Republican Gerald P. Nye of North Dakota originally intended to oppose the measure as "a step toward war" but took a neutral position after receiving numerous letters protesting his position.[68]

Ethnic alignments did not affect the outcome appreciably. No single nationality could have enabled passage of the Taft proposal by voting as a solid bloc. Although usually pictured as noninterventionists, Irish and German senators aligned with the interventionists disapproving of reductions in the lending authority. Besides considering Finland to be a democratic nation, they feared that the totalitarian methods of Communism might spread elsewhere. Farmer-Laborite Lundeen of Minnesota and Democrat Edwin C. Johnson of Colorado, Scandinavians who opposed American involvement in war, favored slicing the original amount. Although sympathetic to Finland, they still opposed American intervention in the European war. Traditional noninterventionist sentiments of their native governments and pacifist clergy, coupled with a desire for the United States to concentrate on resolving economic and

---

67. George L. Grassmuck, Julius Turner, H. Bradford Westerfield, and other scholars describe the New England region as internationalist in the Roosevelt era. The Pacific section is pictured as internationalist by Westerfield; Robert A. Dahl; Duncan Mac Rae, Jr., *Dimensions of Congressional Voting: A Statistical Study of the House of Representatives in the 81st Congress*, p. 276; and Leroy N. Rieselbach, "The Demography of the Congressional Vote on Foreign Aid, 1939–1958," p. 583. Ray A. Billington, Selig Adler, Ralph H. Smuckler, Jeannette P. Nichols, and other scholars stress the Middle West as the core of isolationist strength.

68. Sobel, *Interventionism*, pp. 143–44; *New York Times*, 11 January 1940.

social problems at home, convinced these members to coalesce with the noninterventionists[69] (see table 31).

Economic and ideological forces also contributed to the rejection of the noninterventionist Taft amendment. Since Finland was the only European nation to repay its World War I debts on schedule, several senators remarked that the United States should assist the Scandinavian country in its time of need. Proponents of the Taft amendment, however, countered that the funds should be used to alleviate depressed conditions at home. Ideologically, Finland received considerable support as a democratic nation bravely resisting totalitarian Communist Russia.

Before the Senate completed action, Brown again defended his interventionist measure. American farmers and manufacturers, he insisted, would benefit from the program because the Finns would purchase merchandise in the United States. Denying that the measure violated international law, he stressed that the Havana Convention of 1928 permitted belligerents to use credits to buy noncombat materials. Besides reiterating that Finland had not defaulted on loans to the United States, Brown added that the legislation would assist the Ryti government. ''A vote for this bill,'' he stated, ''is a vote to aid Finland.''[70]

Shortly afterward, the Senate approved the interventionist Brown bill by a 49 to 27 margin, nearly identical to the margin against the Taft amendment. Voting alignments, however, changed considerably this time. Political loyalties declined markedly, with neither major party able to command 75 percent unity. Democrats, despite considerable defections among conservatives, took advantage of their vast numercial superiority to guarantee acceptance of the interventionist Brown measure. Besides hoping to balance the federal budget, some anti-Roosevelt members objected to increasing funding for New Deal agencies. Several Democrats believed federal charity should be doled out instead at home and pointed out that domestic farmers required increased assistance. Republicans were sharply divided on the Brown bill, leaning slightly against the federal loan. Although usually considered a noninterventionist party, nearly one-half aligned with the interventionist camp favoring more federal aid for Finland. Holding staunch anti-Communist sentiments, they feared the Russian seizure might lead to other expansionist efforts elsewhere. Budget-conscious conservatives were impressed that Finland, unlike any other European nation, had not defaulted on World War I loans. A few Republican senators served Scandinavian or Eastern European constituents upset over the Soviet assault (see table 19).

Regional loyalties influenced voting behavior markedly among only the Middle Atlantic and Border delegations. Middle Atlantic members unanimously backed the Brown legislation and aligned with Border senators to provide the interventionists with victory. Both sections were controlled by administration Democrats, primarily were closer geographically to the European conflict, and were anti-Communist. In

69. The ethnic origins of members are derived from Elsdon Coles Smith, *New Dictionary of American Family Names*.

70. *Washington Star*, 14 February 1940; *Grand Rapids Press*, 14 Februay 1940.

addition, the Middle Atlantic states included a variety of Eastern European nationalities suspecting that Stalin might seek to attack other nations. Southern Democrats still leaned toward favoring the loan, but six of the fourteen opposed the interventionist Brown bill. Southern Democrats coalesced to a greater extent with the noninterventionists this time than they had on any other foreign policy roll call at the Seventy-sixth Congress. Besides representing very few Scandinavian constituents, Southern Democrats often urged reducing national expenditures and believed American farmers merited federal assistance more than did the distant Finns[71] (see table 19).

On the noninterventionist side, the Great Plains bloc provided the principal resistance and proportionately was the only delegation furnishing a clear majority against the Brown measure. A predominantly Republican section, the Great Plains distrusted Roosevelt and opposed aiding the Finns through a New Deal agency. Geographically, Great Plains members served an inland area far removed from the European conflict. Besides including German and Russian constituents counseling isolationism, the region depended relatively little on overseas markets for trade. Great Plains senators also urged reducing federal spending abroad and proposed assistance targeted to alleviate depressed agricultural conditions in the United States. They received considerable support from the neighboring Great Lakes senators, who opposed the interventionist Brown bill for similar reasons. On the other hand, the New England and Pacific blocs abandoned the isolationist camp this time and backed the interventionist Export-Import Bank measure (see table 19).

Other considerations affected the outcome. Ideologically, the Scandinavian nation attracted sizeable emotional sympathy from senators as a country valiantly defending its homeland against the Russian onslaught. If the Stalin government launched similar attacks elsewhere, many legislators feared American security would be endangered. Public opinion polls and pro-Finnish newspaper editorials contributed to the Senate acceptance of limited economic assistance. Nationality patterns did not change substantially, continuing to have relatively little impact. Retaining an unusual interventionist posture, Irish and German senators supported making Export-Import Bank loans to Finland (see table 31).

Twenty senators, including fifteen Democrats and five Republicans, did not vote. Several prominent neutrality figures, such as Bailey of North Carolina, Harry F. Byrd of Virginia, Clark of Missouri, Nye of North Dakota, Elbert D. Thomas of Utah, Charles W. Tobey of New Hampshire, and Vandenberg of Michigan, missed both roll calls. Democratic absentees came principally from the South, while Republican absentees served either Great Lakes, Great Plains, or New England constituents.[72]

For the first time, the Senate had approved a measure for limited federal intervention in the European conflict. At the special session, internationalists had authorized indirect military assistance by private American businesses on a cash-and-carry basis. This time the Senate had permitted an executive branch agency to

71. *CR*, 13 February 1940, p. 1404; *New York Times*, 14 February 1940.
72. *CR*, 13 February 1940, p. 1404.

loan money enabling Finland to purchase economic supplies to use in its battle against Russia. On the other hand, the upper chamber had opposed massive federal intervention, denying the Ryti government an opportunity to buy military equipment from the United States.

Most internationalists backed federal intervention in the Finnish case. Forty-six internationalist members, including thirty-eight Democrats and eight New England and Middle Atlantic Republicans who had endorsed neutrality revision, supported the interventionist Export-Import Bank aid. Comprising nearly one-half of the membership, the internationalist-interventionist faction usually represented states east of the Mississippi River. At the special session, they had supported lifting the arms embargo and other internationalist steps to assist the European allies. This time they backed interventionism by endorsing a direct federal loan to a specific European country against an aggressor nation. Several prestigious senators, including Democrat Wagner of New York and Republican Austin of Vermont, belonged to the internationalist-interventionist group. On the other hand, the isolationist-noninterventionist faction continued to diminish numerically. Fourteen members, including seven Democrats, six Republicans, and one third-party man, opposed both the internationalist Pittman and interventionist Brown measures. A more heterogeneous group, they received the largest following, proportionately, in the Great Lakes and Great Plains states. They not only rejected internationalist steps revising neutrality laws, but also disapproved of direct federal intervention against Russia in the Finnish conflict. Noninterventionists were not as influential but did include Republicans Borah of Idaho and Johnson of California. The sudden death in January of Borah, however, left a serious leadership vacuum in the noninterventionist quarter.

Over one-third of the senators had shifted sides. Without support from these influential legislators, majorities could have been secured for either neutrality revision or Finnish assistance. These senators distinguished between internationalism and interventionism, endorsing one and rejecting the other. Fifteen members, mostly serving Southern, Great Lakes, and Great Plains constituents and including senators George of Georgia, Harrison of Mississippi, George W. Norris of Nebraska, and Taft of Ohio, favored arms embargo repeal and opposed direct federal intervention in the specific Finnish case. Eighteen Great Lakes, Great Plains, Mountain, and Pacific senators, led by Vandenberg of Michigan, La Follette of Wisconsin, and Nye of North Dakota, took a more interventionist stance on the credit measure. Despite the outbreak of World War II, they had urged retaining mandatory neutrality legislation toward the European conflict. On the Finnish issue, however, they advocated American intervention against the Soviet Union. Vandenberg was a close friend of Finnish Ambassador Procopé, while La Follette and other members faced reelection campaigns and followed the pro-Finnish views of their constituents.[73]

Despite shifting alignments, Senate voting behavior had resembled neutrality

73. Vandenberg Diary, 30 November 1939; Sobel, *Interventionism*, pp. 136–45, discusses the voting shifts by individual senators.

patterns. Political partisanship continued to play a moderate role, affecting the outcome slightly less this time. Since most delegations did not average 75 percent unity, sectionalism also had diminished in importance. Ideological considerations prevailed in both cases, while economics had become more significant as a determinant. Ethnic groups did not affect the result materially in either instance.

Finnish Ambassador Procopé, who had watched the debate from the gallery, welcomed the limited interventionist Senate action. Following the final tally, Procopé held a press conference. "I am very gratified," he remarked, "at the vote of the Senate. My country will highly appreciate this renewed sign of the sympathy of a great Nation." Upon returning to his Washington home that evening, Procopé wrote Senator Brown of Michigan a laudatory note. "I hope you will allow me to express to you," he commented, "on behalf of my Country and my own name, my sincerest thanks for your efforts and your achievements in favor of Finland, and my very best congratulations to your splendid success."[74]

Interventionist representatives, meanwhile, nearly terminated American relations with the Soviet Union. During debate on the State Department appropriations bill in early February, the Russian army began further penetrating the formidable Mannerheim forces. Several anti-Communists, including Democrat John W. McCormack of Massachusetts and Republican Hamilton Fish of New York, urged punitive action against the Stalin government. McCormack introduced an amendment to delete the $17,500 salary of American Ambassador Laurence Steinhardt, but the House barely rejected 108 to 105 the motion. Since anti-Soviet sentiments were widespread, the McCormack amendment was rejected "only after the Administration had brought pressure to bear upon its supporters in Congress." Majority Leader Sam Rayburn of Texas had warned that the McCormack proposal could provoke further Soviet aggression. "The action here today," Rayburn remarked, "will not help Finland. It will not hurt Russia. It will make a more determined and a more irresistible Russia."[75]

By the middle of February, the Roosevelt administration began exhibiting a less cautious attitude. The decisive Senate approval of the interventionist Brown bill, coupled with the Russian advance in Finland, influenced the executive branch to play a more dynamic role. At Banking and Currency Committee hearings, Federal Loan Administrator Jones insisted that the sooner American economic aid could be given, "the better for our country, the Finns, and everybody else." Jones, on the other hand, stressed that the White House still opposed sending military assistance to the Ryti government.[76]

Democrat Clyde Williams of Missouri directed the interventionist campaign in the House Banking and Currency Committee for the Brown bill. Born on a farm near Grubville, Missouri, he had attended the State Normal School at Cape Girardeau and

74. Hjalmar Procopé to Prentiss M. Brown, 13 February 1940, Box 24, Scrapbooks, Brown Papers. For a comparison of neutrality and Finnish votes, see Sobel, *Interventionism*, pp. 136–44.

75. *CR*, 7 February 1940; *New York Times*, 8 February 1940; David J. Dallin, *Soviet Russia's Foreign Policy, 1939–1942*, p. 179.

76. U.S., Congress, House, Committee on Banking and Currency, "Extension of Lending Authority of Export-Import Bank of Washington," *Hearings*, 16, 19 February 1940.

had graduated from the University of Missouri Law School. After commencing practice in Hillsboro, Missouri, Williams had served as prosecuting attorney for Jefferson County. He was elected in 1926 to the U.S. House of Representatives but was defeated two years later. After returning to the House in 1931, he had supported most New Deal programs and coauthored the Federal Reserve Act. The sixty-six-year-old Missouri Democrat also consistently had backed both the foreign policy and defense programs of President Roosevelt. Besides remaining loyal politically, he believed German expansion jeopardized the safety and democratic institutions of Western Europe and the United States. After the Nazis seized Czechoslovakia in March 1939, he complained that the strict neutrality legislation favored aggressor nations and wanted to grant the president discretionary authority. Williams in June 1939 supported the Bloom bill repealing the arms embargo to belligerent nations. Following the outbreak of World War II, he wholeheartedly endorsed neutrality revision and urged American military assistance to Great Britain and France. Williams championed interventionist Export-Import Bank loans to the Finnish government for political, economic, ideological, and security reasons. Besides seeking to remain loyal to the president, the Missouri Democrat considered the Finns a good financial risk. Economically, Williams believed the loan program would benefit American farmers and help alleviate depressed conditions because the Ryti administration would use the money to purchase American goods. In addition, he lauded the determined Finns for battling bravely to uphold democratic ideals against the spread of Communism and contended that the fall of the Scandinavian country would endanger further the security of the Western world. On the other hand, he advocated economic rather than military assistance to Finland because he did not want to risk breaking American diplomatic relations with the Soviet Union.[77]

Under the direction of Williams, the Banking and Currency Committee steered a moderate interventionist course. The committee on 23 February overwhelmingly approved 18 to 5 the Brown measure after having rejected attempts by both militant interventionists and strict noninterventionists to alter the bill. Led by Progressive Merlin Hull of Wisconsin, ardent interventionists unsuccessfully sought to loan Finland $30 million for the purchase of arms and other commodities. The committee also rejected an attempt by noninterventionist Republican Jessie Sumner of Illinois to slice the proposed lending authority to $50 million. On the other hand, moderate interventionists consented to two changes in the bill. The committee adopted a noninterventionist proposal prohibiting credits to governments defaulting on debts. In an attempt to placate interventionists, Williams's group permitted the sale of commercial airplanes to Finland and other countries.[78]

On this issue, representatives formed three groups. Around one hundred moderate interventionists hoped to preserve the committee version of the bill. Primarily Southern and Border Democrats, they supported the Roosevelt administra-

77. U.S., Congress, *Biographical Directory of the American Congress, 1774–1961 (BDAC)*, p. 1819; *New York Times*, 13 November 1954.

78. U.S., Congress, House of Representatives, Committee on Banking and Currency, "Extension of Lending Authority," *Reports*, no. 1670; *New York Times*, 24 February 1940.

tion's approach of giving Finland limited federal economic assistance. The Scandinavian nation, according to moderate interventionists, was bravely defending its democratic form of government against the spread of Communism. An economy-minded group, they viewed the Finnish administration as a good risk likely to honor its financial obligations. Southern and Border states also praised the accomplishments of the Export-Import Bank, which often had made loans to Latin American nations. Due to this financial assistance, Latin American countries had increased their volume of trade with both Southern and Border states. On the other hand, moderate interventionists opposed selling arms and ammunition to Finland or other victims of aggression. Besides representing comparatively few ethnic groups, they interpreted Eastern European developments as less vital to American security than those directly affecting either Great Britain or France. Banking and Currency Committee member Williams of Missouri directed the floor fight for this faction.

Around fifty representatives were more militant interventionists. Denying that the Brown bill would provide substantial relief, they included numerous Democrats favoring arms embargo repeal and several New England, Middle Atlantic, Great Lakes, and Great Plains isolationists. A heterogeneous group, they preferred a direct credit enabling the Finns to purchase combat supplies. Militant internationalists believed Finland required armaments and ammunition at once to resist the Russian onslaught. By late February, the Soviet army was penetrating the Finnish resistance and threatening to occupy the entire Scandinavian nation. If the United States supplied immediate military assistance, these senators argued, the Ryti government might avert such a takeover. Many militant interventionists were ardent anti-Communists who lauded Finland as a democratic nation valiantly resisting the totalitarian aggression. If the Communists controlled Finland, the militant interventionists argued, the security of Western Europe and possibly the United States would be jeopardized. They also believed that Finland would continue to honor all financial obligations. Several traditional isolationists, particularly from the upper Great Lakes and Great Plains, came from districts containing numerous Scandinavians urging American military assistance to Finland. Democrats Emanuel Celler of New York and Dingell of Michigan joined Republicans Fish of New York and Charles A. Eaton of New Jersey in determining floor strategy for this faction.

Of the four representatives, Eaton came from the most varied background. A native of Nova Scotia, Canada, the seventy-one-year-old Eaton had earned degrees from Acadia University, McMaster University, and Newton Theological Seminary. Eaton had served twenty-seven years as a Baptist minister, holding pastorates in Natick, Massachusetts; Toronto, Ontario; Cleveland, Ohio; and New York City. To supplement his income, he had been a correspondent for several urban newspapers and magazines. Eaton also had written two religious works and delivered incisive, witty sociological lectures. In 1919, he had resigned as pastor of the Madison Avenue Baptist Church in New York City and became director of industrial relations for the General Electric Company in New Jersey. Six years later, the Republican had joined the U.S. House of Representatives from New Jersey. Although an anti-New Dealer, he acted less isolationist on foreign policy measures than did most of his

Republican colleagues. Eaton, a dynamic personality, usually had supported both American international and defense commitments. During World War I, he backed American intervention against Germany and delivered numerous speeches defending the Allied cause and the preservation of democracy against totalitarianism. "If the war has decided any issue," he remarked, "it is that the whole world must adopt the principle of democracy in the entirety of its life." Eaton headed the National Service Section of the United States Shipping Board and worked toward increasing the production of ships. Unlike most Republicans, he defended an internationalist policy in the 1930s as an active member of the powerful Foreign Affairs Committee. He opposed the strict neutrality legislation of the mid-1930s, preferring instead for the United States to rely on international law and freedom of the seas as guiding principles. The Neutrality Act of 1937, the New Jersey Republican complained, did not safeguard American neutral rights and placed too many restraints on American commerce. Eaton, who insisted that domestic economic welfare depended heavily on other nations, warned that the cash-and-carry system would cause severe problems for the shipping industry. The Neutrality Act, he also claimed, would hinder the industrialists and shippers of his home state of New Jersey and would encourage Nazi aggression in Europe. At the special session in 1939, he aligned with internationalists rejecting the Vorys and Shanley amendments to restore the arms embargo. Eaton, however, disapproved of the Neutrality Act of 1939 and still preferred depending on international law. After Russia attacked Finland, the New Jersey Republican urged Congress to provide military assistance to the Scandinavian nation. He particularly considered the spread of Communism a threat to the life of democratic institutions in the Western world. The Finns, he also stressed, needed federal intervention quickly because they faced overwhelming odds against the powerful Russians. Eastern industrialists and shipping interests, Eaton believed, would benefit from a military loan because the Ryti government would spend the money to buy American defense products. The New Jersey Republican moreover was impressed that Finland, unlike other European nations, had repaid its World War I obligations on schedule.[79]

At the other extreme, fifty to seventy noninterventionists attacked the Brown bill as too committal. Basically Great Lakes and Great Plains Republicans, they had disapproved of arms embargo repeal and vigorously opposed American entry into the European conflict. Noninterventionists usually favored balancing the federal budget and therefore had protested increased financing for the Export-Import Bank and other Roosevelt New Deal agencies. In addition, they served a region geographically more remote and insulated from the European conflict. Although anti-Communist, they denied that Russian aggression endangered the security of the United States or the Western Hemisphere. The Great Lakes and Great Plains states, which had a sizeable number of Russian and particularly German groups opposing American entry into World War II, also had relied less than the New England and

79. "Charles A. Eaton," *Current Biography* 6 (1945):163–64; *BDAC*, p. 884. Robert A. Divine, *The Illusion of Neutrality*, p. 188.

Middle Atlantic regions upon European trade. Congress, some Great Lakes and Great Plains representatives holding progressive views insisted, should increase federal spending to solve domestic problems rather than authorize loans to distant lands.

In this instance, Republican Sumner of Illinois directed the noninterventionist strategy. A native of Milford, Illinois, a town eighty miles south of Chicago, she was the daughter of a wealthy banker and a descendant of former President Zachary Taylor and Massachusetts Sen. Charles Sumner. After earning an economics degree from Smith College, Sumner had taken law courses at the University of Chicago, Oxford University, and Columbia University and had studied business at New York University and the University of Wisconsin. Sumner, who never married, had practiced law for several years in Chicago and then had worked for Chase National Bank in New York City. She had returned to Milford to practice law and had defeated two male opponents for the Iroquois County judgeship left vacant by the death of her uncle, thus becoming the first woman county judge in state history. With strong editorial support from the the *Chicago Tribune*, she had been elected to the U.S. House of Representatives in 1938 from a predominantly Republican district. The chubby, gregarious, blue-eyed, fast-talking, witty blonde exhibited enormous physical and emotional energy on the Banking and Currency Committee. She deplored the New Deal policies of the president, whom she referred to in speeches as "Papa Roosevelt." A rabid isolationist, the Illinois Republican insisted that Roosevelt already had gained too much power and opposed granting him discretionary authority to determine aggressors. Sumner shared the *Chicago Tribune*'s view that Roosevelt deliberately was leading the nation into World War II. She denied that German expansion in Europe threatened American security, since the Atlantic Ocean adequately protected the United States. During 1939, Sumner vigorously opposed repeal of the arms embargo and any other changes in the strict neutrality legislation. On the Finnish issue, the Illinois Republican stood at the forefront of noninterventionists rejecting the Brown bill. The staunchly anti-Roosevelt Republican disapproved of funding New Deal agencies that might embroil the United States in overseas conflicts. Since the federal government already was spending too much money at home, she adamantly resisted extending financial commitments abroad. An exponent of noninterventionism, she did not believe that the spread of the European war endangered American safety. Sumner, although anti-Communist, also did not want the United States to provoke Russia into launching additional adventures.[80]

On the eve of House debate, meanwhile, Brown on 26 February delivered another nationwide radio address. By this time the Russian army had begun to penetrate the Mannerheim line in southeastern Finland. Brown still favored providing massive combat assistance but ruled this step out, contending, "There is no doubt but that a loan for military purposes, for the purchase of munitions of war,

---

80. "Jessie Sumner," *Current Biography* 6 (1945):579–81; Hope Chamberlin, *A Minority of Members: Women in the U.S. Congress*, pp. 157–60.

would be a violation of international law." On the other hand, Brown stressed that the Havana Agreement of 1928 permitted the United States to provide transportation, communications, food, clothing, medicine, and other nonmilitary supplies. Deploring the Russian attack on Finland, he lauded the Mannerheim army for battling against overwhelming odds. "Without the slightest provocation," Brown remarked, "this modern barbarian power . . . launched its attack in the dead of winter." In regard to Finland, he commented, "Their stand has aroused the admiration of the world." The Michigan Democrat urged the United States to intervene as much as possible to assist the brave Finns in their battle against Communist domination. Unless the House approved the interventionist bill quickly, Brown warned, the Stalin regime might launch further aggression. "But let the unholy doctrine of these Communists who control the most extensive country in the world, with a population of 180,000,000 succeed in Finland," he cautioned, "and then it is but a step to Sweden, to Norway, and to Denmark." Believing "Finland now holds the front for Christendom," he remarked, "let not powerful America fail them."[81]

During the two-day floor debate, interventionists again defended the loan on ideological grounds. Moderates and militants pictured Finland as a bastion for freedom and individual liberties struggling against totalitarian aggression. "There has not been," Fish of New York claimed, "a more dastardly, abominable, or treacherous attack in recent history." Fish urged the United States to help the Scandinavian nation "defend its liberties, its independence, and its freedom against Communism," while Republican William A. Pittenger of Minnesota added that the Ryti government was "fighting our battle—the battle of civilization against communism." Pittenger insisted the Roosevelt administration should terminate diplomatic relations with Russia and refuse to ship any goods the Soviet Union might use militarily against Finland.[82] Moderate interventionists supported the economic assistance, but the militant wing preferred permitting Finland to purchase military materials. "We restrict the loan," Dingell of Michigan complained, "for powder puffs, silken scanty panties, and for cream puffs, when we know the Finns need shrapnel, buckshot, barbed wire, and all the fiercest instruments of hell because they are fighting to stop anti-Christ and the hosts of hell." Similarly, Eaton of New Jersey protested, "We hide behind a barricade of sentimental twaddle, of cringing cowardice, and political flim flamism that is absolutely disgraceful."[83]

Militant interventionists also backed the loan for security, economic, and legal reasons. Citing the Scandinavian experience, they warned that the Stalin government might attempt to spread the Communist ideology to Western Europe and to the United States. Finland's "annihilation," Republican Harold Knutson of Minnesota warned, "would completely change the situation all over Europe, giving the totalitarian states complete control, not only over the Baltic Sea but over northern Europe

81. Brown Radio Address, 26 February 1940.
82. *CR*, 27 February 1940, pp. 2036–37, 2074, Appendix, p. 1042.
83. *CR*, 28 February 1940, pp. 2105, 2107.

and in the Balkans as well.'' Democrat Adolph J. Sabath of Illinois, a native of Czechoslovakia, argued that the interventionist measure would help revive American commerce, agriculture, and employment, while Republican Robert B. Chiperfield of Illinois contended that the legislation would not violate either the Neutrality Act or international law. Since neither Russia nor Finland had declared war, he explained, the Neutrality Act would not be applicable. In addition, Chiperfield noted that the measure did not contravene international law because it specifically prohibited sending military supplies.[84]

Ideological and economic themes were highlighted by the noninterventionists. Besides disapproving of further American involvement abroad, noninterventionists feared that Export-Import Bank loans would increase the already rising national debt. Sumner of Illinois insisted, ''The people have tried to make it very plain that they do not want to finance another foreign war purely to defend principles of democracy.'' Foreign aid, Democrat John E. Rankin of Mississippi predicted, would plunge the United States into ''another holocaust of destruction, probably costing us millions of men and billions of dollars.''[85] Noninterventionists also argued that charity should begin at home. ''We have run into debt,'' Republican Joshua L. Johns of Wisconsin noted, ''at the rate of over $10,000,000 a day since we started this fiscal year.'' According to Democrat Lee Geyer of California, the money should be allocated ''to assist our own unemployed, our small business man, our small farmer, our four million unemployed youth, our aged persons who need assistance, and our needy veterans.''[86]

Republican noninterventionists also dwelled on political and legal issues. The Brown measure, they contended, would centralize authority in Washington and discriminate against business corporations. Conservative Fred L. Crawford of Michigan argued against creating ''any more Government lending agencies or adding to their capital structure so they can compete with private industry.'' Although the Brown bill was intended to assist Finland, noninterventionists were alarmed that the power of the Export-Import Bank would increase. James E. Van Zandt of Pennsylvania termed the Brown legislation ''a request for a New Deal agency to grab an additional $100,000,000 of the American taxpayers' money and disburse same at their own pleasure under the guise of aiding war-torn Finland.''[87] Andrew C. Schiffler of West Virginia urged that Neutrality Act restrictions be applied to the Russo-Finnish conflict, while Vorys of Ohio stressed that lawyers considered a federal loan an illegal action that could provoke Soviet reprisals and thus recommended that Americans instead donate to the Hoover fund.[88]

On 28 February, moderate interventionists steered the measure through the House unscathed. By a decisive 82 to 35 margin, the House rejected a motion by Fish of New York to loan the Ryti government $20 million for the purchase of military

84. *CR*, 27 February 1940, pp. 2034, 2058, 2060, 2064.
85. *CR*, 28 February 1940, pp. 2112, 2102.
86. *CR*, 27 February 1940, p. 2078, 28 February 1940, p. 2109.
87. *CR*, 27 February 1940, pp. 2064, 2072.
88. *CR*, 29 January 1940, Appendix, p. 402, 27 February 1940, p. 2040.

equipment. To the dismay of the militant interventionists, the representatives also decisively defeated 106 to 49 an amendment by Democrat William Miller of Connecticut to remove restrictions on exporting combat equipment. Moderates allied with noninterventionists to prevent federal credits to any governments defaulting on financial obligations. In anticlimactic fashion, the House easily approved 168 to 51 the Brown measure.[89]

For the first time, the House had adopted legislation for limited federal intervention in the European conflict. Representatives in late 1939 had permitted private American industries to provide military aid to the Allies on an indirect cash-and-carry system. Congressmen this time had authorized an agency of the executive branch to loan money to the Ryti government to be used for purchasing nonmilitary supplies in its war against the Soviet Union. Although rejecting military aid, representatives were more receptive to direct, limited federal intervention in Finland than they had been to repeal of the arms embargo.

No roll-call votes were conducted. Numerous congressmen probably did not wish to have their official views recorded and left their constituents unclear as to how they had voted. The mixed attitude of the House members also may have been reflected in the absenteeism, which incredibly exceeded 50 percent on the Brown measure. Numerous representatives were undecided about what type of federal assistance, if any, the Finnish government should receive.

Within a week, the interventionist Brown bill became law. As on neutrality, a conference committee reconciled differences between the Senate and House versions. The House Banking and Currency Committee had amended the interventionist bill by permitting the Export-Import Bank to finance the purchase of commercial airplanes and by prohibiting advances to debt-defaulting nations. House conferees consented to delete the airplane section, thus preventing the Ryti government from receiving any assistance convertible to military use. Conferees quickly sent the Brown bill to the White House, where the president on 2 March immediately signed it. Following a different procedure than he had after the special session, however, Roosevelt did not invite any congressmen or photographers to witness the event.[90]

The interventionist Brown Act, although doubling the capital of the Export-Import Bank from $100 million to $200 million, had several major restrictions. Neither Finland nor any other country could receive additional loans exceeding $20 million. The loans could not be used to purchase military supplies or to otherwise violate either international law or the Neutrality Act of 1939. In addition, the legislation prevented credits from being made to any country defaulting on debts at the time of the Johnson Act of 1934.

American economic intervention fell short of what Finland needed. The Ryti government, even though grateful for American sympathy and help, was disappointed that the credits could not be used to buy military equipment. They also protested that the United States continued to ship large quantities of gasoline and

89. *CR*, 28 February 1940, pp. 2103–16; *New York Times*, 29 February 1940.
90. *New York Times*, 1, 3 March 1940; Sobel, *Interventionism*, p. 130.

other war materials to the Soviet Union. Although disliking the restrictions of the Brown Act, the Ryti administration received some military assistance from private American business firms. By 21 February, the Finns had ordered $5.5 million in armaments, including 44 fighter planes, 176 machine guns, 60 million cartridges, and spare parts for aircraft.[91]

During late February, however, Finland began peace negotiations with the Soviet Union. The Russian army was defeating the Mannerheim forces, compelling the Finnish commander to signal the Ryti government to seek an end to hostilities. Although the Allies had promised to assist the Finnish troops, Mannerheim concluded that the aid would not come for at least one more month and probably would not be sufficient to defeat the formidable Soviet army. On 12 March, the Ryti administration capitulated to the Russians and signed a peace treaty at Moscow. Finland ceded 25,000 square miles of territory, including the entire Karelian Isthmus, its second largest city, several islands in the Gulf of Finland, and vast northern territory. The Soviet Union received a thirty-year lease to the port at Hanko but consented to remove its forces from the Petsamo area. Besides losing 12 percent of its population, mainly in the Karelian area, 18,000 Finns were killed, 40,000 wounded, and there was incalculable physical damage. In sum, the treaty subjected the Finns strategically to the whims of the Soviet Union and the Stalin regime.[92]

These developments both surprised and dismayed most Americans. The mass media, particularly newspapers, had led people to believe that the Mannerheim army was waging successful counterattacks against the Soviet forces and was defending the Scandinavian country. Since Americans still refused to believe that Mannerheim's troops had lost the war, they attributed the outcome partly to the ineffectiveness of the Ryti government and its diplomatic corps. In addition, they concluded that the Roosevelt administration, Congress, and the Allies had provided too little assistance too late to prevent a Soviet takeover. Americans also began to realize, however, that they had expressed much sympathy and given relatively little concrete aid to the Scandinavian nation and thus tried to compensate in subsequent months. Fighting Funds for Finland collected money to help rebuild the Finnish army, the Export-Import Bank funds still were made available, and Senator Brown proposed another $20 million loan to Finland. Despite these overtures, the Finnish government began to turn elsewhere for assistance. Most Finns desired revenge against the Soviet Union and backed the Nazis in June 1941, when Germany attacked Russia.[93]

The Finnish capitulation saddened the entire Congress. Senators and representatives lauded the Scandinavians' bravery and courage in fighting against both overwhelming odds and the potent Soviet army. On 4 March, Senator Vandenberg wrote his close friend Ambassador Procopé:

Your gloriously brave little country has won the war and lost the peace—and

91. Schwartz, *Russo-Finnish War*, pp. 24–25; *New York Times*, 3 March 1940.
92. Max Beloff, *The Foreign Policy of Soviet Russia*, 2:147; Schwartz, *Russo-Finnish War*, pp. 33–34. For an overview, see William L. Langer and S. Everett Gleason, *The Challenge to Isolation, 1937–1940*, pp. 329–42.
93. Sobel, *Interventionism*, pp. 164–66, 170.

lost it only because of the inevitable pressure of an enormously outnumbering foe. But as long as written history survives, Finland's heroic defense of her birth-right will be one of the epics of human courage. There is nothing comparable in the story of a thousand years.

Most legislators, including Vandenberg, were confident that the Finns ultimately would regain independence from Russian control. Vandenberg predicted, "The fortitude which magnificently faced the unholy and unequal challenge of the battle line will rise above the burdens of this unhappy and inhuman outcome, biding the day when God's justice will prevail."[94]

Congress had made a moderate interventionist response to a highly emotional issue. The Brown Act did not constitute a complete victory for either the interventionists or the noninterventionists. Interventionists interpreted the adoption of the Export-Import Bank legislation as a sign that the United States was ready to take a more active role in the European conflict, while noninterventionists stressed that the loans could not be used for military purposes. Although the economic assistance fell short of what many desired, the Brown Act reflected the pro-Finnish and anti-Russian sentiments of the American people. The loan was presented in emotional and ideological terms, thus diminishing the effectiveness of the noninterventionists in resisting federal aid to Finland. On the other hand, the amorphous nature of, and the various limitations in, the Brown Act rendered the measure ineffective in aiding Finland. Despite sympathizing with the Scandinavian nation, Congress did not provide the military assistance the Mannerheim army needed to wage a successful resistance against the powerful Russian forces. The Stalin regime did not even protest the Brown Act, realizing the Roosevelt administration was not anxious to take any action disrupting diplomatic relations.

Above all, the Brown Act made much more impact on the United States than on the Russo-Finnish conflict. The congressional response marked the first specific example of direct American intervention in the European conflict to help one specific belligerent against an aggressor nation. Although Congress had shifted to internationalism at the special session, it had not enacted direct interventionist legislation on behalf of a particular European country. Following the outbreak of World War II, most internationalist senators and representatives had seen neutrality revision as a means of keeping the United States out of the European conflict rather than of intervening on behalf of either Great Britain or France. Arms embargo repeal was an internationalist action considerably aiding the Allies, but the cash-and-carry restrictions prevented the United States from transporting goods to Allies and intervening directly in the European war. Neutrality revision permitted private business firms to sell arms to belligerents, while the Brown Act for the first time authorized a particular federal agency to intervene directly against an aggressor nation in World War II.

In the final analysis, the Roosevelt administration and the legislative branch shared responsibility for the ineffective assistance given to Finland. Despite the

94. Arthur H. Vandenberg to Hjalmar Procopé, 4 March 1940, 1939–1940, Vandenberg Papers.

multifaceted effort by Senator Brown, neither the president nor Congress answered the real needs of the Finns. Roosevelt should have provided more direct leadership from the outset and recommended legislation authorizing military help to the Ryti government. Since public opinion overwhelmingly supported the Scandinavians, Congress probably would have approved an unrestricted loan. Although American economic assistance did not thwart the Russian army, Congress had expanded on the internationalist pattern established at the special session. Vocal isolationists no longer controlled the legislative branch and could not block limited American intervention in specific European conflicts.

6

The Campaign for Preparedness

During the spring of 1940, Congress entered a fourth phase characterized by the most extensive peacetime preparedness campaign in American history. After a period of relative calm on the European scene, Hitler in the spring suddenly attacked Scandinavia and the Low Countries. By early summer, German armies had conquered France and prepared to assault Great Britain by air. The legislative branch quickly approved over $8 billion in emergency appropriations for defense facilities, equipment, ammunition, airplanes, and ships. Besides unanimously approving a 70 percent increase in naval strength, the House and Senate permitted the purchase of 4,000 planes and 200 new fighting vessels, the expansion of shipbuilding facilities, and the development of a two-ocean fleet. They also overwhelmingly adopted a record peacetime army supply bill, whereby the army could procure tanks, guns, artillery, and ammunition for 2 million troops and 15,000 planes.[1] "Congress," Democrat Carter Glass of Virginia remarked, "has made vaster appropriations than ever before in history for national defense." Anti-New Dealers, along with isolationists and noninterventionists, even backed the rapid increase in arms spending. If "we do not go as far as we can in building up our own defense," Republican John Taber of New York warned, we "are going to be the next easy victim for the dictator nations."[2] Other preparedness issues, such as peacetime selective service, however, provoked much more intense controversy.

On the selective service issue, congressional focus changed from a debate between interventionists and noninterventionists to one involving preparedness advocates and rearmament opponents. During early 1940, the interventionists and noninterventionists had clashed over American foreign policy toward the Russo-Finnish War and over to what extent, if any, the federal government should aid the Risto Ryti government. Interventionists had supported either military or at least economic assistance to Finland, while the noninterventionists had opposed executive branch aid to the Scandinavian country. The nature of the debate changed in the spring and summer of 1940, when the legislative branch switched attention to defense manpower recruitment policies. Congress debated whether to retain voluntary enlistment for recruiting soldiers or to implement the first peacetime draft in American history. Preparedness advocates urged the United States to help defend against the Axis expansion by adopting conscription of soldiers. On the other hand, rearmament opponents preferred that the army continue relying on voluntary enlist-

1. For background on international and congressional developments, see Robert A. Divine, *The Reluctant Belligerent: American Entry into World War II*, and William L. Langer and S. Everett Gleason, *The Challenge to Isolation, 1937–1940*.

2. Carter Glass to Henry Taylor, 14 May 1940, Box 384, Carter Glass Papers; John Taber to Caspar Gregory, 20 June 1940, Box 67, John Taber Papers.

ments and did not want to take any action risking further American involvement in the European war.

At this time, the United States Army was ill prepared to handle changing European developments. The American army, including the National Guard, comprised slightly more than 500,000 troops. Chief of Staff Gen. George Catlett Marshall advocated an army of over 2 million soldiers, but voluntary enlistments had dropped markedly. Besides being unable to handle a possible invasion by the Axis powers, the military force lacked adequate manpower to protect Latin America. The army had only one fully armored unit available and needed to prepare as quickly as possible to meet rapidly changing conditions abroad.[3]

Initial impetus for the draft came from a pressure group. The Military Training Camps Association, comprising World War I officers, had trained 100,000 soldiers at Plattsburg, New York, for involvement in World War I. Graduates of Ivy League schools, the officers subsequently had become prominent lawyers, doctors, and businessmen in New England and Middle Atlantic states. On 8 May 1940, nine association members met at the Harvard Club in New York City to organize the twenty-fifth anniversary celebration of the Plattsburg camps. At the meeting, distinguished Manhattan lawyer Grenville Clark proposed that the MTCA launch a preparedness campaign for compulsory military training and service. Believing that Germany was endangering the security of Western Europe, the Plattsburgers welcomed the idea.[4]

Clark was asked to direct the MTCA preparedness campaign. Fifty-seven years old, Clark had grown up in an aristocratic family and graduated from Harvard University and Harvard Law School. In 1906 he had joined Root, Clark, Buckner, and Ballantine, one of the largest and most prestigious American firms. According to U.S. Supreme Court Justice Felix Frankfurter, Clark was "a man of independence, financially and politically, who devotes himself as hard to public affairs as private citizen as he would were he in public service." An advocate of conservation, Negro rights, academic freedom, veterans legislation, and judicial reform, he had appeared "in critical or confusing times, as a lobby for particular impulses of the national conscience." Clark avoided the limelight, conducting his public activities as an independent critic whenever the need arose. A rugged six-footer, he was a close friend of President Franklin D. Roosevelt and numerous other leading federal officials.

For over two decades, Clark had exhibited interest in military preparedness. During World War I, he had assisted Gen. Leonard Wood in organizing Military Instruction Camps for Business and Professional Men at Plattsburg, New York.

3. William E. Leuchtenburg, *Franklin D. Roosevelt and the New Deal, 1932–1940*, pp. 306–7.

4. John G. Clifford, "Grenville Clark and the Origins of Selective Service," pp. 17–19. For background on selective service, see John Garry Clifford, *The Citizen Soldiers: The Plattsburg Training Camp Movement*, and Martin L. Fausold, *James W. Wadsworth, Jr.: The Gentleman from New York*, pp. 112–23. The principal works on the Selective Service Act of 1940 are Samuel R. Spencer, Jr., "A History of the Selective Training and Service Act of 1940 from Inception to Enactment" (Ph.D. diss.), and John Joseph O'Sullivan, "From Voluntarism to Conscription: Congress and Selective Service, 1940–1945" (Ph.D. diss.).

After the sinking of the *Lusitania* in May 1915, Clark and other Ivy League professionals had trained nearly 100,000 officers for military duty in Western Europe. Plattsburgers performed distinguished combat service in France, receiving military honors at the battles of Argonne and Belleau Wood. Clark and other Plattsburgers retained their memberships in the MTCA after the war and assisted the army in recruiting personnel aged eighteen to twenty-four for the Citizens Military Training Camps. In addition, Clark often met with other MTCA members at luncheons in New York City to discuss world affairs. He was alarmed over Hitler's aggression across Europe and urged the United States to provide military assistance to Great Britain. Since the Nazis threatened the security of the Western Hemisphere, Clark insisted the War Department should at once intensify rearmament efforts. Shortly before Germany launched a blitzkrieg through the Low Countries, Clark on 8 May 1940 proposed that the Plattsburgers launch a preparedness campaign for legislation enacting peacetime selective service. He denied that voluntary enlistments could meet American defense requirements and instead recommended that the War Department draft soldiers as the quickest and most effective means of raising and training troops for possible combat duty.[5]

MTCA preparedness activity quickly intensified on several fronts. A policy committee framed a resolution depicting the peacetime draft as "the only means that will suffice to protect this country in the present world emergency." On 22 May, Clark, former Secretary of State Henry L. Stimson, Gen. John McCauley Palmer, and ninety-seven other organization members gathered at the Harvard Club. These preparedness advocates vigorously supported a compulsory military service measure and designated *New York Times* Vice-president Julius Ochs Adler to head a subcommittee to write legislation.[6]

During May, the MTCA also sought endorsements of selective service from President Roosevelt and the War Department. Clark on 16 May wired Roosevelt about the "absolute necessity of compulsory military training now," but the president preferred voluntary recruitment methods. Although conceding that "a very strong public opinion" advocated "universal service of some kind," Roosevelt on 18 May replied that the peacetime draft was a "political question."[7] Since the president was contemplating a possible third-term candidacy, he cautiously avoided making any verbal or written commitment. A pragmatist, Roosevelt also did not want to alienate Americans on this controversial question. MTCA officials twice met in late May in Washington with Chief of Staff Marshall and urged him to back peacetime selective service. Although recognizing that the army needed trained manpower quickly, Marshall indicated that the draft would not be used unless Congress declared war. Unless the president supported selective service publicly, Marshall declined to endorse the MTCA preparedness approach.[8]

    5. Clifford, "Clark," pp. 17–19.
    6. Ibid., pp. 19–21.
    7. Grenville Clark to Franklin D. Roosevelt, 16 May 1940, Series IX, Box 6, Grenville Clark Papers; Elliott Roosevelt, ed., *FDR: His Personal Letters, 1928–1945*, 2:1026.
    8. Clifford, "Clark," pp. 22–23; Forrest G. Pogue, *George C. Marshall: Ordeal and Hope*,

Initial lobbying activities on Capitol Hill also were fruitless. On 31 May, Clark visited Democrat James F. Byrnes of South Carolina and outlined MTCA preparedness plans. "You're wasting your time," Byrnes remarked, because "no such bill can get through the Senate" in peacetime and in an election year. Unless Roosevelt announced support, Byrnes warned, less than one-third of the senators would vote for selective service.[9]

In early June, Clark attempted to draft a bill with Maj. Lewis Hershey of the War Department. Clark proposed registering all males between ages eighteen and sixty-five and making all men between twenty-one and forty-five liable for military duty. He also recommended training inductees for six months and paying recruits five dollars monthly plus any travel expenses. Hershey, however, did not believe Congress would accept such a comprehensive measure. Besides limiting draftees to the ages of twenty-one to thirty-one, Hershey suggested preparing soldiers for eighteen months and paying them the same twenty-one dollars monthly remuneration given to enlistees. Although meeting several times, Clark and Hershey could not agree on a common version.[10]

The MTCA still sought to secure backing from the cautious president. After Italy attacked France on 10 June, Clark wired Roosevelt that compulsory military training was "absolutely essential for our integrity and institutions." Clark wanted an appointment with the president, but the latter politely declined. At a press conference on 16 June, Roosevelt instead proposed mandatory vocational training for American youth.[11]

Several MTCA members, including Clark, sought to find congressional sponsors for a selective service bill. Since the legislative branch planned to adjourn 21 June for the national political conventions, the lobbyists had to move quickly. On the Senate side, MTCA members visited the offices of Republican Henry Cabot Lodge, Jr., of Massachusetts, conservative Democrat Millard E. Tydings of Maryland, and New Deal Democrat Kenneth D. McKellar of Tennessee. Of the three members, only Lodge initially expressed even mild interest in introducing such preparedness legislation. Tydings, stressing the same theme as Byrnes of South Carolina, preferred not to endorse the rearmament measure until Roosevelt and the American people accepted selective service. McKellar, meanwhile, did not have time to discuss the issue with MTCA lobbyists.[12]

Clark's group still did not have a definite Senate sponsor. On 20 June, Clark

1939–1942, pp. 57–58; Mark S. Watson, *Chief of Staff, Prewar Plans and Preparations*, pp. 190–91; Spencer, "Selective Training and Service Act," pp. 92–96.

9. "Byrnes," n.d., Series IX, Part B, Box 1, Clark Papers.

10. Spencer, "Selective Training and Service Act," pp. 136–39.

11. Grenville Clark to Franklin D. Roosevelt, 10 June 1940, Official Files (OF) 1413, Box 7, Franklin D. Roosevelt Papers; Grenville Clark to Edwin Watson, 14 June 1940, Edwin Watson to Grenville Clark, 15 June 1940, Series IX, Box 6, Clark Papers; *New York Times*, 17 June 1940.

12. Grenville Clark to John McAuley Palmer, 17 June 1940, Series IX, Box 6, Henry Cabot Lodge, Jr., to Grenville Clark, 22 June 1940, Grenville Clark to Henry Cabot Lodge, Jr., 27 June 1940, Series IX, Box 4, Samuel R. Spencer, Jr., Interviews with Edward R. Burke, 8 July 1947, with Julius Ochs Adler, 10 July 1947, and with Philip Carroll, 31 July 1947, Series IX, Parts A, B, Box 1, Clark Papers.

invited Democrat Edward R. Burke of Nebraska to join Lodge in introducing the preparedness bill. Burke, who already had been defeated in an April primary for renomination, gladly consented. A native of Running Water, South Dakota, the fifty-nine-year-old Burke had graduated from Beloit College and played tackle on the football team. After studying at Harvard Law School, he had joined the air service in World War I. Burke had developed a successful practice in corporation law in Omaha, Nebraska, where he was active in the American Bar Association. In 1932 the Democrat had been elected to the U.S. House of Representatives and initially backed Roosevelt's domestic policies. After moving to the U.S. Senate in 1935, Burke opposed both the president's Supreme Court reorganization plan and his labor legislation. Burke had further alienated Roosevelt by seeking a constitutional amendment limiting a chief executive to one six-year term in office. On the other hand, he let domestic differences with the White House stop at the water's edge and supported both the president's internationalist and defense programs. Unlike a majority of Great Plains senators, he stressed that American security depended on British and French supremacy in Western Europe. German aggression, he contended, not only threatened democratic institutions in Western Europe, but also jeopardized the safety of the Western Hemisphere. The Nebraska Democrat viewed the strict neutrality laws of the mid-1930s as discriminatory acts favoring the Allies against Germany. Shortly after the outbreak of World War II, Burke delivered one of the most candid internationalist speeches of the entire Senate debate in urging repeal of the arms embargo. "I see no justification," he remarked, "for permitting a law to stand that favors Hitlerism." Burke particularly supported the Pittman bill because it would "go far toward winning victory for the European democracies." During the late 1930s, the Nebraska Democrat also insisted upon strengthening both the army and navy and especially favored intensification of manpower recruitment. Burke argued that voluntary methods were not securing enough enlistees to fulfill defense needs and pictured peacetime selective service as the most effective and quickest way to raise an army. Along with other preparedness advocates, he recalled how the United States had sent numerous unprepared soldiers to fight on the European battlefield in World War I and wanted to begin training more troops at an earlier date this time.[13]

Buoyed by Burke's cooperation, Clark immediately telephoned Lodge's office. Since the Massachusetts Republican was not there, Clark left a message hoping Lodge still would cosponsor the measure. Lodge's secretary, however, misunderstood Clark and told her boss Burke would serve as sole sponsor. The Massachusetts senator erroneously concluded that the MTCA had decided to bypass him in introducing the legislation. "I had formed a favorable opinion of it," Lodge wrote Clark two days later, "and was interested in pursuing the matter further without delay—when your message arrived. I trust that the change in procedure which you finally adopted will be satisfactory to you and productive of good results." In retrospect, Lodge may not have been the best salesman for selective service because

13. Spencer Interview with Burke, 8 July 1947; "Edward Raymond Burke," *Current Biography* 1 (1940):125–26.

he favored limiting the draft to eligible men between ages nineteen and twenty-three.[14]

Clark accordingly dropped plans to seek bipartisan cosponsors. In order to avoid any further delay, Clark asked Burke to introduce the MTCA preparedness proposal. Burke, who liked the idea of having a major bill named after him, quickly consented. Around noon Burke introduced the first peacetime selective service legislation in American history. The Burke rearmament measure required registration of an estimated 40 million men between ages twenty-one and forty-five eligible for an eight-month training period. Clergymen, industrial and agricultural employees considered vital to the national interest, and those either with dependents or considered unfit were exempted.[15]

On the House side, MTCA lobbyists encountered little difficulty in finding a sponsor. Upon the recommendation of William Chadbourne, the MTCA asked New York Republican James W. Wadsworth to introduce the preparedness bill. The son of a gentleman farmer and national Republican politician, sixty-two-year-old Wadsworth had been born in Geneseo, New York, and had attended a prep school in Southboro, Massachusetts. After graduation from Yale University, he had raised livestock on a 14,000-acre farm near Geneseo. He had belonged to the New York State Assembly and subsequently had served two terms in the U.S. Senate. Although defeated in 1926 by Democrat Robert F. Wagner, the six-foot, 170-pound Wadsworth had returned to Washington in 1933 as a member of the House of Representatives. The wealthy anti-New Dealer had attacked farm legislation and had denounced the growing national debt. In 1939, the Washington press corps ranked the reserved, intelligent New Yorker as one of the six ablest members of the House.

Throughout his career, Wadsworth had lobbied for national military preparedness. He had fought in Puerto Rico during the Spanish-American War and later had joined the National Guard. An advocate of universal military training, he had followed the jingoist philosophy of former President Theodore Roosevelt. In the Senate, he particularly was active in urging military preparedness and by 1916 had backed peacetime selective service as the most equitable and efficient means to raise an army. Following World War I, he had opposed both American entry into the League of Nations and the World Court and had continued to stress military preparedness. Wadsworth chaired the Senate Military Affairs Committee, where he had authored the National Defense Act of 1920. The legislation maintained a 280,000-man standing army, placed federalized National Guard troops and World War I veterans into the reserves, and boosted the principle of the citizen-soldier. An active participant in the Loyal Legion, the Spanish War Veterans, and other military organizations, the New York Republican usually cooperated with President

14. Lodge to Clark, 22 June 1940; Clark to Lodge, 27 June 1940; Spencer Interview with Burke, 8 July 1947.

15. *New York Times*, 21 June 1940; Spencer Interview with Burke, 8 July 1947; Grenville Clark to James W. Wadsworth, Jr., 1 May 1947, Series IX, Part B, Box 1, Clark Papers; Spencer, "Selective Training and Service Act," pp. 165–67. For a summary of the bill, see Military Training Camps Association, "The Selective Training and Service Bill," 21 June 1940, Sen. 76A–E1, Box 116, Legislative Division, National Archives.

Roosevelt on foreign policy issues. Besides endorsing the Naval Expansion Bill of 1938, he had supported lifting the arms embargo.[16]

Wadsworth defended a selective service measure largely for military and historical reasons. Alarmed over ominous European developments, he feared German expansion might endanger the internal security of the United States and of its Latin American neighbors. Compulsory service, he believed, "would help put Uncle Sam in a better position to defend himself." In addition, Wadsworth considered a peacetime draft synonymous with "the spirit of democracy." The New York Republican claimed, "Every man, regardless of his station in life, owes an obligation to defend it [the United States]."[17] The United States, he also recalled, had begun the Plattsburg camps too late in World War I. During that conflict, the War Department had sent thousands of untrained, ill-equipped soldiers to the European battlefield. A few preparations, Wadsworth cautioned, should be made so as to avoid a repetition of that unfortunate experience. If Hitler employed military force against the United States, the New York Republican argued, troop levels of the regular army and the National Guard reserves would be too low to offer effective resistance. Wadsworth stressed that voluntary enlistments were too unpredictable and would not meet national defense requirements. "We had no military policy worthy of name," Wadsworth later recalled, for raising troops, "and the Army hadn't filled the structure with men."[18] He also denied that changing recruitment policies would involve giving any military assistance to Great Britain or sending troops to Europe unless the United States was attacked.

In mid-June, Wadsworth joined the manpower preparedness campaign. Over the phone, MTCA members Chadbourne and Clark urged the New York representative to consider introducing a selective service bill. Chadbourne also sent him a copy of the proposed preparedness legislation. On 20 June, Senator Burke invited the New York Republican to join him in cosponsoring the rearmament measure. Wadsworth, who did not belong to the Military Affairs Committee, regarded the request as "a great [personal] compliment" and quickly accepted.[19] "The Military Affairs Committee," he remarked, "didn't mind a bit" and was "perfectly willing to see an outsider stick his neck out." The following day, he presented the compulsory draft bill in the House.[20]

During the next few weeks, the selective service issue was overshadowed by

16. Samuel R. Spencer, Jr., Interview with William Chadbourne, 9 July 1947, Series IX, Part B, Box 1, Clark Papers; "James W. Wadsworth," *Current Biography* 4 (1943):796–99; David L. Porter, "The Man Who Made the Draft—Representative James Wadsworth," p. 29; "Washington Correspondents Name Ablest Members of Congress in *Life* poll." For additional background, see Alden Hatch, *The Wadsworths of the Genesee*, and Fausold, *Wadsworth*.

17. James W. Wadsworth, Jr., to Mrs. William Preston, 10 August 1940, James W. Wadsworth, Jr., to Mrs. Charles Williams, 13 July 1940, James W. Wadsworth, Jr., to Mrs. Anna Spacher, 17 June 1940, Box 21, Wadsworth Family Papers.

18. James W. Wadsworth, Jr., Memoirs, p. 439.

19. Spencer Interview with Chadbourne, 9 July 1947; Samuel R. Spencer, Jr., Interview with Howard Petersen, 8 July 1947, Clark to Wadsworth, 1 May 1947, James W. Wadsworth, Jr., to Grenville Clark, 5 May 1947, Series IX, Part B, Box 1, Clark Papers.

20. Wadsworth, Memoirs, p. 435; *New York Times*, 22 June 1940.

other events. Roosevelt on 19 June unexpectedly had appointed Republican preparedness advocates Stimson as Secretary of War and Frank Knox as Secretary of the Navy. At Philadelphia, Republicans nominated utilities magnate Wendell L. Willkie of Indiana to run for the presidency in the November election. Senator Burke, meanwhile, had made arrangements with Military Affairs Committee Chairman Morris Sheppard of Texas to commence hearings.[21]

Committee hearings, which began on 3 July, produced spirited debate. Several MTCA preparedness advocates, including Clark, Adler, General Palmer, and Col. William Donovan, defended the selective service measure on military and ideological grounds. Besides warning that Hitler's moves threatened American security and democratic systems, they criticized the existing recruitment system. Clark insisted sufficient manpower was "just as important as the possession of modern mechanized arms," while Palmer termed "literally absurd" the hopes of securing "an effective national defense under the voluntary system."[22] Preparedness advocates also endeavored to avoid a repetition of the American experience in World War I. In a letter to Chairman Sheppard, Gen. John J. Pershing claimed, "If we had adopted compulsory military training in 1914 it would not have been necessary for us to send partially trained boys into battle against the veteran troops of our adversary." Pershing concluded, "Certainly we could have ended the conflict much sooner, with the saving of many thousands of lives and billions of treasure."[23] Congressional approval of selective service, preparedness advocates believed, would expedite troop mobilization.

On the other hand, rearmament opponents testified about the adverse ideological and moral implications of the draft. The National Council for Prevention of War, the Keep America Out of War Congress, and other pacifist organizations questioned compelling individuals to serve in the armed forces. Quakers and other Protestant denominations protested that selective service would expedite American involvement in foreign wars, while educational groups warned that changing recruitment policies would interrupt the academic progress of students. In addition, labor, Socialist, Communist, and Fascist groups denounced the selective service bill. Hitler, rearmament opponents argued, did not threaten American security. Frederick J. Libby, executive secretary of the National Council for Prevention of War, argued that the draft created "more of an emergency than a threat from Hitler." According to rearmament opponents, peacetime selective service was a dangerous precedent. Socialist Norman Thomas claimed, "No proposal could be more in line with Fascist

21. Elting E. Morison, *Turmoil and Tradition: A Study of the Life and Times of Henry L. Stimson*, p. 399, and Henry L. Stimson and McGeorge Bundy, *On Active Service in Peace and War*, pp. 323–24, describe the Stimson appointment. For the nomination of Willkie, see Herbert S. Parmet and Marie B. Hecht, *Never Again: A President Runs for a Third Term*, and Donald Bruce Johnson, *The Republican Party and Wendell Willkie*. Burke's activities are summarized in Spencer Interview with Burke, 8 July 1947; Howard Petersen to Grenville Clark, 25 June 1940, Series IX, Box 6, Clark Papers.

22. U.S., Congress, Senate, Committee on Military Affairs, "Compulsory Military Training and Service," *Hearings* (hereafter cited as "Compulsory Military Training"), 3 July 1940, pp. 23–29, 45–46.

23. John J. Pershing to Morris Sheppard, 3 July 1940, Sen. 76A–E1, Box 116, Legislative Division, National Archives.

regimentation and less in accord with American tradition.''[24] Numerous lobbyists testified against the selective service preparedness measure, prolonging hearings for nearly a month.

The cautious Roosevelt administration still opposed the draft too. Roosevelt, who favored voluntarism, initially declined to send anyone to testify. The selection of anti-New Dealers Burke and Wadsworth as cosponsors of the measure also dismayed the president. ''Their mouths were closed,'' Wadsworth remarked, ''and in turn the mouths of the Chief of Staff, of the Chief of Naval Operations, and of all the subordinates down the military line were closed. The two committees sat waiting.''[25]

Preparedness advocate Stimson persuaded the executive branch to reevaluate its position. After considerable debate, the Senate on 9 July had approved Stimson 56 to 28 to replace isolationist Harry Woodring as secretary of war. Stimson immediately urged General Marshall and other War Department officials to support the selective service rearmament measure. Roosevelt indirectly endorsed the peacetime draft the next day by requesting that weapons ''be placed in the hands of troops trained, seasoned, and ready.''[26] During the next few days, Marshall and Stimson both defended the preparedness legislation before Sheppard's committee. On 12 July, Marshall warned Congress not to ''speculate with regard to the safety of the United States,'' while Stimson classified the existing method as ''a costly failure.'' According to Stimson, selective service was ''an imperative first step or element in preparedness.'' Although welcoming the administration policy change, preparedness advocates claimed the executive branch could have cooperated sooner. ''It took us about five or six weeks,'' Wadsworth commented, ''to get that statement from the White House. There was politics in it—no doubt about it—and it had come up too close to the [political] conventions.''[27]

Roosevelt eventually adopted compulsory military service, but the cautious president did not make further public commitments until the Democratic convention had nominated him for a third presidential term. A political pragmatist, he also waited until public opinion polls showed around two-thirds of Americans favoring a peacetime draft. At a press conference on 2 August, Roosevelt criticized voluntarism. ''I am in favor,'' he declared, ''of a selective service training bill'' as ''essential to adequate defense.'' He did not endorse the Burke-Wadsworth measure when questioned by reporters but privately favored the preparedness legislation. In a letter to Sen. A. Victor Donahey of Ohio, the president recommended that Congress ''take immediate steps'' to meet the ''real danger'' to national safety. The selective

24. For testimony by selective service opponents, see ''Compulsory Military Training,'' 5 July 1940, pp. 121–31, 10 July 1940, pp. 143–49, 160–65, 182–96, 11 July 1940, pp. 255–57. 294–97.

25. Clifford, ''Clark,'' pp. 30–31; Hatch, *Wadsworths*, p. 253.

26. Diary of Henry L. Stimson, 8–9 July 1940, Henry L. Stimson Papers; *New York Times*, 11 July 1940.

27. ''Compulsory Military Training,'' 12, 31 July 1940; Henry L. Stimson to Morris Sheppard, 30 July 1940, Sen. 76A–E1, Box 116, Legislative Division, National Archives; Wadsworth, Memoirs, p. 437.

service bill, he stressed, was "the last place" for any public official to consider "national defense in terms of party advantage."[28]

By early August, Sheppard's Military Affairs Committee still was considering the selective service measure. The eldest of seven children, Sheppard was the son of a lawyer, district judge, and Democratic U.S. congressman residing near Wheatville, Texas. After earning degrees from the University of Texas and Yale University, he had become an attorney in Pittsburg, Texas. At age twenty-seven, Sheppard had been elected in 1902 to fill his father's unexpired term in the U.S. House of Representatives. Joining the U.S. Senate in 1913, the eloquent Methodist had sponsored the Eighteenth Amendment implementing prohibition across the United States. He had defended most New Deal measures until his special committee unearthed extensive Works Progress Administration interference in the 1938 elections. Sheppard had played a major role in securing adoption of the Hatch Acts of 1939 and 1940 to prevent political coercion of WPA workers.

The Texas Democrat consistently had supported internationalist, interventionist, and preparedness legislation. During the Mexican Civil War, he had urged strengthening military fortifications along the Texas border. Sheppard also had recommended rapid development of air power and had backed American intervention in World War I against Germany. In the interwar period, he had endorsed the League of Nations and World Court and had become chairman of the Military Affairs Committee. The strict neutrality legislation of the mid-1930s, he claimed, benefited aggressor nations and hurt Great Britain and France. A loyal Democrat, he had advocated neutrality revision and favored granting the president more discretionary authority. Sheppard, who represented predominantly pro-British constituents, warned that Nazi expansion in Europe threatened the security of the Western Hemisphere. After the outbreak of World War II, he had endorsed the internationalist Neutrality Act of 1939 repealing the arms embargo and the interventionist Brown Act of 1940 granting economic assistance to Finland. The Texas Democrat in 1940 contended the War Department could not raise sufficient volunteers and recommended selective service as the surest way to raise troops.[29]

Preparedness advocates controlled the Military Affairs Committee. Under the direction of Sheppard, defenders of the compulsory draft included nine Democrats and four Republicans representing nearly all sections of the United States. There was, preparedness advocates emphasized, "an immediate necessity to provide an orderly, predictable, efficient, and fair method for procuring the men which should be trained and disciplined to use these arms effectively." Three rearmament opponents, led by Farmer-Laborite Ernest Lundeen of Minnesota, rejected the selective service measure. A bipartisan group, rearmament opponents served Mountain or Great Plains constituents. They called a peacetime draft "abhorrent to the ideals of

28. *New York Times*, 3 August 1940; Franklin D. Roosevelt to A. Victor Donahey, 3 August 1940, OF 1413, Box 8, Roosevelt Papers.

29. "John Morris Sheppard," *Dictionary of American Biography* 22, supp. 3, pp. 706–7; Escal F. Duke, "Political Career of Morris Sheppard, 1875–1941" (Ph.D. diss.).

patriotic Americans" and "utterly repugnant to American democracy and American traditions."

Preparedness advocates, although making several concessions to rearmament opponents, ultimately controlled the committee decisionmaking. Besides extending the training period from eight to twelve months and broadening deferment categories, the committee approved an amendment narrowing registration to adult males between ages twenty-one and thirty-one. On 5 August, the preparedness-minded committee easily approved the selective service measure 13 to 3 and sent it to the Senate floor for debate. With the exception of Republican Rufus C. Holman of Oregon and Democrat Robert R. Reynolds of North Carolina, the thirteen preparedness advocates backing selective service had supported the internationalists repealing the arms embargo. Of the three rearmament opponents, two had aligned with the isolationists objecting to the sale of munitions to belligerents.[30] This action marked the first time a Senate committee had abandoned the voluntary recruitment method in peacetime and adopted selective service instead.

MTCA preparedness advocates protested the committee changes. Clark, upset over age limitations, urged Sheppard's group to restore the original twenty-one to forty-five figure. The narrower range, he feared, would "put the entire burden and risk on our youth."[31] Besides blaming the large volume of hostile constituent mail, Clark attributed the outcome to the army's attitude. "The bill has had a little hard sledding lately," Clark explained, "due to a flood of adverse letters which put a panic into some of the Senate and the Senate Committee had emasculated it." "The Army people," he claimed, "might have stopped this if they had been convinced that wide registration and wide liability to service were as important as we think them, but, as you know, they never had their hearts in this."[32]

Several surveys, along with Senate action on the National Guard bill, encouraged selective service proponents. In late July, the MTCA concluded that fifty-five of seventy-four committed members backed selective service and listed twenty-two as uncertain. During August, three polls predicted closer margins of victory for the selective service measure. The *New York Times, PM*, and *Congressional Intelligence* indicated that preparedness advocates held a thirteen-to-eighteen-vote majority. On 8 August, the Senate overwhelmingly approved 71 to 7 Roosevelt's request ordering all National Guard and retired army personnel into active service for one year of intensive training.[33]

Political and sectional alignments differed markedly from those on the Finnish

30. U.S., Congress, Senate, Committee on Military Affairs, "Compulsory Military Training and Service," *Reports*, no. 2002.

31. Grenville Clark to Members of U.S. Senate Military Affairs Committee, 3 August 1940, Series IX, Box 2, Clark Papers.

32. Grenville Clark to John McAuley Palmer, 3 August 1940, Series IX, Box 6, Clark Papers.

33. Memorandum, "Position of Senators on Burke-Wadsworth Bill," 25 July 1940, Series IX, Box 2, Clark Papers; Spencer, "Selective Training and Service Act," pp. 426–27; *Congressional Record*, 76th Cong., 3d sess., vol. 86, 8 August 1940, pp. 10067–68.

loan. Selective service advocates attracted less numerical support and were more heterogeneous than the interventionists favoring federal credits. Democrats provided the nucleus of support for preparedness but experienced more defections this time. On the other hand, Republicans furnished less resistance to rearmament than they had to the interventionist Export-Import Bank bill. Southern Democrats proportionately directed the preparedness campaign for changing recruitment methods and aligned with New England, Border, and Middle Atlantic delegations. Preparedness generated greater enthusiasm among the Southern and New England blocs but received less backing west of the Mississippi River. By contrast, rearmament opponents attracted more followers and held majorities in more geographical areas. As on the interventionist Finnish issue, a majority of Republicans opposed altering the voluntary approach. Sectionally, the rearmament opponents registered striking gains among the Pacific members. The Pacific delegation proportionately led the resistance to preparedness and was joined by the Great Lakes, Great Plains, and Mountain senators[34] (see table 20).

Ideological, demographic, economic, and constituent pressures caused several internationalists to oppose rearmament. They feared a conscript army would violate democratic principles and unduly regiment the American people. Great Lakes, Great Plains, Mountain, and Pacific senators complained that MTCA preparedness advocates represented the interests of the northeastern establishment. Since the United States still faced unemployment and agricultural problems, rearmament opponents insisted priority be given to settling internal discontent. Hostile constituent mail and intense pacifist activities also caused several internationalists to oppose rearmament.

Preparedness advocates stressed military considerations. Since the regular army had dwindled from 280,000 to 165,000 men, preparedness advocates did not believe the existing system could fill manpower requirements. An extensive War Department campaign between January and June 1940 had netted only 14,000 volunteers.[35] Republican Warren R. Austin of Vermont contended the method was "a total failure in building an army," while youthful Rep. Lyle H. Boren of Oklahoma even contemplated joining the armed forces. According to Boren, "the Nation as a whole provided only one-half as many enlistments as were necessary to build our army even to 400,000 soldiers when we need at least a million and perhaps two million soldiers."[36]

Historically, parallels were drawn by preparedness advocates with the World War I experience. During that conflict, the War Department had provided inadequate facilities for training troops and had sent thousands of unprepared soldiers to Europe. As Representative Wadsworth recalled, "We had to throw men into battle who never had fired their rifles," resulting in "unnecessary and ghastly sacrifice." Continued dependence upon the voluntary approach, he warned, was

34. The tables referred to in this chapter are based on data from the Inter-University Consortium for Political Research, University of Michigan.

35. Watson, *Chief of Staff*, pp. 15–36; "Compulsory Military Training," 3 July 1940, pp. 23–29.

36. Warren R. Austin Speech, New York City, 4 July 1940, Speech File, Warren R. Austin Papers; Lyle H. Boren to Rev. Willmoore Kendall, 27 August 1940, Box 87, Lyle H. Boren Papers.

"dangerous to the country and bitterly unfair to the young men who must defend it.''[37] In order to avoid a repetition of the numerous World War I casualties, rearmament advocates urged switching to a peacetime draft. Selective service, they maintained, would not establish a dangerous precedent. Democrat Carl Hayden of Arizona remarked, ''Conscription is an entirely democratic process which is no way contrary to American ideals,'' while Rep. Robert L. Doughton of North Carolina recalled, ''We did adopt the draft system during the World War before Hitler was ever heard of.''[38]

Compulsory duty, preparedness advocates argued, would benefit American youth without draining American taxpayers. A peacetime draft, they insisted, would help American youth develop strong, healthy bodies and an appreciation for training. Rep. William T. Byrne of New York affirmed, ''Surely it can do no harm and can give people some exercise and an outlook on life which they cannot possibly get unless they have discipline and the regularity of living.''[39] Protecting American and British defense was considered more vital than reducing armaments. ''There has never been any doubt in my mind,'' Democrat Joseph C. O'Mahoney of Wyoming declared, ''that our future security depends upon the success achieved by Great Britain in its defense against Hitler.'' War and Navy department programs already approved by Congress required manpower to operate them. ''It seems so absurd to me,'' Majority Whip Sherman Minton of Indiana commented, ''to appropriate billions of dollars to buy a lot of defense weapons and then not to provide the men to use them.''[40]

Ideologically, the preparedness advocates pictured the European struggle as a battle between democracy and totalitarianism. In spring 1940, the Nazis had overrun Norway, Denmark, Holland, Belgium, and France. The draft, preparedness advocates claimed, afforded the best protection against possible German expansion into the Western Hemisphere. ''Had we had such a program for the past few years,'' Republican J. Chandler Gurney of South Dakota remarked, ''we would have been ready for the emergency that we are now in.'' Democrat Theodore G. Bilbo of Mississippi endorsed changing recruitment policies ''so we will be ready to defend America if the 'big bullies' across the sea attempt to invade our country.''[41] Selective service was viewed by preparedness advocates as the best means of protecting the free world against dictatorial rule. Rep. John H. Kerr of North Carolina insisted, it ''is imperative for this Nation to equip itself to defend our ideals and cherished rights against all hazards.''[42]

Preparedness advocates deemphasized political considerations. Despite the fact

37. Wadsworth, Memoirs, p. 439; Wadsworth to Williams, 13 July 1940.
38. Carl Hayden to Mrs. Edwin Pendleton, 23 August 1940, 379/28, Carl Hayden Papers; Robert L. Doughton to Boyden Walter, 7 September 1940, Folder 848, Robert L. Doughton Papers.
39. William T. Byrne to Edward Scheiberling, 24 July 1940, Series IX, Box 1, Clark Papers.
40. Joseph C. O'Mahoney to A. N. Talcott, 22 August 1940, Box 50, Joseph C. O'Mahoney Papers; Sherman Minton to William G. McAdoo, 22 August 1940, Box 473, William G. McAdoo Papers.
41. J. Chandler Gurney to Grenville Clark, 6 August 1940, Series IX, Box 3, Clark Papers; Theodore G. Bilbo to Mrs. Sally Collins, 9 July 1940, Subject File D, Theodore G. Bilbo Papers.
42. John H. Kerr to A. Roy Moore, 11 June 1940, Box 15, John H. Kerr Papers.

that they were jeopardizing their reelection prospects, several preparedness advocates considered the peacetime draft the most effective means of preparing the military forces for possible combat duty. Freshman Rep. Thomas V. Smith of Illinois declared to one disenchanted constituent, "Of course I shall vote for conscription." "And you can't terrify me," he added, "by telling me of the political consequences of my doing so. If you don't like this then go out and elect somebody to Congress who's coward enough to follow the conscience of a cad instead of one that he ought to have for himself."[43]

Rearmament opponents, meanwhile, relied on ideological themes, According to rearmament opponents, selective service would violate American constitutional principles and encourage the regimentation characteristic of dictator nations. Republican Arthur Capper of Kansas charged that the compulsory draft was "unAmerican, undemocratic, and the undoubted road to military dictatorship." "It is the duty of the American people," American-Laborite Rep. Vito Marcantonio of New York asserted, "to rally against the Nazification of America." Republican Rep. Ben F. Jensen of Iowa warned, "History records that every nation that has put peace time conscription into effect has very soon gone into a complete military dictatorship" and considered selective service "a much greater threat to the peace and security of America than any enemy force could possibly be in this war today."[44] Numerous casualties might result from sending conscripted American youths overseas to battle. If voluntarism was abandoned, Independent George W. Norris of Nebraska feared the United States "would be armed to the teeth, ready to quarrel or fight at the drop of a hat." "We are not at war with anyone," Republican Rep. Joshua L. Johns of Wisconsin remarked, "but in my opinion this act means war."[45]

Furthermore, rearmament opponents considered selective service unwarranted. Denying that German expansion threatened American security, rearmament opponents insisted the Atlantic Ocean protected the United States from foreign invasion. Republican Rep. Bartel J. Jonkman of Michigan declared, "There is no danger of probable attack," while party colleague Rep. Clarence McLeod of Michigan contended, "So far, the Administration has failed to prove that a national emergency now exists." "Until we are threatened, and definitely not until then," McLeod vowed, "will I ever vote to conscript the youths of America into war machine."[46] By continuing voluntarism, rearmament opponents believed, the War Department could raise a formidable army on short notice. "Before any nations of Europe could prepare to invade the United States," Norris gave assurance, "we would have ample time to prepare and to train a large army, without its being necessary to prepare years

43. Thomas V. Smith to Alfred Ames, 21 August 1940, Box 7, Thomas V. Smith Papers.

44. Arthur Capper to *United States News*, 31 July 1940, General Correspondence, Arthur Capper Papers; Vito Marcantonio Press Release, 19 September 1940, Box 22, Vito Marcantonio Papers; Ben F. Jensen to Roscoe S. Jones, 11 September 1940, Personal Correspondence, Box 18, Folder 97, Ben F. Jensen Papers.

45. George W. Norris to Rev. C. A. Moon, 23 July 1940, Tray 104, Box 4, George W. Norris Papers; Joshua L. Johns to Grenville Clark, 5 September 1940, Series IX, Box 4, Clark Papers.

46. Bartel J. Jonkman Press Release, 24 May 1940, Box 1, Bartel J. Jonkman Papers; Clarence McLeod to Amos Pinchot, 6 September 1940, Box 67, Amos Pinchot Papers.

in advance." In addition, rearmament opponents claimed the armed forces had not encountered manpower shortages. Republican Arthur H. Vandenberg of Michigan pointed out, "The Army and the Navy have fitted every volunteer quota they have sought this year."[47]

As on neutrality, several Republican rearmament opponents stressed political considerations. They feared Roosevelt would use selective service to embroil the United States further in the European war. If "we authorize the President to declare an emergency in *his* judgment and thereupon to launch general conscription at his option," Vandenberg of Michigan protested, "we have left too much power in the hands of an impulsive Executive who (to say the least) is not as peace-minded as I could wish."[48] Democrat Donahey of Ohio charged that the measure was "fraught with political disaster," while Republican Hiram W. Johnson of California claimed the "only war we are in at present is a 'wordy' war started by the President."[49] Rearmament opponents warned that Roosevelt would attempt to retain the peacetime draft permanently. Republican Rep. Clifford R. Hope of Kansas predicted, "If we once fasten a policy of conscription on this country in peacetime, we may not be able to get rid of it. Most certainly, we shall not, if Mr. Roosevelt should be reelected."[50]

Economic themes also abounded. Rearmament opponents cautioned that Wall Street and munitioners could make considerable profits at public expense from American involvement in the European war. "This conscription bill drive," youthful Democrat Rush Dew Holt of West Virginia argued, "is financed by those who have interests to protect and expect the boys to do it." In addition, rearmament opponents stressed that the United States still experienced serious economic problems from the depression and believed the federal government should concentrate on lowering unemployment and improving housing conditions rather than on drafting soldiers. "America has nothing to fear from any isms," American-Laborite Marcantonio of New York commented, "if we take care of youth unemployment, general unemployment, and secure economic security for the American people." Rearmament opponents claimed the War Department lacked adequate facilities and equipment to train a large-scale military force. "A conscript Army made up of youths trained for a year or two, compared to Hitler's army," Democrat James E. Murray of Montana stated, "is like a high school football team going up against the professional teams they have in Chicago and New York."[51]

Across the nation, Americans debated the merits of selective service. On 1

47. Norris to Moon, 23 July 1940; Arthur H. Vandenberg to Katherine Pantlind, 30 September 1940, Arthur H. Vandenberg Papers.
48. Arthur H. Vandenberg to Charles Kerr, 24 July 1940, Vandenberg Papers.
49. A. Victor Donahey to Franklin D. Roosevelt, 1 August 1940, OF 1413, Box 8, Roosevelt Papers; Hiram W. Johnson to Hiram W. Johnson, Jr., 28 July 1940, Part VI, Box 8, Hiram W. Johnson Papers.
50. Clifford R. Hope to Lyle Yancey, 30 August 1940, Legislative Correspondence, Box 182, Clifford R. Hope Papers.
51. Rush Dew Holt Press Release, 10 August 1940, A&M 1701, Box 102, Rush Dew Holt Papers; Vito Marcantonio to L. B. Harrison, 16 February 1940, Civil Liberties, Box 1, Marcantonio Papers; James E. Murray to Hugh Daly, 31 August 1940, as quoted in Leuchtenburg, *Franklin D. Roosevelt*, p. 308.

June, a Gallup poll showed the populace evenly divided on compulsory one-year military duty. After the fall of France, the proportion favoring a peacetime draft rose to 64 percent. By August, a majority from every state favored abandoning voluntarism.[52] Constituents also deluged senators and representatives with telegrams and letters. Despite public opinion surveys, most correspondence repudiated the selective service measure. Senator Donahey of Ohio remarked, "Letters from Ohio are pouring in and they show 100 to 1 against the conscription measure." "Our West Virginia letters," Senator Holt added, "show a margin of more than 90% in opposition."[53] Senator Johnson of California, whose office daily was "swamped" with around 2,000 communications, observed, "There is a drive on *against* conscription." On the House side, Republican Thomas E. Martin of Iowa reported that 90 percent of his mail favored retaining voluntarism.[54] "This office," Republican Bruce Barton of New York indicated, "received something like 3,000 letters in a ratio of about 10 to 1 against the bill." "Their letters to me indicate great fear of conscription during peacetime," Republican Karl Stefan of Nebraska added, "because they feel it will lead us into war."[55]

The passionate national debate quickly spread to Capitol Hill. Encouraged by constituent mail, rearmament opponents intensified their public campaign against the draft. Before a large gathering in Washington, D.C., Holt of West Virginia, Gerald P. Nye of North Dakota, and other senators on 1 August accused preparedness advocates of arousing war "hysteria."[56] On the other hand, the MTCA heightened its lobbying activity. According to Grenville Clark, "hundreds of thousands of people got a totally wrong idea of how the bill would operate and got the impression that millions of men were going to be pulled away from their homes all at once." MTCA lobbyists advocating preparedness concentrated on the Senate, where floor debates would begin shortly and where opponents were extremely vocal. Setting up headquarters at the Hotel Carlton, Clark and others visited around twenty-two undecided senators and eleven members leaning against the bill. At these sessions, MTCA personnel declared that the German army held a vast numerical advantage over American troops and recalled how United States citizens had been drafted in both the Civil War and World War I.[57]

The MTCA preparedness campaign netted mixed results. Clark found most New England, Middle Atlantic, and Great Lakes senators receptive to the selective service rearmament measure. Republicans Vandenberg of Michigan and Taft of

52. Hadley Cantril and Mildred Strunk, eds., *Public Opinion, 1935–1946*, pp. 458–89.

53. Donahey to Roosevelt, 1 August 1940; Rush Dew Holt Washington Newsletter, 13 August 1940, A&M 1701, Box 97, Holt Papers.

54. Hiram W. Johnson to Rolan Curran, 12 August 1940, Hiram W. Johnson to Frank Doherty, 13 August 1940, Part III, Box 19, Johnson Papers; Joseph Drake Notes on Representative Martin, 13 August 1940, Series IX, Box 5, Clark Papers.

55. Bruce Barton to Constituents Favoring Burke-Wadsworth Bill, 11 September 1940, OF 1413, Box 8, Roosevelt Papers; Karl Stefan to W. B. Sadilek, 30 July 1940, Box 24, Karl Stefan Papers.

56. *New York Times*, 2 August 1940.

57. Grenville Clark to Francis Maloney, 29 August 1940, Series IX, Box 5, "Lining Up Support," Series IX, Part B, Box 1, Clark Papers.

Ohio, however, told Clark they opposed selective service on political and ideological grounds.[58] New York City lawyers Malcolm Langford and Franklin Canfield encountered more formidable resistance from Great Plains and Mountain rearmament opponents. Nye of North Dakota, Norris of Nebraska, and others rejected the compulsory draft. Democrat William J. Bulow of South Dakota told Langford his father had emigrated from Germany "to escape such evils as compulsory military training."[59] On the other hand, Alabama lawyer Douglas Arant reported a very favorable response to preparedness from Southern Democrats.[60]

During midsummer, selective service neared a showdown. For the first time, President Roosevelt had endorsed the principle of selective service. On the other hand, rearmament opponents were gaining momentum in Congress because of the avalanche of hostile constituent mail. The resurgence by rearmament opponents indicated that MTCA lobbyists and public opinion polls may have overestimated the extent of the pro-selective service sentiments. Norris of Nebraska predicted, "I do not believe Congress will pass that kind of law" because "opposition to compulsory military training, I think, is quite universal."[61] Amidst the flurry of activity, the ninety-six senators were preparing to begin one of the most spirited floor debates ever held on Capitol Hill.

58. "Lining Up Support"; Grenville Clark to Robert A. Taft, 16 August 1940, Series IX, Box 7, Clark Papers.
59. Malcolm Langford Notes on Senator Nye, 1 August 1940, Series IX, Box 5, Malcolm Langford Notes on Senator Gillette, 1 August 1940, Series IX, Box 3, Malcolm Langford Notes on Senator Bulow, 10 August 1940, Series IX, Box 1, Malcolm Langford Notes on Senator O'Mahoney, 10 August 1940, Series IX, Box 5, Clark Papers.
60. Douglas Arant to Grenville Clark, 27 July, 2, 8 August 1940, Series IX, Box 1, Clark Papers.
61. George W. Norris to Edgar Barratt, 2 August 1940, Tray 104, Box 4, Norris Papers.

7

The Triumph of Preparedness

The mood on Capitol Hill was tense. Journalists, lobbyists, and constituents anxiously awaited the impending floor debates and votes, which would affect countless Americans. Preparedness advocates and rearmament opponents alike scrutinized the provisions and implications of the Burke-Wadsworth bill. "Nothing more important has come before Congress in my memory," Republican Charles W. Tobey of New Hampshire admitted, because the United States "never attempted [selective service] in peacetime before."[1]

Two senators did not wait until the scheduled 9 August opening date to begin floor debate. Three days earlier, Democrat Rush Dew Holt of West Virginia, a rearmament opponent, had accused the Military Training Camps Association of plotting American entry in the European war in order to preserve overseas investments. Besides arguing that munitioners and bankers had drawn the United States into the last world conflict, he described Grenville Clark, Secretary of War Henry L. Stimson, and other MTCA lobbyists as "dollar patriots." These men, Holt claimed, had "interests to protect in this war" and were "willing to sacrifice American boys in European battlefields." In a spirited rebuttal, Majority Whip Sherman Minton of Indiana praised the members of Clark's organization as "high class, patriotic gentlemen" sponsoring essential preparedness legislation. "I did lose my head a little," Minton admitted later, "and spoke when I was very angry." "I probably did violate the rules of the Senate," he confessed, "but I was angry enough to have done even more."[2]

After this preliminary exchange, the Senate on 9 August commenced the long-awaited floor debate. As dignitaries approached the Capitol building, numerous photographers snapped pictures. Members of Congress, reporters, and spectators rapidly filled the Senate and heard Democrat Morris Sheppard of Texas deliver the initial speech. In a lively manner, Sheppard defended the preparedness bill on security and ideological grounds. Alarmed over European conditions, he warned, "Doctrines and aggressions of certain dictator-controlled countries become every day more menacing toward free and independent democratic countries." "Every day of delay," Sheppard cautioned, "now tends to place this country in the category of 'Another France.' "[3]

From the outset, rearmament opponents controlled floor debate. They sought to delay action, thus enabling them to organize anticonscription sentiment across the

1. Charles W. Tobey to Alva Allen, 10 August 1940, Box 79, Charles W. Tobey Papers.
2. *Congressional Record (CR)*, 76 Cong., 3d sess., vol. 86, 6 August 1940, pp. 15166–71; Sherman Minton to William G. McAdoo, 22 August 1940, Box 473, William G. McAdoo Papers.
3. *New York Times*, 10 August 1940; *CR*, 9 August 1940, pp. 10093–96; *Dallas News*, 10 August 1940.

United States. During the first few days, Democrats Holt of West Virginia, Burton K. Wheeler of Montana, and Bennett Champ Clark of Missouri, Republicans Arthur H. Vandenberg of Michigan and Robert A. Taft of Ohio, and Independent George W. Norris of Nebraska denounced a peacetime draft on ideological grounds and geographical lines. Labeling compulsory military training regimentation, rearmament opponents urged continuing the voluntary recruitment method. Selective service, Wheeler warned, would "slit the throat of the last democracy still living" and would "accord to Hitler his greatest and cheapest victory." Norris argued that changing mobilization policy meant "turning the clock back a thousand years," while Vandenberg predicted, "The Army and the Navy can get what they want by the traditional, peacetime volunteer system." Geographically, the rearmament opponents denied that totalitarian countries threatened American security. "I do not believe," Taft stated, "that any of these nations will attack the United States." In addition, Taft affirmed, "Our present forces can defend us against an attack across 3,000 miles of water."[4]

Rearmament opponents particularly benefited from Taft's assistance. The son of a former U.S. president and Supreme Court chief justice, the fifty-year-old Taft was a native of Cincinnati, Ohio. After graduating from Yale University and Harvard Law School, he had opened a law practice in Cincinnati. Hard-working and intelligent, Taft had served in the Ohio House of Representatives and in 1938 had been elected to the U.S. Senate. Taft quickly became a Republican leader because of his name, his ability, and his party's minority position. Several Republicans had supported Taft for the presidency in 1940, but the Ohio senator had neither participated in the primaries nor sought the nomination. Taft adamantly had opposed the New Deal programs and the growth of federal government powers.

Although from the Great Lakes region, Taft was more internationalist than most of his colleagues. He had traveled abroad extensively as a youth and had lived in the Philippines, where his father was chief commissioner. During World War I, the Ohio Republican was assistant counsel for the U.S. Food Administration and an American relief administrator in Europe. Taft disagreed with many party members by favoring the Treaty of Versailles and supporting American entrance into the League of Nations. During the 1930s, however, he usually had aligned with the isolationists. Taft adamantly had disapproved of American intervention in European affairs and had insisted that the president was magnifying the dangers inherent abroad. Roosevelt, he charged, deliberately was attempting to conceal failures in New Deal programs and to enlarge his personal authority. Alarmed over the growth of the federal bureaucracy, the Ohio Republican warned that a totalitarian dictatorship gradually was replacing democratic rule at home. Until September 1939, Taft had supported the strict neutrality legislation and had argued that arms embargo repeal would unduly commit the United States overseas. He also did not believe the Nazis would attack the Western Hemisphere, claiming the three-thousand-mile-wide

4. *CR*, 12 August 1940, pp. 10113, 10117, 10123, 10126, 14 August 1940, p. 10308. For a description of the debates, see *New York Times*, 13–15 August 1940.

Atlantic Ocean afforded natural protection against invasion. Following the outbreak of World War II, Taft had supported internationalism and opposed interventionism. The German attack on Poland in September 1939 had persuaded the Ohio Republican that the United States should take more concrete measures to help prevent the spread of Hitler's totalitarianism. At the special session in 1939, he had supported the internationalist Pittman measure removing the ban on munitions sales and endorsed comprehensive aid short of war to Great Britain. Taft had also advocated increasing defense expenditures to strengthen coastal fortifications in case the European war spread to the Western Hemisphere. On the other hand, the Ohio Republican had opposed economic assistance to Finland and selective service. Taft charged that a peacetime draft would embroil the United States further in the European conflict and claimed the War Department still could recruit a sufficient number of army volunteers.[5]

Taft's three-hour presentation on the Senate floor both impressed and alarmed preparedness advocates. Selective service backers hoped the remaining speeches would maintain the same high standards. "Sen. Taft," Republican Warren R. Austin of Vermont commented, "made a fine argument this afternoon against the Conscription bill—the most free from the sloppy talk about 'war mongering,' 'militarizing,' 'anti-American' etc. which has come from Senators Vandenberg, Norris, and Wheeler." "It was refreshing to one like myself," he remarked, "who is persuaded that the bill ought to be agreed to." Taft's address, however, irritated MTCA lobbyist Franklin Canfield, who was seated in the Senate gallery. "Taft," Canfield protested, "is consuming the time, if not occupying the attention of the Senate today." Canfield warned, "The bill is becoming more and more enmeshed in politics where it will strangle unless something is done to pull it out."[6]

Since Taft held considerable prestige in Republican circles, Clark attempted to persuade him to stop criticizing selective service. "I was surprised at the complete certainty with which you expressed your point of view," Clark wrote Taft, "to the effect that those who have serious apprehensions, all have hysteria." Inasmuch as European events "may soon make any cocksure attitude on this subject look very foolish," he urged the Ohio Republican to show "more *tolerance* . . . towards those with whom you so sharply disagree." "Isn't it just *possible*," Clark asked, "that they may turn out to be less foolish than by implication at least you and Senator Wheeler and Senator Vandenberg and Senator Holt make them out to be?" Taft, however, intensified his opposition to the compulsory draft. Nearly a month later, Taft wrote Clark, "I think the conscription bill is a great mistake."[7]

During the first ten days, preparedness advocates kept a low profile and seldom participated in floor debates. Majority Leader Alben W. Barkley of Kentucky did not

5. "Robert A. Taft," *Current Biography* 1 (1940):787–89; James T. Patterson, *Mr. Republican: A Biography of Robert A. Taft.*

6. Warren R. Austin to Mrs. Chauncey Austin, 14 August 1940, Correspondence with Mother, Box 1939–1940, Warren R. Austin Papers. Franklin Canfield to Grenville Clark, 14 August 1940, Series IX, Box 2, Grenville Clark Papers.

7. Grenville Clark to Robert A. Taft, 16 August 1940, Robert A. Taft to Grenville Clark, 13 September 1940, Series IX, Box 7, Clark Papers.

attempt to discipline Democrats or break up the delaying tactics. Besides lacking a clear-cut directive from the White House to intervene, Barkley considered the preparedness issue too controversial for political partisanship. Along with Sheppard, he hoped a majority of senators would become disenchanted with the dilatory strategy.

In their infrequent floor remarks, preparedness advocates reiterated ideological and security themes. The rapid expansion of German totalitarianism into Western Europe, they argued, endangered individual freedoms and liberties at home. Democrat Edward R. Burke of Nebraska asserted, "The safety and welfare of the United States require the prompt passage of a compulsory training and service act." In addition, selective service was pictured by preparedness advocates as the only effective method of recruiting army personnel. "I don't want them," Democrat Tom Connally of Texas declared, "to have to wait until we are plunged into war to receive their training in the battlefield amidst blood and slaughter."[8]

In order to break the impasse, Democrat Francis T. Maloney of Connecticut proposed a compromise solution. Maloney, a forty-six-year-old native of Meriden, Connecticut, had attended public and parochial schools there. After working as a counterman in an all-night café, he had joined the *Meriden Record* as a cub reporter. Maloney quickly had become city editor and mayor of Meriden. Following one term in the U.S. House of Representatives, he had been elected in 1934 to the U.S. Senate. Maloney had supported New Deal programs and became an expert on financial, monetary, and commercial problems. He had declined an invitation from President Roosevelt to become national Democratic party chairman in 1940, when James A. Farley resigned that position.

During the 1930s, Maloney usually had aligned with the internationalists and interventionists on Capitol Hill. Following the outbreak of World War II, he had supported the Pittman measure repealing the arms embargo because he believed the existing neutrality measure aided aggressor nations. Maloney not only maintained that German expansion endangered the safety and democratic institutions of Western Europe, but also represented numerous Polish constituents concerned over Hitler's sudden attack upon their homeland. Besides remaining loyal politically, the Connecticut Democrat came from a highly industrialized state likely to benefit economically from munitions sales. On the Finnish issue, Maloney had approved of granting federal economic assistance to the Ryti government. He was an anti-Communist opposed to Russian expansion and contended that the Scandinavian nation needed American intervention quickly. Maloney considered Finland a good financial risk and figured his section might gain economically from purchases by the Ryti government. Since he came from a highly maritime region, the Connecticut Democrat favored military preparedness and particularly espoused strengthening naval fortifications. On the other hand, he opposed immediate selective service and urged instead retaining voluntary enlistment, Maloney, who was campaigning for reelection in 1940, faced considerable pressure from constituents opposing conscription as an antidemocratic step leading to more involvement in war. A gifted speaker and frequent mediator of internal party disputes, he considered offering an alternative solution to manpower recruitment. At a press conference in early August, Maloney suggested that Congress postpone consideration of a peacetime draft and continue voluntary methods for the remainder of 1940.[9]

MTCA lobbyists, however, sought to dissuade Maloney from introducing the compromise proposal. In a letter to the Connecticut Democrat, Clark cautioned, "The postponement would do a great deal of harm." The compromise, he warned, would "create confusion and delay" in "the orderly development of the plans which our best informed advisers tell us are necessary." Maloney replied that immediate adoption of selective service would provoke greater "emotion and confusion and bitterness" among many Americans. "Until you have a chance to examine Congressional mail," he remarked, "I doubt that you can realize the feelings of our people and how 'bitterly' so many of them feel about immediate conscription." On 20 August, Maloney, who viewed his compromise "as a possible cushion against a shock to our national life," formally introduced his amendment.[10]

Wavering members and rearmament opponents welcomed the Maloney plan. Senators facing reelection particularly found the compromise attractive because they were receiving large volumes of anticonscription mail. The Maloney amendment also delighted rearmament opponents, who continued to control floor debate. On 23 August, Holt of West Virginia occupied the floor most of the session and often yielded to sympathetic colleagues. "I am working day and night," Holt remarked, "doing research to prove the weak points in the measure."[11]

Dismayed over these developments, preparedness advocates eventually sought to seize the initiative. "The patience of Senators," Austin of Vermont admitted, "is stretched to the limit by the prolonged debate on the conscription bill." Majority Whip Minton commented, "We are having the damnedest time here getting this Conscription Bill through." "I only hope," he added, "we are not fiddling while Rome burns."[12] "To call this a filibuster," Democrat Harry H. Schwartz of Wyoming declared, "is to put it mildly. One isolationist speaks and then the others all get up and agree with him."[13] On 19 August, Majority Leader Barkley temporarily broke the impasse. Democrats Lister Hill of Alabama and Millard E. Tydings of Maryland delivered speeches supporting the selective service preparedness measure. By discarding voluntary enlistment, Tydings counseled, "We would better overdo on the side of preparedness rather than underdo."[14] The momentum returned to the

9. U.S., Congress, *Biographical Directory of the American Congress, 1774–1961 (BDAC)*, p. 1258; *New York Times*, 17 January 1945.

10. Grenville Clark to Francis T. Maloney, 12 August 1940, Francis T. Maloney to Grenville Clark, 16 August 1940, Series IX, Box 5, Clark Papers; *CR*, 20 August 1940, p. 10559.

11. *CR*, 23 August 1940; Rush Dew Holt to F. E. Watson, 26 August 1940, A&M 1701, Box 42, Rush Dew Holt Papers.

12. Warren R. Austin to Mrs. Chauncey Austin, 21 August 1940, Correspondence with Mother, Box 1939–1940, Austin Papers; Minton to McAdoo, 22 August 1940.

13. *New York Times*, 23 August 1940.

14. *CR*, 19 August 1940, pp. 10472–73, 10491.

rearmament opponents the next day, when Maloney introduced his compromise amendment.

MTCA preparedness advocates, meanwhile, sought White House intervention to break the impasse. On 21 August, MTCA lobbyist Canfield remarked, "The 'ball' had been taken away from the sponsors of the bill." According to Canfield, "opponents were running with it for a touchdown in the form of the Maloney amendment." Senators Burke and Barkley, he complained, had provided ineffective leadership for the preparedness advocates. Canfield predicted Congress would approve the compromise motion unless "the President and Mr. Willkie at least pass the word to their spokesmen that they disagree with Senator Maloney's suggestions."[15]

Roosevelt, however, continued to exhibit cautious leadership, Although he favored selective service, the president had not publicly endorsed the Burke-Wadsworth legislation. House Appropriations Committee Chairman Edward T. Taylor of Colorado already had urged Roosevelt to reach a "mutually satisfactory" position with Republican presidential nominee Wendell L. Willkie on the measure. Such consensus, Taylor predicted, would "pave the way for smooth, orderly, expeditious passage" of the measure. Declining this suggestion, the president instead stated, "The best approach is an appeal to the patriotism of [Republican congressional leaders] Joe Martin and Charlie McNary."[16] In an effort to avoid making the legislation a personal issue, he did not instruct Senate leaders to intervene in the first two weeks of debate to block the filibuster. Instead the cautious president quietly signaled both Barkley and Byrnes to commence lining up affirmative votes. Roosevelt subsequently gave only one direct signal to his party members—on 23 August Secretary of War Stimson publicly urged the president to repudiate the Maloney amendment. Later that day Roosevelt told reporters, "I am absolutely opposed to the postponement because it means . . . nearly a year of delay." If Congress did not pass a selective service bill within two weeks, the president warned, "we are going to have a real delay in getting our team together."[17]

Willkie also was courted by the preparedness advocates. Unless Willkie supported selective service, MTCA leaders feared most Republicans would reject the compulsory draft. Burke and Wadsworth both had endorsed the presidential candidacy of Willkie, thus diminishing this possibility. In addition, Wadsworth and Clark made written appeals for rearmament to the presidential aspirant. During late July, Wadsworth warned Willkie that the army could not rely upon enlistments and urged him to back selective service "as the only dependable method of obtaining men." Above all, Wadsworth stressed that the preparedness measure "did not originate in the White House" and instead was framed by the MTCA. A few days later, Clark also implored the Republican candidate to make "a forthright endorsement" of the

15. Franklin Canfield to Elihu Root, Jr., 21 August 1940, Series IX, Box 2, Clark Papers.

16. Edward T. Taylor to Franklin D. Roosevelt, 5 August 1940, Franklin D. Roosevelt to Edward T. Taylor, 12 August 1940, President's Personal File 5665, Franklin D. Roosevelt Papers.

17. Diary of Henry L. Stimson, 23 August 1940, Henry L. Stimson Papers; *New York Times*, 24 August 1940.

selective service proposal.[18] In his initial campaign speech on 17 August, Willkie favored abandoning the voluntary system. Before a huge throng at Ellwood, Indiana, Willkie asserted, "Some form of selective service is the only democratic way to secure the trained and competent manpower we need for defense." On 26 August, Willkie told reporters an "immediate" peacetime draft was preferable to the Maloney amendment.[19] Willkie's attitude particularly on preparedness placed Minority Leader Charles L. McNary of Oregon, his vice-presidential running mate, in a predicament. Although opposing any change in American recruitment policy, McNary did not want to make selective service a partisan issue.

The statements by Roosevelt and Willkie helped preparedness advocates break the Senate filibuster. Buoyed by these remarks, preparedness advocates on 24 August seized the initiative. Republican Ernest W. Gibson of Vermont, along with Democrats Hill of Alabama and Harry F. Byrd of Virginia, urged quick Senate approval of the selective service measure. Willkie especially had played a key role in shifting the momentum against the rearmament opponents. Republican Hiram W. Johnson of California charged that Willkie "really broke the back of the opposition to the conscription law and lent a great deal of assistance to the Austins, and others, in the Senate who were playing the game of Roosevelt and Great Britain." "If he had not broken the force of our opposition and taken weak men into the Roosevelt camp on the conscription bill," Johnson claimed, "we might have stood a chance of defeating it."[20]

Rearmament opponents made several unsuccessful attempts to amend the measure. On 26 August, the Senate rejected motions by Massachusetts Republican Henry Cabot Lodge, Jr., to reduce trainees from 1 million to 800,000 and to limit eligible conscripts to ages twenty-one to twenty-five. Missouri Democrat Clark's proposal to confine draftees to the United States and its possessions produced similar results.[21] A day later, the Senate defeated 54 to 29 an amendment by Democrat David I. Walsh of Massachusetts to keep the existing recruitment method until Congress had declared war. By a 56 to 22 margin, the upper chamber repudiated Taft's plan restricting the regular army to 500,000 men and creating a special corps of 1.5 million volunteer reservists.[22] The decisive tallies indicated that some form of selective service would be adopted. Rearmament opponents thus concentrated on proposals to delay the implementation of a peacetime draft.

The selective service measure, however, was changed in two significant ways. The Senate on 26 August overwhelmingly endorsed Lodge's motion limiting induct-

18. James W. Wadsworth, Jr., to Wendell L. Willkie, 24 July 1940, Box 21, Wadsworth Family Papers; Grenville Clark to Wendell L. Willkie, 2 August 1940, Series IX, Box 2, Clark Papers; Martin L. Fausold, *James W. Wadsworth, Jr.: The Gentleman from New York*, pp. 316–17.

19. David L. Porter, "The Man Who Made the Draft—Representative James Wadsworth," p. 32; Fausold, *Wadsworth*, p. 318; *New York Times*, 18 August 1940; *New York Herald-Tribune*, 27 August 1940.

20. *CR*, 24 August 1940, pp. 15561–63; Hiram W. Johnson to Hiram W. Johnson, Jr., 30 August, 1 September 1940, Part VI, Box 8, Hiram W. Johnson Papers.

21. *CR*, 26 August 1940, pp. 10870, 10888, 10912–14.

22. *CR*, 27 August 1940, pp. 11035–36, 11043.

ees to the Western Hemisphere and American territorial possessions. Preparedness advocates and rearmament opponents both disapproved of sending troops to European battlefields. Two days later, the upper chamber resoundingly accepted 69 to 16 an amendment by Democrats Richard B. Russell of Georgia and John H. Overton of Louisiana. This proposal empowered the president to seize control of industries refusing to cooperate with the national defense program.[23] Overton argued that the War Department should ''draft plants, whose owners by reason of their exhorbitant [sic] profits, refused to supply the men with the equipment and materiel necessary for their service.'' Norris of Nebraska, Gerald P. Nye of North Dakota, and Wheeler of Montana, and other Great Lakes, Great Plains, and Mountain members especially welcomed the Russell-Overton plan. Munitioners and Wall Street businesses, they charged, sought American involvement overseas to secure monetary profits. Wheeler predicted that the financiers, ''the bankers and the great newspapers of the City of New York, who are parading and shouting for this bill in the interest of doing patriotic service, will raise a howl when this amendment is put into the bill.''[24]

As senators prepared to debate the controversial Maloney amendment, Democrat Carl Hayden of Arizona on 28 August submitted another compromise solution. A native of Tempe, Arizona, the sixty-two-year-old Hayden had graduated from Arizona Normal School and attended Stanford University. In 1902, he had opened a flour milling business in Tempe. During the next decade, Hayden had served on the Tempe Town Council and was treasurer and sheriff of Maricopa County. He had been elected in 1912 as the first Arizona member of the U.S. House of Representatives. Hayden in 1926 had joined the U.S. Senate, where he was an expert on irrigation, flood control, and roads. Besides advocating highway construction, the Arizona Democrat supported increased federal assistance for organized labor, farmers, and retired persons. ''The highly respected Hayden,'' the *Washington Post* remarked, ''works hard, speaks little, generally votes for the little fellow.'' The Arizona Democrat usually aligned with the internationalists and preparedness spokesmen on Capitol Hill. During World War I, he had supported the American declaration of war against Germany, backed appropriations for improving military fortifications, and urged furnishing defensive arms to merchant vessels. Hayden continued his interest in military affairs after World War I and voted for construction of the navy and marine corps. In the 1930s, he had usually endorsed internationalist, interventionist, and preparedness programs. After the outbreak of World War II, he had warned that strict neutrality legislation discriminated in favor of the aggressor nations and therefore supported the internationalist Pittman measure repealing the arms embargo. The Arizona Democrat had also sympathized with the Finnish people and advocated the interventionist Brown legislation authorizing a federal loan to the Ryti government for purchasing nonmilitary materials. Hayden believed Nazi activities in Western Europe adversely affected American interests

23. *New York Times*, 27 August 1940; *CR*, 28 August 1940, p. 11112.
24. John H. Overton to J. F. Hall, 10 September 1940, Box X–44, John H. Overton Papers; *CR*, 28 August 1940, p. 11090.

and therefore supported strengthening military fortifications. In regard to raising an army, however, Hayden preferred continuing the voluntary approach. Although not opposed to the principle of peacetime selective service, he contended that the War Department could meet manpower requirements through traditional enlistments. If a sufficient number of enlistees could not be secured, he then would consent to a peacetime draft.[25]

The Hayden plan was a modified version of the earlier Maloney amendment. Maloney had proposed that if 400,000 men did not enroll before 1 January 1941, the peacetime draft should be implemented. Hayden recommended instead allotting a sixty-day grace period for enlistments. Under the Hayden plan, the president would issue orders upon enactment of the selective service bill and again on 1 January. In each instance, Roosevelt could resort to selective service after sixty days to fill any quota deficits. Besides ensuring that the army would reach manpower goals, the amendment would determine the wisdom of continuing existing recruitment methods. According to Hayden, "enough voluntary enlistments could be secured within the next two months to fill the immediate needs of the War Department."[26]

Hayden's proposal encountered a mixed reception on Capitol Hill. Rearmament opponents strenuously supported postponement of the compulsory draft. "I would do anything in the way of amendment of the Bill," Republican Johnson of California remarked, "that would smear it, or might demonstrate its uselessness." On the other hand, Majority Leader Barkley, a preparedness advocate who deplored the Hayden motion as "the wrong way to raise an army," attempted to discipline party members to reject the compromise plan.[27]

By a narrow 43 to 41 margin, Senate preparedness advocates the same day defeated the Hayden amendment. On this issue, political considerations made less impact than usual. Despite Barkley's pleas, Democrats divided more sharply on this preparedness question than they had on any other foreign policy roll call during the Seventy-sixth Congress. Roosevelt had exhibited little direct leadership, providing party members with an outlet to deemphasize political considerations this time. The president had not endorsed the principle of selective service publicly until early August and had declined to indicate specifically whether he backed the Burke-Wadsworth measure. In hopes of averting a personal confrontation with Congress, he had given hardly any direct signals to party members and had left the direction to Senate heads.

A slight majority of the Democrats opposed the Hayden amendment, barely preventing another experimental round with voluntary enlistments. Representing mainly the eastern half of the United States, they asserted that the Nazi blitzkrieg across Western Europe and especially the fall of France threatened American

25. "Carl Hayden," *Current Biography* 12 (1951):261–63; *BDAC*, p. 1028.

26. *New York Times*, 29 August 1940; Carl Hayden to Mrs. Edwin Pendleton, 23 August 1940, 379/28, Carl Hayden Papers.

27. Hiram W. Johnson to Hiram W. Johnson, Jr., 8 September 1940, Part VI, Box 8, Johnson Papers; Samuel R. Spencer, Jr., "A History of the Selective Training and Service Act of 1940 from Inception to Enactment" (Ph.D. diss.), pp. 463–64.

security. If Hitler defeated Great Britain, these Democrats warned, Germany next might attack the Western Hemisphere. The army, preparedness advocates urged, should draft and train soldiers as quickly as possible to meet this changing situation. On the other hand, nearly one-half of the Democrats supported the compromise proposal made by their Arizona colleague. Serving mainly states west of the Mississippi River, these rearmament opponents claimed that the Atlantic Ocean afforded adequate protection against foreign invasion. These Democrats denounced selective service as forced regimentation and still preferred recruiting an army through voluntary enlistments.

Similarly, the Republicans divided sharply and thus failed to take advantage of the Democratic division. The sentiments of Republican senators reflected the national schism within the minority party on selective service. One-half of the Republicans, particularly those from the New England and Middle Atlantic States, agreed with presidential candidate Willkie and rejected the compromise proposal. Since the Nazis were spreading westward, these preparedness advocates insisted the United States should act quickly to implement the draft. Other members, especially from inland regions, distrusted Roosevelt, did not believe the United States faced imminent danger, and denounced conscription as a totalitarian tactic (see table 21).

Sectional delegations likewise were quite divided on the Hayden amendment. Southern Democrats proportionately led the preparedness battle for an immediate draft and aligned with the New England and Middle Atlantic blocs to prevent another trial period for voluntary enlistments. Although largely anti-New Deal, Southern Democrats increasingly had supported President Roosevelt's foreign policy programs. The German takeover of France and the subsequent blitzkrieg of Great Britain especially alarmed these members. Besides serving predominantly British-American constituents, the Southerners had traded extensively with Western Europe and geographically were separated from the European conflict only by the Atlantic Ocean. They also had a strong military tradition and usually had backed American preparedness efforts. The New England and Middle Atlantic delegations similarly represented a less insulated region bartering considerably with Great Britain and including a large number of British-Americans. A bipartisan group, they came from a more industrial section that might profit economically from federal government defense contracts (see table 21).

Pacific members proportionately directed the unsuccessful campaign to delay the draft sixty days and coalesced with the Mountain, Great Lakes, and Great Plains senators.[28] Anti-Roosevelt Republicans, who held considerable influence in the Pacific bloc, favored giving voluntary enlistments another chance. Situated a vast distance from the overseas conflict, the Pacific states had relied comparatively little on European commerce. Ethnically, Russian and Scandinavian constituents living there deplored the draft as un-American and as a belligerent step. The Mountain members, although they had favored arms embargo repeal, this time backed the

28. *CR*, 28 August 1940, p. 11124. The tables cited in this chapter are based on data from the Inter-University Consortium for Political Research, University of Michigan.

compromise proposal made by their Arizona colleague. The largely Democratic Mountain delegation rejected Barkley's pleas to support selective service, while the Great Lakes and Great Plains Republicans repudiated Willkie's proconscription views. The Mountain, Great Lakes, and Great Plains sections geographically were quite removed from the European conflict and did not lose much trade because of the Nazi activity overseas. Ever mindful of American entry into World War I, they suspected rearmament would benefit primarily the eastern financial and industrial interests. German and Russian constituents residing there feared conscription might expedite American entry into war against their homelands (see table 21).

Other considerations contributed to the demise of the Hayden amendment. Ideologically, many preparedness advocates urged increased manpower because Western European democracies were struggling for survival against the totalitarian nations. They feared that if Great Britain was conquered by the Nazis, Hitler might attack the Western Hemisphere and endanger the cherished freedoms enjoyed by American citizens. Preparedness-minded pressure groups, most notably the MTCA, favored an immediate draft and helped avert postponement of peacetime conscription. Marked public opinion shifts in favor of selective service also diminished the political consequences some preparedness advocates feared from opposing the Hayden compromise. On the other hand, ethnic factors played a subordinate role this time. Irish and German senators split very sharply on the question of peacetime selective service, thus decreasing the impact of nationalities. After the surrender of France, several Irish and German legislators increasingly realized Hitler threatened the future of the world and became preparedness advocates. Other Irish and German senators, however, rejected selective service as too authoritarian and opposed the American rearmament campaign[29] (see table 31).

Hayden's solution produced unusual alignments. Seven Democrats and two Republicans who ultimately supported the selective service measure also backed the compromise Hayden Plan. Of the nine, Democrats Key Pittman of Nevada, Robert F. Wagner of New York, and Republican Wallace H. White of Maine served on the prestigious Foreign Relations Committee. Democrats Maloney of Connecticut and William H. King of Utah were embroiled in strenuous reelection campaigns. If all rearmament opponents had united, the Senate would have approved the sixty-day delay. Four rearmament opponents, including Republicans John A. Danaher of Connecticut and Taft of Ohio and Democrats Lewis P. Schwellenbach of Washington and D. Worth Clark of Idaho, also rejected the Hayden proposal. Danaher was an anti-Roosevelt Republican from a heavily Irish state, while the other three rearmament opponents served more insulated, highly ethnic regions. According to Taft, the compromise was "a means of proving that the voluntary system will not work."[30]

29. The ethnic origins of members are derived from Elsdon Coles Smith, *New Dictionary of American Family Names*.
30. Spencer, "Selective Training and Service Act," p. 465. The four other senators supporting both the Hayden amendment and the Burke-Wadsworth measure were Republican Charles W. Tobey of New Hampshire and Democrats James M. Mead of New York, Matthew M. Neely of West Virginia, and Millard E. Tydings of Maryland.

By a much wider 50 to 35 margin, Senate preparedness advocates the same day rejected the Maloney amendment. Although still disunited, Democrats displayed sufficient cohesion this time in support of preparedness to cause the defeat of the Maloney motion. Republicans leaned toward retaining voluntary recruitment methods but still remained more divided than Roosevelt's party. Once again, the minority did not capitalize on the widespread Democratic split. Border state senators joined the Southern members this time in directing preparedness advocates resisting postponement of the draft. Besides being overwhelmingly Democratic, both sections included mainly British-Americans, engaged in considerable commerce with Western European nations, and mostly were located closer to the European scene. Exponents of the domino theory, these preparedness advocates feared Hitler would extend the European war to the Western Hemisphere and insisted that the United States should train conscripts quickly. Several Border and Mountain Democrats who had supported the earlier Hayden proposal disapproved of the Maloney motion, thus creating the wider vote margin. As earlier, the Pacific delegation led proportionately the drive for the Maloney amendment and coalesced with the Great Lakes and Great Plains members against rearmament[31] (see table 21).

On 28 August, the upper chamber adopted 58 to 31 the Burke measure. Solidifying ranks, Democrats largely supported the compulsory draft and insured victory for the preparedness advocates. Even though Roosevelt had not demonstrated dynamic direction, most Democrats rallied to the preparedness side. Aware that Germany might attack the Western Hemisphere, they urged the United States to recruit more soldiers promptly to meet such a contingency. On the other hand, they still were less united than they had been on either the internationalist neutrality revision or the interventionist Finnish legislation. Republicans remained sharply divided, leaning slightly against conscription. The abstention by Minority Leader McNary symbolized the widespread disagreement within the opposition party. The preparedness-minded New England and Middle Atlantic Republicans recommended the training of conscripts because of German activity overseas and Willkie's pro-conscription attitude. In addition, New England and Middle Atlantic industries and commerce would benefit financially from federal defense contracts. By contrast, Great Lakes and Great Plains Republicans opposing rearmament charged that selective service was antidemocratic, feared profiteering from rearmament by eastern interests, and denied that Nazi expansion endangered American security. On this roll call, sectionalism played a more vibrant role than political partisanship. Southern and Border delegations almost unanimously backed selective service and cast nearly one-half of the affirmative preparedness votes. The New England and Middle Atlantic senators, who also achieved at least 75 percent cooperation, also helped insure success for the selective service measure. For rearmament opponents, the Pacific, Great Lakes, and Great Plains blocs directed the movement to retain voluntary recruitment and were joined by one-half of the Mountain senators. Pacific members continued to vote less for preparedness than historians have thought, while

31. *CR*, 28 August 1940, p. 11137.

the opposite pattern prevailed among the Mountain delegation[32] (see table 21).

As on the Hayden amendment, other considerations influenced the outcome. Ideologically, a majority of senators feared the Germans might continue to expand and contended the United States should prepare militarily to help preserve democratic institutions. Preparedness interest groups, especially the MTCA, had lobbied extensively to rally senatorial support for selective service. Public opinion nationally increasingly favored adoption of the draft, thus aiding adoption. Ethnic factors, on the other hand, continued to have marginal impact. Defying traditional stereotypes, Irishmen aligned with the preparedness advocates. Germans reached no consensus, while the Scandinavians opposed rearmament and disapproved of the selective service bill[33] (see table 31).

Preparedness voting alignments resembled those on the internationalist neutrality revision issue more than those on the interventionist Finnish question. Internationalists, who had supported repeal of the arms embargo, overwhelmingly favored the selective service measure. Of the fifty-eight preparedness advocates defending selective service, fifty (86 percent) also favored neutrality revision. The preparedness coalition, however, differed considerably from that on Finnish intervention. Thirty-four (59 percent) of the preparedness advocates had cast affirmative votes on the interventionist Brown Act. On the other hand, there was much less continuity among the isolationists, noninterventionists, and rearmament opponents. Of the thirty-one rearmament opponents, twenty (64 percent) were isolationists favoring retention of the arms embargo and only thirteen (42 percent) were noninterventionists against federal credits to Finland (see appendixes 3, 4).

The three issues provide a clearer portrait of the internationalists, interventionists, and preparedness advocates on the one hand and the isolationists, noninterventionists, and rearmament opponents on the other hand. Politically, the internationalists, interventionists, and preparedness advocates received over twice as much backing from Democrats as from Republicans. Sectionally, the Border delegation led proportionately the campaign to increase American overseas commitments and aligned with Middle Atlantic and Southern senators. Republican and third-party senators consistently directed the isolationists, noninterventionists, and rearmament opponents. The Pacific and Great Plains blocs usually sided with the opposition on the three issues. On the other hand, the Mountain, Great Lakes, and New England delegations did not follow consistent patterns (see tables 22, 23).

Voting determinants resembled previous alignments. As on the interventionist Finnish issue, political party affiliation played a moderate role on the preparedness question. Democrats averaged 70 percent unity on major roll calls, while Republicans managed only 54 percent. Sectional considerations influenced behavior more decisively, repeating patterns on the internationalist neutrality revision legislation.

32. *CR*, 28 August 1940, p. 11142; *New York Times*, 29 August 1940. H. Bradford Westerfield, Robert A. Dahl, Duncan Mac Rae, Jr., Leroy N. Rieselbach, and other scholars picture the Pacific section as internationalist in this era.

33. Samuel Lubell, Mark Lincoln Chadwin, T. Ryle Dwyer, Lawrence H. Fuchs, and others describe the Irish as isolationist in the Roosevelt period.

On the preparedness question, around one-half of the delegations averaged at least 75 percent cooperation (see table 21). As with the internationalist arms embargo repeal measure, interest groups made an enormous impact upon preparedness legislation. Besides framing the selective service measure, the MTCA lobbied numerous senators. Ideological factors figured prominently on the Finnish and other two issues, while ethnicity usually was subordinate.

Several individuals contributed substantially to the Senate outcome. MTCA leader Grenville Clark performed the most instrumental role, helping draft the legislation and directing preparedness lobbying activities. At the request of the MTCA, Senator Burke of Nebraska gladly had introduced the controversial measure."You have earned the gratitude of the people of America." Clark wrote Burke, "for your effective and patriotic service." Sheppard of Texas vigorously had steered the selective service bill through the Military Affairs Committee and had defended preparedness on the Senate floor. In a letter to Sheppard, MTCA member Julius Ochs Adler remarked, "We are fortunate that in this emergency you were directing the consideration of the measure."[34] Although President Roosevelt had continued to act cautiously, Republican nominee Willkie had made selective service a more bipartisan issue.

MTCA preparedness advocates welcomed the final Senate outcome. "The Senate's action by such a decisive majority," Clark commented, "is now proof that the American system is still capable of meeting a crisis." The Plattsburgers, however, still would have preferred to change the upper age limit from thirty-one to forty-five. Besides including more experienced, older men, this change would have lessened the burden on American youth. Otherwise, the Senate version pleased the MTCA preparedness advocates. The army was authorized to draft 800,000 single men by early 1941 for service in the United States, the Western Hemisphere, and American territorial possessions. If the United States became engaged in war or if Congress considered the national interest to be suddenly endangered, selective service could be extended beyond one year. Conscientious objectors and persons in designated occupations were exempted. In order to insure steady production of defense materials, the federal government was empowered to recruit private plants.[35]

The Senate action marked a major step in the preparedness movement. Since the outbreak of World War II, the upper chamber had approved the internationalist Pittman measure repealing the arms embargo and the limited interventionist Brown bill for federal assistance to Finland. This time the Senate had agreed to abandon the traditional voluntary enlistment method for recruiting soldiers and had endorsed the first peacetime draft in American history. On the other hand, they had sanctioned this step as a precautionary measure to help defend the Western Hemisphere against

34. Grenville Clark to Edward R. Burke, 29 August 1940, Series IX, Box 1, Clark Papers; Julius Ochs Adler to Morris Sheppard, 29 August 1940, Scrapbook, 1935–1942, Morris Sheppard Papers.
35. Grenville Clark to Members of House of Representatives, 3 September 1940, Series IX, Box 8, Clark Papers; *New York Times*, 29 August 1940.

foreign invasion and had vigorously opposed sending American troops to European battlefields.

The House Military Affairs Committee, meanwhile, was considering the preparedness bill. Under the direction of Kentucky Democrat Andrew J. May, the group had conducted an extensive investigation in July of American recruitment policies. Hearings were extended to permit all interested witnesses to testify. After completing proceedings, the committee recessed to await final Senate action. Chairman May, a sixty-five-year-old native of Langley, Kentucky, had taught at public schools in Floyd and Magoffin counties. He had graduated from Southern University Law School and commenced practice at Prestonburg, Kentucky. For several years, May had served as county attorney, special circuit court judge, and director of coal and mining companies. The Kentucky Democrat, who had been elected in 1930 to the U.S. House of Representatives, had befriended Vice-president John Nance Garner and aligned with anti-New Dealers defending private enterprise and opposing the growth of the federal government's powers. As head of the Military Affairs Committee, May enthusiastically supported internationalist, interventionist, and preparedness policies. Besides championing army expansion, the Kentucky Democrat favored strengthening military fortifications along the Atlantic Coast and increasing national authority to mobilize the armed forces. May advocated preparedness not only because the Axis nations endangered world security, but also because American munitions industries could reap substantial profits. A vociferous critic of the Ludlow war referendum proposals, he also urged military training for Civilian Conservation Corps members and in 1938 had written legislation for complete wartime mobilization of civilians and industries. The internationalist Kentucky Democrat had approved of lifting the arms embargo and relaxing cash-and-carry restrictions. Denying that the voluntary system could secure a sufficient number of volunteers, he insisted that selective service afforded the best means of preserving peace.[36]

The preparedness-minded Military Affairs Committee made two major changes in the selective service bill. In late August, May's group attached an amendment by Republican Walter G. Andrews of New York, a preparedness advocate, to extend from thirty-one to forty-five the upper age limit for draftees. A motion by Connecticut Democrat J. Joseph Smith granted the army authority to control plants of recalcitrant manufacturers on a forced rental basis. The Smith proposal narrowed the scope of the earlier Russell-Overton plan. This change came at the insistence of New York Republican James W. Wadsworth, Jr., who protested allowing Roosevelt indefinitely to seize control of domestic industries. Wadsworth argued that the War Department could not secure military equipment "as quickly or in as great numbers if the government took charge."[37]

Preparedness advocates easily controlled decisionmaking in the Military Af-

36. "Andrew Jackson May," *Current Biography* 2 (1941):565–66; *BDAC*, p. 1278.
37. Gilbert Y. Steiner, *The Congressional Conference Committee: Seventieth to Eightieth Congresses*, p. 78; James W. Wadsworth, Jr., to Robert P. Patterson, 24 August 1940, Box 21, Wadsworth Papers.

fairs Committee and by a wide 17 to 8 margin on 29 August sent the selective service bill to the House floor. Preparedness advocates comprised thirteen Democrats and four Republicans and came predominantly from Southern, Border, and Middle Atlantic states. If Congress rejected the selective service measure, draft defenders argued, "it would be a crime against the country." Four preparedness advocates, Democrats Smith of Connecticut and John M. Costello of California and Republicans Charles R. Clason of Massachusetts and Albert Rutherford of Pennsylvania, had voted against the internationalist measure repealing the arms embargo. Led by Republican Dewey Short of Missouri, rearmament opponents consisted of six Republicans and two Democrats representing Great Plains and Great Lakes constituents. Rearmament opponents denounced conscription as a "dangerous departure" laying the foundation for "a military dictatorship." With the exception of Democrat Edwin M. Schaefer of Illinois, they had favored retaining the ban on munitions sales.[38]

At the outset, preparedness advocates controlled the House. Wadsworth of New York, along with the MTCA, already had lobbied extensively for preparedness in the lower chamber. On 20 August, Wadsworth had entertained May of Kentucky, Majority Leader Sam Rayburn of Texas, Naval Affairs Committee Chairman Carl Vinson of Georgia, and eleven other influential representatives at the Army and Navy Club. At this dinner, Grenville Clark and Gen. George Catlett Marshall had delivered speeches defending selective service preparedness. Wadsworth also had attempted to persuade several Republican colleagues to support the draft, while MTCA lobbyist Joseph Drake had encountered favorable responses from several Democratic representatives. To the delight of Clark's organization, the Rules Committee on 30 August restricted floor debate to two days.[39]

From the beginning, party heads did not attempt to discipline party members. Majority Leader Rayburn particularly played a less active role on this preparedness issue than he had at the special session. The House, he predicted, would approve the selective service measure within a week by at least a two-to-one margin. Since the middle of August, two related actions had enhanced the prospects of preparedness advocates.[40] On 15 August, the representatives overwhelmingly has passed rearmament legislation ordering all National Guard members and retired army personnel into active service for one year of intensive training. Six days later, the House had consented 183 to 144 to increase from $200 million to $700 million the lending authority of the Export-Import Bank. The latter measure had authorized the additional $500 million to help Latin American nations develop resources, stabilize

38. U.S., Congress, House of Representatives, Committee on Military Affairs, "Compulsory Military Training and Service," *Reports*, no. 2093, 29 August 1940.

39. Joseph Drake Memorandum, 15 August 1940, Series IX, Box 8, Clark Papers; James W. Wadsworth, Jr., to J. W. Wainwright, 17 September 1940, Box 21, Wadsworth Papers; Joseph Drake Notes on Representative Robertson, 13 August 1940, Series IX, Box 6, Clark Papers; Spencer, "Selective Training and Service Act," p. 470.

40. Joseph Drake Notes on Representative Rayburn, 13 August 1940, Series IX, Box 6, Clark Papers; *New York Times*, 31 August 1940.

economies, and market products.[41] On the other hand, Republicans were divided nationally on preparedness and on the peacetime draft. Minority Leader Martin therefore freed party colleagues to vote their personal convictions this time.

House alignments had shifted considerably since the special session. Preparedness advocates were more heterogeneous politically than internationalists had been on neutrality revision. They received backing from 80 percent of the Democrats and registered 10 percent gains among Republicans. Regionally, there was more continuity between the internationalists and preparedness advocates than in the Senate. Southern Democrats proportionately led the campaign for internationalists favoring arms embargo repeal and for preparedness advocates defending selective service and aligned with a substantial majority of the Border and Middle Atlantic congressmen. New England representatives were much more receptive to changing preparedness policies than to altering neutrality legislation. This time opposition forces had more numerical support. Rearmament opponents comprised over three-fourths of the Republicans and attracted 7 percent wider following from Democrats. Great Lakes members proportionately led the anticonscription movement and were joined by the Great Plains and Mountain delegations. Sectionally, rearmament opponents recorded the most substantial gains among the Great Plains and Mountain blocs (see table 24).

The House on 3 September began floor debate. Newspaper reporters, radio commentators, photographers, and numerous spectators came to Capitol Hill to witness the representatives determine manpower recruitment policies. "There is lots of interest in it," Democrat J. Wilburn Cartwright of Oklahoma remarked, and "the galleries and halls are full. Have to have a lot of extra policemen and plain-clothes men."[42] The colorful discussion, however, provided few perceptive insights. "If you read all the speeches," Republican Ralph A. Gamble of New York stated, "you must have done so out of doors, otherwise I am afraid you would have been asphyxiated."[43]

During the two days, preparedness advocates stressed rearmament and ideological themes. Led by Wadsworth of New York and May of Kentucky, they argued that voluntarism had failed to meet defense manpower quotas. Preparedness advocates insisted that German expansion threatened American security and supported selective service as the quickest way to build an effective army. Wadsworth, who delivered their most effective speech, contended that the United States could no longer afford "to indulge in a wait-and-see policy." According to him, the War Department should train troops "as soon as we can get them" for "the safe defense of the Monroe Doctrine."[44]

For the rearmament opponents, Republican Hamilton Fish of New York

41. CR, 15 August 1940, p. 10448, 21 August 1940, pp. 10704–5.
42. New York Times, 4 September 1940; J. Wilburn Cartwright to Relatives, 4 September 1940, Box 126, J. Wilburn Cartwright Papers.
43. Ralph A. Gamble to A. G. Thacher, 2 October 1940, Series IX, Box 3, Clark Papers.
44. CR, 4 September 1940, pp. 11440–43; Porter, "Wadsworth," p. 32; Fausold, Wadsworth, p. 318.

directed floor strategy. A native of Garrison, New York, the fifty-one-year-old Fish was the grandson of a former secretary of state. He had graduated cum laude from Harvard University, where he was an all-American tackle in football. After a stint in the New York State Assembly, Fish had commanded a National Guard regiment in World War I. He had been elected in 1918 to the U.S. House of Representatives, where he defended the interests of veterans groups and introduced legislation to pay bonuses and erect monuments. A die-hard politician, Fish thrived on newspaper publicity and always sought to please his constituents. The New York Republican, who usually aligned with conservatives against New Deal measures, had supported the Liberty League movement. Although serving the district in which Roosevelt lived, Fish continually criticized the president and believed the chief executive already had assumed too much power. Roosevelt likewise detested Fish, ranking him with Representatives Joseph W. Martin, Jr., of Massachusetts and Bruce Barton of New York as one of his principal foes in Congress.

Fish backed the militant isolationists on Capitol Hill. An advocate of American entry into World War I, he had contended that Germany had violated American neutral maritime rights. During the 1930s, he had disagreed with those isolationists who wished to avoid American involvement in war either by sacrificing neutral rights on the high seas or by curtailing trade to belligerent nations. Fish was one of the few isolationists opposing the strict Neutrality Act of 1937, charging that it empowered the president to terminate commerce with countries at war. Two years later, the New York Republican had disapproved of the internationalist Neutrality Act of 1939 and endorsed the Vorys amendment restoring the arms embargo. Hostility toward both Roosevelt and war, coupled with an intense hatred of Communism and the Soviet Union, prompted Fish to protest American actions to aid the Allies. Besides believing that the president deliberately was seeking to involve the United States in the European conflict, he denied that the Nazis threatened the Western world. Rabid anti-Soviet attitudes caused him to make questionable associations and engage in disreputable activities. The recipient of wide press coverage, Fish often had spoken at rallies of the German-American Bund. He also had abused his franking privileges by mailing to constituents Nazi-inspired speeches and pamphlets. Joining American-Laborite Vito Marcantonio of New York, he denounced conscription as an undemocratic method and claimed that dropping voluntary recruitment would draw the United States closer to war against Germany.[45]

Ideological arguments were elucidated by rearmament opponents. Along with denying that Nazi activity abroad threatened American democratic institutions, they insisted that voluntary enlistments met War Department quotas. A peacetime draft, rearmament opponents warned, would violate American freedoms and encourage further participation in the European conflict. Fish denounced the selective service measure as "an evil and ruinous experiment" on a "direct road to Hitlerism,

45. "Hamilton Fish," *Current Biography* 2 (1941):278–80; Richard N. Current, "Hamilton Fish: 'Crusading Isolationist,' " in J. T. Salter, ed., *Public Men In and Out of Office*, pp. 210–24; Manfred Jonas, *Isolationism in America, 1935–1941*, pp. 52–54.

dictatorship and national socialism." "The day is not far off," Marcantonio of New York added, "when these weapons of destruction and this army built by conscription will be used not for defense but for participation in an imperialist war."[46]

Two skirmishes enlivened the floor action. In an address, Democrat Martin L. Sweeney of Ohio, a rearmament opponent, criticized President Roosevelt for drawing the United States closer to the European war. The impassioned speech irked Kentucky Democrat Beverly M. Vincent, who was seated in the adjoining chair. A preparedness advocate, Vincent jumped up and declared he would not sit next to a "traitor." Vincent and Sweeney briefly sparred, landing penetrating blows to the face. Before colleagues could stop the fracas, both representatives had bloody noses. In the gallery, meanwhile, several members of organizations opposing rearmament interrupted speeches being delivered by preparedness advocates. In an effort to restore order, security forces removed the demonstrators from the premises. The lobbyists' tactics may have influenced several undecided representatives to support the selective service measure. "A lot of 'bums' and the 'hoodlum' element, pacifists, and Communists," Cartwright of Oklahoma remarked, "are doing more for the bill by fighting it than they are doing against it." "I don't think," he added, "the opposition will get over 100 votes now."[47]

Preparedness advocates clashed with rearmament opponents over the age range. Since rearmament opponents considered the House upper limit of forty-five too broad, they favored restoration of the Senate version. Rearmament opponents supported an amendment by Democrat Arthur Anderson of Missouri to restrict to ages twenty-one to thirty-one the parameters for draftees. On the other hand, preparedness advocates preferred the more comprehensive twenty-one to forty-five range. The MTCA sent every congressman a letter defending the larger range. Clark's group asserted, "The wider age range would make for national unity and morale."[48]

The timing of selective service likewise provoked controversy. Rearmament opponents urged delaying for at least sixty days any peacetime draft. Fish of New York introduced a carbon copy of the original Hayden amendment continuing voluntarism for at least two months. If 400,000 Americans did not enlist within that time period, the War Department could institute compulsory service to fill quotas. Rearmament opponents still chose not to change manpower recruitment policies. Republican Karl Stefan of Nebraska opposed resorting to the draft "unless and until every honest effort has been made to secure the necessary enlistments through the American voluntary system."[49] On the other hand, preparedness advocates recommended immediate selective service because Nazi aggression already endangered American security. They argued that delaying troop mobilization would render

46. CR, 3 September 1940, p. 11361; New York Times, 5 September 1940.
47. Spencer, "Selective Training and Service Act," p. 472; Cartwright to Relatives, 4 September 1940.
48. New York Times, 7 September 1940; Clark to Representatives, 3 September 1940.
49. New York Times, 6 September 1940; Karl Stefan to Chris Wunderlich, 8 August 1940, Box 24, Karl Stefan Papers.

ineffective army expansion plans. "Time there was for England, for Belgium, for France," Rayburn of Texas recalled, "and they didn't use it. Sixty days would have meant a great deal."[50]

Preparedness advocates prevailed on two major votes. On 6 September, representatives decisively rejected 161 to 47 Anderson's proposal lowering to thirty-one the upper age limit for draftees. Democrat Lyle H. Boren of Oklahoma, who aligned with the majority, commented, "It is difficult to convince me that *I* would not make a better soldier" than considerably younger men. A day later, the House overwhelmingly approved 330 to 83 the Smith amendment authorizing the government to operate certain defense plants on a forced rental basis.[51]

Rearmament opponents, however, revived the voluntary system. In a teller vote, the House on 5 September approved 185 to 155 the Fish motion delaying for at least sixty days the peacetime draft. An estimated 45 Democrats joined around 140 Republican rearmament opponents in securing postponement. During the next two days, preparedness advocates lobbied behind-the-scenes in an attempt to change the attitudes of rearmament opponents. Nevertheless, representatives on 7 September upheld 207 to 200 the Fish proposal on a roll call. The House, thus, was more reluctant than the Senate to abandon voluntary enlistment and wanted to give the traditional system another trial period.[52]

In contrast to the Senate, political considerations figured prominently in the House. Nearly 80 percent of the representatives adhered to party lines on the crucial amendment. Republicans, along with third-party members, solidly aligned with rearmament opponents in postponing selective service at least sixty days. Distrustful of Roosevelt, Republicans believed the chief executive already wielded too much power and opposed granting him additional authority. "I believe," Democrat Robert L. Doughton of North Carolina charged, "that it was only a political move by the Republicans" to discredit the president. Republican Ben F. Jensen of Iowa, on the other hand, insisted, "The concensus [sic] among the Republicans in Congress regarding this matter is that the people are thoroughly fedup with rubber stamp representation in Congress." Wadsworth, a prominent Republican, asserted, "Their distrust of Roosevelt is so deep and incurable that it sways their judgment completely on any measure which may directly or indirectly give him more power."[53] Hitler, Republican rearmament opponents claimed, would not attempt to conquer the Western Hemisphere. Besides considering voluntary enlistments sufficient, the minority party labeled conscription authoritarian and antidemocratic. On the other hand, approximately three-fourths of the Democrats aligned with the preparedness advocates preferring an immediate draft. Led by Southern and Border congressmen,

50. Spencer, "Selective Training and Service Act," p. 476.
51. *CR*, 6 September 1940, p. 11657, 7 September 1940, pp. 11749–50; Lyle H. Boren to Hec Bussey, 12 August 1940, Box 85, Lyle H. Boren Papers.
52. *CR*, 5 September 1940, p. 11572, 7 September 1940, pp. 11748–49.
53. Robert L. Doughton to Mr. & Mrs. C. A. Millsaps, 9 September 1940, Folder 849, Robert L. Doughton Papers; Wadsworth to Wainwright, 17 September 1940; Ben F. Jensen to Roscoe S. Jones, 11 September 1940, Personal Correspondence, Box 18, Folder 97, Ben F. Jensen Papers.

they usually supported the national defense programs. They warned that Hitler's assault on Great Britain jeopardized American defense and thus backed an immediate draft as a precautionary measure. One-fourth of the Democrats, mainly from the Great Lakes, Great Plains, and Mountain states, aligned with rearmament opponents in favor of giving voluntary enlistments another test and provided the slight margin for the Fish amendment (see table 25). Denying a domino theory, these Democrats considered conscription an overreaction to the existing world situation. The vastly outnumbered Republicans thus received sufficient backing from Roosevelt's party to change the intent of the selective service measure. Democratic defections resembled those exhibited in June 1939 on the Vorys arms embargo motion.

Great Lakes and Great Plains representatives, aligning with New England and Mountain colleagues, proportionately led the campaign by rearmament opponents for postponement. The largely Republican Great Lakes and Great Plains delegations opposed permitting the president and executive branch to draft an army. Representing inland regions, these rearmament opponents argued that the three-thousand-mile-wide Atlantic Ocean afforded the United States adequate protection against foreign invasion. Besides serving many anticonscription ethnic groups, Great Lakes and Great Plains congressmen suspected eastern financial interests of hoping to reap profits from increased American involvement in the war. They rejected the draft as regimentation and preferred giving voluntary enlistment another test. Mountain representatives, although consisting largely of Democrats more sympathetic to Roosevelt, used similar arguments for opposing rearmament. Contrary to traditional viewpoints, the New England congressmen again aligned with rearmament opponents in favor of extending the time period for enlistment. The Republican-controlled delegation found the compromise attractive because they distrusted the president. On the other hand, Southern and Border blocs favoring selective service proportionately led the resistance by preparedness advocates to the Fish motion. Besides usually backing the administration's internationalist programs, these overwhelmingly Democratic groups warned that the Nazis endangered American democracy and security. Most of the Southern and Border states were separated from the overseas conflict only by the Atlantic Ocean, they contained mainly pro-British nationalities, and they engaged in enormous European trade. Backing selective service also conformed with the military traditions of these two sections. Although a large group numerically, the Middle Atlantic representatives divided along party lines and reached no consensus on the issue. Democrats urged adoption of selective service, while Republicans wished to retain the voluntary enlistment method (see table 25).

Ethnic groups were divided on the Fish amendment. Most Germans and Scandinavians aligned with rearmament opponents supporting postponement of conscription, contributing to the adoption of the Fish amendment. Inhabitants of inland states, the German representatives did not consider the Nazis a geographical threat to American safety, repudiated the draft as antidemocratic, and believed voluntary enlistments could meet American manpower needs. German congressmen described conscription as a major step toward involving the United States in a war against their homeland. Scandinavians adamantly opposed rearmament, again following the strict neutrality tenets of their home governments and pacifist ministers. Although usually considered rearmament opponents, the Irish legislators allied with the preparedness advocates on this issue. Belonging predominantly to the Democratic party, they supported Rayburn's pleas to resort to the draft. Irish representatives typically resided in industrial states located closer geographically to the European war and benefiting financially from rearmament efforts. Casting aside their traditional anti-British attitudes, they pictured Hitler as a serious threat to democratic institutions and especially to the freedom of religion (see table 31).

The Fish amendment changed markedly the status of the preparedness legislation. Until the teller vote, preparedness advocates had appeared to be in firm control of the House situation and had seemed virtually assured of securing immediate enactment of selective service. Rearmament opponents, however, had unexpectedly controlled decisionmaking on this amendment and had given the traditional voluntary enlistment method another trial period. Under the able direction of Fish, rearmament opponents were well organized on both the teller and roll-call votes and waged a very effective battle in altering the intent of the Wadsworth measure. The overconfident attitude of preparedness advocates, combined with indecisive leadership by Roosevelt, had contributed to the legislative outcome. Although Wadsworth had performed ably in floor debates and in arranging speakers, other leading congressional preparedness advocates had been less effective. Speaker William B. Bankhead of Alabama and Majority Leader Rayburn initially had not attempted to command party loyalty on the issue and had intervened too late to make up the wide differential on the teller vote. Roosevelt, who privately favored selective service, had proceeded cautiously and exhibited little direct leadership. If the president had taken more direct leadership, fewer Democrats probably would have aligned with the rearmament opponents on the Fish amendment.

In anticlimactic fashion, the House on 7 September overwhelmingly approved 263 to 149 the sharply modified selective service measure. Although 77 percent still followed party lines, political considerations declined in importance. Around thirty Democrats and thirty Republicans who had aligned with rearmament opponents supporting the Fish amendment earlier endorsed the final selective service bill. Since the House already had postponed the draft, this bipartisan group found the preparedness measure more palatable. If the voluntary method did not work, these congressmen were prepared to recruit an army through peacetime conscription. Democrats overwhelmingly approved the revised legislation and solidified ranks more than did Republicans, thus guaranteeing adoption of the selective service measure. On the other hand, 68 percent of the Republicans aligned with rearmament opponents rejecting any peacetime selective service. Minority Leader Martin, Fish of

New York, and several other New England and Middle Atlantic Republicans approved the markedly amended legislation, thus splitting their party ranks[54] (see table 25).

On the preparedness measure, sectionalism also played a dynamic role. Demographically, representatives displayed more unity than they had on most other major foreign policy or defense roll calls at the Seventy-sixth Congress. With the exception of the Pacific bloc, every delegation attained at least 70 percent cohesion. Southern and Border Democrats again stood proportionately at the forefront of the preparedness campaign for selective service and attracted support this time from the New England, Middle Atlantic, Mountain, and Pacific delegations. Nearly one-half of the New England and Mountain members voted with rearmament opponents for the Fish amendment and with preparedness advocates for the final measure. If the voluntary method did not secure the required number of men, these representatives were willing to authorize the drafting of soldiers. Geographically, the New England and Middle Atlantic states were more vulnerable to the European conflict than was any other section. Since Great Britain was being assaulted by the Nazis, New England and Middle Atlantic congressmen insisted the United States should be prepared militarily to counter any expansion by Hitler into the Western Hemisphere. Besides having ethnic links to Great Britain, the New England and Middle Atlantic states traded extensively with Western Europe and had numerous industries likely to benefit from a rearmament program. Although normally considered rearmament opponents, Mountain congressmen also approved of the modified Wadsworth legislation. Along with their Pacific Coast colleagues, they were largely affiliated with Roosevelt's Democratic party and espoused the domino theory. Great Lakes and Great Plains members still proportionately directed the resistance to any peacetime selective service, furnishing over two-thirds of the votes by rearmament opponents against the selective service measure (see table 25).

Other forces also influenced congressional voting behavior. Ethnic groups, particularly the Irish, helped enact the modified bill. Despite prevailing stereotypes, most Irish and several German representatives aligned with the preparedness advocates approving the revised version. Since Hitler's totalitarian methods threatened democratic institutions and individual freedoms, they urged the United States to intensify recruitment efforts. On the other hand, most German and Scandinavian congressmen aligned with rearmament opponents resisting any changes in manpower policies (see table 31). Ideological factors, along with interest groups and public opinion, likewise determined House voting patterns. Due to ominous European developments, many representatives advocated rapid preparedness to help safeguard democracy in the Western Hemisphere. MTCA lobbying activity, coupled with increasing public support for selective service, also contributed to the decisive roll-call margin.

Voting determinants of senators and representatives contrasted markedly. Political partisanship and ethnic background loomed larger in the House, where

54. *CR*, 7 September 1940, pp. 11754–55.

members faced reelection more often. In the lower chamber, several nationalities coalesced with rearmament opponents desiring postponement of the compulsory draft. Sectional delegations also registered impressive cooperation on both sides of the Capitol. On the other hand, ideological and defense considerations loomed larger in the Senate. Due to MTCA preparedness activity, pressure groups affected more decisively the Senate voting behavior.

House alignments resembled those on the neutrality question. Isolationists who had opposed repeal of the arms embargo resoundingly rejected the preparedness measure. Of the 149 rearmament opponents, 123 (83 percent) also had aligned with isolationists vetoing munitions sales to belligerent nations. To a lesser extent, representatives advocating preparedness maintained impressive unity. Of the 263 preparedness advocates, 206 (78 percent) also had supported the internationalists on lifting the arms ban (see appendix 5).

In the House, both issues furnished lucid pictures of the internationalists and preparedness advocates on the one hand and the isolationists and rearmament opponents on the other. Politically, the internationalists and preparedness advocates received four times as much backing from Democrats as from Republicans. Sectionally, Southern Democrats proportionately led the internationalists and preparedness advocates and aligned with Mountain and especially Border congressmen. On the other hand, Republicans vastly outnumbered Roosevelt's party in the camp of the isolationists and rearmament opponents. Regionally, the Great Lakes bloc proportionately directed the battle against internationalism and preparedness and was joined by the Great Plains group. On the two issues, Pacific and Middle Atlantic delegations did not follow consistent patterns (see table 26).

Voting determinants fluctuated moderately on the two issues. Political party affiliation played a major role on both neutrality and selective service. Democrats and Republicans consistently averaged at least 75 percent unity, but partisanship decreased on preparedness. Republican solidarity declined 10 percent, while the number of Democratic defections also increased. On the other hand, sectionalism figured more prominently on preparedness legislation. The number of delegations achieving at least 75 percent solidarity doubled on the selective service measure (see tables 17, 26). Ethnic forces continued to have a profound impact on the voting behavior of representatives. Due mainly to German congressmen, nationalities had a more dramatic effect on selective service than they had had on neutrality (see table 31).

Representative Wadsworth had played the most crucial congressional role in the preparedness campaign. Besides sponsoring the House measure, he had influenced Willkie to back a peacetime draft. The Military Affairs Committee had been convinced by Wadsworth to widen age limits for induction and to soften the industrial amendment. In addition, he had asked numerous Republican colleagues to support his legislation. Wadsworth had not succeeded, however, in preventing adoption by rearmament opponents of the Fish amendment. The conference committee, he hoped, would restore the senate version instituting immediate selective service. He also regretted that most of his Republican colleagues had not joined the internationalists this time. "If any other man had been in the White House," Wadsworth declared, "there would not have been 25 or 30 votes against the bill on the Republican side."[55]

MTCA preparedness advocates, meanwhile, influenced the conferees to remove the controversial Fish proposal. On 9 September, Grenville Clark warned House conferees that retention of the Fish motion would "cause confusion and delay." Clark also feared the plan would "draw distinction between volunteers and selected men, and unnecessarily damage the selective service system."[56] At MTCA insistence, presidential candidate Willkie conferred with Republican leaders McNary and Martin in Indianapolis and persuaded them that conferees should discard the amendment.[57] To the delight of both the MTCA preparedness advocates and Willkie, the House conferees agreed to restore the original Senate version. Nearly all the House conferees, including Democrats May of Kentucky, Dow W. Harter of Ohio, and R. Ewing Thomason of Texas and Republican Andrews of New York, favored an immediate peacetime draft.[58]

A temporary deadlock developed over age limits. House conferees still insisted upon keeping the broader twenty-one to forty-five range for inductees. Wadsworth protested that lowering the figure to thirty-one would make older men "incensed at being left out" and eliminate from active duty every World War I veteran. Older personnel, Wadsworth claimed, would make excellent noncommissioned officers and provide "a steadying influence upon the youngsters."[59] Senate managers, though, rejected this solution and preferred restricting to thirty-one the upper age limit. In order to break the impasse, Andrews of New York suggested that the existing army age range be adopted. After Maj. Lewis Hershey indicated the upper limit was thirty-five years, the conferees unanimously accepted that figure. Democrat Elbert D. Thomas of Utah particularly commended the compromise arrangement. "I fought myself hoarse yesterday," Thomas remarked, "but I had my way on everything so I certainly shall not complain."[60]

Conferees encountered more difficulty in settling the controversial industrial

55. Porter, "Wadsworth," pp. 29–32; Wadsworth to Wainwright, 17 September 1940.

56. Grenville Clark to Walter G. Andrews, 9 September 1940, Sen. 76A–El, Box 116, Legislative Division, National Archives.

57. Donald Bruce Johnson, *The Republican Party and Wendell Willkie*, p. 134; Grenville Clark to Wendell L. Willkie, 11 September 1940, Series IX, Box 8, Clark Papers.

58. U.S., Congress, House of Representatives, Committee on Conference, "Selective Training and Service Act of 1940," *Reports*, no. 2937; Spencer, "Selective Training and Service Act," p. 482; Steiner, *Congressional Conference Committee*, p. 80

59. James W. Wadsworth, Jr., to William Sloan, Jr., 3 September 1940, Box 21, Wadsworth Papers.

60. John G. Clifford, "Grenville Clark and the Origins of Selective Service," pp. 37–38; Elbert D. Thomas to Will Cates, 12 September 1940, Box 29, Elbert D. Thomas Papers. Some senators favored narrowing the age limits further. Democrat Harry S. Truman of Missouri, who preferred restricting draftees to ages nineteen to twenty-four, warned that the United States should "not use the older brackets except in case of a real emergency." Harry S. Truman to District Manager, D. W. Haering Company, 19 February 1941, Senatorial Files, Box 160, Harry S. Truman Papers.

draft issue. Senate managers agreed to drop the Russell-Overton amendment and accept a milder version. Seizure of plants was permitted only where the public necessity was immediate and where the national emergency was very acute.[61] A majority of senators, however, favored restoration of the Russell-Overton proposal. Southern Democrats complained that conferees had unduly restricted executive power. "The Conferees," Russell of Georgia protested, "have gone out of their way to find restrictions and limitations on the power of the Government to force industry to cooperate." Other senators noted that numerous businesses had not honored War Department requests for military supplies. Democrat Joseph C. O'Mahoney of Wyoming complained that the Smith amendment would "grant exemptions to industrial corporations which had refused to accept government orders for arms, ammunition, and other necessary supplies for national defense."[62] In a rare move, the Senate rejected the conference report. By a narrow 37 to 33 margin, it adopted a motion by Democrat Matthew M. Neely of West Virginia to restore the Russell-Overton proposal. Conferees quickly reconvened and increased the authority of the government to handle recalcitrant industries.[63]

Preparedness advocates clearly had controlled decisionmaking in the conference committee. Senate and especially House conferees, all members of the Military Affairs Committee, advocated preparedness more wholeheartedly than did either the typical senator or the typical representative. Although clashing over age limits and drafting industries, the preparedness-minded committee members had eliminated the Fish amendment and thus insured that selective service would begin immediately.

Preparedness advocates greeted the final outcome, while rearmament opponents were dismayed. The Burke-Wadsworth measure, which the preparedness advocates had championed, ultimately had emerged relatively intact. "I am really astounded," Wadsworth observed, "that our bill has not suffered more. As a matter of fact, it comes out practically intact so far as fundamentals go." In addition, preparedness advocates were relieved that the first peacetime draft in American history would not be delayed. "It was a terrific battle," Military Affairs Committee Chairman May remarked, "and I am glad it is finished."[64] By contrast, rearmament opponents still were leery of selective service and preferred voluntary recruitment. "I don't know," Republican Taft of Ohio confided, "that I have ever voted on a measure with as much confidence that my view is the correct one." Taft predicted, "The great bulk of the American people will in the end come to the same conclusion."[65] Rearmament opponents especially were afraid the compulsory draft would

61. U.S., Congress, House of Representatives, Committee on Conference, "Selective Training," *Reports*, no. 2937; *New York Times*, 12–13 September 1940.

62. Steiner, *Congressional Conference Committee*, p. 80; Joseph C. O'Mahoney to Frank Clark, 14 September 1940, Box 50, Joseph C. O'Mahoney Papers.

63. *CR*, 13 September 1940, p. 12113; Steiner, *Congressional Conference Committee*, p. 80.

64. James W. Wadsworth, Jr., to Grenville Clark, 12 September 1940, Box 21, Wadsworth Papers; Fausold, *Wadsworth*, pp. 318–19; Andrew J. May to Grenville Clark, 21 September 1940, Series IX, Box 5, Clark Papers.

65. Taft to Clark, 13 September 1940.

have an adverse impact on American life. Republican Vandenberg of Michigan deplored the Burke-Wadsworth measure as "an unfortunate and dangerous trend," while Republican Johnson of California denounced it "as the most insidious that has been passed in my long service here."[66] On the House side, Republican Clifford R. Hope of Kansas warned, "Peacetime conscription is the first step toward dictatorship in this country." On 19 September, Marcantonio of New York introduced a bill to repeal selective service. "It is the duty of the American people," he declared, "to rally against the Nazification of America."[67]

Roosevelt signed the Burke-Wadsworth bill on 16 September at the White House. Before giving his approval, the president reminded Americans of the worsening European situation. Compulsory service, he predicted, would promote "greater preparedness to meet the threat of war" and help citizens better "enjoy the blessings of peace."[68] Cameras flashed constantly while Roosevelt signed the Burke-Wadsworth measure. In a buoyant mood, the normally cautious president gave pens to Burke, Wadsworth, and other officials present. Wadsworth, who personally disliked the chief executive, took his souvenir pen home and quickly discarded it.[69]

External forces also had interceded in the outcome. If Hitler had not attacked Western Europe in the spring, Congress would have postponed action on selective service. Willkie had made statements supporting conscription, while newly appointed Secretary of War Stimson had persuaded the president to favor a peacetime draft. The preparedness-minded MTCA, especially Grenville Clark, had played the most instrumental role in guiding the Burke-Wadsworth measure through various stages. Secretary Stimson claimed, "There would have been no Selective Service Act of 1940" without the "private initiative" of the MTCA and the "indefatigable and intelligent work" of Clark. Similarly, Wadsworth commended Clark and his group for "starting this thing and carrying on the battle so bravely." "Your emergency committee," Wadsworth wrote Clark, "has performed a vital public service. It performed it unselfishly and with a vision not often possessed by any group in these hectic days."[70]

Selective service provided the nucleus for the American defense effort in World War II. Before the Japanese attack on Pearl Harbor, the War Department trained nearly 1.7 million troops from thirty-six divisions for combat duty. With the aid of the compulsory draft, America helped thwart Hitler's offensive in Europe and Japanese expansion in Asia. The new manpower recruitment program indeed

66. Arthur H. Vandenberg to Katherine Pantlind, 30 September 1940, Arthur H. Vandenberg Papers; Johnson to Johnson, 1 September 1940.

67. Clifford R. Hope to Frank Russell, 20 September 1940, Legislative Correspondence, Box 182, Clifford R. Hope Papers; Vito Marcantonio Press Release, 19 September 1940, Box 22, Vito Marcantonio Papers.

68. Samuel I. Rosenman, ed., *The Public Papers and Addresses of Franklin D. Roosevelt*, 9:428–34.

69. Clifford, "Clark," p. 38; Alden Hatch, *The Wadsworths of the Genesee*, p. 255.

70. Henry L. Stimson and McGeorge Bundy, *On Active Service in Peace and War*, p. 346; Wadsworth to Clark, 12 September 1940.

ultimately fulfilled the expectations of MTCA leader Clark. On 17 September 1940, Clark had predicted, "I think time will show that it was a *sine qua non* to any real effort to stand up to Hitler *et al.*" "Much more needs to be done to that end," he added, "but without this I don't think we'd have got to first base."[71]

Congress in the summer of 1940 had moved from an interventionist to a preparedness stage. During the Russo-Finnish War, the legislative branch had approved limited federal intervention by permitting Export-Import Bank loans to the Ryti government. After Germany had conquered the Low Countries and France, Congress had shifted attention to building American defense and to mobilizing manpower quickly. Besides calling up the National Guard, the legislative branch had replaced voluntary enlistment with the first peacetime draft in American history. Congress thus had taken the most comprehensive step toward preparing American defense since World War I.

As on foreign policy, Congress wielded considerable control over preparedness legislation. Roosevelt, although privately preferring selective service, proceeded very cautiously and let the MTCA and the legislative branch handle the specific details. The president did not endorse publicly the principle of a peacetime draft until August and exhibited little direct leadership, hoping to avoid making the issue a personal one. Congress, cognizant of the president's timid attitude, controlled decisionmaking on this issue and often acted quite independently of the White House. Rearmament opponents in the Senate delayed action on the Burke-Wadsworth bill for over two weeks and nearly adopted the Hayden amendment, which would have postponed the draft. To the chagrin of Roosevelt, the House attached the Fish amendment, temporarily reviving voluntary enlistment. The legislative branch thus had continued to wield the extensive independent authority exhibited earlier on both the neutrality and Finnish questions.

The mobilizing of American troops had completed a twenty-month period marked by rapidly changing developments both on the European scene and in Congress. Since the Seventy-sixth Congress had convened, the Nazis had conquered Czechoslovakia, Poland, Denmark, Norway, the Low Countries, and France. During the same period, the legislative branch had moved from isolationism to internationalism, had intervened more directly in the European conflict, and had taken a major step toward strengthening American defense.

71. Kent R. Greenfield, Robert R. Palmer, Bell I. Wiley, *The Organization of Ground Combat Troops*, pp. 199–203; Grenville Clark to James W. Wadsworth, Jr., 17 September 1940, Box 21, Wadsworth Papers.

8

Summary

During the next fifteen months, internationalists and interventionists controlled congressional decisionmaking. They still argued that American assistance to the Allied nations would strengthen the defense of Western Europe and would help deter Hitler from invading the Western Hemisphere. Roosevelt defeated Republican Wendell L. Willkie in the November elections to win an unprecedented third term in office, thus giving encouragement to many internationalist and interventionist Democrats. The legislative branch in early 1941 approved the Lend-Lease Act authorizing the president to sell, transfer, lend, or lease arms, equipment, and supplies to Great Britain and other countries whose defense was considered vital to American security. In late 1941, Germany's undeclared warfare in the Atlantic Ocean compelled the internationalist, interventionist Congress to revise the Neutrality Act. Roosevelt was authorized to arm American merchant ships carrying supplies from Iceland to belligerent European ports. Following the sudden Japanese attack on Pearl Harbor in December 1941, the legislative branch almost unanimously declared a state of war against Japan and thus sanctioned direct American intervention in World War II.[1]

Preparedness advocates, meanwhile, held a slim majority on Capitol Hill. President Roosevelt in the summer of 1940 deliberately did not consult with the legislative branch when he arranged for the United States to transfer fifty World War I destroyers to Great Britain in exchange for ninety-nine-year leases to several naval and air bases in the Western Hemisphere because he was fearful that rearmament opponents might block the transaction. In the summer of 1941, Congress reluctantly extended the selective service system for recruiting soldiers. Although Roosevelt

---

1. The principal works on the election of 1940 are Bernard F. Donahoe, *Private Plans and Public Dangers: The Story of FDR's Third Nomination*; Donald Bruce Johnson, *The Republican Party and Wendell Willkie*; Herbert S. Parmet and Marie B. Hecht, *Never Again: A President Runs for a Third Term*; and Arthur M. Schlesinger, Jr., Fred L. Israel, and William P. Hansen, eds., *History of American Presidential Elections*, pp. 2917–47. For the impact of the election on American diplomacy, see Robert A. Divine, *Foreign Policy and U.S. Presidential Elections, 1940–1960*, pp. 3–89. The principal account of Lend-Lease is Warren F. Kimball, *The Most Unsordid Act: Lend-Lease, 1939–1941*. For the impact of Lend-Lease, consult George C. Herring, Jr., *Aid to Russia, 1941–1946: Strategy, Diplomacy, the Origins of the Cold War*, and Robert H. Jones, *The Roads to Russia: United States Lend-Lease to the Soviet Union*. Works discussing the Atlantic war include Thomas A. Bailey and Paul B. Ryan, *Hitler vs. Roosevelt: The Undeclared Naval War*; Samuel Eliot Morison, *History of the United States Naval Operations in World War II*; Elmer B. Potter and John R. Fredland, eds., *The United States and World Sea Power*; William L. Langer and S. Everett Gleason, *The Undeclared War, 1940–1941*; and Theodore A. Wilson, *The First Summit: Roosevelt and Churchill at Placentia Bay 1941*. For background to Pearl Harbor, consult Robert J. C. Butow, *Tojo and the Coming of the War*; Herbert Feis, *The Road to Pearl Harbor: The Coming of the War Between the United States and Japan*; Paul W. Schroeder, *The Axis Alliance and Japanese-American Relations*; and Roberta Wohlstetter, *Pearl Harbor: Warning and Decision*, 1941.

wanted the peacetime draft for the duration of the war, preparedness advocates barely secured a one-year extension of selective service.[2]

On the other hand, isolationists, noninterventionists, and rearmament opponents still held considerable influence on Capitol Hill. Besides denying that any emergency situation existed, they stressed the geographical protection afforded by the Atlantic Ocean and protested that foreign aid programs eventually would compel direct American entry into the European war. Isolationists, noninterventionists, and rearmament opponents enthusiastically supported the America First Committee, a largely Great Lakes, Great Plains, and Mountain organization attracting 850,000 members. Senators Gerald P. Nye of North Dakota and Burton K. Wheeler of Montana, along with aviator Charles A. Lindbergh, appeared at rallies to mobilize public opinion against American intervention in the European conflict.[3] It was because rearmament opponents were so vocal on Capitol Hill that Roosevelt did not seek legislative approval for the destroyer-base deal. Besides posing formidable resistance to Lend-Lease and the arming of merchant vessels, the isolationists, noninterventionists, and rearmament opponents nearly terminated the peacetime selective service system. The Japanese attack on Pearl Harbor, however, quickly silenced the opponents, who joined the internationalists, interventionists, and preparedness advocates in declaring a state of war against the Asian nation.

During 1939 and 1940, the Seventy-sixth Congress passed through four distinct stages contingent to changing European developments. Isolationists had controlled legislative decisionmaking until the outbreak of World War II. Although Germany seized Czechoslovakia in March 1939, Congress did not revise the neutrality statutes to take punitive action against the Nazis. Isolationists adamantly opposed American involvement in the European war but disagreed over whether the United States should retaliate if any foreign belligerents infringed upon neutral rights. Besides favoring the retention of the strict neutrality laws, they particularly disapproved of lifting the arms embargo. Representatives adopted the isolationist Vorys amendment restoring the controversial ban on munitions sales to belligerents, while vocal isolationists on the Senate Foreign Relations Committee prevented any floor action on neutrality revision. At the regular 1939 session, isolationist strategists provided much more effective leadership than did internationalists on Capitol Hill.

The Seventy-sixth Congress in September 1939 entered a second stage in which internationalists determined the course of American foreign policy. After the German invasion of Poland and the eruption of World War II, the isolationists no longer could prevent the legislative branch from changing the mandatory neutrality measures. At the special session, Congress approved internationalist legislation repeal-

2. Philip Goodhart, *Fifty Ships that Saved the World: The Foundation of the Anglo-American Alliance*, details the destroyer-base deal, while John Joseph O'Sullivan, "From Voluntarism to Conscription: Congress and Selective Service, 1940–1945" (Ph.D. diss.), describes the 1941 extension.

3. For committee activities, see Wayne S. Cole, *America First: The Battle Against Intervention, 1940–41*. The impact of participants is assessed in Wayne S. Cole, *Charles A. Lindbergh and the Battle Against American Intervention in World War II*; Wayne S. Cole, *Senator Gerald P. Nye and American Foreign Relations*; and Burton K. Wheeler, *Yankee from the West: Turbulent Life Story of the Yankee-Born U.S. Senator from Montana*.

ing the arms embargo and restoring the indirect cash-and-carry system. Great Britain, France, and other belligerents could purchase military weapons from the United States if they paid cash and transported the goods in their own vessels. On the other hand, the internationalist-minded Congress was reluctant to commit the United States either to direct intervention in World War II or to specific defense alliances. They also argued that neutrality revision afforded the best means of keeping the United States from direct involvement in the European conflict. Although the isolationists still were well-organized, especially in the Senate, the internationalists furnished more dynamic leadership this time on Capitol Hill.

The third stage, which occurred in early 1940, was characterized by limited interventionist control of foreign policy decisionmaking. Although Germany did not launch further attacks for several months, the Soviet Union in late November 1939 invaded Finland. Interventionists insisted the United States should assist the Ryti government but disagreed over whether to send direct military relief or merely economic aid. Under limited interventionist control, the Senate and House in February 1940 approved legislation doubling to $200 million the capital of the Export-Import Bank and enabling Finland to receive $20 million in nonmilitary assistance. The Brown Act of 1940 marked the first time the Seventy-sixth Congress authorized a federal agency to intervene directly in a specific European conflict to aid a particular democratic country in World War II. On the other hand, the legislative branch did not want to alienate the Soviet Union and thus acted against providing military assistance to the Mannerheim army. The measure consequently was ineffective because Finland needed American combat supplies to defend against the numerically superior Russian forces.

By the summer of 1940, the Seventy-sixth Congress had embarked on a fourth stage in which preparedness advocates determined decisionmaking. Between April and July, German armies attacked Scandinavia and the Low Countries, conquered France, and planned an air invasion of Great Britain. Preparedness advocates claimed the 500,000-man army could not protect either the United States or Latin America from a German blitzkrieg. Since the number of voluntary enlistments had declined, they urged adoption of the first peacetime selective service system in American history. Despite determined resistance by rearmament opponents, the Senate in August approved a peacetime draft. Rearmament opponents the next month temporarily delayed the draft in the House, but the preparedness-minded conference committee quickly revived immediate selective service. This action, which restricted troops to defending the Western Hemisphere, enabled the training of nearly 1.7 million men for combat duty prior to Pearl Harbor and was the most comprehensive preparedness step taken by Congress since World War I.

The Seventy-sixth Congress determined the course of American foreign policy more than I anticipated. Although James T. Patterson ably describes how the Senate and House wielded considerable authority on domestic issues in Roosevelt's second term, historians usually picture the executive rather than the legislative branch as the controller of American diplomacy.[4] The decline in presidential prestige, which had occurred at home since 1937, had also extended to international affairs. At the regular session in 1939, Congress clearly determined foreign policy decisionmaking. The Senate Foreign Relations Committee repeatedly procrastinated action on the controversial neutrality revision issue. Chairman Key Pittman of Nevada provided ineffective leadership, while vocal isolationists exercised an influence disproportionate to their actual numbers. Under isolationist control, the House in June restored the embargo on the sale of munitions to belligerent nations. The Senate Foreign Relations Committee, following shrewd maneuvering by isolationists, in July again postponed action on changing neutrality legislation.

During this period, Roosevelt was extremely cautious in handling neutrality legislation. The Supreme Court "packing" incident, the attempted purge of conservative Democratic senators in primaries, and other presidential actions had diminished markedly Roosevelt's influence on Capitol Hill. Although favoring complete repeal of neutrality statutes, Roosevelt instead let Congress decide the legislative details and designated too much authority to ineffective leaders there. Before Roosevelt had attempted to play a more direct role, the representatives in June restored the isolationist arms embargo and the Senate Foreign Relations Committee in July pigeonholed neutrality revision.[5] In retrospect, it is debatable whether more direct White House intervention at an earlier date could have influenced Congress to lift the ban on the sale of armaments to belligerents at the regular session. Public opinion polls indicated that a majority of Americans consented to munitions sales to belligerents, but isolationists controlled the legislative branch and probably would have prevented any attempt to alter strict neutrality statutes.

At the special session, Congress still largely determined the course of American foreign policy. Although it repealed the arms embargo, the legislative branch continued to act quite independently of the White House. Senate isolationists not only prevented immediate action on neutrality revision by conducting a lengthy filibuster, but also retained several restrictive features of the Neutrality Act of 1937. Besides preventing American ships from entering combat zones, Congress still prohibited United States citizens from traveling on belligerent vessels or extending credits to warring nations. Cash-and-carry was revived, thus only limited, indirect American relief to European Allies was sanctioned. Although internationalists held numerical control, the legislative branch still did not authorize direct American intervention in the European conflict to help specific democracies attacked by totalitarian aggressors.

Roosevelt, meanwhile, played a more active role than at the regular session. Before convening the special session, the president outlined his legislative program

4. For domestic role, see James T. Patterson, *Congressional Conservatism and the New Deal*.

5. Robert A. Divine, James T. Patterson, and others also note that the president exhibited indecisive leadership at the regular session in 1939. This image of Roosevelt contrasts sharply with the portrait presented by Harry Elmer Barnes, Charles A. Beard, Charles C. Tansill, and other revisionist historians.

and summoned several prominent senators and representatives to discuss strategy.[6] In addition, he slowly had begun to regain some of the prestige and influence he had lost since 1937 on Capitol Hill. On the other hand, the president still wanted to avoid making the neutrality issue a personal one and thus was reluctant to assume direct personal leadership. Congressional leaders again handled the specific legislative details, while State Department personnel lobbied for neutrality revision behind-the-scenes. Roosevelt still preferred complete repeal of the neutrality statutes, but the Senate and House instead granted only two of the changes he desired—repeal of the arms embargo and wider personal discretionary authority.

The Seventy-sixth Congress likewise played a major role in determining American policy toward the Russo-Finnish War. Historians have concentrated primarily on the executive branch following the outbreak of World War II and consequently have underestimated the amount of independent power exercised by the legislative branch over foreign policy.[7] Although the Ryti government pleaded for American military assistance to resist the Russian army, senators and representatives refused to sanction unrestricted relief. Instead Congress permitted limited intervention by granting Export-Import Bank loans to Finland for purchasing non-military supplies. Besides carefully avoiding any specific mention of Finland in the bill, the legislative branch attached other restrictions rendering the Brown Act of 1940 ineffective in halting Russian aggression. On the other hand, the Seventy-sixth Congress had for the first time in World War II authorized a federal agency to intervene on behalf of a particular European nation against an aggressor country.

Roosevelt, meanwhile, demonstrated the considerable caution evident on neutrality at the regular 1939 session. Historians often picture the president as asserting more internationalist leadership following the outbreak of World War II, but he declined such a role on the Finnish question. Although sympathetic with Finland, Roosevelt publicly opposed an unrestricted federal loan to the Ryti government and preferred to let Congress decide the legislative details. Besides fearing the vocal isolationist influence on Capitol Hill, the president did not want to make the issue a personal matter or to risk breaking diplomatic relations with the Soviet Union.[8] In retrospect, Congress probably would have complied if Roosevelt had publicly supported direct American military assistance to Finland. American public opinion overwhelmingly sided with Finland against Russia, and numerous isolationist legislators favored granting an unrestricted loan to the Ryti government.

The selective service issue indicated that historians have underemphasized congressional power on preparedness legislation too.[9] The Seventy-sixth Congress wielded authority on this preparedness issue comparable to that on earlier inter-

6. Similar conclusions concerning Roosevelt's more active role at the special session are reached by Divine, and Langer and Gleason.
7. James MacGregor Burns, Robert Dallek, Dexter Perkins, Basil Rauch, and others primarily concentrate on the executive branch following the outbreak of World War II.
8. Robert Sobel likewise finds that the president approached the Finnish loan question with considerable caution.
9. Burns, Dallek, Perkins, Rauch, and others mainly stress the role of the executive branch on preparedness questions.

nationalist measures. Although the preparedness advocates held a slight numerical advantage, Senate rearmament opponents had more effective leadership and prevented floor action on a peacetime draft for over two weeks. Vocal rearmament opponents almost precluded the Senate from adopting immediate selective service and temporarily revived the voluntary enlistment method in the House. Congress, however, ultimately approved the first peacetime selective service in American history.

Timidity characterized Roosevelt's approach to the preparedness question. The president once more in 1940 did not exhibit the direct, dynamic leadership often attributed to him by historians. Despite privately preferring selective service, Roosevelt acted cautiously and let the Military Training Camps Association and the legislative branch determine the specific details. Besides refusing to endorse the principle of selective service until August, he was reluctant to support publicly the Burke-Wadsworth measure. Roosevelt, already nominated for a third term, did not want to make selective service a personal issue either and still feared the vocal isolationist influence on Capitol Hill.[10] Even if the president had demonstrated more forthright leadership, it is uncertain whether Congress would have acted differently. Senate rearmament opponents probably still would have filibustered the legislation, and the House still might have attached the Fish amendment delaying the peacetime draft.

In the House, alignments of the internationalists and preparedness advocates remained consistent. Democratic representatives usually defended both international and preparedness measures and received very limited support from Republicans. Southern congressmen proportionately directed campaigns for those urging greater American commitments abroad and were joined by Border members. On most occasions, the Pacific, Mountain, and Middle Atlantic delegations also aligned with the internationalists and preparedness advocates.

On the side of isolationists and rearmament opponents, representatives formed a homogeneous group politically and sectionally. Republican congressmen supplied the nucleus of resistance to neutrality revision and selective service. New England representatives led proportionately the isolationist struggle against lifting the arms embargo at the regular session, while Great Plains congressmen performed this function for the isolationists following the outbreak of World War II. Great Lakes members proportionately directed the rearmament opponents against selective service (see table 27).

By contrast, Senate coalitions varied considerably. Democrats consistently led the internationalists and preparedness advocates in the upper chamber but received fluctuating Republican support. Southern senators usually spearheaded the drive proportionately for the internationalists and preparedness advocates and allied with Border, Middle Atlantic, and New England delegations. Border and Middle Atlantic senators exhibited far greater enthusiasm for the internationalists seeking neutrality

10. Similar findings concerning the president's course on selective service are made by John G. Clifford, O'Sullivan, and Spencer.

revision, while New England members rallied much more behind the advocates of selective service. On the other hand, alignments of isolationists and rearmament opponents were more consistent. Republicans dominated the isolationists and rearmament opponents and attracted limited Democratic backing. The Great Plains members furnished the largest numerical support for the isolationists and rearmament opponents, while the Pacific delegation gave the highest percentage of backing (see table 28).

Finnish alignments, meanwhile, did not conform to these patterns. Democrats remained interventionist, but Republican senators strikingly were less interventionist than on other issues. Middle Atlantic and Border senators rather than Southern members proportionately directed the interventionist campaign to provide economic assistance for the Ryti government. Five of the eight regional blocs favored a federal nonmilitary loan to Finland, with the noninterventionist Great Plains senators furnishing the principal resistance. In the House, numerous New England and Middle Atlantic Republicans abandoned noninterventionism on this issue.

Senators typically acted more internationalist and preparedness-minded than representatives. They not only endorsed the internationalist arms embargo repeal by a wider margin, but also rejected an amendment by rearmament opponents to delay the start of the peacetime draft. Senators responded more favorably to internationalist and preparedness measures than did representatives because senators were less subject to political constraints, represented broader ethnic constituencies, and included a higher proportion of Southern members. On the other hand, the Senate did not prevent isolationists and rearmament opponents from monopolizing floor debate on the neutrality and selective service legislation.

Some unexpected alignments occurred. Coastal blocs frequently acted proportionately less internationalist, interventionist, and preparedness-minded than inland delegations. Historians usually picture the Great Lakes, Great Plains, and Mountain blocs as the leaders of the isolationists, noninterventionists, and rearmament opponents on Capitol Hill.[11] On the neutrality issue, New England representatives acted proportionately more isolationist than did Mountain representatives. The New England delegation included a high proportion of anti-Roosevelt Republicans who resisted granting further power to a president from the opposite party. Numerous Irish constituents residing in New England disapproved of sending American military relief to their homeland's traditional rival—Great Britain. On the Senate side, the Pacific bloc was proportionately less internationalist and preparedness-minded than were the Great Lakes and Great Plains delegations.[12] Under the direction of Minority Leader Charles L. McNary of Oregon and Hiram W. Johnson of Califor-

11. Ray A. Billington, Selig Adler, Ralph H. Smuckler, Jeannette P. Nichols, and others consider the Middle West as the least internationalist, interventionist, and preparedness-minded in the Roosevelt period.

12. The New England region is pictured as internationalist in this era by George L. Grassmuck, Julius Turner, H. Bradford Westerfield, and others. Westerfield, Robert A. Dahl, Duncan Mac Rae, Jr., Leroy N. Rieselbach, and other scholars emphasize the internationalism and preparedness attitudes of the Pacific section.

nia, these Republicans distrusted Roosevelt and refused to accept legislation designating additional authority to a Democratic president. German and Russian constituents living in the Pacific states opposed any American assistance to Western European countries fighting against their homeland and disapproved of preparedness efforts involving the United States in war. Besides having relatively little Atlantic Ocean trade, the Pacific states geographically were located furthest from the European conflict and consequently did not believe Hitler threatened American security.

An unusually high number of party defections occurred in the Senate on selective service. Historians have pictured the Democrats as preparedness advocates and the Republicans as rearmament opponents.[13] Majority Leader Alben W. Barkley and Minority Leader McNary, however, did not secure united party backing on this issue. Thirty percent of the Democrats, including mainly members from states west of the Mississippi River, equated the peacetime draft with forced regimentation and preferred voluntary enlistment. Since Roosevelt had asserted little direct leadership, Barkley encountered difficulty in rallying majority support. Several Great Plains, Mountain, and Pacific senators did not want to alienate constituents hostile to conscription, while others believed the Atlantic Ocean insulated the United States from a foreign invasion. Nearly one-half of the Republicans, particularly those from the New England and Middle Atlantic states, supported peacetime selective service. New England and Middle Atlantic Republicans came from the sections geographically closest to the European conflict and consequently believed the United States should prepare defensively against a possible Nazi invasion. Minority Leader McNary of Oregon, who opposed conscription, particularly faced a dilemma because he was the vice-presidential running mate of preparedness advocate Willkie.

In the House, Republicans acted surprisingly interventionist on the Finnish loan. Hamilton Fish of New York and other traditional isolationists became militant interventionists this time favoring American defense commitments to the Ryti government. Many Republican interventionists were staunch anti-Communists who lauded Finland as a democratic nation bravely resisting totalitarian aggression. If the Communists conquered the Scandinavian nation, they warned, both Western European and American defense would be threatened. The Ryti government, Republican interventionists remarked, had repaid its World War I debts to the United States and probably would continue to fulfill all financial obligations. Upper Great Lakes Republicans represented numerous Scandinavians favoring American military assistance to Finland.[14]

Unexpected ethnic patterns also occurred. Historians normally portray the Irish and German members as isolationists and rearmament opponents in the prewar period. Many Irish and German legislators, however, supported the internationalist arms embargo repeal and selective service preparedness. Numerous Irishmen re-

13. Turner, Grassmuck, Dahl, Rieselbach, and others describe the Democrats as much more preparedness-minded than the Republicans in the Roosevelt era.
14. In his study of Finnish-American relations, Sobel also finds that a considerable number of isolationist Republican representatives supported an unrestricted federal loan to the Ryti government.

mained loyal to the internationalist and preparedness programs of the Democratic party, responding to appeals by Rayburn and other congressional leaders. The immediate dangers posed by Nazi Germany to the Western world, they stated, overshadowed any traditional hostile attitudes toward Great Britain. Besides deploring Hitler's authoritarian tactics, Irish legislators denounced Nazi suppression of individual liberties and religious freedoms of Roman Catholics. A majority of Irish senators and representatives resided in the industrial New England and Middle Atlantic states, which were closer geographically to Europe, included a high proportion of Anglo-Saxon constituents, and would benefit from defense mobilization. Several German legislators, although proud of their ethnic heritage, feared that Hitler's dictatorial policies jeopardized individual civil liberties in their homeland and the security of democratic nations in Western Europe. The Nazi attack on Poland and particularly the subsequent invasions of the Low Countries and France influenced many German legislators to support both internationalist and preparedness programs. In addition, some German senators and representatives served states or districts containing numerous Anglo-Saxon and other pro-British constituents[15] (see table 32).

Political party was the most important variable on internationalist and preparedness legislation in the House. Representatives averaged at least 79 percent overall party cooperation on the neutrality revision and selective service issues. Democrats disagreed considerably with Republicans on both munitions sales and preparedness. Democratic congressmen usually supported internationalist and preparedness programs, following Rayburn's leadership. Since a Democratic president occupied the White House, they were less reluctant to increase executive power. A majority of Democratic representatives served New England, Middle Atlantic, or Southern states located closer to the European conflict and more vulnerable to a Nazi invasion. They had primarily Anglo-Saxon constituents who supported American military aid to Great Britain and advocated preparedness to defend the Western Hemisphere. In most instances, Democratic congressmen represented either industrial and commercial sections benefiting from military preparedness contracts or agricultural regions thriving on foreign trade.

On the other hand, most Republicans in the House opposed internationalist and preparedness programs. Anti-Roosevelt sentiments, sparked by the president's attempts to "pack" the Supreme Court, reorganize the executive branch, and raise federal spending, primarily caused the Republican resistance. Several Republicans who otherwise might have welcomed neutrality revision and peacetime conscription disapproved of increasing the authority of a president from the opposite party. Republicans frequently represented inland Great Lakes or Great Plains states less vulnerable to Nazi invasion and served German, Russian, or Scandinavian isolationists and rearmament opponents. These predominantly Republican sections relied less on European trade and believed eastern financial and industrial interests

15. These ethnic groups are depicted as isolationists and rearmament opponents by Mark Lincoln Chadwin, T. Ryle Dwyer, Lawrence H. Fuchs, Samuel Lubell, and others.

deliberately were attempting to draw the United States into the European conflict against the national interest.[16]

Political party was a less significant variable in the Senate, where party defections were more commonplace. Since senators faced reelection campaigns less often, they confronted fewer risks in deviating from party line or ignoring constituent pressure. Some Democratic senators opposed internationalist or preparedness programs primarily because they distrusted Roosevelt and feared that he was attempting to usurp legislative power. These Democrats, led by Bennett Champ Clark of Missouri, came from inland regions and did not believe Hitler endangered American security. Internationalists and preparedness advocates, they warned, were seeking to involve the United States in the European conflict against American interests. In addition, some Democratic isolationists, noninterventionists, and rearmament opponents served German, Russian, or Scandinavian constituents opposed to greater American commitments overseas or preparedness at home. On the other hand, a number of Republican senators supported internationalist and particularly preparedness programs. These predominantly New England and Middle Atlantic senators served industrial areas profiting economically from European trade and domestic defense contracts and located closer geographically to the European conflict. Subordinating anti-Roosevelt attitudes, they warned that the Nazis threatened American security and thus urged preparedness against a possible invasion of the Western Hemisphere.

The importance of partisanship diminished somewhat with the rapidly deteriorating European conditions. Representatives achieved the most political cooperation before the outbreak of World War II—in June 1939 on the arms embargo issue. At the regular session, most congressmen voted according to political affiliation rather than ideological considerations on international issues. Party solidarity declined among Republican representatives on international questions at the special session and on the interventionist Finnish matter. The German attack on Poland, coupled with the Russian invasion of Finland, convinced some Republican congressmen to subordinate political differences with Roosevelt. Besides believing the Nazis seriously threatened world security, they also staunchly opposed the spread of Communism into Scandinavian countries. On the Senate side, Democratic unity declined significantly on the Finnish interventionist legislation. Noninterventionist Democratic senators either opposed taking provocative action against the Soviet Union, preferred federal relief at home rather than for distant Finland, or represented almost exclusively Anglo-Saxon constituents. Since Roosevelt had furnished little direct leadership, it was difficult for Barkley to secure political cohesion. Political unity declined markedly among Democrats and particularly Republicans on the selective service legislation. Senators and representatives alike indicated greater willingness to subordinate political considerations on preparedness than on internationalist or interventionist questions. For reasons indicated earlier, numerous Mountain and Pacific Democrats and New England and Middle Atlantic Republi-

16. Turner, Dahl, Grassmuck, and others find political party loyalty stronger than sectional loyalty.

cans influenced the decline in partisanship on the peacetime draft (see tables 20, 24).

Congressional party leadership fluctuated in importance. Party chiefs were more effective in the House and especially among the Democratic majority. Following the directives of Sam Rayburn of Texas, Democratic representatives displayed at least 79 percent unity on neutrality revision and selective service. Rayburn made dramatic floor speeches before the final roll calls on the internationalist and preparedness questions. Minority Leader Joseph W. Martin of Massachusetts commanded at least 76 percent loyalty on the three issues and experienced sizeable defections only on selective service. A first-term Republican leader, Martin had to rebuild an essentially disorganized party in order to make it an effective opposition force. In the Senate, members displayed more political independence on the three issues. Democratic boss Barkley secured 82 percent backing on the internationalist neutrality revision question at the special session but witnessed widespread party defections on the interventionist Export-Import Bank bill and compulsory draft. Barkley exhibited mediocre leadership because he still lacked the confidence of party conservatives who had supported Pat Harrison of Mississippi in 1937 and often had no clear directive from the White House. Minority Leader McNary faced even greater resistance from his party, which particularly was divided on preparedness and, to a lesser extent, was disunified on internationalist and interventionist issues. Since the Republicans lacked national consensus on arms embargo and selective service, McNary abandoned plans to make any partisan appeals on the Senate side.[17]

Sectionalism, on the other hand, was a more important variable in the Senate than in the House. Southern, Border, Middle Atlantic, and Pacific senators usually displayed considerable regional loyalty, averaging over 75 percent loyalty on the internationalist, interventionist, and preparedness issues. Southern and Border senators all belonged to the Democratic party, while 62 percent of the Middle Atlantic and 50 percent of the Pacific members were affiliated with the same party. Regional unity among Senate delegations was substantial on both internationalist and interventionist legislation but declined on the highly ideological preparedness question. Although geographical considerations made less impact in the House, representatives serving predominantly one-party regions were quite cohesive on foreign policy and defense legislation through the Seventy-sixth Congress. Southern and Border congressmen, nearly all of whom belonged to the Democratic party, displayed very impressive sectional unity.[18]

Several sectional delegations followed consistent patterns. Casting aside anti-Roosevelt sentiments, Southern and Border senators and representatives proportion-

17. Grassmuck, Donald R. Matthews, and David B. Truman, *The Congressional Party: A Case Study*, also report the majority party as more united than the minority party. For Republican problems in the 1939–1940 period, consult Joseph Boskin, "Politics of an Opposition Party: The Republican Party in the New Deal Period" (Ph.D. diss.), and Patrick E. McGinnis, "Republican Party Resurgence in Congress, 1936–1946" (Ph.D. diss.).

18. Lubell; Frank Freidel, *F.D.R. and the South*; V. O. Key, Jr., *Southern Politics in State and Nation*; George Brown Tindall, *The Disruption of the Solid South*; and others show the importance of sectionalism in the Roosevelt period. On the Senate side, five of the eight Middle Atlantic members and three of the six Pacific members belonged to the Democratic party. In the House, the ninety-nine Southern representatives and forty of the forty-five Border congressmen affiliated with the Democratic party.

ately directed the campaigns for internationalist, interventionist, and preparedness measures. Besides having a military tradition, they resided closer than most other sections to the European conflict and believed Germany endangered American security. Southern and Border Democrats also served predominantly Anglo-Saxon constituents supporting American military assistance to Great Britain. In addition, they relied extensively on foreign trade, which was jeopardized by German aggression, and derived economic benefits from defense spending.[19] The Middle Atlantic senators, however, replaced the Southern members proportionately at the forefront of interventionists advocating either military or economic assistance to Finland. Historians usually have pictured the Southern Democrats as the leading spokesmen of interventionism, but the Middle Atlantic senators were decidedly anti-Communist and warned that Russian expansion might threaten democracy elsewhere.[20] Under the direction of Banking and Currency Committee Chairman Robert F. Wagner of New York, the largely Democratic delegation considered Finland a good financial risk and supported increased funding for Roosevelt's New Deal agency.

Great Lakes and Great Plains legislators, along with Pacific senators and New England representatives, usually directed the isolationists, noninterventionists, and rearmament opponents. Primarily Republicans, they distrusted Roosevelt and feared the chief executive was seeking American intervention in World War II. Besides denying that German activity threatened American security, Great Lakes and Great Plains constituents claimed that greedy eastern bankers, munitioners, and industrialists deliberately were conspiring to ally the United States with Great Britain and mobilize the army. In addition, the Great Lakes and Great Plains states relied much less than the New England and Middle Atlantic areas on European trade. Great Lakes and Great Plains members holding progressive attitudes insisted the United States should solve domestic problems and feared that internationalist, interventionist, and preparedness programs would drain financial resources. German, Scandinavian, and Russian constituents residing in the Great Lakes and Great Plains states urged their legislators to oppose internationalist and preparedness legislation. For reasons outlined above, New England representatives and Pacific senators defied historical stereotypes and often aligned with opposition forces on Capitol Hill (see table 30).

Ideology was an important variable in the House and especially in the Senate. Although difficult to measure in quantitative terms, ideology helped determine congressional voting behavior on interventionist, preparedness, and, to a lesser extent, internationalist legislation. Interventionists lauded Finland as a democratic nation resisting the spread of Communism and, therefore, favored federal assistance to the Ryti government. On the other hand, noninterventionists argued that American intrusion in the Russo-Finnish conflict might embroil the United States further in the European war and insisted charity should begin at home. Preparedness advocates, meanwhile, urged the United States to adopt immediate selective service

19. The internationalist, interventionist, and preparedness attitudes of the South in the 1939–1940 period also are described by Cole, Marian D. Irish, Grassmuck, Lubell, and others.
20. Cole, Irish, Grassmuck, Lubell, and others stress the interventionist role of Southern Democrats.

because totalitarianism was spreading across Europe and endangering the safety of democratic institutions. Since they viewed the compulsory draft as regimental and undemocratic, rearmament opponents preferred traditional voluntary enlistments. On the neutrality question, internationalists favored lifting the arms embargo to help the Allies preserve democratic institutions in Western Europe against the Nazi dictatorship. Isolationists, by contrast, feared further American commitments abroad not only would hinder reform efforts at home, but also ultimately would mean direct entrance into World War II.

Other significant variables were ethnic and economic considerations. Ethnic forces played an important role in the House, where metropolitan areas with foreign nationalities held wider representation. German representatives helped restore the isolationist arms embargo and the Fish proposal delaying the draft. Defying historical stereotypes, the Irish congressmen helped the internationalists remove the ban on munitions sales to belligerents at the special session. Economic factors were stressed by the isolationists on neutrality, the noninterventionists on the Finnish issue, and the rearmament opponents on selective service. Great Lakes and Great Plains isolationists and rearmament opponents denounced neutrality revision and selective service as attempts by eastern financial and industrial interests to reap profits from internationalist and preparedness commitments. On the Finnish legislation, Great Lakes, Great Plains, and Southern noninterventionists insisted relief spending should begin at home and urged increased federal assistance for farmers rather than the distant Finns.

Interest groups also held considerable influence on internationalist and particularly preparedness issues. On preparedness, the MTCA framed the Burke-Wadsworth selective service legislation and secured congressional sponsors. In addition, the MTCA testified before congressional committees and helped rally support for preparedness on Capitol Hill. Under the able tutelage of Grenville Clark, the MTCA played an indispensable role in securing enactment of the first peacetime draft in American history. Lobbyists, particularly the White committee, helped secure adoption of the internationalist neutrality revision measure. Conducting an extensive national publicity campaign, the White committee solidified public opinion behind repeal of the arms embargo. Several maritime organizations were instrumental in inserting congressional amendments loosening travel restrictions.[21] On the other hand, interest groups made little impact on the more ideological Finnish legislation.

The public, meanwhile, was more internationalist, interventionist, and preparedness-minded than the Seventy-sixth Congress. The legislative branch usually lagged behind public opinion polls, being more reluctant to commit the United States to internationalist, interventionist, and preparedness measures. Although a majority of Americans supported repeal of the arms embargo in the spring of 1939, the legislative branch retained the isolationist neutrality statutes. The hostile mail

21. Spencer and O'Sullivan likewise stress the importance of interest groups on selective service, while Divine reaches similar conclusions on neutrality revision.

received by Congress did not reflect accurately the internationalist public sentiment on the issue. At the special session, senators and representatives followed public opinion somewhat more closely by repealing the arms embargo. Congress acted more cautiously than public opinion on the Finnish question, permitting the Ryti government to purchase only nonmilitary supplies. Since Americans overwhelmingly sympathized with the Scandinavian nation, they probably would have supported direct military assistance against the Russian army. After the Nazis conquered France, public opinion was more preparedness-minded than the legislative branch and favored selective service by a considerable margin. Congress, deluged with hostile mail not representative of prevailing sentiment, nearly delayed implementing the first peacetime draft.[22]

In summary, the Seventy-sixth Congress made a significant impact on American foreign and preparedness policy. The legislative branch journeyed through isolationist, internationalist, interventionist, and preparedness stages and enacted three major measures—neutrality revision lifting the arms embargo, federal economic assistance to the Finnish government, and the first peacetime draft in American history. Congress exercised more control over foreign policy and defense legislation than has previously been thought, while President Roosevelt furnished surprisingly little direct leadership. On the three legislative issues, some unusual political, sectional, and ethnic alignments occurred. Over 25 percent of the Democratic representatives aligned with isolationists and rearmament opponents, while several Republican senators supported selective service and many Republican representatives were interventionist on the Finnish question. Sectionally, coastal delegations—particularly the Pacific senators and New England representatives—often voted less internationalist and interventionist than inland blocs. Ethnically, Irish representatives were quite internationalist and preparedness-minded, and the German members occasionally followed suit. Political party was the most important voting determinant in the House, while sectionalism and ideology played very important roles in the Senate.

Further examination will be required to determine if these trends and patterns applied to other legislation submitted to the Seventy-sixth Congress. During 1939, the legislative branch debated over the Spanish civil war, the sale of 555 combat airplanes to France, and Japanese expansion in China. Congress also considered increasing military supplies and strengthening national defense, expanding naval bases, and revitalizing American armaments. At the 1940 session, it called out the National Guard, enacted excess profits legislation, and financed Latin American defense. An investigation of these issues could further illuminate the period characterized by shifts from isolationism to internationalism, interventionism, and preparedness.

22. Hadley Cantril, ed., *Public Opinion 1935–1946*, includes surveys of public attitudes on the three issues. Divine, Sobel, and Spencer describe public opinion on neutrality revision, Finnish assistance, and selective service, respectively, while Rowena Wyant and Herta Herzog assess congressional mail on the peacetime draft.

Table 1. Political Party Affiliation of Members of Congress, 1939

Party	Internationalists		Isolationists		Moderates		Total
	%	N	%	N	%	N	N
Senate							
Democrats	49	34	23	16	28	19	69
Republicans	4	1	74	17	22	5	23
Other	--	--	75	3	25	1	4
House							
Democrats	69	178	10	27	21	54	259
Republicans	0	0	96	159	4	7	166
Other	25	1	50	2	25	1	4

Source: (Senate) "Congressional Poll on Neutrality," Congressional
Intelligence 4(7 April 1939); (House) Congressional Record, 30 June
1939, pp. 8511-13, compiled from roll-call votes of Vorys and Tinkham amendments and Bloom bill.

Note: Other senators include two Farmer-Laborites, one Progressive,
and one Independent; other representatives include one Farmer-Laborite, two Progressives, and one American-Laborite.

Table 2. Region of Residence of Members of Congress, 1939

Region	Internationalists		Isolationists		Moderates		Total
	%	N	%	N	%	N	N
Senate							
New England	17	2	33	4	50	6	12
Middle Atlantic	62	5	25	2	13	1	8
Great Lakes	30	3	50	5	20	2	10
Great Plains	14	2	57	8	29	4	14
South	50	10	15	3	35	7	20
Border	60	6	20	2	20	2	10
Mountain	37	6	50	8	13	2	16
Pacific	17	1	66	4	17	1	6
House							
New England	14	4	76	22	10	3	29
Middle Atlantic	33	31	56	52	11	10	93
Great Lakes	22	20	70	62	8	7	89
Great Plains	17	8	64	30	19	9	47
South	88	80	1	1	11	10	91
Border	53	20	11	4	37	14	38
Mountain	50	7	36	5	14	2	14
Pacific	32	9	43	12	25	7	28

Source: (Senate) "Congressional Poll on Neutrality," Congressional
Intelligence 4(7 April 1939); (House) Congressional Record, 30 June
1939, pp. 8511-13, compiled from roll-call votes of Vorys and Tinkham amendments and Bloom bill.

Table 3. Age of Members of Congress, 1940

Age	Internationalists		Isolationists		Moderates	
	%	N	%	N	%	N
Senate						
30–39	3	1	8	3	--	--
40–49	15	5	14	5	20	5
50–59	15	5	36	13	24	6
60–69	58	19	28	10	40	10
70 and over	9	3	14	5	16	4
Total	100	33	100	36	100	25
Mean		64		58		62
House						
25–29	1	1	--	--	--	--
30–39	12	21	10	18	15	9
40–49	29	51	31	57	43	26
50–59	26	46	33	62	29	18
60–69	24	42	19	35	8	5
70 and over	8	14	8	14	5	3
Total	100	175	100	186	100	61
Mean		54		53		48

Source: U.S., Congress, Biographical Directory of the American Congress, 1774–1961. Totals do not include two senators and seventeen representatives who no longer served in Congress as of January 1940.

Table 4. Birthplace and Region of Residence of Members of Congress, 1939

Birthplace	Internationalists		Isolationists		Moderates	
	%	N	%	N	%	N
Senate						
Same State	66	23	67	24	52	13
Different State, Same Region	6	2	11	4	4	1
Different Region	23	8	22	8	40	10
Foreign Country	6	2	--	--	4	1
Total	100	35	100	36	100	25
House						
Same State	76	138	68	127	69	43
Different State, Same Region	6	10	10	19	3	2
Different Region	16	28	15	29	27	17
Foreign Country	2	3	7	13	--	--
Total	100	179	100	188	100	62

Source: U.S., Congress, Biographical Directory of the American Congress, 1774–1961.

Table 5. Type of Residence of Members of Congress, 1939

Residence	Internationalists		Isolationists		Moderates	
	%	N	%	N	%	N
Senate						
Rural (under 2,500)	11	4	28	10	16	4
Town (2,500–9,999)	26	9	11	4	20	5
Small City (10,000–24,999)	20	7	17	6	20	5
Large City (25,000–99,999)	20	7	28	10	24	6
Metropolitan (over 100,000)	23	8	17	6	20	5
Total	100	35	100	36	100	25
House						
Rural	17	30	21	39	20	12
Town	19	34	21	39	34	21
Small City	17	30	13	24	13	8
Large City	10	19	23	43	18	11
Metropolitan	37	66	23	43	16	10
Total	100	179	100	188	100	62

Source: U.S., Congress, Biographical Directory of the American Congress, 1774–1961; The World Almanac, 1940.

Table 6. Education of Members of Congress, 1939

Education	Internationalists		Isolationists		Moderates	
	%	N	%	N	%	N
Senate						
Grade School	--	--	6	2	4	1
High School	--	--	17	6	12	3
Attended College	17	6	19	7	16	4
College Graduate	11	4	11	4	4	1
Post-College	72	25	47	17	64	16
Total	100	35	100	36	100	25
House						
Grade School	2	4	2	3	--	--
High School	14	25	13	25	6	4
Attended College	13	24	18	34	26	16
College Graduate	6	11	10	19	15	9
Post-College	65	115	57	107	53	33
Total	100	179	100	188	100	62

Source: U.S., Congress, Biographical Directory of the American Congress, 1774–1961.

Table 7. Previous Occupation of Members of Congress, 1939

Occupation	Internationalists		Isolationists		Moderates	
	%	N	%	N	%	N
Senate						
Professional						
Law	86	30	50	18	72	18
Other	3	1	22	8	16	4
Agriculture	--	--	6	2	--	--
Business						
Outdoor	--	--	--	--	--	--
Manufacturing	--	--	14	5	--	--
Commerce	9	3	--	--	4	1
Services	3	1	8	3	4	1
Government	--	--	--	--	--	--
Unskilled						
Laborers	--	--	--	--	4	1
Total	100	35	100	36	100	25
House						
Professional						
Law	61	110	47	88	48	30
Other	7	12	16	30	6	4
Agriculture	3	5	5	10	6	4
Business						
Outdoor	5	9	4	8	5	3
Manufacturing	2	4	4	8	2	1
Commerce	7	12	8	14	11	7
Services	8	13	12	23	10	6
Government	6	11	3	5	10	6
Unskilled						
Laborers	2	3	1	2	2	1
Total	100	179	100	188	100	62

Source: U.S., Congress, Biographical Directory of the American
Congress, 1774-1961.

Table 8. Religious Affiliation of Members of Congress, 1939

Religion	Internationalists		Isolationists		Moderates	
	%	N	%	N	%	N
Senate						
Protestant						
Reformation	31	11	44	16	40	10
Pietistic	34	12	33	12	32	8
Fundamentalist	9	3	--	--	8	2
Nontraditional	3	1	3	1	--	--
General	11	4	3	1	--	--
Roman Catholic	9	3	14	5	8	2
Jewish	--	--	--	--	4	1
None	3	1	3	1	8	2
Total	100	35	100	36	100	25
House						
Protestant						
Reformation	23	41	40	75	40	24
Pietistic	27	49	22	42	26	16
Fundamentalist	15	26	1	2	8	5
Nontraditional	2	4	4	7	3	2
General	1	2	8	15	1	1
Roman Catholic	23	41	14	26	20	12
Jewish	3	6	--	--	--	--
None	6	10	11	21	3	2
Total	100	179	100	188	100	62

Source: Margaret Blackly, Library of Congress, Legislative Reference Service, "Religious Affiliation of Members of 75th Congress, typewritten manuscript, 9 October 1940; Who's Who in America, 1940-1941. The denominations included in the above categories are: (Reformation) Presbyterian, Lutheran, Congregational, Evangelical and Reformed, Dutch Reformed, United Church of Christ, Episcopal; (Pietistic) Methodist, African Methodist Episcopal, United Brethren, Evangelical Reformed, American Baptist, Disciples of Christ; (Fundamentalist) Church of God, Church of God in Christ, Pentecostal or Assembly of God, Church of Christ, Salvation Army, Primitive Baptist, Free Will Baptist, Seventh Day Baptist, Southern Baptist; (Nontraditional) Christian Scientist, Spiritualist, Latter Day Saints, Unitarian, Jehovah's Witnesses, Quakers, Unity, Universalist.

Table 9. Military Service of Members of Congress, 1939

Service	Internationalists		Isolationists		Moderates	
	%	N	%	N	%	N
Senate						
Yes	46	16	19	7	36	9
No	54	19	81	29	64	16
Total	100	35	100	36	100	25
House						
Yes	32	58	42	79	45	28
No	68	121	58	109	55	34
Total	100	179	100	188	100	62

Source: U.S., Congress, Biographical Directory of the American Congress, 1774–1961.

Table 10. Political Experience of Members of Congress, 1939

Total Years	Internationalists		Isolationists		Moderates	
	%	N	%	N	%	N
Senate						
None	9	3	9	3	4	1
1–5	19	6	26	9	17	4
6–10	19	6	29	10	4	1
11–15	22	7	18	6	35	8
16–20	9	3	12	4	26	6
Over 20	22	7	6	2	13	3
Total	100	32	100	34	100	23
House						
None	15	27	22	40	28	16
1–5	22	40	23	42	28	16
6–10	26	45	21	38	23	13
11–15	22	38	20	37	17	10
16–20	10	17	7	13	1	1
Over 20	5	9	8	14	3	2
Total	100	176	100	184	100	58

Source: U.S., Congress, Biographical Directory of the American Congress, 1774–1961. Totals do not include three internationalists, two isolationists, and two moderates in the Senate, and three internationalists, four isolationists, and four moderates in the House.

Table 11. Type of Political Experience of Members of Congress, 1939

Type	Internationalists %	Internationalists N	Isolationists %	Isolationists N	Moderates %	Moderates N
Senate						
U.S. Executive	11	4	14	5	16	4
U.S. Senate	6	2	8	3	4	1
U.S. House	37	13	14	5	48	12
U.S. Judicial	3	1	6	2	8	2
State Executive	31	11	42	15	40	10
State Legislative	40	14	39	14	40	10
State Judicial	26	9	17	6	24	6
Local Executive	14	5	17	6	16	4
Local Legislative	9	3	3	1	4	1
Local Judicial	40	14	17	6	16	4
	N = 35		N = 36		N = 25	
House						
U.S. Executive	8	14	10	19	11	7
U.S. Senate	--	--	1	1	1	1
U.S. House	7	12	11	21	8	5
U.S. Judicial	4	7	3	5	1	1
State Executive	19	34	16	31	11	7
State Legislative	36	64	32	60	24	15
State Judicial	17	31	6	12	3	2
Local Executive	19	34	25	47	16	10
Local Legislative	9	16	9	16	11	7
Local Judicial	28	51	22	42	24	15
	N = 179		N = 188		N = 62	

Source: U.S., Congress, Biographical Directory of the American
Congress, 1774-1961.

Table 12. Political Party and Region of Residence of Members of
Congress, 1939-1940

Region	Democrats %	Democrats N	Republicans %	Republicans N	Other %	Other N
Senate	70	73	26	27	4	4
New England	31	4	69	9	--	--
Middle Atlantic	62	5	38	3	--	--
Great Lakes	58	7	33	4	8	1
Great Plains	40	6	40	6	20	3
South	100	20	--	--	--	--
Border	100	11	--	--	--	--
Mountain	89	16	11	2	--	--
Pacific	57	4	43	3	--	--
House	60	277	39	178	1	4
New England	23	7	77	23	--	--
Middle Atlantic	47	46	53	52	1	1
Great Lakes	39	36	60	55	2	2
Great Plains	37	18	61	30	2	1
South	100	99	--	--	--	--
Border	89	40	11	5	--	--
Mountain	80	12	20	3	--	--
Pacific	66	19	35	10	--	--

Source: U.S., Congress, Biographical Directory of the American
Congress, 1774-1961. Totals include replacement congressmen
for those who resigned or died during their terms.

Table 13. House Views on Neutrality, 30 June 1939

	Vorys Amendment				Final Bloom Bill			
	Yes		No		Yes		No	
Party	%	N	%	N	%	N	%	N
Democrats	27	61	73	164	85	193	15	33
Republicans	95	149	5	7	3	5	97	151
Other	67	4	33	2	50	3	50	3
Region								
New England	75	18	25	6	17	4	83	20
Middle Atlantic	63	55	38	33	38	33	62	54
Great Lakes	75	61	25	20	28	23	72	58
Great Plains	79	33	21	9	32	14	68	29
South	13	10	87	69	99	79	1	1
Border	41	14	59	20	85	29	15	5
Mountain	55	6	45	5	45	5	55	6
Pacific	61	17	39	11	50	14	50	14

Source: Congressional Record, 30 June 1939, pp. 8511-14. Internationalists voted no on the Vorys amendment and yes on the final
Bloom bill. Isolationists voted yes on the Vorys amendment and no
on the final Bloom bill.

Table 14. Internationalism of Senators, October 1939

Party	% Internationalist
Democrats	78-85
Republicans	32-36
Other	25-33
Region	
New England	58
Middle Atlantic	75
Great Lakes	60-78
Great Plains	36-50
South	89-94
Border	90
Mountain	60-75
Pacific	20

Source: Congressional Record, 10 October 1939, p. 237;
27 October 1939, pp. 1023-24. The percentages indicate
the range of votes against the Tobey and Clark amendments
and for the final Pittman bill.

Table 15. Senate Views on Neutrality, October 1939

Party	Tobey Amendment 10 October 1939				Clark Amendment 27 October 1939				Final Pittman Bill 27 October 1939			
	Yes		No		Yes		No		Yes		No	
	%	N	%	N	%	N	%	N	%	N	%	N
Democrats	15	10	85	57	22	15	78	52	81	54	19	13
Republicans	67	14	33	7	68	15	32	7	36	8	64	14
Other	67	2	33	1	75	3	25	1	25	1	75	3
Region												
New England	42	5	58	7	42	5	58	7	58	7	42	5
Middle Atlantic	25	2	75	6	25	2	75	6	75	6	25	2
Great Lakes	22	2	78	7	40	4	60	6	60	6	40	4
Great Plains	54	7	46	6	64	9	36	5	50	7	50	7
South	6	1	94	17	11	2	89	17	89	17	11	2
Border	10	1	90	9	10	1	90	9	90	9	10	1
Mountain	25	4	75	12	40	6	60	9	67	10	33	5
Pacific	80	4	20	1	80	4	20	1	20	1	80	4

Source: Congressional Record, 10 October 1939, p. 237; 27 October 1939, pp. 1023–24. Internationalists voted no on the Tobey and Clark amendments and yes on the final Pittman bill. Isolationists voted yes on the Tobey and Clark amendments and no on the final Pittman bill.

Table 16. Internationalism of Representatives, November 1939

Party	% Internationalist
Democrats	86–88
Republicans	12–13
Other	50
Region	
New England	29–38
Middle Atlantic	50–54
Great Lakes	32–35
Great Plains	28–30
South	93–99
Border	85–87
Mountain	62
Pacific	64–68

Source: Congressional Record, 2 November 1939, pp. 1343–45; 3 November 1939, p. 1389. The percentages indicate the range of votes against the Vorys and Shanley amendments and for the final Pittman bill.

Table 17. House Views on Neutrality, November 1939

	Vorys Amendment				Shanley Amendment			
	2 November 1939				2 November 1939			
	Yes		No		Yes		No	
Party	%	N	%	N	%	N	%	N
Democrats	13	34	87	221	14	36	86	219
Republicans	87	142	13	21	87	142	13	21
Other	50	3	50	3	50	3	50	3
Region								
New England	62	18	38	11	69	20	31	9
Middle Atlantic	50	45	50	45	49	44	51	46
Great Lakes	65	57	35	31	67	59	33	29
Great Plains	70	33	30	14	72	34	28	13
South	7	6	93	84	4	4	96	86
Border	13	5	87	34	15	6	85	33
Mountain	38	5	62	8	38	5	62	8
Pacific	36	10	64	18	32	9	68	19

Source: Congressional Record, 2 November 1939, pp. 1343–45;
3 November 1939, p. 1389. Internationalists voted no on the
Vorys and Shanley amendments; Isolationists voted yes on
these two amendments.

Table 18. Interventionism of Senators, February 1940

Party	% Interventionist	Percent Change Since October 1939
Democrats	71–81	2–7 decrease
Republicans	11–47	3–7 decrease
Other	50–75	25–42 increase
Region		
New England	40–70	3 decrease
Middle Atlantic	75–100	13 increase
Great Lakes	50	10–28 decrease
Great Plains	36–45	5–19 increase
South	57–86	17–22 decrease
Border	80	10 decrease
Mountain	64–71	unchanged
Pacific	33–67	30 increase

Source: Congressional Record, 13 February 1940, pp. 1403–4.
The percentages indicate the range of votes against the Taft
amendment and for the final Brown bill. The percentage
change was determined by comparing the range of interventionist votes with the range of internationalist votes on the
Tobey and Clark amendments and the final Pittman bill. An
increase means that the party or section favored federal intervention in Finland more than neutrality revision, while a decrease means the party or section favored neutrality revision
more than federal intervention in Finland.

Table 19. Senate Views on Finnish Aid, February 1940

	Taft Amendment				Final Brown Bill			
	13 February 1940				13 February 1940			
	Yes		No		Yes		No	
Party	%	N	%	N	%	N	%	N
Democrats	19	10	81	45	71	39	29	16
Republicans	89	16	11	2	47	8	53	9
Other	25	1	75	3	50	2	50	2
Region								
New England	60	6	40	4	70	7	30	3
Middle Atlantic	25	2	75	6	100	8	--	--
Great Lakes	50	3	50	3	50	3	50	3
Great Plains	55	6	45	5	36	4	64	7
South	14	2	86	12	57	8	43	6
Border	20	2	80	8	80	8	20	2
Mountain	29	4	71	10	64	9	36	5
Pacific	67	2	33	1	67	2	33	1

Source: Congressional Record, 13 February 1940, pp. 1403-4.
Interventionists voted no on the Taft amendment and yes on
the final Brown bill. Noninterventionists voted yes on the
Taft amendment and no on the final Brown bill.

Table 20. Preparedness Views of Senators, August 1940

Party	% Preparedness Advocates	Percent Change Since February 1940
Democrats	55-84	10 decrease
Republicans	44-50	17 increase
Other	0-25	50 decrease
Region		
New England	64-82	18 increase
Middle Atlantic	50-84	21 decrease
Great Lakes	30-60	5 decrease
Great Plains	36-42	2 increase
South	83-100	20 increase
Border	50-90	10 decrease
Mountain	33-62	19 decrease
Pacific	25	25 decrease

Source: Congressional Record, 27 August 1940, p. 11043;
28 August 1940, pp. 11124, 11137-38, 11142. The percentages indicate the range of votes against the Taft, Hayden, and Maloney amendments and for the final Burke bill.
The percentage changes were determined by comparing the
range of votes of preparedness advocates with the range
of interventionist votes on the Taft amendment and the
final Brown bill. An increase means the party or region
favored selective service more than federal intervention
in Finland, while a decrease means the party or region
favored federal intervention in Finland more than selective service.

Table 21. Senate Views on Selective Service, August 1940

	Hayden Amendment 28 August 1940				Maloney Amendment 28 August 1940				Final Burke Bill 28 August 1940			
	Yes		No		Yes		No		Yes		No	
Party	%	N	%	N	%	N	%	N	%	N	%	N
Democrats	45	28	55	34	35	22	65	42	75	50	25	17
Republicans	50	9	50	9	56	10	44	8	44	8	56	10
Other	100	4	--	--	100	3	--	--	--	--	100	4
Region												
New England	33	4	67	8	36	4	64	7	82	9	18	2
Middle Atlantic	43	3	57	4	50	4	50	4	75	6	25	2
Great Lakes	70	7	30	3	67	6	33	3	30	3	70	7
Great Plains	64	7	36	4	60	6	40	4	36	4	64	7
South	17	3	83	14	12	2	88	15	95	18	5	1
Border	50	4	50	4	10	1	90	9	90	9	10	1
Mountain	67	10	33	5	56	9	44	7	50	8	50	8
Pacific	75	3	25	1	75	3	25	1	25	1	75	3

Source: Congressional Record, 28 August 1940, pp. 11124, 11137-38, 11142. Preparedness advocates voted no on the Hayden and Maloney amendments and yes on the final Burke bill. Rearmament opponents voted yes on the Hayden and Maloney amendments and no on the final Burke bill.

Table 22. Senate Views on Neutrality, October 1939, and Selective Service, August 1940

	For Neutrality Revision Only		For Selective Service Only		For Both		Against Both	
Party	%	N	%	N	%	N	%	N
Democrats	11	7	5	3	71	45	13	8
Republicans	6	1	17	3	27	5	50	9
Other	25	1	--	--	--	--	75	3
Region								
New England	--	--	25	3	58	7	17	2
Middle Atlantic	--	--	--	--	75	6	25	2
Great Lakes	30	3	--	--	30	3	40	4
Great Plains	9	1	--	--	36	4	55	6
South	6	1	12	2	82	14	--	--
Border	--	--	--	--	90	9	10	1
Mountain	21	3	7	1	50	7	21	3
Pacific	33	1	--	--	--	--	67	2

Source: Congressional Record, 27 October 1939, pp. 1023-24; 28 August 1940, p. 11142. These figures are based on the final Senate votes on the Pittman and Burke bills.

Table 23. Senate Views on Finnish Loan, February 1940, and Selective
Service, August 1940

Party	For Finnish Loan Only		For Selective Service Only		For Both		Against Both	
	%	N	%	N	%	N	%	N
Democrats	14	7	18	9	58	30	10	5
Republicans	14	2	14	2	29	4	43	6
Other	50	2	--	--	--	--	50	2
Region								
New England	25	2	--	--	75	6	--	--
Middle Atlantic	11	1	22	2	56	5	11	1
Great Lakes	33	2	--	--	17	1	50	3
Great Plains	11	1	11	1	22	2	56	5
South	--	--	36	5	64	9	--	--
Border	--	--	13	1	75	6	13	1
Mountain	31	4	15	2	39	5	15	2
Pacific	50	1	--	--	--	--	50	1

Source: Congressional Record, 13 February 1940, p. 1404; 28 August
1940, p. 11142. These figures are based on the final Senate votes
on the Brown and Burke bills.

Table 24. Preparedness Views of Representatives, September 1940

Party	% for Preparedness	Percent Change Since November 1939
Democrats	74-86	7 decrease
Republicans	14-33	10 increase
Other	17	33 decrease
Region		
New England	29-86	23 increase
Middle Atlantic	53-73	11 increase
Great Lakes	14-22	15 decrease
Great Plains	19-26	7 decrease
South	95-100	unchanged
Border	75-89	4 decrease
Mountain	27-70	14 decrease
Pacific	48-63	11 decrease

Source: Congressional Record, 7 September 1940, pp.11748-49;
New York Times, 8 September 1940. The percentages indicate
the range of votes against the Fish amendment and for the
final Wadsworth bill. The percentage changes were determined
by comparing the range of votes of preparedness advocates
with the range of internationalist votes on the Vorys and
Shanley amendments and the final Pittman bill. An increase
means the party or region favored selective service more
than neutrality revision, while a decrease means the party
or region favored neutrality revision more than selective
service.

Table 25. House Views on Selective Service, September 1940

	Fish Amendment 7 September 1940				Final Wadsworth Bill 7 September 1940			
	Yes		No		Yes		No	
Party	%	N	%	N	%	N	%	N
Democrats	26	64	74	176	86	210	14	33
Republicans	86	138	14	23	32	52	68	111
Other	83	5	17	1	17	1	83	5
Region								
New England	71	20	29	8	86	24	14	4
Middle Atlantic	47	42	53	47	73	66	27	24
Great Lakes	86	73	14	13	21	18	79	69
Great Plains	81	37	19	9	26	12	74	35
South	5	4	95	80	100	85	--	--
Border	25	9	75	27	89	34	11	4
Mountain	73	8	27	3	70	7	30	3
Pacific	52	14	48	13	63	17	37	10

Source: Congressional Record, 7 September 1940, pp. 11748-49;
New York Times, 8 September 1940. Preparedness advocates
voted no on the Fish amendment and yes on the final Wadsworth
bill, while rearmament opponents voted yes on the Fish amendment and no on the final Wadsworth bill.

Table 26. House Views on Neutrality, November 1939, and Selective
          Service, September 1940

	For Neutrality Revision Only		For Selective Service Only		For Both		Against Both	
Party	%	N	%	N	%	N	%	N
Democrats	7	15	4	10	82	188	7	17
Republicans	1	1	20	30	12	18	67	104
Other	50	2	--	--	--	--	50	2
Region								
New England	--	--	56	15	30	8	14	4
Middle Atlantic	3	2	19	15	54	42	24	19
Great Lakes	9	8	--	--	21	18	70	60
Great Plains	9	4	7	3	20	9	64	28
South	--	--	1	1	99	80	--	--
Border	--	--	3	1	88	31	9	3
Mountain	--	--	10	1	60	6	30	3
Pacific	15	4	15	4	47	12	23	6

Source: Congressional Record, 3 November 1939, pp. 1389; New York Times,
8 September 1940. Figures are based on the final House votes on the
Pittman and Wadsworth bills.

Table 27. Internationalist and Preparedness Views of Representatives, 1939–1940

	Neutrality Revision	Neutrality Revision	Selective Service	Average
	For June 1939	For November 1939	For September 1940	For
Party	%	%	%	%
Democrats	79	87	80	82
Republicans	3	14	24	14
Other	42	50	17	36
Region				
New England	21	35	58	38
Middle Atlantic	38	52	63	51
Great Lakes	27	33	18	26
Great Plains	26	30	23	26
South	93	98	98	96
Border	72	86	82	80
Mountain	50	63	49	54
Pacific	55	67	56	59

Source: Congressional Record, 30 June 1939, pp. 8511–14; 2 November 1939, pp. 1343–45; 7 September 1940, pp. 11748–49; New York Times, 8 September 1940. Figures are based on the final House votes on the Vorys, Shanley and Fish amendments and the Bloom and Wadsworth bills.

Table 28. Internationalist, Interventionist, and Preparedness Views of Senators, 1939–1940

	Neutrality Revision	Finnish Loan	Selective Service	Average
	For October 1939	For February 1940	For August 1940	For
Party	%	%	%	%
Democrats	82	76	65	74
Republicans	34	29	47	37
Other	28	63	--	30
Region				
New England	58	55	75	63
Middle Atlantic	75	88	61	75
Great Lakes	69	50	30	50
Great Plains	44	41	36	40
South	92	72	89	84
Border	90	80	70	80
Mountain	68	68	44	59
Pacific	20	50	25	31

Source: Congressional Record, 10 October 1939, p. 237; 27 October 1939, pp. 1023–24; 13 February 1940, pp. 1403–4; 28 August 1940, pp. 11124, 11142. Figures are based on the final Senate votes on the Tobey, Clark, Taft, and Hayden amendments and the Pittman and Brown bills.

Table 29. Average Political Party Unity, 1939–1940

	Neutrality Revision	Neutrality Revision	Finnish Loan	Selective Service	Party Unity
	June 1939 %	October 1939 %	February 1940 %	August 1940 %	Average %
Senate					
Democrats	--	81	76	65	74
Republicans	--	66	71	54	64
Other	--	72	63	100	78
House					
Democrats	99	87	--	80	82
Republicans	96	87	--	77	87
Other	59	50	--	83	64

Source: (Senate) Congressional Record, 10 October 1939, p. 237; 27
October 1939, pp. 1023–24; 13 February 1940, pp. 1403–4; 28 August
1940, pp. 11124, 11137–38; (House) Congressional Record, 30 June 1939,
pp. 8511–14; 2 November 1939, pp. 1343–45; 7 September 1940, pp.
11748–49; New York Times, 8 September 1940. The Tobey and Clark
amendments and the final Pittman bill on neutrality revision, the
Taft amendment and final Brown bill on the Finnish loan, and the
Hayden and Maloney amendments, and the final Burke bill were the roll-
calls used to determine the average regional unity of senators. The
Vorys amendment and the final Bloom bill on neutrality revision, the
Vorys and Shanley amendments on neutrality revision, and the Fish
amendment and final Wadsworth bill were the roll-calls used to determine the average regional unity of representatives.

Table 30. Average Regional Unity, 1939–1940

Issue	Senate Delegations With 75% Unity	House Delegations With 75% Unity
Neutrality Revision June 1939	–	4
Neutrality Revision October, November 1939	5	2
Finnish Loan February 1940	3	–
Selective Service August, September 1940	3	4

Source: (Senate) Congressional Record, 10 October 1939, p. 237;
27 October 1939, pp. 1023–24; 13 February 1940, pp. 1403–4;
28 August 1940, pp. 11124, 11137–38, 11142; (House) Congressional Record, 30 June 1939, pp. 8511–13; 2 November 1939, pp. 1343–
45; 7 September 1940, pp. 11748–49; New York Times, 8 September
1940. Figures are based on those roll-call votes cited in
Table 29.

Table 31. Ethnic Alignments of Members of Congress

	Irish				German				Scandinavian			
	Yes		No		Yes		No		Yes		No	
	%	N	%	N	%	N	%	N	%	N	%	N
Senate												
Neutrality Revision												
Tobey Amendment October 1939	33	4	67	8	25	1	75	3	67	2	33	1
Pittman Bill October 1939	67	8	33	4	75	3	25	1	33	1	67	2
Finnish Loan												
Taft Amendment February 1940	30	3	70	7	25	1	75	3	100	2	--	--
Brown Bill February 1940	70	7	30	3	75	3	25	1	50	1	50	1
Selective Service												
Hayden Amendment August 1940	50	5	50	5	50	2	50	2	100	1	--	--
Burke Bill August 1940	70	7	30	3	50	2	50	2	--	--	100	2
House												
Neutrality Revision												
Vorys Amendment June 1939	37	19	63	32	81	29	19	7	67	8	33	4
Bloom Bill June 1939	67	35	33	17	33	12	67	25	42	5	58	7
Vorys Amendment November 1939	29	16	71	40	62	25	38	15	69	9	31	4
Selective Service												
Fish Amendment September 1940	40	22	60	33	74	31	26	11	69	9	31	4
Wadsworth Bill September 1940	78	43	22	13	48	20	52	22	17	2	83	10

Source: (Senate) Congressional Record, 10 October 1939, p. 237;
27 October 1939, p. 1024; 13 February 1940, pp. 1403-4; 28 August
1940, pp. 11124, 11142; (House) Congressional Record, 30 June
1939, pp. 8511-14; 2 November 1939, pp. 1343-45; 7 September
1940, pp. 11748-49; New York Times, 8 September 1940. Figures
are based on those roll-call votes cited in Table 29.

Table 32. Internationalism of Ethnic Groups

Ethnic Group	Neutrality Revision	Neutrality Revision	Finnish Loan	Selective Service	Average
	For June 1939	For October/ November 1939	For February 1940	For August/ September 1940	For
Senate	%	%	%	%	%
Irish	--	67	70	60	66
German	--	75	75	50	67
Scandinavian	--	33	25	--	19
House					
Irish	65	71	--	69	68
German	26	38	--	37	34
Scandinavian	38	31	--	24	31

Source: Same as for Table 31. Ethnic figures are based upon those roll-call votes cited in Table 29.

Appendix 1. Classification of Senators

Internationalists (35)			Moderates (25)			Isolationists (36)		
Member	Party	State	Member	Party	State	Member	Party	State
Adams	D	CO	Bailey	D	NC	Barbour	R	NJ
Andrews	D	FL	Bulow	D	SD	Bone	D	WA
Ashurst	D	AZ	Burke	D	NB	Borah	R	ID
Austin	R	VT	Byrd	D	VA	Bridges	R	NH
Bankhead	D	AL	Byrnes	D	SC	Capper	R	KS
Barkley	D	KY	Danaher	R	CT	Chavez	D	NM
Bilbo	D	MS	Davis	R	PA	Clark, B.	D	MO
Brown	D	MI	Downey	D	CA	Clark, D.	D	ID
Caraway	D	AR	George	D	GA	Donahey	D	OH
Connally	D	TX	Gerry	D	RI	Frazier	R	ND
Ellender	D	LA	Gibson	R	VT	Gurney	R	SD
Gillette	D	IA	Glass	D	VA	Holman	R	OR
Green	D	RI	Hale	R	ME	Holt	D	WV
Guffey	D	PA	Harrison	D	MS	Johnson, E.	D	CO
Hayden	D	AZ	Hatch	D	NM	Johnson, H.	R	CA
Hill	D	AL	Herring	D	IA	King	D	UT
Hughes	D	DE	Lee	D	OK	La Follette	P	WI
Lewis	D	IL	Lucas	D	IL	Lodge	R	MA
Logan	D	KY	Maloney	D	CT	Lundeen	F-L	MN
McKellar	D	TN	Norris	I	NB	McCarran	D	NV
Mead	D	NY	Russell	D	GA	McNary	R	OR
Miller	D	AR	Schwartz	D	WY	Nye	R	ND
Minton	D	IN	Tydings	D	MD	O'Mahoney	D	WY
Murray	D	MT	Van Nuys	D	IN	Overton	D	LA
Neely	D	WV	White	R	ME	Reed	R	KS
Pepper	D	FL				Reynolds	D	NC
Pittman	D	NV				Shipstead	F-L	MN
Radcliffe	D	MD				Smith	D	SC
Schwellenbach	D	WA				Stewart	D	TN
Sheppard	D	TX				Taft	R	OH
Smathers	D	NJ				Tobey	R	NH
Thomas, Elb.	D	UT				Townsend	R	DE
Thomas, Elm.	D	OK				Vandenberg	R	MI
Truman	D	MO				Walsh	D	MA
Wagner	D	NY				Wheeler	D	MT
						Wiley	R	WI

Appendix 2. Classification of Representatives

Internationalists (179)

Voted Internationalist on Three Roll Calls (149)

Member	Party	State	Member	Party	State	Member	Party	State
Barden	D	NC	Ferguson	D	OK	McKeough	D	IL
Barnes	D	IL	Flaherty	D	MA	McMillan, John	D	SC
Bates, Joe	D	KY	Flannagan	D	VA	Magnuson	D	WA
Beam	D	IL	Ford, Aaron	D	MS	Mahon	D	TX
Beckworth	D	TX	Fulmer	D	SC	Maloney	D	LA
Bell	D	MO	Garrett	D	TX	Marcantonio	D	NY
Bland	D	VA	Gavagan	D	NY	Martin, John	D	CO
Bloom	D	NY	Geyer	D	CA	Martin, John	D	IL
Boykin	D	AL	Gibbs	D	GA	May	D	KY
Bradley, Michael	D	PA	Gore	D	TN	Merritt	D	NY
Brown, Paul	D	GA	Gossett	D	TX	Mills, Wilbur	D	AR
Bryson	D	SC	Grant	D	AL	Mitchell	D	IL
Buckley	D	NY	Green, Lex	D	FL	Monroney	D	OK
Burch	D	VA	Hare	D	SC	Mouton	D	LA
Burgin	D	NC	Hart	D	NJ	Myers	D	PA
Byrne	D	NY	Harter	D	OH	Nelson	D	MO
Byrns	D	TN	Hendricks	D	FL	Norrell	D	AR
Caldwell	D	FL	Hennings	D	MO	Pace	D	GA
Cannon, Pat	D	FL	Hobbs	D	AL	Parsons	D	IL
Celler	D	NY	Izac	D	CA	Patman	D	TX
Chandler	D	TN	Jarman	D	AL	Pearson	D	TN
Clark	D	NC	Johnson, Jed	D	OK	Peterson, Hugh	D	GA
Claypool	D	OH	Johnson, Luther	D	TX	Peterson, J.	D	FL
Cochran	D	MO	Johnson, Lyndon	D	TX	Pierce, Walt H.	D	OR
Coffee, John	D	WA	Jones, Marvin	D	TX	Ramspeck	D	GA
Cooper	D	TN	Kee	D	WV	Randolph	D	WV
Courtney	D	TN	Keller	D	IL	Rayburn	D	TX
Cox	D	GA	Kennedy, Michael	D	NY	Richards	D	SC
Creal	D	KY	Keogh	D	NY	Robertson	D	VA
Crowe	D	IN	Kilday	D	TX	Robinson	D	UT
Cullen	D	NY	Kirwan	D	OH	Rogers, Will	D	OK
Darden	D	VA	Kitchens	D	AR	Romjue	D	MO
Delaney	D	NY	Kleberg	D	TX	Sacks	D	PA
Dempsey	D	NM	Kocialkowski	D	IL	Sasscer	D	MD
DeRouen	D	LA	Kramer	D	CA	Satterfield	D	VA
Dickstein	D	NY	Lanham	D	TX	Schuetz	D	IL
Dingell	D	MI	Larrabee	D	IN	Sirovich	D	NY
Doughton	D	NC	Lea	D	CA	Smith, Howard	D	VA
Doxey	D	MS	Lesinski	D	MI	Smith, T. V.	D	IL
Drewry	D	VA	Lewis, Lawr.	D	CO	Snyder	D	PA
Duncan	D	MO	McAndrews	D	IL	Somers	D	NY
Dunn	D	PA	McArdle	D	PA	South	D	TX
Durham	D	NC	McCormack	D	MA	Sparkman	D	AL
Eberharter	D	PA	McGehee	D	MI	Steagall	D	AL
Fay	D	NY	McGranery	D	PA	Sullivan	D	NY

Member	Party	State	Member	Party	State	Member	Party	State
Tarver	D	GA	Vinson	D	GA	Whelchel	D	GA
Terry	D	AR	Wallgren	D	WA	Whittington	D	MS
Thomas, Albert	D	TX	Ward	D	MD	Williams	D	MO
Thomason	D	TX	Weaver	D	NC	Woodrum	D	VA
Vincent	D	KY	West	D	TX			

Internationalists Absent on Three Roll Calls (30)

Member	Party	State	Member	Party	State	Member	Party	State
Bankhead	D	AL	Disney	D	OK	Patrick	D	AL
Boehne	D	IN	Ellis	D	AR	Sabath	D	IL
Boland	D	PA	Fitzpatrick	D	NY	Scrugham	D	NV
Bulwinkle	D	NC	Folger	D	NC	Shannon	D	MO
Byron	D	MD	Kelly	D	IL	Smith, Joe	D	WV
Cannon, Clarence	D	MO	Kerr	D	NC	Starnes	D	AL
Cartwright	D	OK	McMillan, T.	D	SC	Sumners	D	TX
Casey	D	MA	McReynolds	D	TN	Taylor, Edward	D	CO
Cummings	D	CO	Mansfield	D	TX	Warren	D	NC
Dies	D	TX	Norton	D	NJ	Wood	D	MO

Moderates (62)

For Vorys Amendment, Against Recommital, For Bloom Bill (37)

Member	Party	State	Member	Party	State	Member	Party	State
Allen, A. L.	D	LA	Griffith	D	LA	O'Neal	D	KY
Boren	D	OK	Havenner	D	CA	O'Toole	D	NY
Brooks	D	LA	Hill	D	WA	Polk	D	OH
Buckler	F-L	MN	Houston	D	KS	Rankin	D	MS
Chapman	D	KY	Johnson, George	D	WV	Ryan, Elmer	D	MN
Coffee, Harry	D	NB	Leavy	D	WA	Schulte	D	IN
Cole, W. P.	D	MD	Maciejewski	D	IL	Schwert	D	NY
Collins	D	MS	Massingdale	D	OK	Smith, Martin	D	WA
Colmer	D	MS	Mills, Newton	D	LA	Spence	D	KY
Fernandez	D	LA	Moser	D	PA	Voorhis	D	CA
Flannery	D	PA	Murdock, John	D	AZ	Walter	D	PA
Gathings	D	AR	Nichols	D	OK	Zimmerman	D	MO
Gregory	D	KY						

Against Vorys Amendment, For Recommittal, Against Bloom Bill (15)

Member	Party	State	Member	Party	State	Member	Party	State
Arnold	D	IL	Faddis	D	PA	Maas	R	MN
Ball	R	CN	Harrington	D	IA	Murdock, Abe	D	UT
Buck	D	CA	Hook	D	MI	Sheppard	D	CA
Cole, W. S.	R	NY	Kean	R	NJ	Stearns	R	NH
Edmiston	D	WV	Kennedy, Ambrose	D	MD	Wadsworth	R	NY

Other Moderates Splitting Votes on Three Roll Calls (10)

Member	Party	State	Member	Party	State	Member	Party	State
Allen, Robert	D	PA	Patton	D	TX	Shanley	D	CN
Barton	R	NY	Poage	D	TX	Smith, J. J.	D	CN
Ford, Tom	D	CA	Secrest	D	OH	White, Compton	D	ID
O'Leary	D	NY						

Isolationists (188)

Voted Isolationist on Three Roll Calls (168)

Member	Party	State	Member	Party	State	Member	Party	State
Alexander	R	MN	Elston	R	OH	Kinzer	R	PA
Allen, Leo	R	IL	Englebright	R	CA	Knutson	R	MN
Andersen, H. C.	R	MN	Evans	D	NY	Kunkel	R	PA
Anderson, C. A.	D	MO	Fenton	R	PA	Lambertson	R	KS
Anderson, John	R	CA	Ford, Leland	R	CA	Landis	R	IN
Andresen	R	MN	Fries	D	IL	LeCompte	R	IA
Angell	R	OR	Gamble	R	NY	Lemke	R	ND
Arends	R	IL	Gartner	R	PA	Lewis, Earl	R	OH
Austin	R	CN	Gearhart	R	CA	Luce	R	MA
Barry	D	NY	Gehrmann	P	WI	Ludlow	D	IN
Bates, George	R	MA	Gerlach	R	PA	McDowell	R	PA
Bender	R	OH	Gilchrist	R	IA	McLean	R	NJ
Blackney	R	MI	Gillie	R	IN	McLeod	R	MI
Bolles	R	WI	Graham	R	PA	Marshall	R	OH
Bolton	R	OH	Grant, Robert	R	IN	Martin, Thomas	R	IA
Bradley, Fred	R	MI	Griswold	R	WI	Michener	R	MI
Brewster	R	ME	Gross	R	PA	Miller	R	CT
Brown, Clarence	R	OH	Guyer	R	KS	Monkiewicz	R	CT
Burdick	R	ND	Gwynne	R	IA	Mott	R	OR
Carlson	R	KS	Hall	R	NY	Mundt	R	SD
Carter	R	CA	Halleck	R	IN	Murray	R	WI
Case	R	SD	Hancock	R	NY	O'Brien	R	NY
Chiperfield	R	IL	Harness	R	IN	O'Connor	D	MT
Church	R	IL	Harter, J. F.	R	NY	O'Day	D	NY
Clason	R	MA	Hartley	R	NJ	Oliver	R	ME
Clevenger	R	OH	Hawks	R	WI	Osmers	R	NJ
Cluett	R	NY	Healey	D	MS	Pfeifer	D	NY
Cooley	D	NC	Heinke	R	NB	Pierce, Wallace	R	NY
Corbett	R	PA	Hess	R	OH	Pittenger	R	MN
Costello	D	CA	Hinshaw	R	CA	Powers	R	NJ
Crawford	R	MI	Hoffman	R	MI	Rabaut	D	MI
Crosser	D	OH	Holmes	R	MA	Reed, Chauncey	R	IL
Crowther	R	NY	Hope	R	KS	Reed, Daniel	R	NY
Culkin	R	NY	Horton	R	WY	Rees	R	KS
Curtis	R	NB	Hull	P	WI	Rich	R	PA
D'Allesandro	D	MD	Hunter	D	OH	Risk	R	RI
Darrow	R	PA	Jarrett	R	PA	Robsion	R	KY
Dirksen	R	IL	Jeffries	R	NJ	Rockefeller	R	NY
Ditter	R	PA	Jenkins	R	OH	Rodgers	R	PA
Dondero	D	MI	Jensen	R	IA	Rogers, Edith	R	MA
Douglas	R	NY	Johnson, Anton	R	IL	Routzohn	R	OH
Dowell	R	IA	Johnson, Noble	R	IN	Rutherford	R	PA
Dworshak	R	ID	Jones, Robert	R	OH	Sandager	R	RI
Eaton	R	NJ	Keefe	R	WI	Schafer	R	WI
Elliott	D	CA	Kennedy, Martin	D	NY	Schiffler	R	WV

Member	Party	State	Member	Party	State	Member	Party	State
Seccombe	R	OH	Talle	R	IA	Welch	R	CA
Seger	R	NJ	Tenerowicz	D	MI	White, Dudley	R	OH
Shafer	R	MI	Thill	R	WI	Wigglesworth	R	MA
Simpson	R	PA	Thomas, J.P.	R	NJ	Williams, George	R	DE
Smith, Clyde	R	ME	Thorkelsen	R	MT	Winter	R	KS
Smith, Fred	R	OH	Tibbott	R	PA	Wolcott	R	MI
Springer	R	IN	Tinkham	R	MA	Wolfenden	R	PA
Stefan	R	KS	Tolan	D	CA	Wolverton	R	NJ
Sumner	R	IL	Treadway	R	MA	Woodruff	R	MI
Sutphin	D	NJ	Van Zandt	R	PA	Youngdahl	R	MN
Sweeney	D	OH	Vreeland	R	NJ			
Taber	R	NY						

Voted Isolationist Except on Final Roll Call (7)

Fish	R	NY	Reece	R	TN	Taylor, J.W.	R	TN
Jenks	R	NH	Schaefer	D	IL	Vorys	R	OH
McLaughlin	D	NB						

Isolationists Absent on Three Roll Calls (13)

Andrews	R	NY	Jacobsen	D	IA	Mason	R	IL
Ashbrook	D	OH	Johns	R	WI	Plumley	R	VT
Connery	D	MA	Mapes	R	MI	Short	R	MO
Engel	R	MI	Martin, Joe	R	MA	Wheat	D	NC
Gifford	R	MA						

Appendix 3. Senate Alignments on Neutrality and Selective Service

Members Favoring Both Measures			Members Opposing Both Measures		
Member	Party	State	Member	Party	State
Andrews	D	FL	Borah/Thomas, J.	R	ID
Austin	R	VT	Bulow	D	SD
Bailey	D	NC	Capper	R	KS
Bankhead	D	AL	Clark, Bennett	D	MO
Barbour	R	NJ	Clark, D. W.	D	ID
Barkley	D	KY	Danaher	R	CT
Bridges	R	NH	Davis	R	PA
Burke	D	NB	Donahey	D	OH
Byrd	D	VA	Downey	D	CA
Byrnes	D	SC	Holt	D	WV
Caraway	D	AR	Johnson, Hiram	R	CA
Chandler	D	KY	La Follette	P	WI
Connally	D	TX	Lundeen	F-L	MN
Ellender	D	LA	McCarran	D	NV
George	D	GA	Nye	R	ND
Gerry	D	RI	Shipstead	F-L	MN

Members Favoring Both Measures				Members Opposing Both Measures		
Member	Party	State		Member	Party	State
Green	D	RI		Townsend	R	DE
Guffey	D	PA		Vandenberg	R	MI
Gurney	R	SD		Walsh	D	MA
Hale	R	ME		Wiley	R	WI
Harrison	D	MS				
Hatch	D	NM				
Hayden	D	AZ		**Members Favoring Neutrality Only**		
Herring	D	IA				
Hill	D	AL		Adams	D	CO
Hughes	D	DE		Brown	D	MI
King	D	UT		Johnson, Edwin	D	CO
Lee	D	OK		Murray	D	MT
Lucas	D	IL		Norris	I	NB
McKellar	D	TN		Schwellenbach	D	WA
Maloney	D	CT		Smith	D	SC
Mead	D	NY		Taft	R	OH
Miller	D	AR		Van Nuys	D	IN
Minton	D	IN				
Neely	D	WV				
O'Mahoney	D	WY		**Members Favoring Selective Service Only**		
Pepper	D	FL				
Pittman	D	NV		Chavez	D	NM
Radcliffe	D	MD		Lodge	R	NH
Russell	D	GA		Overton	D	LA
Schwartz	D	WY		Reynolds	D	NC
Sheppard	D	TX		Tobey	R	NH
Slattery	D	IL		White	R	ME
Smathers	D	NJ				
Stewart	D	TN				
Thomas, Elbert	D	UT				
Thomas, Elmer	D	OK				
Truman	D	MO				
Tydings	D	MD				
Wagner	D	NY				

Ashurst, Bone, and Glass did not vote on neutrality revision, while Bilbo, Frazier, Gibson, Gillette, Holman, McNary, and Reed were absent on the selective service vote. John Thomas replaced Borah, who died in January 1940.

Appendix 4. Senate Alignments on Finland and Selective Service

Members Favoring Both Measures			Members Opposing Both Measures		
Member	Party	State	Member	Party	State
Andrews	D	FL	Adams	D	CO
Austin	R	VT	Bulow	D	SD
Bankhead	D	AL	Capper	R	KS
Barbour	R	NJ	Danaher	R	CT
Barkley	D	KY	Holt	D	WV
Burke	D	NB	Johnson, Hiram	R	CA
Byrnes	D	SC	Lundeen	F-L	MN
Chandler	D	KY	McCarran	D	NV
Green	D	RI	Norris	I	NB
Guffey	D	PA	Taft	R	OH
Hale	R	ME	Thomas, John	R	ID
Hatch	D	NM	Van Nuys	D	IN
Hayden	D	AZ	Wiley	R	WI
Herring	D	IA			
Hill	D	AL	**Members Favoring Finnish Loan Only**		
Hughes	D	DE	Ashurst	D	AZ
King	D	UT	Brown	D	MI
Lee	D	OK	Clark, D.W.	D	ID
Maloney	D	CT	Davis	R	PA
McKellar	D	TN	Johnson, Edwin	D	CO
Mead	D	NY	La Follette	P	WI
Miller	D	AR	Murray	D	MT
Minton	D	IN	Schwellenbach	D	WA
Neely	D	WV	Shipstead	F-L	MN
Pepper	D	FL	Townsend	R	DE
Pittman	D	NV	Walsh	D	MA
Radcliffe	D	MD			
Schwartz	D	WY	**Members Favoring Conscription Only**		
Sheppard	D	TX	Chavez	D	NM
Smathers	D	NJ	Connally	D	TX
Stewart	D	TN	George	D	GA
Tydings	D	MD	Gerry	D	RI
Wagner	D	NY	Gurney	R	SD
White	R	ME	Harrison	D	MS
			Lodge	R	MA
			O'Mahoney	D	WY
			Reynolds	D	NC
			Russell	D	GA
			Thomas, Elmer	D	OK

Holman missed both votes, while Bailey, Bone, Bridges, Byrd, Caraway, Bennett Clark, Donahey, Downey, Ellender, Glass, Lucas, Nye, Overton, Slattery, Elbert Thomas, Tobey, Truman, Vandenberg, and Wheeler did not vote on the Finnish loan. Bilbo, Frazier, Gibson, Gillette, Holman, McNary, and Reed were absent on the selective service vote.

Appendix 5. House Alignments on Neutrality and Selective Service

Members Favoring Both Measures

Member	Party	State	Member	Party	State	Member	Party	State
Allen, A. L.	D	LA	Culkin	R	NY	Hobbs	D	AL
Allen, Robert	D	PA	Cullen	D	NY	Houston	D	KS
Anderson, John	R	CA	Cummings	D	CO	Izac	D	CA
Ball	R	CT	D'Alesandro	D	MD	Jarman	D	AL
Barden	D	NC	Darden	D	VA	Johnson, George	D	WV
Barnes	D	IL	Delaney	D	NY	Johnson, Jed	D	OK
Bates	D	KY	DeRouen	D	LA	Johnson, Luther	D	TX
Beam	D	IL	Dickstein	D	NY	Johnson, Lyndon	D	TX
Beckworth	D	TX	Disney	D	OK	Jones, Marvin	D	TX
Bell	D	MO	Doughton	D	NC	Kean	R	NJ
Bland	D	VA	Doxey	D	MS	Kee	D	WV
Bloom	D	NY	Drewry	D	VA	Kefauver	D	TN
Boland	D	PA	Duncan	D	MO	Keller	D	IL
Boren	D	OK	Dunn	D	PA	Kelly	D	IL
Boykin	D	AL	Durham	D	NC	Kennedy, Michael	D	NY
Bradley, Michael	D	PA	Eberharter	D	PA	Kerr	D	NC
Brewster	R	ME	Edmiston	D	WV	Kilday	D	TX
Brooks	D	LA	Elliott	D	CA	Kirwan	D	OH
Brown, Paul	D	GA	Faddis	D	PA	Kitchens	D	AR
Bryson	D	SC	Fay	D	NY	Kleberg	D	TX
Buck	D	CA	Ferguson	D	OK	Kocialkowski	D	IL
Buckley	D	NY	Fitzpatrick	D	NY	Kramer	D	CA
Bulwinkle	D	NC	Flaherty	D	MA	Lanham	D	TX
Burch	D	VA	Flannagan	D	VA	Larrabee	D	IN
Burgin	D	NC	Flannery	D	PA	Lea	D	CA
Byrne	D	NY	Folger	D	NC	Leavy	D	WA
Byrns	D	TN	Ford, Aaron	D	MS	Lewis, Lawrence	D	CO
Byron	D	MD	Ford, Leland	R	CA	McCormack	D	MA
Camp	D	GA	Ford, Thomas	D	CA	McGehee	D	MS
Cannon, Clarence	D	MO	Fulmer	D	SC	McGranery	D	PA
Cannon, Pat	D	FL	Gamble	R	NY	McKeough	D	IL
Cartwright	D	OK	Gathings	D	AR	McLean	R	NJ
Casey	D	MA	Gavagan	D	NY	McMillan	D	SC
Celler	D	NY	Gifford	R	MA	Maciejewski	D	IL
Clark	D	NC	Gore	D	TN	Mahon	D	TX
Claypool	D	OH	Gossett	D	TX	Maloney	D	LA
Cluett	R	NY	Grant, George	D	AL	Martin, John	D	IL
Cole, W. S.	R	NY	Green, Lex	D	FL	Massingale	D	OK
Colmer	D	MS	Gregory	D	KY	May	D	KY
Cooley	D	NC	Griffith	D	LA	Merritt	D	NY
Cooper	D	TN	Hare	D	SC	Mills, Newton	D	LA
Courtney	D	TN	Hart	D	NJ	Mills, Wilbur	D	AR
Cox	D	GA	Harter	D	OH	Mitchell	D	IL
Cravens	D	AR	Havenner	D	CA	Monroney	D	OK
Creal	D	KY	Hendricks	D	FL	Moser	D	PA
Crowe	D	IN	Hennings	D	MO	Mouton	D	LA

212 · **Seventy-sixth Congress**

Member	Party	State	Member	Party	State	Member	Party	State
Murdock, John	D	AZ	Robertson	D	VA	Sumners	D	TX
Myers	D	PA	Robinson	D	UT	Tarver	D	GA
Nelson	D	MO	Rogers, Will	D	OK	Taylor, Edward	D	CO
Nichols	D	OK	Romjue	D	MO	Terry	D	AR
Norrell	D	AR	Sabath	D	IL	Thomas, Albert	D	TX
Norton	D	NJ	Sacks	D	PA	Thomas, J.P.	R	NJ
O'Neal	D	KY	Sasscer	D	MD	Thomason	D	TX
Osmers	R	NJ	Satterfield	D	VA	Vincent	D	KY
O'Toole	D	NY	Schuetz	D	IL	Vinson	D	GA
Pace	D	GA	Schwert	D	NY	Voorhis	D	CA
Parsons	D	IL	Scrugham	D	NV	Vreeland	R	NJ
Pearson	D	TN	Sheppard	D	CA	Wadsworth	R	NY
Patman	D	TX	Smith, Joe	D	WV	Walter	D	PA
Patton	D	TX	Smith, T.V.	D	IL	Ward	D	MD
Peterson, Hugh	D	GA	Snyder	D	PA	Warren	D	NC
Peterson, J. H.	D	FL	Somers	D	NY	Weaver	D	NC
Pierce, Wallace	R	NY	South	D	TX	West	D	TX
Plumley	R	VT	Sparkman	D	AL	Whelchel	D	GA
Poage	D	TX	Spence	D	KY	Whittington	D	MS
Ramspeck	D	GA	Starnes	D	AL	Williams, Clyde	D	MO
Randolph	D	WV	Steagall	D	AL	Woodrum	D	VA
Rayburn	D	TX	Stearns	R	NH	Zimmerman	D	MO
Richards	D	SC	Sullivan	D	NY			

Members Opposing Both Measures

Member	Party	State	Member	Party	State	Member	Party	State
Alexander	R	MN	Dirksen	R	IL	Hope	R	KS
Allen	R	IL	Dondero	R	MI	Hull	P	WI
Andersen, H.C.	R	MN	Douglas	R	NY	Hunter	D	OH
Anderson, C.A.	D	MO	Dworshak	R	ID	Jacobsen	D	IA
Andresen, A.H.	R	MN	Elston	R	OH	Jarrett	R	PA
Angell	R	OR	Engel	R	MI	Jenkins	R	OH
Arends	R	IL	Evans	D	NY	Jensen	R	IA
Bender	R	OH	Fries	D	IL	Johns	R	WI
Blackney	R	MI	Gartner	R	PA	Johnson, Anton	R	IL
Bolles	R	WI	Gehrmann	P	WI	Johnson, Noble	R	IN
Bradley, Fred	R	MI	Geyer	D	CA	Jones, Robert	R	OH
Brown, Clarence	R	OH	Gilchrist	R	IA	Keefe	R	WI
Burdick	R	ND	Gillie	R	IN	Kinzer	R	PA
Carlson	R	KS	Graham	R	PA	Knutson	R	MN
Carter	R	CA	Grant, Robert	R	IN	Kunkel	R	PA
Case	R	SD	Gross	R	PA	Lambertson	R	KS
Church	R	IL	Guyer	R	KS	Landis	R	IN
Clevenger	R	OH	Halleck	R	IN	LeCompte	R	IA
Coffee, Harry	D	NB	Harness	R	IN	Lemke	R	ND
Corbett	R	PA	Hartley	R	NJ	Lewis, Earl	R	OH
Crawford	R	MI	Hawks	R	WI	Ludlow	D	IN
Crosser	D	OH	Hess	R	OH	McDowell	R	PA
Crowther	R	NY	Hinshaw	R	CA	McLeod	R	MI
Curtis	R	NB	Hoffman	R	MI	Marshall	R	OH

Member	Party	State	Member	Party	State	Member	Party	State
Martin, Thomas	R	IA	Rodgers	R	PA	Thill	R	WI
Mason	R	IL	Routzohn	R	OH	Tibbott	R	PA
Michener	R	MI	Ryan	R	MN	Tinkham	R	MA
Miller	R	CT	Schafer	R	WI	Tolan	D	CA
Mundt	R	SD	Schiffler	R	WV	Van Zandt	R	PA
Murray	R	WI	Seccombe	R	OH	Vorys	R	OH
O'Connor	D	MT	Secrest	D	OH	Welch	R	CA
Oliver	R	ME	Shafer	R	MI	Wheat	R	IL
Pittenger	R	MN	Shanley	D	CT	White, Compton	D	ID
Rabaut	D	MI	Shannon	D	MO	White, Dudley	R	OH
Reece	R	TN	Short	R	MO	Williams, Geo.	R	DE
Reed, Chauncey	R	IL	Smith, Fred	R	OH	Winter	R	KS
Reed, Daniel	R	NY	Springer	R	IN	Wolcott	R	MI
Rees	R	KS	Stefan	R	NB	Wolfenden	R	PA
Rich	R	PA	Sumner	R	IL	Wolverton	R	NJ
Robsion	R	KY	Sweeney	D	OH	Woodruff	R	MI
Rockefeller	R	NY	Talle	R	IA	Youngdahl	R	MN

Members for Neutrality Revision Only

Member	Party	State	Member	Party	State	Member	Party	State
Boehne	D	IN	Hill	D	WA	Marcantonio	A-L	NY
Buckler	F-L	MN	Hook	D	MI	Polk	D	OH
Cochran	D	MO	Lesinski	D	MI	Schulte	D	IN
Coffee, John	D	WA	McAndrews	D	IL	Smith, Martin	D	WA
Dingell	D	MI	McArdle	D	PA	Tenerowicz	D	MI
Gwynne	R	IA	Magnuson	D	WA	Wood	D	MO

Members for Selective Service Only

Member	Party	State	Member	Party	State	Member	Party	State
Austin	R	CT	Hall, L.	R	NY	O'Brien	R	NY
Barton	R	NY	Hancock	R	NY	O'Leary	D	NY
Bates, George	R	MA	Harrington	D	IA	Powers	R	NJ
Clason	R	MA	Harter	R	NY	Rankin	D	MS
Cole, W.P.	D	MD	Healey	D	MA	Rogers, Edith	R	MA
Connery	D	MA	Holmes	R	MA	Rutherford	R	PA
Costello	D	CA	Horton	R	WY	Sandager	R	RI
Ditter	R	PA	Jencks	R	NH	Simpson	R	PA
Eaton	R	NJ	Luce	R	MA	Smith, Clyde	R	ME
Englebright	R	CA	McLaughlin	D	NB	Smith, J. Joseph	D	CT
Fenton	R	PA	Maas	R	MN	Taber	R	NY
Fish	R	NY	Martin, Joe	R	MA	Treadway	R	MA
Gearhart	R	CA	Mott	R	OR	Wigglesworth	R	MA
Gerlach	D	PA						

Bibliography

Unpublished Sources

MANUSCRIPT COLLECTIONS

Warren R. Austin Papers. Guy Bailey Library, University of Vermont, Burlington.
Josiah W. Bailey Papers. William Perkins Library, Duke University, Durham, N.C.
Alben W. Barkley Papers. Margaret I. King Library, University of Kentucky, Lexington.
Theodore G. Bilbo Papers. University of Southern Mississippi Library, Hattiesburg.
Sol Bloom Papers. New York Public Library, New York City.
William E. Borah Papers. Library of Congress, Washington, D.C.
Lyle H. Boren Papers. University of Oklahoma Library, Norman.
Prentiss M. Brown Papers. Bentley Historical Library, University of Michigan, Ann Arbor.
Clarence Cannon, Jr., Papers. Western Historical Manuscripts Collection, University of
    Missouri, Columbia.
Arthur Capper Papers. Kansas State Historical Society, Topeka.
J. Wilburn Cartwright Papers, University of Oklahoma Library, Norman.
Grenville Clark Papers. Baker Memorial Library, Dartmouth College, Hanover, N.H.
W. Sterling Cole Papers. Cornell's Collection of Regional History and University Archives,
    Cornell University, Ithaca, N.Y.
Thomas Connally Papers. Library of Congress, Washington, D.C.
Fred L. Crawford Papers. Bentley Historical Library, University of Michigan, Ann Arbor.
James J. Davis Papers. Library of Congress, Washington, D.C.
Robert L. Doughton Papers. Southern Historical Collection, University of North Carolina
    Library, Chapel Hill.
Ernest W. Gibson Papers. Guy Bailey Library, University of Vermont, Burlington.
Carter Glass Papers. Alderman Library, University of Virginia, Charlottesville.
Lex Green Papers. P. K. Yonge Library of Florida History, University of Florida, Gainesville.
Theodore F. Green Papers. Library of Congress, Washington, D.C.
Pat Harrison Papers. In possession of William S. Coker, Pensacola, Fla.
Carl Hayden Papers. Hayden Library, Arizona State University, Tempe.
Joseph Hendricks Papers. P. K. Yonge Library of Florida History, University of Florida,
    Gainesville.
Clyde L. Herring Papers. University of Iowa Library, Iowa City.
Rush Dew Holt Papers. West Virginia University Library, Morgantown.
Clifford R. Hope Papers. Kansas State Historical Society, Topeka.
Cordell Hull Papers. Library of Congress, Washington, D.C.
Inter-University Consortium for Political Research, University of Michigan, Ann Arbor.
Ben F. Jensen Papers. University of Iowa Library, Iowa City.
Hiram W. Johnson Papers. Bancroft Library, University of California, Berkeley.
Bartel J. Jonkman Papers. Bentley Historical Library, University of Michigan, Ann Arbor.
Eugene J. Keogh Papers. George Arents Research Library, Syracuse University, Syracuse,
    N.Y.
John H. Kerr Papers. Southern Historical Collection, University of North Carolina Library,
    Chapel Hill.
Alfred M. Landon Papers. Kansas State Historical Society, Topeka.
Karl M. LeCompte Papers. University of Iowa Library, Iowa City.
William G. McAdoo Papers. Library of Congress, Washington, D.C.
Charles L. McNary Papers. Library of Congress, Washington, D.C.
Vito Marcantonio Papers. New York Public Library, New York City.

George W. Norris Papers. Library of Congress, Washington, D.C.

Mary T. Norton Papers. Rutgers University Library, New Brunswick, N.J.

Gerald P. Nye Papers. Herbert C. Hoover Library, West Branch, Iowa.

Joseph C. O'Mahoney Papers. Western History Research Center, University of Wyoming, Laramie.

John H. Overton Papers. Louisiana State University Library, Baton Rouge.

Claude D. Pepper Papers. Washington National Records Center, Suitland, Md.

J. Hardin Peterson Papers. P. K. Yonge Library of Florida History, University of Florida, Gainesville.

Amos Pinchot Papers. Library of Congress, Washington, D.C.

Key Pittman Papers. Library of Congress, Washington, D.C.

Franklin D. Roosevelt Papers. Franklin D. Roosevelt Library, Hyde Park, N.Y.

Lewis P. Schwellenbach Papers. Library of Congress, Washington, D.C.

Morris Sheppard Papers. University of Texas Library, Austin.

Thomas V. Smith Papers. University of Chicago Library, Chicago, Ill.

Karl Stefan Papers. Nebraska State Historical Society, Lincoln.

Henry L. Stimson Papers. Yale University Library, New Haven, Conn.

John Taber Papers. Cornell's Collection of Regional History and University Archives, Cornell University, Ithaca, N.Y.

Elbert D. Thomas Papers. Franklin D. Roosevelt Library, Hyde Park, N.Y.

Elmer Thomas Papers. University of Oklahoma Library, Norman.

Charles W. Tobey Papers. Baker Memorial Library, Dartmouth College, Hanover, N.H.

Harry S. Truman Papers. Harry S. Truman Library, Independence, Mo.

U.S., House of Representatives, Committee Papers. National Archives, Legislative Division.

U.S., Senate, Committee Papers. National Archives, Legislative Division.

Arthur H. Vandenberg Papers. Bentley Historical Library, University of Michigan, Ann Arbor.

John M. Vorys Papers. Ohio State Historical Society, Columbus.

Wadsworth Family Papers. Library of Congress, Washington, D.C.

Robert F. Wagner Papers. Department of History, Georgetown University, Washington, D.C.

Lindsay C. Warren Papers. Southern Historical Collection, University of North Carolina Library, Chapel Hill.

Wallace H. White, Jr., Papers. Library of Congress, Washington, D.C.

William Allen White Papers. Library of Congress, Washington, D.C.

Clyde Williams Papers. Western Historical Manuscripts Collection, University of Missouri, Columbia.

PH.D. DISSERTATIONS

Boskin, Joseph. "Politics of an Opposition Party: The Republican Party in the New Deal Period." University of Minnesota, 1959.

Bowers, Robert C. "The American Peace Movement, 1933–1941." University of Wisconsin, 1950.

Cain, Earl R. "Analysis of the Neutrality Debates, 1935–1941." Northwestern University, 1950.

Cleary, C. Richard. "Congress, the Executive, and Neutrality: 1935 to 1940." Fordham University, 1953.

Coffey, William. "Rush Dew Holt: The Boy Senator, 1905–1942." West Virginia University, 1970.

Coombs, F. Alan. "Joseph Christopher O'Mahoney: The New Deal Years." University of Illinois, 1968.

DeWitt, Howard A. "Hiram Johnson and American Foreign Policy, 1917–1941." University of Arizona, 1972.
Donovan, John C. "Congress and the Making of Neutrality Legislation, 1935–1939." Harvard University, 1949.
Duke, Escal F. "Political Career of Morris Sheppard, 1875–1941." University of Texas, 1958.
Guinsburg, Thomas N. "Senatorial Isolationism in America, 1919–1941." Columbia University, 1969.
Hanks, Richard K. "Hamilton Fish and American Isolationism, 1920–1944." University of California at Riverside, 1971.
Heacock, Walter J. "William Brockman Bankhead: A Biography." University of Wisconsin, 1952.
Henderson, Cary S. "Congressman John Taber of Auburn: Politics and Federal Appropriations, 1923–1962." Duke University, 1964.
Kaner, Norman. "Toward a Minority of One: Vito Marcantonio and American Foreign Policy." Rutgers University, 1968.
Libby, Justin H. "The Irresolute Years: American Congressional Opinion Towards Japan, 1937–1941." Michigan State University, 1971.
Lorentz, May Rene. "Henrik Shipstead: Minnesota Independent, 1923–1946." Catholic University of America, 1963.
McFarland, Keith. "Secretary of War Harry H. Woodring and the Problems of Readiness, Rearmament, and Neutrality, 1936–1940." Ohio State University, 1969.
McGinnis, Patrick E. "Republican Party Resurgence in Congress, 1936–1946." Tulane University, 1967.
Manheimer, Eric. "The Public Career of Elmer Thomas." University of Oklahoma, 1952.
Mickey, David H. "Senatorial Participation in Shaping Certain United States Foreign Policies, 1921–1941." University of Nebraska, 1954.
Mulvihill, Peggy M. "The United States and the Russo-Finnish War." University of Chicago, 1965.
O'Sullivan, John Joseph. "From Voluntarism to Conscription: Congress and Selective Service, 1940–1945." Columbia University, 1971.
Roberts, Walter K. "The Political Career of Charles Linza McNary, 1924–1944." University of North Carolina, 1953.
Ruetten, Richard T. "Burton K. Wheeler of Montana: A Progressive Between the Wars." University of Oregon, 1961.
Schmidtlein, Eugene F. "Truman the Senator." University of Missouri, 1962.
Smyrl, Frank H. "Tom Connally and the New Deal." University of Oklahoma, 1968.
Spencer, Samuel R., Jr. "A History of the Selective Training and Service Act of 1940 from Inception to Enactment." Harvard University, 1951.
Stoesen, Alexander R. "The Senatorial Career of Claude D. Pepper." University of North Carolina, 1965.
Ward, Paul E. "A History of the Special Sessions of Congress: Threats of War, War, and Its Effects." St. John's University, 1959.

Published Sources

GOVERNMENT PUBLICATIONS

U.S., Congress. *Biographical Directory of the American Congress, 1774–1961*. Washington: U.S. Government Printing Office, 1961.
U.S., Congress. *Congressional Record*. Vols. 84–86. Washington: U.S. Government Printing Office, 1939–1940.

U.S., Congress, House of Representatives, Committee on Banking and Currency. "Extension of Lending Authority of Export-Import Bank of Washington." *Hearings*, 76th Cong., 3d sess. Washington: U.S. Government Printing Office, 1940.

———. "Extension of Lending Authority of Export-Import Bank of Washington." *Reports*, 76th Cong., 3d sess., no. 1670 (23 February 1940).

U.S., Congress, House of Representatives, Committee on Conference. "Neutrality Act of 1939." *Reports*, 76th Cong., 2d sess., no. 1475 (3 November 1939).

———. "Selective Training and Service Act of 1940." *Reports*, 76th Cong., 3d sess., no. 2937 (12 September 1940).

U.S., Congress, House of Representatives, Committee on Foreign Affairs. "American Neutrality Legislation." *Hearings*, 76th Cong., 1st sess. Washington: U.S. Government Printing Office, 1939.

———. "Neutrality Act of 1939." *Reports*, 76th Cong., 1st sess., no. 856 (17 June 1939).

U.S., Congress, House of Representatives, Committee on Military Affairs. "Compulsory Military Training and Service." *Reports*, 76th Cong., 3d sess., no. 2093 (29 August 1940).

U.S., Congress, Senate, Committee on Banking and Currency. "Extension of Lending Authority of Export-Import Bank of Washington." *Hearings*, 76th Cong., 3d sess. Washington: U.S. Government Printing Office, 1940.

———. "Extension of Lending Authority of Export-Import Bank of Washington." *Reports*, 76th Cong., 3d sess., no. 1166 (25 January 1940).

U.S., Congress, Senate, Committee on Foreign Relations. "Increasing the Lending Authority of the Export-Import Bank." *Hearings*, 76th Cong., 3d sess. Washington: U.S. Government Printing Office, 1940.

———. "Increasing the Lending Authority of the Export-Import Bank." *Reports*, 76th Cong., 3d sess., no. 1185 (7 February 1940).

———. "Neutrality Act of 1939." *Reports*, 76th Cong., 2d sess., no. 1155 (29 September 1939).

———. "Neutrality, Peace Legislation, and Our Foreign Policy." *Hearings*, 76th Cong., 1st sess. Washington: U.S. Government Printing Office, 1939.

U.S., Congress, Senate, Committee on Military Affairs. "Compulsory Military Training and Service." *Hearings*, 76th Cong., 3d sess. Washington: U.S. Government Printing Office, 1940.

———. "Compulsory Military Training and Service." *Reports*, 76th Cong., 3d sess., no. 2002 (5 August 1940).

U.S., Department of the Army. *Annual Report of the Secretary of War to the President, 1939–1940*. Washington: U.S. Government Printing Office, 1939–1940.

———, Greenfield, Kent R.; Palmer, Robert R.; and Wiley, Bell I. *The Organization of Ground Combat Troops*. Washington: Department of the Army, 1947.

———, Kreidberg, Marvin A., and Henry, Merton G. *History of Military Mobilization of the United States Army, 1775–1945*. Washington: Department of the Army, 1955.

———, Watson, Mark S. *Chief of Staff: Prewar Plans and Preparations*. Washington: Department of the Army, 1950.

U.S., Department of State. *Department of State Bulletin*. Washington: U.S. Government Printing Office, 1939–1940.

———. *Foreign Relations of the United States, 1939–1941*. 13 vols. Washington: U.S. Government Printing Office, 1951–1964.

———. *Peace and War: United States Foreign Policy, 1931–1941*. Washington: U.S. Government Printing Office, 1943.

NEWSPAPERS

Chicago Tribune, September–November 1938
Dallas News, July–September 1940
Detroit Free Press, January–February 1940
Detroit News, January–February 1940
Grand Rapids Press, February 1940
Great Falls Tribune, August 1939
New York Herald-Tribune, March 1939–September 1940
New York Times, January 1939–October 1940
Portland Press-Herald, July 1939
Washington Post, January 1939–October 1940.
Washington Star, March 1939–September 1940
Washington Times-Herald, March 1939–September 1940

MAGAZINES

American Journal of International Law, April 1939–July 1940
Current History, December 1938–October 1940
Foreign Affairs, April 1939–October 1940
Nation, January 1939–September 1940
New Republic, January 1939–September 1940
Newsweek, January 1939–September 1940
Time, January 1939–September 1940
Vital Speeches, March 1939–September 1940

MEMOIRS AND BIOGRAPHIES

Barkley, Alben W. *That Reminds Me*. Garden City: Doubleday, 1954
Blackorby, Edward C. *Prairie Rebel: The Public Life of William Lemke*. Lincoln: University of Nebraska Press, 1963.
Bloom, Sol. *The Autobiography of Sol Bloom*. New York: Putnam's, 1948.
Blum, John Morton. *From the Morgenthau Diaries*. 3 vols. Boston: Houghton Mifflin, 1959–1967.
Brown, Prentiss M. Interview with Author. St. Ignace, Mich. 22 August 1972.
Burns, James MacGregor. *Roosevelt: The Lion and the Fox*. New York: Harcourt, Brace, 1956.
———. *Roosevelt: The Soldier of Freedom*. New York: Harcourt Brace Jovanovich, 1970.
Byrnes, James F. *All in One Lifetime*. New York: Harper, 1958.
Chamberlin, Hope. *A Minority of Members: Women in the U.S. Congress*. New York: Praeger, 1973.
Cole, Wayne S. *Charles A. Lindbergh and the Battle Against American Intervention in World War II*. New York: Harcourt Brace Jovanovich, 1974.
———. *Senator Gerald P. Nye and American Foreign Relations*. Minneapolis: University of Minnesota Press, 1962.
Connally, Thomas, and Steinberg, Alfred. *My Name is Tom Connally*. New York: Crowell, 1954.
Dictionary of American Biography. Vol. 22, supps. 2 and 3. New York: Scribner's, 1958–1973.
Dorough, C. Dwight. *Mr Sam*. New York: Random House, 1962.
Fausold, Martin L. *James W. Wadsworth, Jr.: The Gentleman from New York*. Syracuse, N.Y.: Syracuse University Press, 1975.
Freidel, Frank. *Franklin D. Roosevelt*. 4 vols. Boston: Little, Brown, 1952–1973.

Gorman, Joseph B. *Kefauver: A Political Biography*. New York: Oxford University Press, 1971.

Green, Adwin Wigfall. *The Man Bilbo*. Baton Rouge: Louisiana State University Press, 1963.

Hatch, Alden. *The Wadsworths of the Genesee*. New York: Coward-McCann, 1959.

Hooker, Nancy Harrison, ed. *The Moffat Papers*. Cambridge: Harvard University Press, 1956.

Hull, Cordell. *The Memoirs of Cordell Hull*. 2 vols. New York: Macmillan, 1948.

Huthmacher, J. Joseph. *Senator Robert F. Wagner and the Rise of Urban Liberalism*. New York: Atheneum, 1968.

Ickes, Harold L. *The Secret Diary of Harold L. Ickes*. 3 vols. New York: Simon and Schuster, 1953–1954.

Israel, Fred L. *Nevada's Key Pittman*. Lincoln: University of Nebraska Press, 1963.

Israel, Fred L., ed. *The War Diary of Breckinridge Long*. Lincoln: University of Nebraska Press, 1966.

Johnson, Donald Bruce. *The Republican Party and Wendell Willkie*. Urbana: University of Illinois Press, 1960.

Johnson, Walter. *William Allen White's America*. New York: Holt, 1947.

Levine, Ervin L. *Theodore Francis Green: The Washington Years, 1937–1960*. Providence, R.I.: Brown University Press, 1971.

Libbey, James K. *Dear Alben: Mr. Barkley of Kentucky*. Lexington: University Press of Kentucky, 1979.

Lowitt, Richard. *George W. Norris: The Triumph of a Progressive, 1933–1944*. Urbana: University of Illinois Press, 1978.

McKenna, Marian C. *Borah*. Ann Arbor: University of Michigan Press, 1961.

Maddox, Robert James. *William E. Borah and American Foreign Policy*. Baton Rouge: Louisiana State University Press, 1969.

Maney, Patrick J. *"Young Bob" La Follette: A Biography of Robert M. La Follette, Jr., 1895–1953*. Columbia: University of Missouri Press, 1978.

Martin, Joseph W., Jr. *My First Fifty Years in Politics*. New York: McGraw Hill, 1960.

Mazuzan, George T. *Warren R. Austin at the U.N., 1946–1953*. Kent, Ohio: Kent State University Press, 1977.

Miller, Merle. *Plain Speaking: An Oral Biography of Harry S. Truman*. New York: Putnam's, 1974.

Miller, William J. *Henry Cabot Lodge: A Biography*. New York: Heineman, 1967.

Moore, John Robert. *Senator Josiah William Bailey of North Carolina: A Political Biography*. Durham, N.C.: Duke University Press, 1968.

Morison, Elting E. *Turmoil and Tradition: A Study of the Life and Times of Henry L. Stimson*. Boston: Houghton Mifflin, 1960.

Norris, George W. *Fighting Liberal: The Autobiography of George W. Norris*. New York: Macmillan, 1945.

Patterson, James T. *Mr. Republican: A Biography of Robert A. Taft*. Boston: Houghton Mifflin, 1972.

Pogue, Forrest C. *George C. Marshall: Ordeal and Hope, 1939–1942*. New York: Viking, 1966.

Pratt, Julius W. *Cordell Hull, 1933–44*. 2 vols. New York: Cooper Square, 1964.

Roosevelt, Elliott, ed. *FDR: His Personal Letters, 1928–1945*. 2 vols. New York: Duell, Sloan, and Pearce, 1950.

Rosenman, Samuel I., ed. *The Public Papers and Addresses of Franklin D. Roosevelt*. 13 vols. New York: Macmillan, 1938–1950.

Schaffer, Alan. *Vito Marcantonio: Radical in Congress*. Syracuse, N.Y.: Syracuse University Press, 1966.

Socolofsky, Homer E. *Arthur Capper: Publisher, Politician, and Philanthropist*. Lawrence: University of Kansas Press, 1962.

Steinberg, Alfred. *The Man from Missouri: The Life and Times of Harry S. Truman*. New York: Putnam's, 1962.

———. *Sam Rayburn: A Biography*. New York: Hawthorn Books, 1975.

Stimson, Henry L., and Bundy, McGeorge. *On Active Service in Peace and War*. New York: Harper, 1948.

Swain, Martha H. *Pat Harrison: The New Deal Years*. Jackson: University Press of Mississippi, 1978.

Tompkins, C. David. *Senator Arthur H. Vandenberg: The Evolution of a Modern Republican, 1884–1945*. East Lansing: Michigan State University Press, 1970.

Tugwell, Rexford G. *The Democratic Roosevelt*. Garden City: Doubleday, Doran, 1957.

Vandenberg, Arthur H., Jr., ed. *The Private Papers of Senator Vandenberg*. Boston: Houghton Mifflin, 1952.

Voorhis, Jerry. *Confessions of a Congressman*. Garden City: Doubleday, 1947.

Wadsworth, James W., Jr. Memoirs, Columbia University Oral History Collection, Columbia University, N.Y.

Wheeler, Burton K. *Yankee from the West: Turbulent Life Story of the Yankee-Born U.S. Senator from Montana*. Garden Ctiy: Doubleday, 1962.

BOOKS

Adams, Frederick C. *Economic Diplomacy: The Export-Import Bank and American Foreign Policy, 1934–1939*. Columbia: University of Missouri Press, 1976.

Adler, Selig. *The Isolationist Impulse: Its Twentieth Century Reaction*. New York: Abelard-Schuman, 1957.

———. *The Uncertain Giant, 1921–1941: American Foreign Policy Between the Wars*. New York: Macmillan, 1965.

Alsop, Joseph W., and Kintner, Robert. *American White Paper*. New York: Simon and Schuster, 1940.

Atwater, Elton. *American Regulation of Arms Exports*. Washington: Carnegie Endowment for International Peace, 1941.

Bailey, Thomas A., and Ryan, Paul B. *Hitler vs. Roosevelt: The Undeclared Naval War*. New York: The Free Press, 1979.

Barnes, Harry Elmer, ed. *Perpetual War for Perpetual Peace: A Critical Examination of the Foreign Policy of Franklin Delano Roosevelt and Its Aftermath*. Caldwell, Idaho: Caxton, 1953.

Beard, Charles A. *American Foreign Policy in the Making, 1932–1940*. New Haven, Conn.: Yale University Press, 1946.

———. *The Devil Theory of War*. New York: Vanguard Press, 1936.

———. *President Roosevelt and the Coming of the War: A Study in Appearances and Realities*. New Haven, Conn.: Yale University Press, 1948.

Beloff, Max. *The Foreign Policy of Soviet Russia*. 2 vols. London: Oxford University Press, 1949.

Blum, John Morton. *V Was for Victory: Politics and American Culture during World War II*. New York: Harcourt Brace Jovanovich, 1976.

Bolt, Ernest C., Jr. *Ballots before Bullets: The War Referendum Approach to Peace in America, 1914–1941*. Charlottesville: University of Virginia Press, 1977.

Borg, Dorothy. *The United States and the Far Eastern Crisis, 1933–1938*. Cambridge: Harvard University Press, 1964.

Browder, Robert Paul. *The Origins of Soviet-American Diplomacy*. Princeton, N.J.: Princeton University Press, 1953.

Butow, Robert J. C. *Tojo and the Coming of the War*. Princeton, N.J.: Princeton University Press, 1961.

Cantril, Hadley, and Strunk, Mildred, eds. *Public Opinion, 1935–1946*. Princeton, N.J.: Princeton University Press, 1951.

Chadwin, Mark Lincoln. *The Hawks of World War II*. Chapel Hill: University of North Carolina Press, 1968.

Chatfield, Charles. *For Peace and Justice: Pacifism in America, 1914–1941*. Knoxville: University of Tennessee Press, 1971.

Clifford, John Garry. *The Citizen Soldiers: The Plattsburg Training Camp Movement, 1913–1920*. Lexington: University Press of Kentucky, 1972.

Cohen, Warren I. *The American Revisionists: The Lessons of Intervention in World War I*. Chicago: University of Chicago Press, 1967.

Cole, Wayne S. *America First: The Battle Against Intervention, 1940–41*. Madison: University of Wisconsin Press, 1953.

Compton, James V. *The Swastika and the Eagle: Hitler, the United States, and the Origins of World War II*. Boston: Houghton Mifflin, 1967.

Dahl, Robert A. *Congress and Foreign Policy*. New York: Harcourt, Brace, 1950.

Dallek, Robert. *Franklin D. Roosevelt and American Foreign Policy, 1932–1945*. New York: Oxford University Press, 1979.

Dallin, David J. *Soviet Russia's Foreign Policy, 1939–1942*. New Haven, Conn.: Yale University Press, 1942.

DeConde, Alexander, ed. *Isolation and Security*. Durham, N.C.: Duke University Press, 1957.

Divine, Robert A. *Foreign Policy and U.S. Presidential Elections, 1940–1960*. New York: Franklin Watts, 1974.

———. *The Illusion of Neutrality*. Chicago: University of Chicago Press, 1962.

———. *The Reluctant Belligerent: American Entry into World War II*. New York: Wiley, 1965.

———. *Roosevelt and World War II*. Baltimore: Johns Hopkins Press, 1969.

Divine, Robert A., ed. *Causes and Consequences of World War II*. Chicago: Quadrangle, 1969.

Doenecke, Justus D. *The Literature of Isolationism: A Guide to Non-Interventionist Scholarship, 1930–1972*. Colorado Springs: Ralph Myles, 1972.

Donahoe, Bernard F. *Private Plans and Public Dangers: The Story of FDR's Third Nomination*. South Bend, Ind.: University of Notre Dame Press, 1965.

Drummond, Donald F. *The Passing of American Neutrality, 1939–1941*. Ann Arbor: University of Michigan Press, 1955.

Dwyer, T. Ryle. *Irish Neutrality and the USA: 1939–47*. Totowa, N.J.: Rowman and Littlefield, 1977.

Fairchild, Henry Pratt, ed. *Dictionary of Sociology*. Paterson, N.J.: Littlefield Adams, 1962.

Feis, Herbert. *The Road to Pearl Harbor: The Coming of the War Between the United States and Japan*. Princeton, N.J.: Princeton University Press, 1950.

Freidel, Frank. *F.D.R. and the South*. Baton Rouge: Louisiana State University Press, 1965.

Friedlander, Saul. *Prelude to Downfall: Hitler and the United States, 1939–1941*. New York: Knopf, 1967.

Frye, Alton. *Nazi Germany and the American Hemisphere, 1933–1941*. New Haven, Conn.: Yale University Press, 1967.

Gardner, Lloyd C. *Economic Aspects of New Deal Diplomacy*. Madison: University of Wisconsin Press, 1964.

Gerson, Louis L. *The Hyphenate in Recent American Politics and Diplomacy*. Lawrence: University of Kansas Press, 1964.

Goodhart, Philip. *Fifty Ships that Saved the World: The Foundation of the Anglo–American Alliance*. Garden City: Doubleday, 1965.

Gould, Julius, and Kolb, William L., eds. *A Dictionary of the Social Sciences*. New York: Free Press of Glencoe, 1964.

Grassmuck, George L. *Sectional Biases in Congress on Foreign Policy*. Baltimore: Johns Hopkins Press, 1951.

Haight, John McVickar, Jr. *American Aid to France, 1938–1940*. New York: Atheneum, 1970.

Hammond, Paul Y. *Organizing for Defense: The American Military Establishment in the Twentieth Century*. Princeton, N.J.: Princeton University Press, 1961.

Herring, George C., Jr. *Aid to Russia, 1941–1946: Strategy, Diplomacy, the Origins of the Cold War*. New York: Columbia University Press, 1973.

Jakobson, Max. *The Diplomacy of the Winter War: An Account of the Russo-Finnish War*. Cambridge: Harvard University Press, 1961.

Johnson, Walter. *The Battle Against Isolation*. Chicago: University of Chicago Press, 1944.

Jonas, Manfred. *Isolationism in America, 1935–1941*. Ithaca, N.Y.: Cornell University Press, 1966.

Jones, Robert H. *The Roads to Russia: United States Lend-Lease to the Soviet Union*. Norman: University of Oklahoma Press, 1969.

Key, V. O., Jr. *Southern Politics in State and Nation*. New York: Knopf, 1949.

Kimball, Warren F. *The Most Unsordid Act: Lend-Lease, 1939–1941*. Baltimore: Johns Hopkins Press, 1969.

Langer, William L., and Gleason, S. Everett. *The Challenge to Isolation, 1937–1940*. New York: Harper, 1952.

———. *The Undeclared War, 1940–1941*. New York: Harper, 1953.

Leigh, Michael. *Mobilizing Consent: Public Opinion and American Foreign Policy, 1937–1947*. Westport, Conn.: Greenwood Press, 1976.

Leuchtenburg, William E. *Franklin D. Roosevelt and the New Deal, 1932–1940*. New York: Harper, 1963.

Lubell, Samuel. *The Future of American Politics*. 3d ed. New York: Harper, 1965.

Mac Rae, Duncan, Jr. *Dimensions of Congressional Voting: A Statistical Study of the House of Representatives in the 81st Congress*. Berkeley: University of California Press, 1958.

Matthews, Donald R. *U.S. Senators and Their World*. Chapel Hill: University of North Carolina Press, 1960.

Millis, Walter. *Arms and Men: A Study in American Military History*. New York: Putnam's, 1956.

Mitchell, G. Duncan, ed. *A Dictionary of Sociology*. Chicago: Aldine Publishing Co., 1968.

Morison, Samuel Eliot. *History of the United States Naval Operations in World War II*. 15 vols. Boston: Little, Brown, 1947–1962.

Nelson, John K. *The Peace Prophets: American Pacifist Thought, 1919–1941*. Chapel Hill: University of North Carolina Press, 1968.

Offner, Arnold A. *American Appeasement: United States Foreign Policy and Germany, 1933–1938*. Cambridge: Harvard University Press, 1969.

O'Sullivan, John Joseph, and Meckler, Alan M., eds. *The Draft and its Enemies: A Documentary History*. Urbana: University of Illinois Press, 1974.

Parmet, Herbert S., and Hecht, Marie B. *Never Again: A President Runs for a Third Term*. New York: Macmillan, 1968.

Patterson, James T. *Congressional Conservatism and the New Deal*. Lexington: University Press of Kentucky, 1967.

Perkins, Dexter. *The New Age of Franklin Roosevelt, 1932–45*. Chicago: University of Chicago Press, 1957.

Perrett, Geoffrey. *Days of Sadness, Years of Triumph: The American People, 1939–1945*. New York: Coward, McCann, & Geoghegan, 1973.

Polenberg, Richard. *Reorganizing Roosevelt's Government: The Controversy over Executive Reorganization, 1936–1939*. Cambridge: Harvard University Press, 1966.

Potter, Elmer B., and Fredland, John R. *The United States and World Sea Power*. Englewood Cliffs, N.J.: Prentice-Hall, 1955.

Range, Willard. *Franklin D. Roosevelt's World Order*. Athens: University of Georgia Press, 1959.

Rauch, Basil. *Roosevelt from Munich to Pearl Harbor: A Study in the Creation of Foreign Policy*. New York: Creative Age Press, 1950.

Rieselbach, Leroy N. *The Roots of Isolationism*. Indianapolis: Bobbs-Merrill, 1966.

Salter, J. T., ed. *Public Men In and Out of Office*. Chapel Hill: University of North Carolina Press, 1946.

Schlesinger, Arthur M., Jr. *The Age of Roosevelt*. 3 vols. Boston: Houghton Mifflin, 1957–1960.

Schlesinger, Arthur M., Jr.; Israel, Fred L.; and Hansen, William P., eds. *History of American Presidential Elections*. 4 vols. New York: Chelsea House, 1971.

Schroeder, Paul W. *The Axis Alliance and Japanese-American Relations, 1941*. Ithaca, N.Y.: Cornell University Press, 1958.

Schwartz, Andrew J. *America and the Russo-Finnish War*. Washington: Public Affairs Press, 1960.

Sherwood, Robert E. *Roosevelt and Hopkins: An Intimate History*. New York: Harper & Brothers, 1948.

Smith, Elsdon Coles. *New Dictionary of American Family Names*. New York: Harper, 1956.

Sobel, Robert. *The Origins of Interventionism: The United States and the Russo-Finnish War*. New York: Bookman, 1960.

Steiner, Gilbert Y. *The Congressional Conference Committee: Seventieth to Eightieth Congresses*. Urbana: University of Illinois Press, 1951.

Tansill, Charles C. *America Goes to War*. Boston: Little, Brown, 1938.

———. *Back Door to War: The Roosevelt Foreign Policy, 1933–1941*. Chicago: Regnery, 1952.

Taylor, F. Jay. *The United States and the Spanish Civil War*. New York: Bookman, 1956.

Tindall, George Brown. *The Disruption of the Solid South*. Athens: University of Georgia Press, 1972.

Traina, Richard P. *American Diplomacy and the Spanish Civil War*. Bloomington: Indiana University Press, 1968.

Trefousse, Hans L. *Germany and American Neutrality, 1939–1941*. New York: Bookman, 1959.

Truman, David B. *The Congressional Party: A Case Study*. New York: Wiley, 1959.

Turner, Julius. *Party and Constituency: Pressures on Congress*. Baltimore: Johns Hopkins Press, 1951.

Westerfield, H. Bradford. *Foreign Policy and Party Politics: Pearl Harbor to Korea*. New Haven, Conn.: Yale University Press, 1955.

Westphal, Albert C. F. *The House Committee on Foreign Affairs*. New York: Columbia University Press, 1942.

Wilson, Theodore A. *The First Summit: Roosevelt and Churchill at Placentia Bay, 1941*. Boston: Houghton Mifflin, 1969.

Wiltz, John E. *From Isolation to War, 1931–1941*. New York: Crowell, 1968.

———. *In Search of Peace: The Senate Munitions Inquiry, 1934–36*. Baton Rouge: Louisiana State University Press, 1963.

Wohlstetter, Roberta. *Pearl Harbor: Warning and Decision*. Stanford University Press, 1962.

Wuorinen, John Henry, ed. *Finland and World War II, 1939–1944*. New York: Ronald, 1948.
Young, Roland A. *Congressional Politics in the Second World War*. New York: Columbia University Press, 1956.

ARTICLES

Billington, Ray. "The Origins of Middle Western Isolationism." *Political Science Quarterly* 60 (March 1945): 44–64.
Brown, John Crosby. "American Isolationism." *Foreign Affairs* 18 (October 1939):29–44.
Burns, Richard Dean, and Dixon, W. Addams. "Foreign Policy and the Democratic Myth: The Debate on the Ludlow Amendment." *Mid-America* 47 (October 1965): 288–306.
Cantril, Hadley. "America Faces the War: A Study in Public Opinion." *Public Opinion Quarterly* 4 (September 1940):387–407.
Carleton, William G. "Isolationism and the Middle West." *Mississippi Valley Historical Review* 33 (December 1946):377–90.
Clapper, Raymond. "Return of the Two Party System." *Current History* 44 (December 1938):13–15.
Clifford, John G. "Grenville Clark and the Origins of Selective Service." *Review of Politics* 35 (January 1973):17–40.
Coker, William Sidney. "Pat Harrison: The Formative Years." *Journal of Mississippi History* 25 (October 1963):251–78.
Cole, Wayne S. "America First and the South, 1940–1941." *Journal of Southern History* 22 (February 1956):36–47.
———. "American Entry into World War II: A Historiographical Appraisal." *Mississippi Valley Historical Review* 43 (March 1957):597–617.
———. "Senator Pittman and American Neutrality Policies, 1933–1940." *Mississippi Valley Historical Review* 46 (March 1960):644–62.
"Congressional Poll on Loans to Foreign Governments." *Congressional Intelligence* 8 (3 February 1940):1–4.
"Congressional Poll on Neutrality." *Congressional Intelligence* 7 (7 April 1939):1–4.
Deak, Francis. "The United States Neutrality Acts: Theory and Practice." *International Conciliation* 358 (March 1940):71–128.
DeConde, Alexander. "The South and Isolationism." *Journal of Southern History* 24 (August 1958):332–46.
Denney, George V., Jr. "What's Your Opinion? Can and Should America Stay Out of the War?" *Current History* 51 (October 1939):42–46.
Donovan, John C. "Congressional Isolationists and the Roosevelt Foreign Policy." *World Politics* 3 (April 1951):299–316.
Dulles, Allen W. "Cash and Carry Neutrality." *Foreign Affairs* 13 (January 1940):179–95.
Eagleton, Clyde. "The Duty of Impartiality on the Part of a Neutral." *American Journal of International Law* 34 (January 1940):99–104.
Eliot, George Fielding. "The Russian Campaign against Finland." *Life* 7 (15 January 1940):19–28.
Elliston, H.B. "On the Finnish Front." *Atlantic Monthly* 165 (February 1940):243–49.
Everett, Guerra. "The Neutrality Act of 1939." *Annals of the American Academy of Political and Social Science* 211 (September 1940):95–101.
Fensterwald, Bernard, Jr. "The Anatomy of American Isolationism and Expansionism." *Journal of Conflict Resolution* 2 (June 1958):111–38.
Fenwick, Charles G. "Neutrality on the Defensive." *American Journal of International Law* 34 (October 1940):697–99.
Fuchs, Lawrence H. "Minority Groups and Foreign Policy." *Political Science Quarterly* 74 (June 1959):161–75.

Gleeck, L.E. "96 Congressmen Make Up Their Minds." *Public Opinion Quarterly* 4 (March 1940):3–24.

Griffin, Walter R. "Louis Ludlow and the War Referendum Crusade, 1935–1941." *Indiana Magazine of History* 64 (December 1968):267–88.

Guinsburg, Thomas N. "The George W. Norris 'Conversion' to Internationalism, 1939–1941." *Nebraska History* 53 (Winter 1972):477–90.

Irish, Marian D. "Foreign Policy and the South." *Journal of Politics* 10 (May 1948):306–26.

Jacob, Philip E. "Influences of World Opinion on U.S. Neutrality Opinion." *Public Opinion Quarterly* 4 (March 1940):48–65.

Jessup, Philip C. "The Neutrality Act of 1939." *American Journal of International Law* 24 (January 1940):95–99.

——. "Reconsideration of Neutrality Legislation." *American Journal of International Law* 33 (July 1939):549–57.

Libby, Justin H. "The Irreconcilable Conflict: Key Pittman and Japan During the Interwar Years." *Nevada Historical Society Quarterly* 18 (Fall 1975):128–39.

Lindley, Ernest K. "The New Congress." *Current History* 48 (February 1939):15–17.

Little, Dwayne L. "Man in the Middle: Sam Rayburn as Majority Leader, 1937–1940." *Proceedings of the Florida College Teachers of History* (1971).

Masland, John W. "The 'Peace' Groups Join Battle." *Public Opinion Quarterly* 4 (December 1940):664–73.

——. "Pressure Groups and American Foreign Policy." *Public Opinion Quarterly* 6 (Spring 1942):115–22.

Mazuzan, George T. "The Failure of Neutrality Revision in Mid-Summer, 1939: Warren R. Austin's Memorandum of the White House Conference of July 18." *Vermont History* 42 (Summer 1974):239–44.

Nichols, Jeannette P. "The Middle West and the Coming of World War II." *Ohio State Archeological and Historical Quarterly* 62 (April 1953): 122–45.

Norris, George W. "American Neutrality." *Vital Speeches* 5 (1 November 1939):62–64.

Offner, Arnold A. "Appeasement Revisited: The United States, Great Britain, and Germany, 1933–1940." *Journal of American History* 64 (September 1977):373–93.

Patterson, James T. "Eating Humble Pie: A Note on Roosevelt, Congress, and Neutrality Revision in 1939." *Historian* 21 (May 1969):407–14.

Plesur, Milton. "The Republican Comeback of 1938." *Review of Politics* 24 (October 1962):525–62.

Porter, David L. "The Man Who Made the Draft—Representative James Wadsworth." *Aerospace Historian* 22 (Spring 1975):29–32.

——. "Ohio Representative John M. Vorys and the Arms Embargo in 1939." *Ohio History* 83 (Spring 1974):103–13.

——. "Senator Pat Harrison of Mississippi and the Reciprocal Trade Act of 1940." *Journal of Mississippi History* 36 (November 1974):363–76.

——. "Senator Warren R. Austin and the Neutrality Act of 1939." *Vermont History* 42 (Summer 1974):228–38.

Rhodes, Benjamin D. "The Origins of Finnish-American Friendship." *Mid-America* 54 (January 1972):3–19.

Riddick, Floyd M. "First Session of the Seventy-sixth Congress." *American Political Science Review* 33 (December 1939):1022–43.

——. "Third Session of the Seventy-sixth Congress." *American Political Science Review* 35 (April 1941):284–303.

Rieselbach, Leroy N. "The Demography of the Congressional Vote on Foreign Aid, 1939–1958." *American Political Science Review* 58 (September 1964):577–89.

Simsarian, James. "Safeguarding American Neutrality." *American Political Science Review* 24 (February 1940):105–9.

Smuckler, Ralph H. "The Region of Isolationism." *American Political Science Review* 47 (June 1953):386–401.

Stromberg, Roland N. "American Business and the Approach to War, 1935–1941." *Journal of Economic History* 13 (Winter 1953):58–78.

"Washington Correspondents Name Ablest Members of Congress in *Life* Poll." *Life* 6 (20 March 1939):13–17.

Wickware, Francis S. H. "What We Think about Foreign Affairs." *Harper's Magazine* 179 (September 1939):397–406.

Wilcox, Francis O. "The Neutrality Fight in Congress, 1939." *American Political Science Review* 33 (October 1939):811–25.

Wilkins, Robert P. "Middle Western Isolationism: A Re-Examination." *North Dakota Quarterly* 24 (Summer 1957):69–76.

Wyant, Rowena. "Voting Via the Senate Mailbag." *Public Opinion Quarterly* 5 (Fall 1941):359–82.

Wyant, Rowena, and Herzog, Herta. "Voting Via the Senate Mailbag, Part II." *Public Opinion Quarterly* 5 (Winter 1941):591–624.

Index